KU-710-697

UNDERSTANDING GLOBAL SOCIAL POLICY

WITHDRAWN FROM
THE LIBRARY

UNIVERSITY OF
WINCHESTER

KA 0389989 6

Also available in the series

Understanding crime and social policy
Emma Wincup

"An engaging, wide-ranging and up-to-date introductory text for students and practitioners who wish to get to grips with the interconnections between criminology as the study of crime and social policy as the study of human well-being." Dr Ros Burnett, Centre for Criminology, University of Oxford.

PB £21.99 (US$36.95) ISBN 978 1 84742 499 0 HB £65.00 (US$85.00) ISBN 978 1 84742 500 3
224 pages   May 2013
E-INSPECTION COPY AVAILABLE

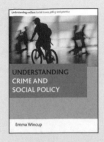

Understanding research for social policy and social work (second edition)
Edited by Saul Becker, Alan Bryman and Harry Ferguson

"Becker and Bryman did a masterful job ... North American public policy students could learn a lot from this book and methodology instructors could have their load considerably eased if URfSPP was more widely read". Kennedy Stewart, Associate Professor, Simon Fraser University School of Public Policy and Member of Parliament for Burnaby-Douglas

PB £24.99 (US$42.95) ISBN 978 1 84742 815 8   HB £65.00 (US$89.95) ISBN 978 1 84742 816 5
448 pages   March 2012
E-INSPECTION COPY AVAILABLE

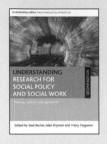

Understanding health and social care (second edition)
Jon Glasby

"This is an ambitious and wide ranging book which provides a valuable historical perspective, as well as a forward looking analysis, based on real experience. It will be a valuable tool for leaders, policy makers and students." Nigel Edwards, Policy Director, The NHS Confederation

PB £21.99 (US$34.95) ISBN 978 1 84742 623 9 HB £65.00 (US$85.00) ISBN 978 1 84742 624 6
224 pages   February 2012
E-INSPECTION COPY AVAILABLE

Understanding 'race' and ethnicity
Edited by Gary Craig, Karl Atkin, Sangeeta Chattoo and Ronny Flynn

"The title of this text belies the far reaching challenge it poses to the discipline, research base and practice of social policy. Its argument that mainstream social policy has consistently marginalised the issue of 'race' and minority ethnic concerns is well founded when judged against the historical record, the evidence base and contemporary shortfalls in policy and practice. This is a deep exploration of the complexities of diversity and difference that speaks to contemporary concerns about substantive citizenship and social justice." Professor Charlotte Williams, OBE, Keele University

PB £22.99 (US$38.95) ISBN 978 1 84742 770 0 HB £65.00 (US$85.00) ISBN 978 1 84742 771 7
336 pages   February 2012
E-INSPECTION COPY AVAILABLE

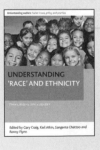

For a full listing of all titles in the series visit www.policypress.co.uk

www.policypress.co.uk

SOCIAL POLICY
ASSOCIATION

INSPECTION COPIES AND ORDERS AVAILABLE FROM:
Marston Book Services Ltd · 160 Eastern Avenue · Milton Park · Oxon OX14 4SB UK
INSPECTION COPIES
Tel: +44 (0) 1235 465500 · Fax: +44 (0) 1235 465500 · Email: inspections@marston.co.uk
ORDERS
Tel: +44 (0) 1235 465500 · Fax: +44 (0) 1235 465500 · Email: direct.orders@marston.co.uk

UNDERSTANDING GLOBAL SOCIAL POLICY

Second edition

Edited by Nicola Yeates

UNIVERSITY OF WINCHESTER
LIBRARY

UNIVERSITY OF WINCHESTER

03899896

First published in Great Britain in 2014 by

Policy Press
University of Bristol
6th Floor
Howard House
Queen's Avenue
Clifton
Bristol BS8 1SD
UK
t: +44 (0)117 331 5020
f: +44 (0)117 331 5369
pp-info@bristol.ac.uk
www.policypress.co.uk

North America office:
Policy Press
c/o The University of Chicago Press
1427 East 60th Street
Chicago, IL 60637, USA
t: +1 773 702 7700
f: +1 773 702 9756
sales@press.uchicago.edu
www.press.uchicago.edu

© Policy Press and the Social Policy Association 2014

British Library Cataloguing in Publication Data
A catalogue record for this book is available from the British Library

Library of Congress Cataloging-in-Publication Data
A catalog record for this book has been requested

ISBN 978 1 44731 024 2 paperback
ISBN 978 1 44731 023 5 hardcover

The right of Nicola Yeates to be identified as editor of this work has been asserted by her in accordance with the Copyright, Designs and Patents Act 1988.

All rights reserved: no part of this publication may be reproduced, stored in a retrieval system, or transmitted in any form or by any means, electronic, mechanical, photocopying, recording, or otherwise without the prior permission of Policy Press.

The statements and opinions contained within this publication are solely those of the editors and contributors and not of the University of Bristol, Policy Press or the Social Policy Association. The University of Bristol, Policy Press and the Social Policy Association disclaim responsibility for any injury to persons or property resulting from any material published in this publication.

Policy Press works to counter discrimination on grounds of gender, race, disability, age and sexuality.

Cover design by Qube Design Associates, Bristol
Front cover: www.jupiterimages.com
Printed and bound in Great Britain by TJ International, Padstow
Policy Press uses environmentally responsible print partners

MIX
Paper from responsible sources
FSC
www.fsc.org
FSC® C013056

UNIVERSITY OF WINCHESTER
LIBRARY

Contents

Detailed contents

List of tables and figures

Tables

Figures

List of abbreviations

ADB	Asian Development Bank
ASEAN	Association of South East Asian Nations
ASEM	Asia-Europe Meeting
AU	African Union
BIAC	Business and Industry Advisory Committee to the OECD
BIT	Bilateral Investment Treaty
BMGF	Bill & Melinda Gates Foundation
BRIC	Brazil, Russia, India and China
CARICC	Central Asian Regional Information and Coordination Centre
CEE	Central and Eastern Europe
CEO	Chief executive officer
CfBT	Centre for British Teachers
CIA	Central Intelligence Agency (US)
CSR	Corporate social responsibility
DAC	Development Advisory Committee (OECD)
DELSA	Directorate for Employment, Labour and Social Affairs (OECD)
DFID	Department for International Development, UK (prior to 1997, known as the Overseas Development Administration, ODA)
EC	European Commission
ECLAC	Economic Commission for Latin America and the Caribbean
EFA	Education for All
ERT	European Round Table
ESCAP	Economic and Social Commission for Asia and the Pacific
ETI	Ethical Trade Initiative
EU	European Union
Europol	European Police Office (an EU law enforcement organisation)
FAO	Food and Agriculture Organisation
FBI	Federal Bureau of Investigation (US)
FCTC	Framework Convention on Tobacco Control
FDI	Foreign direct investment
FLA	Fair Labour Association
G8	Group of 8
G20	Group of 20
G77	Group of 77
GATS	General Agreement on Trade in Services
GATT	General Agreement on Tariffs and Trade
GBIA	Global business interest association

GCCI	Gulf Centre for Criminal Intelligence
GDI	Gross domestic income
GDP	Gross domestic product
GHPPP	Global health public–private partnership
GNI	Gross national income
GUF	Global union federation
HDI	Human Development Index
HFA	Health for All
HIAP	Health in All Policies
HPI	Human Poverty Index
IBRD	International Bank for Reconstruction and Development
ICC	International Chamber of Commerce (Chapters Four, Six)
ICC	International Criminal Court (Chapter Ten)
ICFTU	International Confederation of Free Trade Unions
ICPD	International Conference on Population and Development
ICSW	International Council on Social Welfare
IDA	International Development Association
IDB	Inter-American Development Bank
IFC	International Finance Corporation (the World Bank)
IFI	International financial institution
IGO	International governmental organisation
IHR	International health regulation
ILO	International Labour Organization
IMF	International Monetary Fund
INGO	International non-governmental organisation
Interpol	International Criminal Police Organisation
IPPF	International Planned Parenthood Federation
ITUC	International Trade Union Confederation
IUD	Inter-uterine device
JRR	Justice Rapid Response
MDG	Millennium Development Goal
MFN	Most favoured nation
MNC	Multinational corporation
MPI	Multidimensional Poverty Index
MSF	Médecins sans Frontières
NAFTA	North American Free Trade Agreement
NCD	Non-communicable disease
NGO	Non-governmental organisation
NPM	New public management
OECD	Organisation for Economic Co-operation and Development
PAYG	Pay-as-you-go
PHM	People's Health Movement

PISA	Programme for International Student Assessment (OECD)
PLO	Police liaison officer (overseas)
PPP	Public–private partnership (Chapters Three, Seven, Nine)
PPP	Purchasing power parity (Chapter Two)
PRSP	Poverty Reduction Strategy Paper
R&D	Research and development
SAARC	South Asian Association for Regional Cooperation
SADC	Southern African Development Community
SAP	Structural Adjustment Programme
SDG	Sustainable Development Goal
SDH	Social determinants of health
SOCA	Serious Organised Crime Agency (UK)
SPIAC-B	Social Protection Inter-Agency Cooperation Board
SPF	Social Protection Floor
TAA	Trade Adjustment Assistance
TJM	Trade Justice Movement
TNC	Transnational corporation
TRIPS	Agreement on Trade-Related Aspects of Intellectual Property Rights
UEAPME	European Association of Craft, Small and Medium-Sized Enterprises
UHC	Universal Health Coverage
UN	United Nations
UNAIDS	United Nations Programme on HIV/AIDS
UNASUR	Union of South American Nations
UNCESCR	United Nations Committee on Economic, Social and Cultural Rights
UNCHR	United Nations Commission on Human Rights
UNCHS (Habitat)	United Nations Centre for Human Settlements (renamed UN-HABITAT)
UNCTAD	United Nations Conference on Trade and Development
UNDESA	United Nations Department of Economic and Social Affairs
UNDP	United Nations Development Programme
UNEP	United Nations Environment Programme
UNESCO	United Nations Educational, Scientific and Cultural Organisation
UNFPA	United Nations Population Fund (originally United Nations Fund for Population Activities)
UN-HABITAT	United Nations Human Settlements Programme
UNHCR	United Nations High Commission on Refugees
UNICE	Union of Industrial and Employers' Confederations of Europe

UNICEF	United Nations Children's Fund (originally United Nations International Children's Emergency Fund)
UNITAID	Organisation cooperating with World Health Organization on health-related Millennium Development Goals, in particular HIV/AIDS, malaria and Tuberculosis
UNODC	United Nations Office on Drugs and Crime
UNRISD	United Nations Research Institute on Social Development
USAID	United States Agency for International Development
WEF	World Economic Forum
WHA	World Health Assembly
WHO	World Health Organization
WIPO	World Intellectual Property Organisation
WRC	Worker Rights Consortium
WSF	World Social Forum
WTO	World Trade Organization

Notes on contributors

Roger Dale is Professor of Education at the Graduate School of Education, University of Bristol, UK. His research interests focus on conceptions of the globalisation of education systems and the relationships of regional organisations, especially the EU, and national education systems. He was Academic Coordinator of the EU's Network of Experts in Social Science and Education (NESSE). Together with Susan Robertson he co-founded the journal *Globalisation, Societies and Education*, and co-edited *Globalisation and Europeanisation in Education* (Symposium 2007).

Bob Deacon is Emeritus Professor of International Social Policy at University of Sheffield, UK. His research focuses on the relationship between globalisation and social policy. He is the founding editor of *Critical Social Policy* and *Global Social Policy* and author/editor of 10 books including *Global Social Policy and Governance* (2007, Sage). He has acted as an advisor or consultant to the World Bank, UN Department of Economic and Social Affairs, UNDP, ILO, UNU-CRIS, ITC-ILO, UNDP-TCDC, UNESCO, WHO, EU, Council of Europe, and the ICWS.

Kevin Farnsworth is Senior Lecturer in Social Policy at Sheffield University, UK. His research interests centre primarily on the relative power and influence of business and labour on governments, especially with regard to social and public policy. His recent work examines corporate welfare (state assistance to corporations) and its relationship with social welfare within various welfare systems. He is author of *Social versus Corporate Welfare: Competing Needs and Interests within the Welfare State* (2012, London: Palgrave), *Corporate Power and Social Policy* (2004) and co-editor (with Zoe Irving) (2011) of *Social Policy in Challenging Times: Economic Crisis and Welfare Systems* (Bristol, Policy Press)

Anne Hendrixson is Assistant Director of the Population and Development Program (PopDev), a feminist centre on population and the environment located at Hampshire College in Amherst, Massachusetts in the US. She is a reproductive health advocate, writer, and speaker focused on the politics of global health and population (see http://popdev.hampshire.edu).

Nicholas Hildyard, Larry Lohmann and **Sarah Sexton** are members of The Corner House, a UK-based research and solidarity group focusing on social and environmental justice issues (www.thecornerhouse.org.uk/). They have been trying to understand and to help challenge new manifestations of population thinking and practices when they undermine the rights and welfare of vulnerable groups, weaken grassroots democracy and limit genuine reproductive choice.

Chris Holden is Senior Lecturer in International Social Policy at the University of York, UK, and Honorary Lecturer in Global Health at the London School of Hygiene and Tropical Medicine. He has published widely on the relationships between the global economy, international trade, transnational corporations and health and social policy. He is a member of the Editorial Board of the *Journal of Social Policy* and of the International Advisory Board of the journal *Global Social Policy*. He was an editor of *Social Policy Review* (2009-2011) and co-edited (with Nicola Yeates) (2009) *The Global Social Policy Reader*, Bristol: Policy Press.

Meri Koivusalo is a senior researcher at the National Institute for Health and Welfare, Helsinki, Finland. She has published on international and national health policy, commercialisation and health care, trade and health and globalisation and health. She has co-authored (with Eeva Ollila) *Making a Healthy World: Agencies, Actors and Policies in International Health* (Zed Books, 1997), (with Tritter, Ollila and Dorfman) *Globalisation, markets and healthcare policy: redrawing patient as consumer* (Routledge, 2009).

John Muncie is Emeritus Professor of Criminology at the Open University, UK. He is the author of *Youth and Crime* (Sage, 4th edition, 2014) and has published widely on issues in globalisation, comparative youth justice and international children's rights, including *Criminological Perspectives: Essential Readings* (Sage, 3rd edition, 2013) , *Crime: Local and Global* (Willan, 2010), and *Criminal Justice: Local and Global*, (Willan, 2010). He is co-editor of the Sage journal *Youth Justice: An International Journal.*

Robert O'Brien is LIUNA/Mancinelli Professor of Global Labour Issues and Professor of Political Science at McMaster University, Hamilton, Canada. He has published six books and over twenty journal articles and book chapters in the fields of international relations and global political economy. Amongst his books are: Robert O'Brien and Marc Williams, *Global Political Economy: Evolution and Dynamics 4th Edition* (New York: Palgrave, 2013); Robert O'Brien ed., *Solidarity First: Canadian Workers and Social Cohesion* (Vancouver: University of British Columbia Press, 2008); and Robert O'Brien et al., *Contesting Global Governance* (Cambridge: Cambridge University Press 2000). Robert is associate editor of *Global Labour Journal.*.

Eeva Ollila is a specialist in public health and Associate Professor in health policy at Tampere University, Finland. She currently works as ministerial advisor at the Ministry of Social Affairs and Health (Finland). She has previously worked in WHO, European Commission and as a health policy consultant and researcher. She has published on a range of international health policy issues, including on pharmaceutical policies, population, health and development policies, public/private partnerships and commercial interests in public health policy-making.

Mitchell A. Orenstein is Professor and Chair of the Department of Political Science at Northeastern University in Boston, USA, and an associate of both the Center for European Studies and the Davis Center for Russian and Eurasian Studies at Harvard University. Mitchell is a scholar of international politics focusing on the political economy of transition in Central and Eastern Europe, pension privatisation worldwide, and the role of policy paradigms in economic reform. His research lies at the intersection of comparative politics, international political economy and global public policy. Among his books are *Privatizing Pensions: The Transnational Campaign for Social Security Reform* (Princeton University Press, 2008).

Susan Robertson is Professor of Sociology of Education, Graduate School of Education, University of Bristol, UK. Her research is focused on the study of education and broader social, economic and political forces by analysing the complexities of globalisation and regionalisation. With Professor Roger Dale, Susan is a co-editor of the journal *Globalisation, Societies and Education*.

Nicola Yeates is Professor of Social Policy in the Department of Social Policy and Criminology at The Open University, Milton Keynes, UK. She has published extensively in the areas of globalisation, regionalism, migration, care, social protection and social policy (see Open Research Online www. oro.open.ac.uk for a full list of her research publications), and has acted as advisor or consultant to the World Bank, UNICEF, UNRISD and UNESCO. She was co-editor of *Global Social Policy: journal of public policy and social development* (Sage) to 2010, vice-chair of the UK Social Policy Association to 2013, and is currently chair of the editorial board of *Social Policy and Society*.

Acknowledgements

I am first and foremost grateful to all of the authors for willingly agreeing to make room in their busy schedules to either contribute a new chapter to this second edition of *Understanding Global Social Policy*, or to revise and update their chapter in the first edition of *Understanding Global Social Policy*. I also extend my thanks to the staff at Policy Press – Emily Watt, Laura Greaves, Alison Shaw and Dave Worth – who, as ever, extended their encouragement, practical support, flexibility and efficiency throughout the production process. I also thank the Open University for giving me the time to work on this second edition.

Finally, since the publication of the first edition of *Understanding Global Social Policy* in 2008 the world has become a poorer place with the death of Professor Peter Townsend in 2009. Peter wrote the preface for the first edition; he was an inspiration to me and many, many others around the world. He remains sorely missed. I dedicate this second edition of *Understanding Global Social Policy* to his memory, and in the hope that it will contribute to better understanding the connections between global and domestic politics of social policy that Peter captured with such lucidity in the following sentence:

> A wealthy society which deprives a poor country of resources may simultaneously deprive its own poor classes through maldistribution of those additional resources.[1]

[1] Townsend, P. (ed) (1970) *The Concept of Poverty*, London: Heinneman Educational Books: 42.

The idea of global social policy

Nicola Yeates

Overview

This chapter introduces global social policy as a field of academic study and as a political practice. It contrasts different approaches to the study of social policy in a global context, setting out the essence of globalist approaches to social policy that lie at the heart of this book. The chapter goes on to discuss different perspectives within the field of global social policy and emphasises the importance of historicising global social policy and attending to the different ways in which it plays out across the world. The chapter reviews key themes and debates taken up in the ensuing chapters. Finally, it provides a brief guide to using this book, a summary of the key points covered in the chapter, and suggestions about how to keep up to date with developments in this fast-moving field.

Key concepts

Global social policy; globalisation; methodological transnationalism; methodological nationalism

Introduction

The notion that social policy and human welfare are shaped exclusively by domestic politics, institutions, policies and policy actors, has, over the last two decades, been gradually giving way to an understanding that there is an unmistakably transnational or global dimension to social policy. Global social politics, organisations, policies, programmes and policy actors are powerful forces which have a potent influence on domestic social policy, the terms of social development and the condition of human welfare around the world. They affect everyday lives in a myriad of ways, having an impact on individual and collective subjectivities, shaping major social institutions, framing policy responses and influencing social outcomes in ways that, although not always immediately perceptible, are nevertheless significant.

Building on the first edition of *Understanding global social policy* (Yeates, 2008), this second edition provides an up-to-date, comprehensive and accessible collection of research-based chapters that bring alive and illuminate key issues, debates and themes in contemporary **global social policy**. The book is tangibly concerned with the 'what', 'who', 'why' and 'how' of global social policy. The 11 chapters in this volume examine a wide range of policy areas and issues to uncover what global social policy is, who is involved in making it, why it is needed, how it is enacted, what its consequences and impacts are, and what challenges lie ahead.

The remainder of this chapter provides an introduction to the book as a whole. It discusses the various impetuses in the process of reframing social policy as a global subject and what the prefix 'global' in global social policy signifies and implies. It distinguishes the key features of global social policy as a field of academic study and research and as political practice. It introduces each of the chapters, and concludes with a summary of key points, guidance on using this book and questions for discussion.

Globalisation, social science and policy studies

Global approaches to social policy are located in an approach to social science that emphasises how social institutions, activities, practices and relations cut across, or transcend, individual countries: **methodological transnationalism**. Methodological transnationalism contrasts with **methodological nationalism** that focuses on social institutions, activities and ties at the level of individual countries. The broad differences between these two kinds of **conceptual grammar** and what they mean for the study of social policies and welfare systems are set out in *Box 1.1*.

Box 1.1: Contrasting approaches in social science and social policy

Methodological nationalism	Emphasises the institutions, links, activities and social processes occurring *within* countries	Focuses on the ways in which national welfare states, welfare systems and social policies are influenced by *domestic* politics, policy actors, policies and institutions
Methodological transnationalism	Emphasises the institutions, links, activities and processes *cutting across* countries	Focuses on the ways in which national welfare states, welfare systems and social policies are influenced by *global* politics, policy actors, policies and institutions

The development of Social Policy as a subject of academic study and research has been located in methodological nationalism, and has given rise to a rich interdisciplinary field of study with a distinctive body of theory, concepts, methods and research of practical use across the social sciences, for practitioners and policy makers. From today's vantage point, the assumption that social institutions, policies and practices can be understood exclusively in terms of the domestic realm, it renders invisible the ways in which international actors, institutions and processes of international integration influence the content and development of social policy and the social organisation of welfare. Definitions of social policy as policies enacted in the domestic realm and influenced by domestic considerations neglect and actively obscure the international and transnational dimensions of social policy and the wider global context of social policy making, such as the critical significance of cross-border and **multilateral** spheres of **governance** as sites of social politics and policy making.

Over the last two decades, the conscious embrace of methodological transnationalism has successfully opened up alternative ways of studying key global social institutions and the role of social policy in human welfare. It has been especially formative in capturing a range of transnational social phenomena – often associated with **globalisation** (*Box 1.2*). These range from transnational, border-spanning flows of capital, goods, services, people and ideas, to social formations that channel these social, economic and ideational flows and interactions, links and ties connecting people and places in more than one country, to modes of consciousness that reconstruct a sense of place and locality and give rise to the experience of the world as a shared place (Vertovec, 1999) (see also *Table 1.1*). It has also helped identify a range of transnational policy actors and border-spanning entities. *Table 1.2* sets out five broad kinds of border-spanning entities, along with their motivation and examples. These all feature in the chapters of this volume.

Table 1.1: Conceptual premises of transnationalism

Transnationalism as ...	Main elements and examples
Social morphology	Social formations spanning borders (for example, ethnic diasporas and networks)
Type of consciousness	Identity, memory, awareness; dual/multiple identifications and awareness of multi-locality
Mode of cultural reproduction	Fluidity of constructed styles, social institutions and everyday practices, often channelled through global media and communications (creolisation, hybridity, cultural translation as seen in fashion, music and film)
Avenue of capital	Networks that create the paths along which transnational activities flow (transnational corporations, transnational capitalist class, migrant remittances)
Site of political engagement	Global public spaces and fora (international non-governmental organisations, transnational social movement organisations, ethnic diasporas and transnational communities)
Reconstruction of 'place' or locality	Social fields that connect and position some actors in more than one country; creation of translocal understandings – 'translocalities' – and transnational social spaces

Source: Vertovec (1999, p 447)

Table 1.2: Typology of transnational entities

Type	Definition	Motivation	Examples
Epistemic communities	Experts in different countries linked through the production and dissemination of knowledge	Scientific ideas	Think tanks, international consultancy firms, research institutes
Transnational advocacy networks, transnational social movements	Individuals in different countries linked through a common concern	Moral ideas	Labour, human rights, gender justice, nuclear disarmament
Transnational corporations Transnational criminal networks	Economic entities in different countries linked through the pursuit of economic gain	Profit	Nike (footwear), Shell (oil), Ford (automobiles), Fyffes (bananas) Trafficking and smuggling of humans and commodities such as drugs, tobacco
Transnational professions	Professionals in different countries linked through knowledge and expertise that is not owned by any single society	Technical expertise	Medicine, nursing, accountancy, law, engineering
Transnational governmental networks	Governmental actors in different countries linked through a common issue or concern	Common public mandates	G8, G77, G20; networks of ministers of social development, trade, finance and so on

Source: Adapted from Khagram and Levitt (2005)

Box 1.2: Globalisation

There is a great deal of controversy over the concept of **globalisation** and its onset, causes, effects and universal applicability (see Yeates, 2001, 2007a, 2008). At its core is an emphasis on the ways in which the conditions of human existence are characterised by dense, extensive networks of interconnections and interdependencies that routinely transcend national borders. These include:

- flows of capital, goods and services
- the global integration of business activities and economies
- flows of images, ideas, information and values through media and communications
- worldwide spread of ideologies such as consumerism, individualism and collectivism
- international movements of people (for leisure, work, treatment, personal safety)
- global political institutions, political cooperation, political movements and political action.

One of the main consequences of globalisation is how events happening in one part of the world are able to quickly produce effects in other parts of it. Technology enables the transmission of information around the world within seconds. As the Asian financial crisis of 1997 and the global financial crisis of 2007-08 showed, fluctuations in one economy reverberate around the world and jeopardise jobs and incomes on a mass scale worldwide.

If modern technologies help shape a sense of the world as a single, shared place, culture and politics still matter. Early studies of globalisation emphasised the convergence and 'flattening' of local and national cultures, social systems and welfare states. More emphasis is now placed on how these cultures and systems are 'remade' by global forces, with distinctive national features being retained alongside continued divergence (Yeates and Holden, 2009).

Globalisation Studies, as a field of academic study, builds on significant traditions of thought that understand the world as a single global system. For example, the development of Ecology as a science has seen ecological processes as planetary in scale, with changes in ecological conditions in one part of the planet affecting other parts of it. Here, the impact of human activity on ecological systems was also seen to have a planetary impact, in that toxic chemicals and pollution released in one locality are transported to and have 'impacts on' other proximate and distant parts of the world. Also, in the 1960s world systems and dependency theories were mapping the global systems and mechanisms of unequal exchange that tie the social fates and fortunes of populations in very different parts of the world (Wallerstein, 1979). World systems theory dates the existence of global social systems back (at least) several hundred years.

No new claims can be made for the kinds of interconnectedness associated with globalisation. People, ideas, symbols, capital, goods and services have, for many centuries, 'travelled' across the borders of nation states, facilitated by successive developments in communications and travel technologies and channelled by globe-spanning institutions and networks. However, today's interconnectedness is said to be more extensive in scope than in previous historical periods; the interconnections are also said to be more intensive, and the speed at which such interactions occur is increasing. Globalisation is characterised by an increasing social *enmeshment*, expressed in ways that appear to 'bring together' geographically distant places and peoples around the world (***Box 1.3***).

Box 1.3: Dimensions of enmeshment

Extensity: the degree to which cultural, political, social and economic activities are 'stretching' across national borders to encompass more areas of the world.

Intensity: changes in magnitude and regularity of interconnectedness.

Velocity: changes in the speed of global interactions and processes.

Source: Held et al (1999)

In sum, understandings of the contemporary world have moved away from a world made up of a multitude of bounded national social systems and towards an understanding of a global social system that links **populations** and places in different parts of the world and comprises various global and sub-global hierarchies and networks of border-spanning connections, interactions and effects. How has this understanding come to be reflected in the study of welfare states and social policies? And what does this mean for social policy as a political practice? These issues are discussed in the following two sections.

Global social policy as a field of academic study and analysis

So far, we have seen that a global(isation) perspective challenges the idea that the forces shaping the social organisation of welfare are uniquely or primarily local and national ones, and directs attention to modes of political organisation, social action and economic and cultural forces transcending countries.

In the context of social policy, the last two decades has seen the emergence of a field of study, global social policy (see *Box 1.5*), dedicated to the study of how transnational modes of political organisation, action and forces are implicated in changes to the aims, characteristics and outcomes of welfare states and social policies. Often dated to the mid-1990s, this field in practice built on a substantial body of theory and research by 'early pioneers' of global social policy studies. For example, in the 1950s and 1960s Peter Townsend was developing a *global* analysis of world poverty, combining the insights of global sociology with those of development studies and social policy. In *The concept of poverty*, he set out an 'approach to development and stratification [to explain] how poverty arises, and is perpetuated, in low income and high income countries' (Townsend, 1970, p 30), and argued that '[a] wealthy society which deprives a poor country of resources may simultaneously deprive its own poor classes through maldistribution of those additional resources' (Townsend, 1970, p 42). The riches of those living in high-income countries are, he argued, inextricably linked to the poverty of those living in low-income countries.

In the 1990s global social policy studies came to be more directly informed by ongoing processes of economic and political globalisation, and began emphasising a wide range of possible consequences of globalisation for welfare states and social policies (*Box 1.4*). The anticipated and actual effects of globalisation are diverse and highly contested. They range from predictions of the demise of welfare states where they exist and their stalled development where they don't, to an emphasis on their adaptation and resilience, including, more recently, an emphasis on the possibilities and realities of new areas of social welfare provision; from an emphasis on probable convergence to an emphasis on continued actual divergence; and from an insistence on the continued centrality of governments in international social policy making to an emphasis on how governments as policy actors seem to have been displaced as supranational agencies and transnational actors have grown in strength (Yeates, 2001, 2008a).

Box 1.4: Some possible effects of globalisation on social policy and welfare states

- Creates new or additional social risks and opportunities for individuals, households, workers and communities.
- Sets welfare states in competition with each other. This is said to threaten comprehensive systems of public service provision where they exist or stall their future development where they do not. Among the anticipated effects are:
    - lowering of social and labour standards;
    - privatisation of public services;
    - creation of global health, education and welfare markets; and
    - growing reliance on voluntary and informal provision.
- Raises the issues with which social policy is concerned to supranational and global institutions, agencies and fora.
- Brings new players into the making of social policy (for example, **Bretton Woods** institutions; various United Nations [UN] agencies; development banks; international commercial, voluntary and philanthropic organisations).
- Generates 'new' political coalitions within and between countries (regionally and globally) concerned with social policy reform.

Source: Yeates (2008a)

Box 1.5: Global social policy

Global social policy examines:

- how social policy issues are increasingly being perceived to be global in scope, cause and impact;
- the consequences and implications of international economic and political integration for welfare systems, social policies and human welfare:
    - cross-border flows of people, goods, services, ideas and finance for social policy development and the financing, regulation and provision of social welfare;
    - transnational forms of collective action, including the development of multilateral and cross-border modes of governance (world-regional level [for example, European Union (EU), Union of South American Nations (UNASUR), Association of South East Asian Nations (ASEAN)], trans-regional [for example, Asia-Europe Meeting (ASEM)] and global [the World Bank [WB], UN, International Monetary Fund (IMF)]); and

> the rise of global social movements, international non-governmental organisations (INGOs) and non-state fora such as the World Social Forum (WSF) or the World Economic Forum (WEF); and
>
> – how transnational action, cross-border governance and policy making shape the development of social policies and welfare systems around the world;
>
> • any social policy issues in social development and social governance from transnational and global perspectives.

With the engagement of social policy with globalisation processes so the need to 'globalise' constructs has become more important. One example of how this has been done is the concept of the welfare mix in *Table 1.3*; another is the reformulation articulated by Deacon et al (1997) as follows:

> The classical concerns of social policy analysts with social needs and social citizenship rights becomes [sic] in a globalized context the quest for supranational citizenship. The classical concern with equality, rights and justice between individuals becomes the quest for justice between states. The dilemma about efficiency, effectiveness and choice becomes a discussion about how far to socially regulate free trade. The social policy preoccupation with altruism, reciprocity and the extent of social obligations are put to the test in the global context. To what extent are social obligations to the other transnational? (Deacon et al, 1997, p 195)

Table 1.3: The extended welfare mix

	Domestic	Global
State	National government, regional government, local authorities, town/city councils	International governmental organisations, regional formations; national donors
Market	Domestic markets; local/national firms	Global markets; transnational corporations
Intermediate	National service NGOs, consultancy companies	International non-governmental organisations (charitable and philanthropic bodies); international consultancy companies
Community	Local social movements, neighbourhood associations	Global social movements, diasporic communities
Household	Household strategies	Transnational household survival strategies, international migration

Source: Yeates (2007b)

This kind of work has fed into vibrant scholarship oriented to rethinking the historical foundations and contemporary development of welfare states, and the nature and impacts of ostensibly 'national' social policy. At the same time, shifts of emphasis are taking place in global social policy studies. Some of the key ways in which this is occurring are briefly outlined below.

From global social policy as a practice of elite global institutions and actors...

Deacon and colleagues (1997, p 195) defined global social policy as:

> ... a practice of supranational actors [which] embodies global social redistribution, global social regulation, and global social provision and/or empowerment, and ... the ways in which supranational organisations shape national social policy.

The focus of this definition lay with intergovernmental institutions such as the WB, IMF and UN and international non-state actors such as Oxfam working around social development issues. This definition drew attention to a highly active set of political forces and policy actors that had either been omitted from explanations of national policy change or relegated to the status of 'context'. This work effectively demonstrated how the battle over ideas and policy was being waged at the global level and how national political and policy actors were faced with competing policy reform prescriptions. Deacon et al's definition had a strongly normative, political inflection to it, in the sense that they were not only trying to assess the extent to which global social policy could be said to actually exist but also to identify the kinds of reforms that should be instituted to effect principles of social democracy.

Global social policy embraces a wider range of social policy dialogues

The political forces involved in global social policy formation and the arenas through which it was being played out were much broader than those being focused on by Deacon at the time (Yeates, 1999). Accordingly, the scope of global social policy analysis was broadened to include the range of social dialogues taking place outside the boardrooms and bureaux of **international governmental organisations** (IGOs). This wider definition included the activities of non-elites in global social politics and policy making, notably social movement and non-governmental organisations (NGOs) operating in the numerous shadow congresses and social fora that accompany international governmental meetings. It also opened up the possibility of including citizen movements and NGO campaigns against (for example) local branches of **multinational corporations** (MNCs) as a site of **global social governance**. The 'globalising' strategies of a wide range of social policy actors are evident, whether they be firms and business executives (planning efficiency reforms involving the shedding of staff and relocation of production to another country or outsourcing production), trade unions (protesting about the offshoring of jobs overseas), consumer movements (initiating campaigns against child labour used in the production of commodities or price fixing by cartels) or households (sending a member of the family to work overseas to send home remittances that supplement household income).

This analysis drew attention to the ways in which global social governance was not only multitiered but also multisphered in the sense of encompassing the wider social regulation of economic and political globalisation processes – the activities of corporations and institutionalised political and bureaucratic elites. This work (developed in Yeates, 2001) located the emergence of global social policy within a perceived need to regulate increased social and political conflict worldwide that accompanies contemporary globalisation processes.

Global social policy comes to emphasise codetermination and embeddedness

Extending this focus on a broader range of sites of global social policy and governance, Mitchell Orenstein defined global policies as 'those that are developed, diffused and implemented with the direct involvement of **global policy actors** and coalitions at or across the international, national or local levels of governance' (2005, p 177). This intervention was important because it considered social policies enacted nationally and sub-nationally as 'global' to the extent that they are codetermined by global policy actors and are transnational in scope (2005, pp 177-8).

Hierarchies are implicit in vocabularies of level and tier – with supranational entities placed at the top of the hierarchy and city authorities at the bottom, with power, authority and influence travelling 'downwards'. Recent work has since come to emphasise how these different levels are parts of an overall system in which all parts affect each other, with influence 'travelling' multidirectionally. This opens up questions about the ways in which, and extent to which, actors located in domestic arenas influence the formation of supranational policy, about the 'embeddedness' of transnational policy actors in specific cultural/political territories and about how transnational policy actors operate at different 'levels' of governance – often concurrently (Yeates, 2007b).

These works connect with literature that rejects conceptualisations of 'the global' as something 'out there', 'above' the state or society, and emphasises the ways in which the global is 'in here', 'within' the nation state and something that involves 'us'. This embedded notion of global social policy resonates with scholarship on the existence of transnational spaces within nation states and the playing out of transnational processes within national territories as well as across them. In this sense, transnationalism can be found in 'national' identities, social institutions, economic interactions and political processes as well as in the more visible border-spanning structures and 'high-level' fora and processes.

... and the necessity of locating global social policy in time and place

Global social policy is vulnerable to claims that it is decontextualised from time (history) and place (geography). The emphasis on the rise of contemporary global institutions and globalised welfare states risks exaggerating breaks with the past. Historians of welfare could reasonably point to how the forces behind welfare state building and the social regulation of capitalism operated within a world order characterised by extensive international trade and **migration**, **transnational corporations** (TNCs) and developed international monetary and exchange rate regimes. And while much recent commentary focuses on contemporary transnational political mobilisation in the **anti-globalisation movement**, there are examples of political mobilisation dating back two centuries that were international and extended beyond Europe (Yeates, 2007a).

At the same time, global social policy is played out variably across different countries and regions. The experiences of, for example, African countries differ from those in East Asia, which differ again from those in North America, which differ from those in South America. Many African countries, for example, have experienced the effects of global actors in very particular ways, either being ignored by the globalising corporations or being the subject of intense scrutiny and coercive policy prescriptions by international financial institutions (IFIs). An attentiveness to geography – in particular the political and economic geographies of global social policy – captures the spatially uneven outcomes of political and economic processes of international integration, including the ways in which the interrelationship between people, state and territory is being re-made by global social policies. This better captures how some countries are more embracing of **neoliberal** ideas and policies than others, and how some countries have been able to forge alternative strategies in their social policies to those prescribed by Bretton Woods institutions and Northern governments.

These different emphases and imperatives all find expression in the chapters in this volume. Chapter authors place different emphases in their approach to their topics in ways that reflect their personal intellectual or discipline-specific perspective. However, all chapters address the core tenets of global social policy with their focus on how global forces, governance structures and policy actors are implicated in the (re)making of social policy and its impact on human welfare around the world.

Global social policy as a political practice

Global social policy is not just a field of academic study and research; it is a 'living' political practice. It comprises established institutions, commanding in some cases very substantial resources, diverse policy actors, ranging from governments, to large international bureaucracies, to NGOs, to advocacy and campaign coalitions and **global social movement**s seeking to represent diverse interests (business, labour, environment, health, and so on) in social policy initiatives, and 'real' programmes of social provision and social action. Whether by influencing domestic policy or policies emanating from spheres of cross-border governance, they all contribute to shaping how populations and territories are governed, the broad direction and the specific content of social policy, the terms of social development and the conditions of human welfare.

Each of the chapters of this book survey and illuminate the nature of contemporary global social policy making in practice in the context of specific areas, issues or sectors. They survey global governance structures, policy actors, policy issues, policy goals and content, and effects, consequences and impacts relevant to the chapter topic. Collectively the chapters illustrate the sheer breadth and richness of global social policy as a field of academic study and research and as a set of 'living' political practices. They discuss in tangible and illuminating ways the magnitude and nature of key social issues with which contemporary global policy making is grappling, how global policy responses are, in turn, addressing them, and the challenges that lie ahead.

Part One of the book explores 'Contexts, institutions and actors' and is comprised of four chapters. In Chapter Two, Chris Holden sets out the global context of poverty and inequality. He discusses some of the main ways in which global poverty and inequality have been measured, and explains why these are so politically contested. The chapter presents and analyses key data showing the extent of global poverty and inequality, and it considers the implications of global measures of poverty and inequality for the politics of global social policy.

In Chapter Three, Bob Deacon examines the 'institutional architecture' of global social policy from the perspective of its governance. He provides a broad overview of the policy stances of principal **international organisations** and outlines the extent to which global social policies are promoting **global redistribution**, social regulation and social rights, including attempts to 'green' global social policy in recent years. He reviews some recent proposals to reform global social governance. The increased interest in the potential of sub-global formations in addressing issues of poverty and social inequality is reflected in this discussion.

In Chapter Four, Kevin Farnsworth focuses on the role and influence of business interests and organisations in global social policy making. He examines increasing **corporate power** and business influence on global social policy formation, greater awareness of the social harms and injustices resulting from corporate globalisation and global corporations' activities, the rise of corporate philanthropy in global social policy, and global initiatives to regulate corporate activity. He argues that global social policy making has increasingly reflected business interests overall, while recognising that these interests are in practice quite diverse and are articulated in varied ways in global social policy.

Chapter Five, Chris Holden's second chapter for this volume, examines the relationship between international trade and welfare. He provides a clear guide to the development of the world trading system and the role welfare states play in facilitating capitalist economies' adjustment to global conditions, while protecting workers from the worst social risks and ensuring some modicum of redistribution and social provision. He reviews a major area of political contestation: the effects of international trade and investment agreements on the provision of health, education and welfare services and the setting of policy objectives in these areas.

Part Two of the book, 'Policy domains and issues', covers substantive areas of global social policy making. Each of the six chapters in this section amplify many of the broad issues and themes covered in Part One and discuss how they 'translate' in practice in the context of the specific policy sector that is the subject of the chapter.

In Chapter Six, Robert O'Brien examines the area of global labour policy. This field of global policy making has benefited from the existence of an international organisation dedicated to promoting key labour rights (the **International Labour Organization** [ILO]) for the best part of a century, but, as he notes, the majority of the world's population still does not enjoy adequate working conditions. He examines how states, international organisations, TNCs and civic actors, such as trade unions, are trying to influence the direction and content of global labour policy. The chapter discusses issues in global labour policy such as the extent of adherence to 'core' labour standards and corporate regulation, and considers the effectiveness of key initiatives such as the UN Global Compact.

In Chapter Seven, Meri Koivusalo and Eeva Ollila consider one of the most visible areas of global social policy: health. Global health policy benefits from a relatively extensive set of political commitments backed by a legal framework. It is also marked by intense engagement by a range of public and private transnational policy actors – the UN, IFIs and other IGOs, business corporations and commercial interests, and NGOs, and one of the challenges is how to keep global health policies focused on health objectives rather than trade or industrial objectives. The chapter outlines contemporary issues in global health policy agendas and programmes, such as Health for All (HFA), health reform and access to pharmaceutical drugs. Notable here is the recent turn in policy stances by the WB, UN and EU in their global health policies towards better supporting comprehensive health systems, social equity in access to health and initiatives which address the wider social determinants of health.

In Chapter Eight, Mitchell Orenstein and Bob Deacon examine global policy on pensions and **social protection**. They show how transnational campaigns for pension and social protection have taken shape in recent decades, and chart the 'rise' and stagnation of pensions privatisation alongside the recent campaign for a global Social Protection Floor (SPF). The chapter details some of the methods used in these campaigns, and the ways in which the balance of power between the WB and the ILO in this policy area seems to be shifting. Importantly, the chapter shows that coalitions of domestic actors, acting nationally as well as transnationally, can resist global policy reforms and how reforms that aim to privatise social protection (pensions) can be stalled, even reversed.

In Chapter Nine Roger Dale and Susan Robertson examine the key institutions, actors and policies in global education policy. They contrast different visions and models of education being promoted by different global policies and global actors, the means by which these are progressed, and discuss how these may be reframing education in policy and practice in diverse country contexts worldwide. The increasing interest of commercial businesses in education and the use of public–private partnerships is critically commented on, and they discuss the distinction between constructing education as public services policy and constructing education as part of trade policy – and the implications of these two different policy paradigms for what is taught, how it is taught and under what conditions teaching and learning take place.

In Chapter Ten, John Muncie analyses the realm of global criminal justice policy. The chapter examines the nature and reach of '**global crime**' and the range of policy initiatives to address illicit cross-border trafficking of humans, drugs, body parts and weapons on a global scale. It also discusses the forms that cross-jurisdiction cooperation on crime control currently takes, including initiatives on **transnational policing** and **transnational justice**. States are pooling sovereignty on a range of 'law and order' matters, regionally and internationally, and a 'loosely institutionalised and coordinated crime control system' is emerging. Contrasting with criminological literatures by US and UK academics, which emphasise the dominance of neoliberal punitivity in international policy travel, John Muncie argues that social democratic ideas and practices of criminal justice have not been 'flattened' or eclipsed by neoliberal ones. In this, the chapter resonates with literature emphasising how globalisation processes have an impact on national regimes in markedly different ways, and provides further evidence of the mediating role of domestic cultural, political and socio-institutional formations therein.

In Chapter Eleven, Anne Hendrixson Sarah Sexton, Larry Lohmann and Nicholas Hildyard examine global **population policy**. **Population control** is among the oldest forms of global social policy, and the chapter traces changing concerns and manifestations of global population policy over two centuries. The authors show how Malthusian and **neo-Malthusian** ideas have been taken up by elite groups and spread across the world, facilitated by northern governments through overseas development aid programmes and by international organisations such as the WB and UN. The chapter highlights the enduring influence of 'over-population' discourses in global policy making and how these are taken up in a wide range of areas ranging from the environment, through crime control and national security, to the control of women's fertility.

The plethora of different initiatives and programmes, priorities and issues, identified and discussed in the chapters, testifies to burgeoning global policy activity and to the challenges that lie ahead. Fragmented systems of global governance, deeply entrenched global poverty, inequality and social injustice combine with a reluctance to embrace a global shared responsibility for addressing critical social policy issues, the commercialisation and privatisation of public services, the philanthrocapitalisation of global social financing, the renewal of global trade and investment agreements, and an apparent preference in many areas of global policy making for non-binding agreements and voluntary initiatives. However, recent history shows that politics and ideas still matter, now as much as ever. Global policy is now promoting more universalistic models of health and social protection that disrupt the once seemingly inexorable tide of **neoliberalism**, while the global social harms caused by the global financial crisis and systems of social organisation and governance that enabled it may spur further innovations that address the specific challenges identified in the chapters.

Translating current promising initiatives into a robust and sustained commitment to shared global social responsibility for social development and human welfare will need to involve substantial programmes of global social redistribution, rights and regulation. Now more than ever there is an urgent need for sustained and vigorous collective action – globally, nationally and locally – to capitalise on opportunities to advance progressive forms of action in support of human welfare, social policy and wider social development. In this, the need for a wider and deeper understanding of global social policy is as pressing as ever.

Using this book

This book is written with non-specialist readers in mind looking for an accessible way in to key approaches, debates and issues in global social policy as a field of academic study and as a political practice. Several design features of the book help achieve this:

- Each of the chapters starts with a brief overview of its contents and ends with a summary of the key points covered.
- Chapters make good use of case study material from research, campaigns and policy, and incorporate illustrative and visual material to aid the development of knowledge and understanding.
- Questions for discussion to aid understanding of the chapter contents, further activities to follow up on issues, and further reading and resources.
- Global social policy, like other academic subjects, makes frequent use of abbreviations – a full list of those used in this volume are located at the front of the book.
- A comprehensive glossary of the key terms used in the book, located at the back of the book. The terms are highlighted in bold in each of the chapters the first time they are used.
- A comprehensive index helps easily locate topics of particular interest.

The chapters in this edition of *Understanding global social policy* refer to materials published in the *Global social policy reader* (Yeates and Holden, 2009). The *Global social policy reader* comprises academic publications by international leaders in global social policy and key global policy documents. Together these provide comprehensive coverage of and a guide to key concepts, actors, initiatives and processes in the field.

Finally, the most useful summary overview of many current developments in global social policy making covered in this book is the *Global Social Policy* (GSP) Digest. GSP Digest is freely available variously at: www.ilo.org, www. crop.org and www.gsp–observatory.de.

Summary

- The 'global turn' in social science has opened social policy analysis to the ways that social processes, ties and links between people, places and institutions routinely cut across welfare states.
- Global social policy broadens and invigorates the study of social policy, bringing in a new range of concerns, issues and approaches to social policy and welfare provision.
- Global social policy analysts examine how global forces, governance structures and policy actors are implicated in the (re)making of social policy and its impact on human welfare around the world.

- Global social policy examines a wide range of transnational social policy actors and processes operating across on a range of spheres, sites and scales.
- Global social policy making is embedded in cultural and political contexts. It is historically specific. Place still matters.
- Global social policy is not just an academic subject; it is a set of 'living' political ideas and practices. It is an ongoing (if incomplete) project of major social significance, and a major focus of collective social action and campaigning on a worldwide scale.

Questions for discussion

- Are the effects of globalisation processes on welfare systems and policy making always negative?
- What do people who study and research global social policy examine?
- Why are a sense of history, geography and politics important in global social policy?

References

Deacon, B. with Hulse, M. and Stubbs, P. (1997) *Global social policy: International organisations and the future of welfare*, London: Sage Publications.

Held, D., McGrew, A., Goldblatt, D. and Perraton, J. (1999) *Global transformations*, Cambridge: Polity Press.

Khagram, S. and Levitt, P. (2005) *Towards a field of transnational studies and a sociological transnationalism research program*, Hauser Centre for Non-Profit Organisations, Working Paper no 24 (http://papers.ssrn.com/sol3/papers.cfm?abstract_id=556993).

Orenstein, M. (2005) 'The new pension reform as global policy', *Global Social Policy*, vol 5, no 2, pp 175-202.

Townsend, P. (1970) *The concept of poverty*, London: Heinemann.

Vertovec, S. (1999) 'Conceiving and researching transnationalism', *Ethnic and Racial Studies*, vol 22, no 2, pp 447-62.

Wallerstein, I. (1979) *The capitalist world-economy*, Cambridge: Cambridge University Press.

Yeates, N. (1999) 'Social politics and policy in an era of globalisation', *Social Policy and Administration*, vol 33, no 4, pp 372-93.

Yeates, N. (2001) *Globalisation and social policy*, London: Sage Publications.

Yeates, N. (2007a) 'Globalisation and social policy', in J. Baldock, N. Manning, S. Miller and S. Vickerstaff (eds) *Social policy* (3rd edn), Oxford: Oxford University Press.

Yeates, N. (2007b) 'The global and supra-national dimensions of the welfare mix', in M. Powell (ed) *Understanding the mixed economy of welfare*, Bristol: Policy Press.

Yeates, N. (ed) (2008) *Understanding global social policy*, Bristol: Policy Press.

Yeates, N. and Holden, C. (2009) *The global social policy reader*, Bristol: Policy Press.

Part I
Contexts, institutions, actors

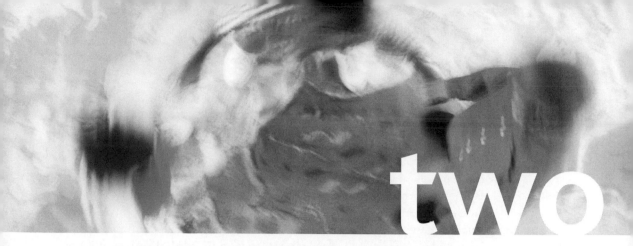

two

Global poverty and inequality

Chris Holden

Overview

Global poverty reduction has been a key goal of international organisations within the United Nations (UN) system for some time. However, the World Bank (WB) has tended to dominate discourses on the measurement and mitigation of global poverty, and global inequality has received far less attention. While it is crucial to understand how global poverty and inequality are measured, these are not simply technical problems but are also fiercely contested political issues. This chapter therefore outlines some of the main ways in which global poverty and inequality have been measured; explains why these are so politically contested; presents some key data; and considers the broader politics of poverty and inequality in the context of globalisation processes.

Key concepts
Global poverty; global inequality

Introduction

The goal of global poverty reduction appears now to be at the heart of an international consensus, enshrined within the UN **Millennium Development Goals** (MDGs) and their successors, and pursued by international institutions such as the **World Bank** (WB) and governments in high- and low-income countries alike. But deciding what poverty is, how it should be measured and the best ways to reduce it is not straightforward.

Furthermore, related phenomena also demand our attention, particularly the current degree of global inequality, its causes and consequences. In addressing these issues, the aim of this chapter is not to summarise the huge volume of literature on poverty and inequality that now exists, nor to explain basic concepts relating to poverty and inequality, which can be found elsewhere. Rather, it aims to explore and explain the challenges of measuring and tackling poverty and inequality at the global level. It discusses some national-level concepts and data for various countries, but its chief aim in doing so is to explain how these are related to processes of **globalisation** and how they are incomplete without a global analysis.

The chapter discusses global poverty and inequality in turn. In both cases, it discusses issues of measurement first before going on to discuss the politics and policies related to tackling the problem. It is worth noting from the beginning, however, that measurement issues are not purely technical matters, but are themselves highly political.

Measuring global poverty

It is useful to begin with the distinction made by Ruth Lister (2004) between concepts, definitions and measures. As Lister argues, 'there is no single concept of poverty that stands outside history and culture. It is a construction of specific societies' (2004, p 3). We might add that it is also politically contested within those societies. *Concepts* thus concern the meanings that people attach to poverty and are 'the framework within which definitions and measurements are developed' (Lister, 2004, pp 3-4). An example given by Lister (2004, p 4) is 'lack of basic security'. *Definitions* are seen as providing 'a more precise statement of what distinguishes the state of poverty and of being poor from that of not being in poverty/poor' (2004, p 4). Examples taken from the British Social Attitudes Survey and reflecting 'absolute' and 'relative' definitions of poverty respectively are where someone does not have 'enough to eat and live without getting into debt' or where someone has 'enough to buy the things they really need, but not enough to buy the things most people take for granted' (Lister, 2004, p 4; see also Hills, 2001). Definitions and concepts may overlap, or become confused, where very broad definitions are used. By contrast, *measures* of poverty 'represent ways of operationalising definitions so that we can identify and count those defined as poor and gauge the depth of their poverty' (Lister, 2004, p 5). Poverty is often measured by income levels, although (particularly in relation to 'absolute' or 'extreme' poverty) income may be a proxy for consumption. Examples of specific measures include whether someone is unable to afford two meals a day, or food containing a certain amount of calories a day. Alternatively, to take a 'relative' example, poverty is sometimes measured in high-income countries on the basis of whether someone has less than 60 per cent of median income.

Lister's reminder that 'there is no single concept of poverty that stands outside history and culture' and that poverty 'is a construction of specific societies' (2004, p 3) raises difficult questions in a period of globalisation. If society is becoming more 'global', with people's reference points being people in other countries as well as in their own, how should we think about poverty? Should we think of ourselves as living within nationally circumscribed societies, or in different countries that are nevertheless part of one 'global' society? Similar questions are pertinent to the issue of inequality, which is discussed below.

Each country usually has its own national poverty line, but these may be derived from different principles or methodologies. If we want to count how many people in the world are living in poverty, we need an agreed methodology for doing so (Townsend, 2009). This will, of course, depend on how we conceptualise and define poverty. If we understand poverty in 'relative' rather than 'absolute' terms, then we are likely to want to agree on a methodology that would allow us to determine what is the minimum necessary for a person to sustain themselves and participate adequately in the social life of the country or particular location where they live. This minimum might vary in monetary terms from place to place, but if we can agree on a common definition and means of measurement, then we could establish the total number of poor people in the world. Gordon, for example, cites a Council of Europe definition of poverty as 'individuals or families whose resources are so small as to exclude them from a minimum acceptable way of life in the Member State in which they live' (EEC, 1981, cited by Gordon, 2009, p 95).

Alternatively, we could measure poverty globally using one 'absolute' definition of poverty, which would allow us to count all the poor people in the world according to one common measure, regardless of where they happened to reside. This is what the WB does when it applies its common measure of extreme poverty throughout the world, initially based on a global poverty line of 'one dollar a day', now US$1.25 a day. This WB measure of global poverty has been extremely influential and the WB is the foremost provider of global poverty statistics and analyses, so it is worth taking some time to examine it more closely. We should start by explaining how the WB classifies countries into the broad categories of 'low', 'middle' or 'high' income countries according to their gross national income (GNI) per capita. GNI per capita is the annual gross national income of a country divided by its **population**, or in other words, the average yearly income of each person in that country. Thus in 2012, 'low' income countries were those with a GNI per capita of US$1,025 or less; 'lower middle' income countries were those with a GNI per capita of US$1,026-4,035; 'upper middle' income countries were those with a GNI per capita of US$4,036-12,475; and 'high' income countries were those with a GNI per capita of US$12,476 or more.

The WB has conceptualised poverty as 'pronounced deprivation in wellbeing' (WB, 2000), with the definition usually stated as 'the inability to attain a minimal standard of living' (WB, 1990). This has been measured by setting a poverty line based on the expenditure necessary to buy a minimum standard of nutrition and other necessities. Although low-income countries, often acting with the advice and assistance of the WB, usually have their own national poverty lines based on these principles, the WB has built on these to derive measures of 'absolute' or 'extreme' poverty that can be applied on a global basis to count the total number of poor people in the world. The 'dollar a day' measure is the most well known of these.

The 'dollar a day' global poverty line was calculated from the official national poverty lines of a sample of low- and middle-income countries. The initial analysis for this in 1990 found that, of 33 countries, eight had national poverty lines at the equivalent of about US$31 a month, that is, approximately US$1 a day (Ravallion et al, 1991). The methodology for calculating this 'extreme poverty' threshold has changed at various points, sometimes provoking much criticism, not least because it can render comparison with poverty rates in previous periods difficult (see, for example, Wade, 2009), although the WB has revised past estimates using its newest methodology (Chen and Ravallion, 2008).

The current version of this measure is US$1.25 a day, calculated as the mean of the national poverty lines of the poorest 15 countries in the world. Since the measure is expressed in US dollars, a method is needed to convert each national currency into US dollars. This is not done using market exchange rates but rather through the use of purchasing power parity (PPP) exchange rates. This is because a dollar converted into the currency of a low-income country at market exchange rates is likely to be able to buy significantly more than the same dollar if spent in the US (Anand et al, 2010; Aten and Heston, 2010). By contrast, a dollar converted at the PPP rate buys about the same in a low-income country that $1 buys in the US. This is important because incomes in low-income countries 'can be three or four times higher when measured at PPP exchange rates than when measured at market exchange rates' (Anand et al, 2010, p 10).

Using PPP exchange rates, the WB measures poverty globally according to a range of different poverty thresholds, in addition to the main US$1.25 a day line. Estimations of the extent of poverty at each threshold are based on data collected from periodic household surveys, carried out by governments and the WB in each country. Obviously, the higher the threshold is set, the greater number of people globally fall below it and are thus counted as poor.

These thresholds are only intended to be relevant to low- and middle-income countries and have little relevance for high-income countries. They have been criticised for being both minimalist and arbitrary (see, for example, Gordon, 2009). Using a poverty threshold like the US$1.25 a day line tells us nothing about the duration of spells of poverty, since people's income tends to move upwards and downwards at different times. Furthermore, the crisp distinction made between poor and non-poor tells us nothing about how many people are just over the line or about the depth of poverty of people who are under the line. At worst, '[a] simple binary measure that classifies households as either poor or non-poor incentivizes policy makers to prioritise people just below the poverty line' (Cimadamore et al, 2013, p 2). These problems can be mitigated somewhat by comparing the numbers of poor people identified at each of the different poverty lines used by the WB. Additionally, we can measure the 'poverty gap', a way of measuring the depth of poverty using the mean shortfall from any given poverty line (counting the non-poor as having zero shortfall), expressed as a percentage of the poverty line (WB, 2013, p 33). However, a further problem, which may lead to underestimations of the extent of female and child poverty, relates to the way that households are assumed to share resources between their members (see **Box 2.1**).

Box 2.1: Gender and household surveys

The surveys that the WB relies on usually employ a unitary model of the household. As Falkingham and Baschieri (2009, p 123) explain, this model 'envisages the household as a single unit, implying the existence of a single household welfare function reflecting the preferences of *all* its members, and assumes that all members of the household pool their resources.' However, in practice members of the household are likely to have different preferences and rarely pool all of their resources. Men tend to spend some of their income on themselves, whereas women are more likely to spend it on their children or general household consumption. The unitary model makes an assumption that the (usually male) household head acts altruistically on behalf of the household as a whole, but we know that this is not always the case. The upshot is that 'gender differentials in welfare are often hidden with the result that policies to combat poverty may be poorly targeted on women and children' (Falkingham and Baschieri, 2009, p 123).

Despite their weaknesses, the poverty measurements provided by the WB do provide us with one way to estimate the number of extremely poor people in the world at any given time; to see how the numbers of extremely poor vary by country or region; and to see how poverty rates have changed over time. *Table 2.1*, for example, shows that using the WB's current preferred measure for extreme poverty, US$1.25 a day, over 25 per cent of the developing world's population, nearly 1.4 billion people, were poor in 2005 (Chen and Ravallion, 2008). At the US$2.5 a day level, more than 3 billion people, over half the developing world's population, were poor.

Table 2.1: Aggregate poverty, developing world,* 2005, as measured by the World Bank

US$ per day	% below each line	Numbers of poor (millions below each line)
1.00	16.1	876.0
1.25	25.2	1,376.7
1.45	32.1	1,751.7
2.00	47.0	2,561.7
2.50	56.6	3,084.7

Note: * 'Developing world' = 84.4% of the world's total population (Chen and Ravallion, 2008, p 23, note 38).

Source: Chen and Ravallion (2008, p 41)

Figure 2.1 shows how the absolute number of poor people in the world has changed by region since 1990, using the US$1.25 a day measure, while *Figure 2.2* shows how the percentage of poor people has changed by region. It is notable that the greatest reduction has taken place in East Asia and the Pacific, and that the percentage of poor people has fallen more sharply than the total numbers, due to **population growth**.

Figure 2.1: People living on less than 2005 PPP US$1.25 a day (billions)

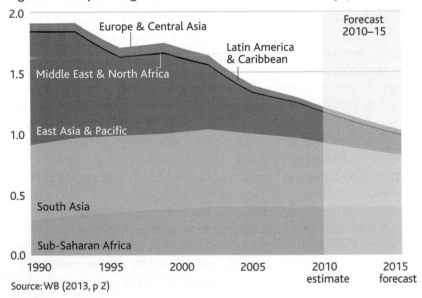

Source: WB (2013, p 2)

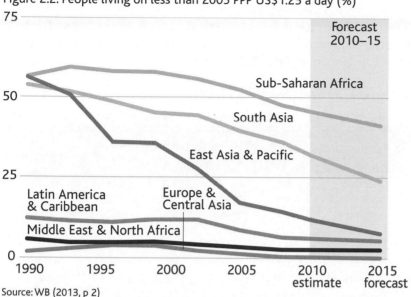

Figure 2.2: People living on less than 2005 PPP US$1.25 a day (%)

Source: WB (2013, p 2)

The US$1.25 a day measure is relatively easy to understand, and the numbers produced by the WB have a certain power in allowing us to state that over a billion people in the world suffer from extreme poverty. However, the WB's definition of poverty is a very narrow one and it produces a very conservative estimate of the number of poor people in the world. Gordon (2009) argues that the WB's approach underestimates the number of poor people because it is based only on the expenditure deemed necessary to buy a minimum amount of nutrition and other basic necessities and does not take into account other features that are necessary for wellbeing, including access to health and education services.

One approach to human wellbeing and development that overcomes some of the limitations of the purely consumption/income-based approach of the WB is that taken by the United Nations Development Programme (UNDP) in compiling the *Human development report* each year since 1990. This is based on the 'capability' concept of Amartya Sen (Sen, 2001), in which human development is defined as 'the process of enlarging people's choices' (UNDP, 1997, p 15). Poverty is thus characterised by a lack of real opportunity to achieve the things a person can do or be and which s/he values, such as living a long and healthy life, being educated and enjoying a decent standard of living (UNDP, 1997, pp 15-16). On the basis of this premise, the UNDP's Human Development Index (HDI) allows us to compare overall levels of human development within each country with those in other countries. The HDI combines indicators of health (life expectancy), education (mean and expected years of schooling) and living standards (GNI per capita) for each country. It assigns each country an overall value between 0 and 1, which then permits countries to be ranked and compared. Rankings for selected countries are shown in *Table 2.2*.

Table 2.2: Human Development Index (HDI) for selected countries, 2011

HDI rank	Country	HDI value	Life expectancy at birth (years)	Mean years of schooling (years)	Expected years of schooling (years)	GNI per capita (constant 2005 PPP$)
1	Norway	0.943	81.1	12.6	17.3	47,557
28	UK	0.863	80.2	9.3	16.1	33,296
50	Romania	0.781	74.0	10.4	14.9	11,046
79	Jamaica	0.727	73.1	9.6	13.8	6,487
101	China	0.687	73.5	7.5	11.6	7,476
123	South Africa	0.619	52.8	8.5	13.1	9,469
145	Pakistan	0.504	65.4	4.9	6.9	2,550
156	Nigeria	0.459	51.9	5.0	8.9	2,069
171	Malawi	0.400	54.2	4.2	8.9	753
187	Congo, Democratic Republic of the	0.286	48.4	3.5	8.2	280

Source: UNDP (2011)

While extremely useful in allowing us to compare mean rates of human development between countries, the HDI does not allow us to measure the total number of poor people in the world, or even in any given country, although the data can be disaggregated to illustrate disparities in human development between social groups within countries (see Grimm et al, 2006). In 1997, therefore, the Human Poverty Index (HPI) was developed to supplement the HDI and to provide a measure of the incidence of poverty in each low-income country, using the same overall approach and dimensions as the HDI: health (the percentage of people expected to die before age 40); education (the percentage of adults who are illiterate); and living standards (a composite of three variables – the percentages of people without access to health services and to safe water, and the percentage of malnourished children under five) (UNDP, 1997). This allowed for the estimation of the percentage of people in a country affected by the forms of deprivation included in the measure, and for the ranking of countries in accordance with this in a similar way to the HDI. However, because the HPI is based on a weighted average of the number of people suffering from the various forms of deprivation, it does not allow for the identification of the specific group of people or number suffering from those deprivations (UNDP, 1997, p 19; 2010, p 95).

The Multidimensional Poverty Index (MPI) thus replaced the HPI in 2010 (UNDP, 2010). Unlike the HPI, it is based on survey data in a similar way to that of the WB's poverty measures. However, unlike monetary income or consumption-based measures such as the WB's US$1.25 a day measure, the MPI considers multiple deprivations and their overlap. It sets deprivation thresholds across the same three dimensions as the HDI and the HPI: health (nutrition and child mortality); education (years of schooling and children enrolled); and living standards (cooking fuel, toilet, water, electricity, floor and assets) (see *Box 2.2*). Those suffering deprivations in at least 33 per cent of these weighted indicators are considered to be 'multidimensionally poor'. As well as providing a headcount of the number of multidimensionally poor people in a country, an MPI value is assigned to each country. This value represents both the incidence of multidimensional poverty in the country (how many people experience overlapping deprivations) and its intensity (how many deprivations they face on average). Importantly, the MPI allows not only the ranking of countries in a similar way to the HDI, but also the estimation of the number of people who are 'multidimensionally poor' for the developing world as a whole and by region. By this method, about 1.7 billion people in the 109 countries covered by the MPI in 2011 – a third of their population – lived in multidimensional poverty (UNDP, 2011, 2013). This is greater than the number produced using the WB's US$1.25 a day threshold, but less than that using the US$2.00 a day threshold (see Table 2.1).

Box 2.2: Deprivation thresholds in the Multidimensional Poverty Index

The MPI identifies multiple deprivations at the individual level in health, education and standard of living, using micro data from household surveys. Each person in a given household is classified as poor or non-poor depending on the number of deprivations his or her household experiences.

The health thresholds are having at least one household member who is malnourished and having had one or more children die. The education thresholds are having no household member who has completed five years of schooling and having at least one school-age child who is not attending school. The standard of living thresholds relate to not having electricity; not having access to clean drinking water; not having access to adequate sanitation; using 'dirty' cooking fuel (dung, wood or charcoal); having a home with a dirt floor; and owning no car, truck or similar motorised vehicle, and owning at most one of these assets: bicycle, motorcycle, radio, refrigerator, telephone or television.

Source: Adapted from Technical Note 4, UNDP (2010, p 221)

Figure 2.3 shows the percentage of people who were MPI poor in selected countries compared to those who were poor by the WB's US$1.25 a day measure. For most countries, the MPI indicates a greater number of poor people than the US$1.25 a day measure, but some countries with relatively good access to services, such as Sri Lanka, Tanzania and Uzbekistan, have an MPI significantly below this monetary-based estimate (UNDP, 2010, pp 96-7). This is an indication of the importance of access to public services in mitigating poverty, not just the need for better incomes. The MPI is an important innovation in the measurement of poverty, but because it only began in 2010 we cannot yet see how global poverty has changed over time using this measure, and even comparisons between countries must be made with caution, since available data cover various years since 2000 (UNDP, 2010, p 100; see also Alkire and Santos, 2010).

The politics of global poverty

Ultimately, there is only a point in measuring poverty if we then want to do something about it. Deciding on the appropriate concepts, definitions and measures is important, because we need to see how poverty changes over time, particularly in response to policy change and political action. The lived experiences of millions of people depend on how governments, **international organisations** and other social actors conceptualise, define and measure poverty, and on whether and how they decide to combat it.

As we have seen, the WB is the primary international organisation influencing the definition and measurement of poverty. Its approach to poverty and to the appropriate policies for its mitigation have developed considerably over time (Marshall, 2008). The key shift came in the 1990s with the initiation of the WB's Comprehensive Development Framework (Pender, 2001; Cammack, 2004) and the **Poverty Reduction Strategy Paper** (PRSP) process (Deacon, 2007, p 29). The latter involves governments of countries in receipt of loans from the WB drawing up strategy papers, alongside **civil society organisations** and WB and **International Monetary Fund** (IMF) staff, detailing how they plan to monitor and reduce poverty. The driver of the introduction of this new process was widespread criticism of the WB and IMF for the negative social consequences of the 'structural adjustment' programmes they had forced debtor countries to adopt as a condition of loans in the 1980s, which involved harsh economic austerity measures.

Figure 2.3: Comparing multidimensional and income poverty

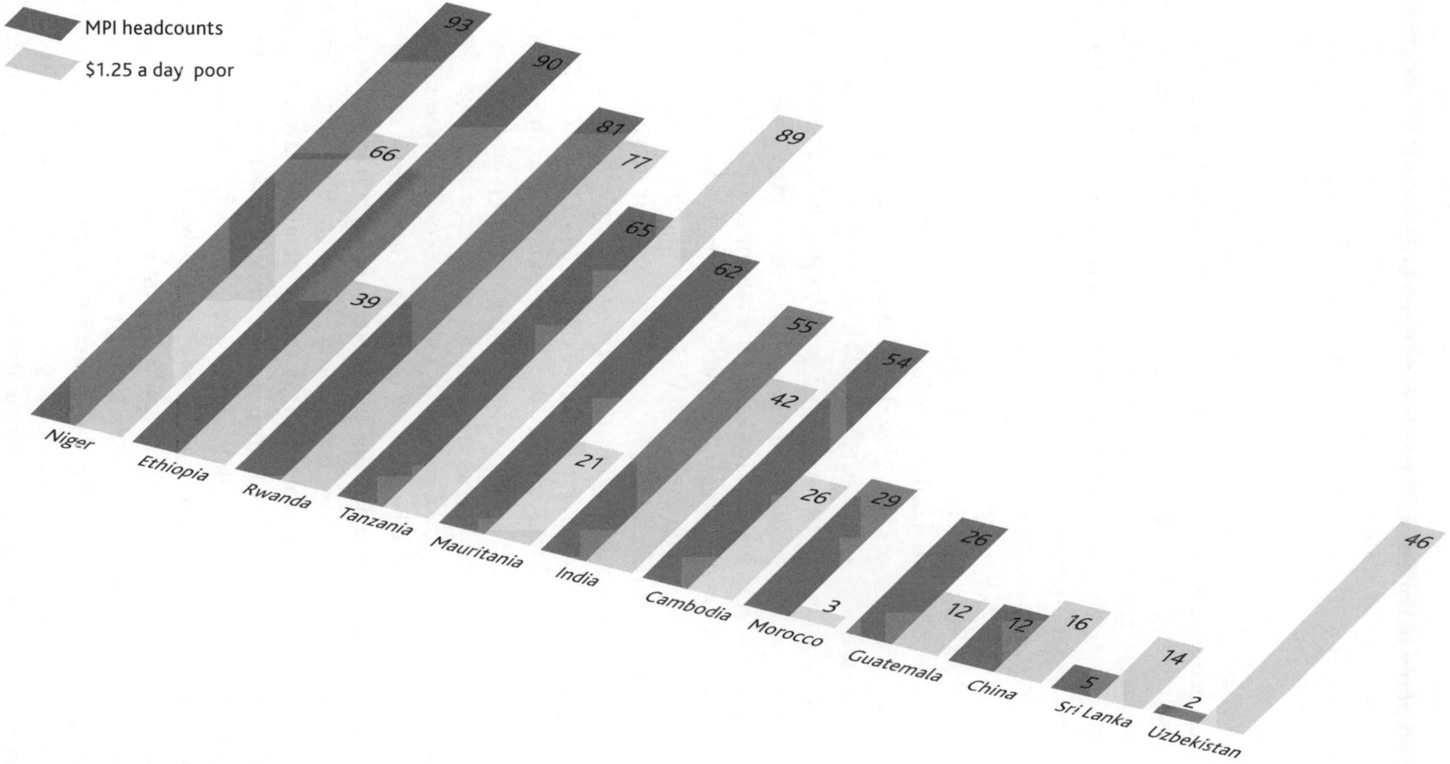

Legend: MPI headcounts, $1.25 a day poor

Source: UNDP (2010, p 97)

The WB and IMF have continued with essentially **neoliberal** policy prescriptions as conditions for debtor countries, premised on the fundamental belief that only **liberalisation** will lead to economic growth and thus poverty reduction in the long term, but the WB now also lays heavy emphasis on the provision of targeted safety nets as a means to protect the poor and the most vulnerable during the economic transition. Its *2012-22 Social protection and labour strategy* (WB, 2012) aims to increase the coherence of **social protection** systems in low- and middle-income countries, which currently suffer from the fragmentation of constituent programmes, and to emphasise three key principles: expanding and better targeting social protection coverage; ensuring that social protection programmes enhance workers' productive potential; and ensuring that systems are able to respond rapidly to economic crises and other shocks. This represents in some ways a maturing of the WB's approach to social protection, recognising as it does the need for comprehensive social protection systems rather than simply poverty alleviation programmes, the importance of social protection systems in underpinning economic growth and the need to learn lessons from the global economic crisis that began in 2007-08. Yet the emphasis on enhancing productive potential and integrating workers into labour markets reflects a continuing neoliberal bias, and critics have long argued that the emphasis on targeted safety nets risks undermining attempts to build more universal social protection systems (see Deacon, 2007, pp 24-45).

Cammack (2004) argues that the WB's commitment to poverty reduction was developed during the 1990s as part of a broader strategy which aimed to situate the WB as the foremost, if not monopoly, provider of development knowledge. This involved a 'deeper' form of intervention in low-income countries than that represented by the old structural adjustment programmes of the 1980s, in which, rather than simply imposing austerity policies on debtor countries, those countries would be compelled to integrate their economies into the global market in a way that could be sustained over the long term and to build the required institutions to facilitate this. The strategy involved 'seeking to legitimate the project through policies of controlled participation and pro-poor propaganda', while simultaneously 'promoting the proletarianisation of the world's poor (their equipping for, incorporation into and subjection to competitive labour markets)' (Cammack, 2004, p 190). Thus the WB 'envisages a global proletariat, on a wage of two dollars a day, with a reserve army of labour acting as a disciplinary force' (Cammack, 2004, p 192). The strategy involves a focus on alleviating extreme poverty while simultaneously trying to get developing countries to build the institutions that are necessary for neoliberal globalisation, including trade openness, pro-competitive forms of regulation, the provision of basic health and education services (which are necessary to build human capital) and a targeted, 'safety net', approach to social security. For this strategy to work, recipient countries must 'buy in' to the project, thus the importance of them demonstrating 'ownership' of the policies agreed with the WB through PRSPs.

The apparent success of the WB's attempt to position itself as the world's primary provider of development knowledge, and the consequent predominance of its ideas within global anti-poverty discourses, is demonstrated by the situation of its poverty measures at the heart of the UN MDGs. Using the WB's measure of one dollar a day (now interpreted as US$1.25 a day), the MDGs set targets for the reduction of global poverty between 1990 and 2015, alongside a number of other related targets (UN, 2013a). Indications are that this key poverty target will be met, but this is largely due to the achievements of economic growth in China following its relative liberalisation since the 1980s (Chen and Ravallion, 2008; UN, 2012). Proponents of neoliberal growth strategies argue that this demonstrates that liberalisation is the best path to economic growth and thus to poverty reduction (Dollar and Kraay, 2004), although critics point out that China's economic model is far from typically liberal (Wade, 2004, pp 169-70). Furthermore, poverty reduction has been slow in other regions, notably Africa, and the global economic crisis that began in 2007-08 has proved a major setback in the fight against poverty (UN, 2012).

As the world approaches 2015, the key year for the MDG targets, the UN system has set in motion the process of deciding how the key challenges relating to poverty and other aspects of development should be tackled in the next period. A host of UN organisations formed the UN System Task Team on the post-2015 UN Development Agenda, which published its initial report in 2012 (UN System Task Team, 2012). Alongside the Task Team, UN Secretary-General Ban Ki-moon appointed a 27-member High-Level Panel composed of **civil society**, private sector and government members to advise him on the post-2015 Development Agenda. The Panel was co-chaired by President Yudoyono of Indonesia, President Johnson Sirleaf of Liberia and UK Prime Minister David Cameron. The Panel's report (UN, 2013b) recommended a continued focus on 'extreme poverty' (as measured by the WB), through a commitment to its complete eradication. This was to be situated within a broader approach than that of the original MDGs, which would promote good **governance**, social inclusion and sustainable growth alongside poverty reduction, since these are 'connected and cannot be addressed in silos' (UN, 2013b, p 14). As well as bringing the number of people living on less than US$1.25 a day to zero, the report suggested targets of reducing the share of people living below each country's 2015 national poverty line and of increasing the number of poor and vulnerable people covered by social protection systems.

UNIVERSITY OF WINCHESTER
LIBRARY

In the latter regard, and overlapping with the work of setting the post-2015 Development Agenda, one particularly positive initiative has been the Social Protection Floor (SPF) Recommendation, agreed by the **International Labour Organization** (ILO) in June 2012 (ILO, 2012). This urges all governments to adopt a number of basic social security guarantees, including access to essential healthcare; basic income security for children; basic income security for people in active age who are unable to earn sufficient income, in particular in cases of sickness, unemployment, maternity and disability; and basic income security for older people. Crucially, the initiative aims both to extend social security 'horizontally' to those currently not covered and to extend it 'vertically' to enhance the contributory, wage-related, social security benefits of workers. Countries are urged to apply several principles, including universality of protection based on social solidarity. The SPF initiative is an important departure because it challenges 'growth first' economists by prioritising social protection *whatever the level of economic development* and because it argues for redistribution both nationally *and internationally* to fund social protection (Deacon, 2012). However, Deacon (2013) has shown how during the progress of its negotiation between the early 2000s until the agreement of the final text in 2012, the initiative was watered down in various ways. This included a shift from the specification of a set of specific benefits to a set of *outcomes* or *guarantees*, to be met by governments in whatever way they saw fit; a shift from a global social floor to *nationally defined floors*, with each country defining its own minimum guarantee level; and a shift from an emphasis on international financial support for the floor to mainly national responsibility for funding it.

Importantly, the initiative appears to have gained support in some of the key forums of global governance (Deacon, 2012), with the WB paying lip service to it in its *2012-22 Social protection and labour strategy* (WB, 2012) and the **G20**'s 2011 Final Communiqué recognising 'the importance of social protection floors in each of our countries, adapted to national situations' (G20, 2011). However, as Deacon (2013) warns, the involvement of the WB (alongside the ILO) in the chairing of the Social Protection Inter-Agency Coordination Board (SPIAC-B) at the behest of the G20 may be a mixed blessing. The ultimate success of the SPF initiative will depend in part on whether the WB uses its influence to ensure that the national interpretations of the floors take its preferred targeted safety net approach rather than a more universal approach; on whether the IMF allows countries the fiscal space to implement the floors; and on whether it forms an important element within the post-2015 UN Development Agenda (Deacon, 2012, 2013; see also **Chapter Eight**).

Measuring global inequality

If poverty is about the lack of certain things that people need for a minimum acceptable level of wellbeing (however defined), inequality is about the distribution of resources (or some other thing that is valued). Inequality can be measured between all individuals within a population or between population sub-groups (such as those based on gender or ethnicity, for example). The latter is important if we want to see how income, poverty rates, health or educational outcomes, or anything else that is valued, differ between sub-groups. Nevertheless, this chapter is primarily concerned with overall inequalities of material resources such as income and wealth. Discussions of this kind of inequality, whether at the national level (that is, within a country) or the global level (that is, within the world taken as a whole), often focus on inequality of *income*, although inequality of *wealth* is just as important. While sufficient income is clearly necessary for people to support themselves on a day-to-day basis, wealth has a disproportionate impact on household wellbeing over time (Davies et al, 2009). This chapter primarily discusses global inequalities of income, but readers are referred to Davies et al (2009) and Yeates (2008a) for further discussions of global inequalities of wealth, and to Ridge and Wright (2008) for broader discussions of the relationships between inequality, poverty and wealth. Here we simply note that global inequality in wealth is even greater than global inequality in income (Davies et al, 2009).

Income inequality can be measured in a number of different ways, including by use of the Gini coefficient and by dividing a population up into fractiles (that is, percentiles, ventiles, deciles or quintiles). The Gini coefficient allocates a score between 1 and 0 (or 100 and 0), where 1 equals absolute inequality and 0 equals absolute equality, so the higher the score, the higher the inequality. Fractiles can be used to show what percentage of total income is held by which segments of the population (so the top 10 per cent, for example, will have a larger share of total income than the bottom 10 per cent).

In a globalising world, how should we approach the study of income inequality? Should we be attempting to measure inequality between individuals (or households) within countries, or between the average incomes of countries, or between individuals (or households) in the world as a whole, regardless of where people live? Income inequality within countries remains important for political, economic and social outcomes, and may be influenced by processes of globalisation, so it is perhaps useful to start by comparing how income inequality has changed within various countries. Work done by the Organisation for Economic Co-operation and Development (OECD) shows that income inequality (measured using the

Gini coefficient) increased in most OECD countries between 1985 and 2008 (OECD, 2011; see **Figure 2.4**).

Figure 2.4: Income inequality in OECD countries, 1985 and 2008

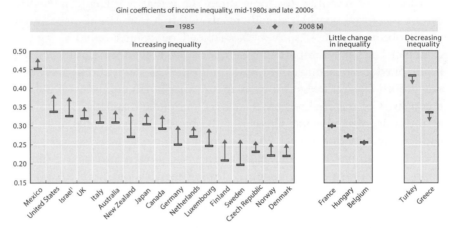

Note: For data years seeTable1, OECD, 2011. "Little change" in inequality refers to changes of less than 2percentage points.
[1] Information on data for Israel: http://dx.doi.org/10.1787/888932315602.
Source: OECD (2011, p 24)

Furthermore, gains have sometimes been concentrated at the very top of the income distribution (OECD, 2011, p 38). Hacker and Pierson (2010, p 155), for example, show that in the US, the share of pre-tax income of the richest 1 per cent increased from around 8 per cent in 1974 to more than 18 per cent in 2007. When investment and dividend income is included, the share of this richest 1 per cent increased from just over 9 per cent to 23.5 per cent during this period (Hacker and Pierson, 2010, p 155). But even focusing on the top 1 per cent can obscure the extent to which gains have been concentrated. The share of the top 0.1 per cent (the richest 150,000 families) increased from 2.7 to 12.3 per cent, while the share of the top 0.01 per cent (the richest 15,000 families) grew from 'less than one in every one hundred dollars in 1974 to more than one of every seventeen – or more than 6 percent of national income accruing to 0.01 percent' (Hacker and Pierson, 2010, p 155).

OECD data (2011) show that large 'emerging economies' had even larger rates of income inequality than most OECD countries, but changes in inequality between the early 1990s and the late 2000s showed some quite big variations (see **Figure 2.5**). Strong economic growth in Brazil and Indonesia, for example, coincided with reductions in income inequality, while in China, India, Russia and South Africa, strong economic growth was accompanied by widening income inequalities (OECD, 2011, p 51). The differences between Brazil and China indicated in *Figure 2.6*, which shows changes in real household income by quintile, are particularly interesting. While the bottom quintile gained most from economic growth in Brazil, in China during the same period it was the top quintile that gained most. Thus while *Figure 2.5* shows that Brazil was more unequal than China in both the early 1990s and the late 2000s, Brazil was becoming less unequal while China was becoming more unequal. These differences in the growth of inequality are at least in part the result of policy action, with the implementation of pro-poor public transfer, minimum wage and education policies in Brazil providing a significant part of the explanation for the downward trend in inequality in that country (Arnal and Forster, 2010, p 44; Neri, 2010). This demonstrates that, even in a period of globalisation, political action at the national level continues to be important. Whether economic growth (where it occurs) is associated with increasing or declining inequality will depend in large part on the actions of governments and other political actors in determining how the proceeds of growth are (re)distributed.

Figure 2.5: Emerging economies – change in inequality levels, early 1990s versus late 2000s[1]

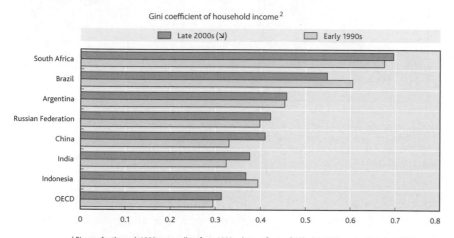

[1] Figures for the early1990s generally refer to1993, whereas figures for the late2000s generally refer to2008.
[2] Gini coefficients are based on equivalised incomes for OECD countries and per capita incomes for all EEs except India and Indonesia for which per capita consumption was used.

Source: OECD (2011, p 51)

However, while these trends in within-country inequality are important, they tell us little about trends in global inequality, that is, for the world taken as a whole. In examining global inequality, it is useful to follow the work of Milanovic, who makes a distinction between *international* and *global* measures of inequality, using three 'concepts' (Milanovic uses the term

Figure 2.6: Emerging economies – change in real household income by quintile

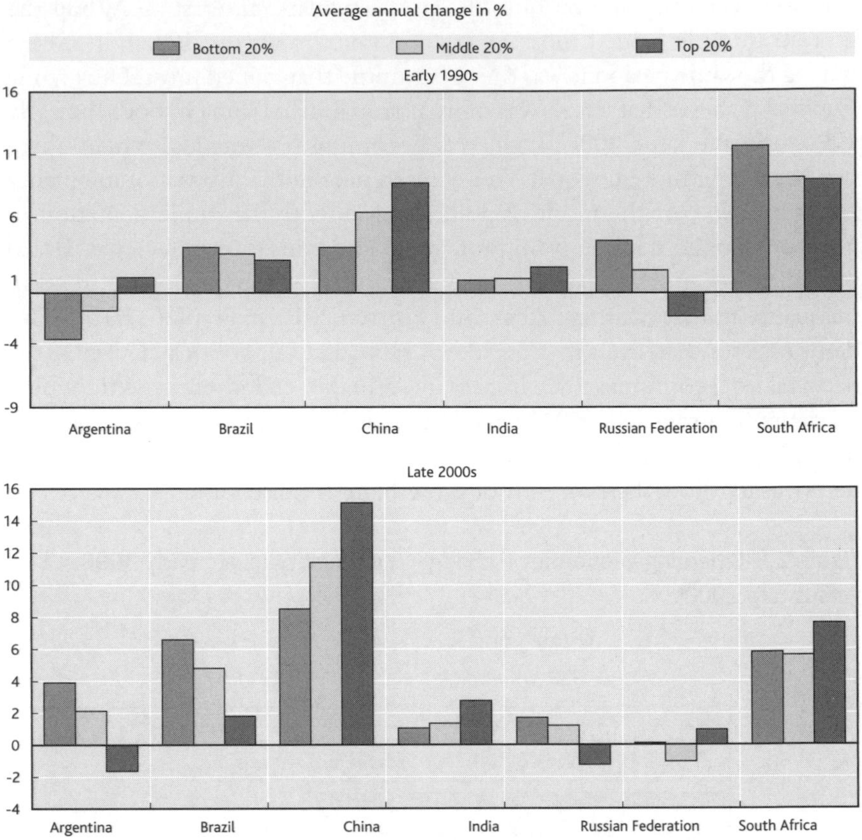

Average annual change in %

Bottom 20%   Middle 20%   Top 20%

Early 1990s

Argentina   Brazil   China   India   Russian Federation   South Africa

Late 2000s

Argentina   Brazil   China   India   Russian Federation   South Africa

[1] Figures for the early1990s generally refer to the period between 1992-93 and1999-2000, whereas figures for the late 2000s generally refer to the period between 2000 and 2008.

[2] For China, data refer to urban areas only and data for India refer to real household consumption.

Source: OECD (2011, p 52)

'concept' in a different way to Lister, meaning not just the broad idea but also some of the specific measurement issues that attach to the concept). We can measure inequality between nations (international inequality) by comparing the gross domestic income (GDI) per capita of each country. This tells us what the differences are between the mean incomes of people in different countries, but it tells us nothing about the distribution of income within those countries. This is what Milanovic calls 'concept 1 inequality' or 'unweighted international inequality' (Milanovic, 2009). 'Concept 2 inequality', or 'weighted international inequality', is the same as concept 1 inequality except that each country is represented in accordance with its population, but still with mean incomes rather than the actual incomes of the people who live there. So, for example, whereas in concept 1 China's weight is the same as any other country, in concept 2 China's weight is approximately 20 per cent of the world because of its large population. Nevertheless, concept 2 still relies on the representative (mean) incomes of people in each country (that is, GDI per capita) rather than their actual incomes, so differences in incomes within countries are still not taken into account (Milanovic, 2009, p 130). 'Concept 3 inequality' measures 'global inequality', that is, inequality between all individuals in the world, regardless of where they live. The data requirements for measuring concept 3 inequality are much more challenging than for the other two concepts, since rather than simply calculating GDI per capita from data in national accounts, it relies on collating data from household surveys undertaken in different countries (Milanovic, 2009, p 130).

Milanovic is able to show how inequality has changed over time using these different measures. *Figure 2.7* illustrates these changes. It is clear from *Figure 2.7* that unweighted international inequality increased substantially between 1950 and 2000 (measured using the Gini coefficient), with the biggest increase starting in the 1980s. Weighted international inequality appears to have reduced, but when China is removed from the calculation it has risen somewhat since the early 1980s. These results are interesting because international inequality seems to have risen most clearly since the early 1980s or late 1970s, that is, during the same period that neoliberal policies were

Figure 2.7: Milanovic's three concepts of inequality, 1950-2000

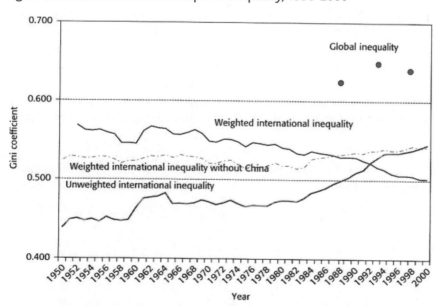

Source: Milanovic (2009, p 134), calculated using WB World Development Indicator data

implemented in many countries and processes of economic globalisation intensified. On the other hand, weighted international inequality declined primarily because of the economic growth of China following its relative economic liberalisation and integration into the world economy. Such varying trends have caused much debate about the impact of economic liberalisation on inequality, just as they have in the case of poverty (see earlier in this chapter and also **Chapter Five**). The challenges of data collection for global inequality (concept 3) mean that Milanovic only has three data points for this, 1988, 1993 and 1998. These show no clear trend, but it is clear that global inequality is much higher than international inequality. As Milanovic notes, this 'is explained by inequality within nations' (Milanovic, 2009, p 135).

Table 2.3 indicates shares of the total global income received by different fractiles of the world population for the latest of these years (1998). This shows that, measured using PPP dollars, the top 5 per cent of the world's population received 33 per cent of global income, whereas the bottom 5 per cent received just 0.2 per cent of global income, a ratio of 165:1 (Milanovic, 2009, p 141). Work by Milanovic using revisions of PPP exchange rates undertaken in 2005 has shown that international and global inequality was even greater than that displayed in *Figure 2.7* and *Table 2.3* (Milanovic, 2012a). Using these new PPP exchange rates and results from a new set of 122 national household surveys, this also shows that in 2005 the top 5 per cent of the world's population received 37.2 per cent of global income (Milanovic, 2012a, p 15). However, we can also measure global inequality using US dollars at market exchange rates, rather than at PPP exchange rates. Whereas we tend to use PPP dollars when measuring global poverty (for reasons discussed above), and can also do so when measuring global inequality, we may instead wish to use market exchange rates when measuring global inequality. This is because the rich will be globally mobile and not rely only on consuming goods bought in their country of residence (Davies et al,

Table 2.3: Share of total global income received by various fractiles of global distribution, 1998

	Top (%)	Bottom (%)	Ratio top to bottom
In US$PPP			
5%	33	0.2	165-1
10%	50	0.7	70-1
In current US$			
5%	45	0.15	300-1
10%	67.5	0.45	150-1

Source: Milanovic (2009, p 141)

2009, p156). Measured using current US dollars at market exchange rates, the disparity between the top and bottom fractiles displayed in *Table 2.3* is greater still, with the top 5 per cent receiving 45 per cent of global income and the bottom 5 per cent receiving just 0.15 per cent of global income, a ratio of 300-1 (Milanovic, 2009, p 141).

The politics of global inequality

We can see that there are extremes of inequality within countries, between the mean incomes of different countries, and between people in the world taken as a whole. For the most part these inequalities have increased substantially over recent decades. The extent of inequality has become a contentious political issue at the national level in high-, middle- and low-income countries alike, especially following the global economic crisis that began in 2007-08. One key debate has been about the impact of economic liberalisation (or 'globalisation') on inequality (see **Chapter Five**). Globalisation has often been thought to affect inequality by having a differential impact on workers with different skill levels, as well as because competition between countries seeking foreign investment leads to a '**race to the bottom**' in tax rates and social protection.

Empirical research has produced no consensus on these issues, in part because researchers do not always focus on the same aspects of globalisation when attempting to understand its impact on inequality (they may choose to focus on tariff reductions, increases in the volume of trade or increases in **foreign direct investment**, for example, or some combination of these or other variables) (Milanovic and Squires, 2005; Dreher and Gaston, 2008). Similarly, they may focus on different aspects of inequality (within-country income inequality or wage inequality, or global income inequality, for example) (Milanovic and Squires, 2005). Furthermore, it is extremely difficult to disentangle the effects of trade and investment liberalisation, reforms to labour laws and technological advances, since these often happen at the same time and each may affect the rewards accruing to different groups of workers (Milanovic and Squires, 2005; OECD, 2011). In particular, increasing openness to the world market through trade and investment liberalisation is often accompanied by liberalisation of labour markets through reforms to make labour contracts more 'flexible'; in other words, both types of liberalisation are often part of a 'package' of neoliberal reforms.

What is clear is the profound effect that government policy can have, for better or worse, on inequality within countries. Effective and well-designed policies on taxation, transfers and public services, on education and on employment protection can play a major role in mitigating inequality (OECD, 2011). Thus, the question for governments is not simply whether they should liberalise, but if they do, how they should combine economic policies of openness with tax and social policies. It is the answers to these questions that will ultimately determine the degree of inequality within a country. China's economy, for example, has grown dramatically during the period of its opening to the world economy, but inequality has also increased, making decisions about how to expand social security and other redistributory policies of the utmost importance. Furthermore, Hacker and Pierson (2010) show how government policies on these issues are not simply the result of a rational, evidence-based process, nor of the inevitable effects of globalisation, but are rather the outcome of long-term struggles between social groups and political actors. In particular, they argue, it is the growing power of business that has facilitated the dramatic increase in inequality in the case of the US (Hacker and Pierson, 2010; see also **Chapter Four**).

However, it is not only national-level policy that is important for inequality, but also how effectively governments coordinate policies through regional or international organisations. As Dreher (2006) points out, supranational political integration might effectively counter the 'race to the bottom'. Inequality therefore needs to be tackled at multiple levels – national, regional and global. At the regional level, the European Union (EU), as the most advanced regional supranational organisation, should have the capacity to set a strong social floor and to redistribute resources in a way that substantially reduces poverty and inequality across the region. Yet the EU's response to the sovereign debt crisis afflicting Greece and other countries has been profoundly neoliberal (see *Box 2.3*).

Box 2.3: Greece, the EU and the global economic crisis

The global economic crisis that began in 2007-08 led to severe recessions and sovereign debt crises in a number of European countries. This was most dramatically the case in Greece, where the crisis led to a 'sudden stop' in the availability of affordable credit and thus to the inability of the government to sustain its budget or service its debts (Papadopoulos and Roumpakis, 2012). The Greek government's ability to fashion its own policy response was severely curtailed by its membership of the Euro currency zone. The 'bailout' package arranged by the European Central Bank, the European Commission and the IMF (the so-called 'troika') imposed harsh austerity measures that 'were unprecedented, in their scope, severity, volume and speed' (Papadopoulos and Roumpakis, 2012, p 214). These included the strengthening of the rights of employers to 'hire and fire'; extensive privatisations and public sector redundancies; huge reductions in public and private sector wages; cuts in unemployment benefits and pensions; and increases in taxes on ordinary citizens alongside reductions in corporate tax (Papadopoulos and Roumpakis, 2012). The result was an estimated total fall in Greek gross domestic product (GDP) of 25 per cent between 2008 and 2013 (Papadopoulos and Roumpakis, 2013a). The impact on welfare outcomes has been dramatic. Unemployment grew from 7.4 per cent in 2008 to 27 per cent by early 2013, with youth unemployment at a staggering 64.2 per cent (Papadopoulos and Roumpakis, 2013a, b). In 2011, 28.4 per cent of the population were suffering from 'material deprivation' (measured as those who could not afford at least four out of a list of nine items), up from 24.1 per cent the year before (ELSTAT, 2013, p 53). In 2011 also, within-country income inequality as measured by the Gini coefficient stood at 33.6, reversing a previous slow decline (ELSTAT, 2013, p 55). Subjective wellbeing decreased dramatically, and the number of suicides doubled (Papadopoulos and Roumpakis, 2012, p 222). Not only has the impact on Greek society been profoundly destructive, but Papadopoulos and Roumpakis (2013b) also argue that the EU's response to the economic crisis represents a decisive shift away from the 'European social model', towards one that forces member states to implement neoliberal policies.

Internationally, the global economic crisis that began in 2007–08 prompted governments, acting through the OECD and the G20, to attempt to combat the 'erosion' of their tax bases by transnational companies (TNCs) engaging in tax avoidance or evasion (OECD, 2013). At the time of writing it was too early to say whether these attempts would be successful. However, it will take a concerted effort to ensure that they do not go the way of previous OECD initiatives, which attempted to limit secrecy in tax havens, but which did little to challenge the neoliberal consensus or to enhance the capacity of states to tax TNCs (Webb, 2004).

As discussed above, the focus of the MDGs and the post-2015 Development Agenda has been very much on combating extreme poverty, but politicians have largely ignored global inequalities of income and wealth. The report of the High-Level Panel on the post-2015 Development Agenda articulated an intention to increase equality of basic outcomes between population sub-groups within countries, so that targets on poverty and other issues would be deemed to have been met only if they were met for every sub-group (defined by income quintile, gender, age, disability, geographical location, and so on). In this way, 'countries would only be able to meet their commitments if they focus on the most vulnerable' (UN, 2013b, p 15). This is an important advance on the approach of the MDGs, yet the report also ducked the issue of income inequality at both the national and global levels, arguing that 'countries differ widely in their view of what levels of income inequality are acceptable and in the strategies they adopt to reduce it' and that therefore 'national policy in each country, not global goal-setting, must provide the answer' (UN, 2013b, p 16). Given that the report envisaged that responsibility for meeting most of the goals should lie at the national level in any case, this is a somewhat weak argument, although it is in keeping with the dominant neoliberal discourse.

Implicit (and sometimes explicit) in perspectives of this kind is an assumption that income inequality is unimportant. Yet, as Milanovic argues (2012b), global and international inequality are of the utmost importance, not least because they give rise to large **migration** flows which politicians in the rich countries will not be able to ignore. Milanovic (2012b) argues that average income differences between countries are now much more important than differences in income between social classes, undermining international class solidarity and making intense **international migration** pressure inevitable. This arguably understates the importance of social classes and the increasing importance of an emerging 'transnational capitalist class' (Robinson and Harris, 2000). Nevertheless, migration could be a key mechanism for reducing global poverty and inequality and facilitating the economic growth of poorer countries, and should be seen as similar to trade policies in this respect (Milanovic, 2012b). Like trade policy and other aspects of economic globalisation, however, migration gives rise to a number of contentious political issues that require careful management (Yeates, 2008b; Betts, 2011). Aid and migration ought therefore to be seen as complementary means for reducing poverty and inequality, especially since, if migration flows are to be reduced, the economies of poorer countries need to be helped to grow faster (Milanovic, 2012b).

As far as aid is concerned, Milanovic (2009, pp 144-5) sets out three key principles that should govern **global redistribution**. These are, first, that transfers should flow from a rich country to a poor country. Second, that they should be 'globally progressive', in other words, transfers should go from a richer person to a poorer person. As Milanovic (2009, p 144) puts it, 'It is not desirable, for instance, for a middle-class Frenchman to make a transfer to somebody who is very rich in South Africa or Brazil.' Third, global transfers should preserve 'national progressivities', that is, they should not worsen national distributions. However, this leads us back to questions of global governance which are not easy to resolve since, as Milanovic (2009, pp 145-6) notes, such transfers would require the existence of some kind of supranational agency to collect and distribute them. This raises difficult questions about the limits of **state sovereignty**, the fairer and more effective representation of lower-income countries in various international institutions, and how collective action at the global level can be made more effective. (These issues are discussed further in **Chapter Three** and in **Section Three** of the *Global social policy reader*).

Based on 2009 data, the OECD calculated that it would cost a little under US$5 billion a year in extra targeted transfers to lift half of the world's poor above the US$1.25 a day poverty line (MDG 1) by 2015 (OECD, 2012).

The total annual costs above current investment, aid and public spending in developing countries to meet the first six MDGs (on poverty, education and health) by 2015 would have been US$120 billion (OECD, 2012). Upper middle-income countries would be capable of meeting these costs themselves from taxation, while lower middle and low-income countries would require improved flows from high-income countries. As the OECD indicates, given the level of inequality in many upper middle-income countries and the austerity politics driving responses to the global economic crisis in many high-income countries, both of these would require the exercise of political will (OECD, 2012), but both are eminently achievable. Global poverty and inequality are intractable problems, but, as Thomas Pogge (2001, p 14) has put it: 'For the first time in human history it is quite feasible, economically, to wipe out hunger and preventable diseases worldwide without real inconvenience to anyone.' That progress is so slow can only be explained by the continued existence of unequal power relations, both between nation states and social classes (within nations and globally).

Conclusion

Much contemporary literature on global poverty and inequality is concerned with their measurement. This chapter has attempted to explain some of the basic measurement issues relating to both global poverty and inequality because an appreciation of these is important to understanding the scale of these interrelated problems, how they have changed over time and what might therefore be done about them. Yet, necessary as the proper measurement of both is, an overemphasis on this risks promoting the fallacy that these are essentially technical problems with technical solutions. Indeed, the debate about how we can best measure global poverty is as fierce as it is only because these are at root deeply political problems that implicitly, if not explicitly, challenge dominant power structures. The debate on the measurement of global inequality has been less politically contested, but only because governments and international organisations have managed to keep issues of inequality off the political agenda for so long. This began to change following the global financial crisis of 2007-08, but issues of inequality now need to be placed centrally on both national and international policy agendas alongside those of poverty.

Summary

- The goal of global poverty reduction has been central to the activities of international organisations for some time, but global inequality has for the most part been kept off of political agendas.

- The WB's measures of extreme poverty have been at the heart of international poverty reduction initiatives, but the measurement of global poverty remains highly contested.
- Some progress on reducing extreme poverty has been made in recent years, but this has varied greatly between different regions and the global economic crisis that began in 2007-08 has been a major setback.
- What the best means are for reducing both global poverty and inequality have been highly contested, with some arguing that liberalisation usually brings economic growth and subsequent poverty reduction. Others question this and highlight the increases in inequality, nationally and globally, that have often accompanied economic liberalisation.
- Comprehensive social policies, designed to complement carefully chosen economic policies, can play a major role in reducing both poverty and inequality. However, differing interests and unequal power relations give rise to intense political struggles over the shape of these policies.
- By most measures, a large part of the world's population continues to live in poverty and global inequality is greater than it has ever been.

Questions for discussion

- Why is the measurement of global poverty so contested?
- What are the relationships between trade and investment liberalisation, economic growth, poverty alleviation and changes in levels of inequality?
- Are reductions in inequality, nationally and/or globally, as important as the reduction of global poverty? Why?

Suggested activities

- Explore the WB's poverty data pages at http://data.worldbank.org/topic/poverty, and look in more detail at the data on poverty for different countries and regions.
- Track the debate on the post-2015 Development Agenda as it progresses, using the websites of different UN agencies and relevant non-governmental organisations (NGOs). What are the different positions and how do they differ from the proposals of the High-Level Panel (www.un.org/sg/management/beyond2015.shtml)?

Further reading and resources

Lister (2004) provides a good general introduction to poverty.

Yeates, N. and Holden, C. (2009) (eds) *The global social policy reader*, Bristol: Policy Press. Section Two contains a number of chapters on both the measurement and politics of global poverty and inequality.

Anand, S., Segal, P. and Stiglitz, J.E. (2010) (eds) *Debates on the measurement of global poverty*, Oxford Scholarship Online. This contains a number of chapters on debates about how global poverty should be measured.

Sen (2001) explains Sen's theory of capabilities, which underpins the HDI and provides a theoretical foundation for rejecting an approach to poverty that relies solely on the measurement of income or consumption.

The WB's website (www.worldbank.org), particularly its pages on Poverty (www.worldbank.org/en/topic/poverty) and Inequality (http://web.worldbank.org/WBSITE/EXTERNAL/TOPICS/EXTPOVERTY/0,,contentMDK:23003479~pagePK:148956~piPK:216618~theSitePK:336992,00.html).

The website of the UNDP (www.undp.org/content/undp/en/home.html), particularly its Poverty Reduction pages: www.undp.org/content/undp/en/home/ourwork/povertyreduction/overview.html, and the MPI pages: http://hdr.undp.org/en/statistics/mpi

The UN's MDGs website: www.un.org/millenniumgoals

The website of the Bretton Woods Project (www.brettonwoodsproject.org), an NGO that monitors the WB and IMF and promotes alternative policies.

References

Alkire, S. and Santos, M.E. (2010) *Acute multidimensional poverty: A new index for developing countries*, New York: United Nations Development Programme.

Anand, S., Segal, P. and Stiglitz, J.E. (2010) 'Introduction', in S. Anand, P. Segal and J.E. Stiglitz (eds) *Debates on the measurement of global poverty*, Oxford: Oxford Scholarship Online.

Arnal, E. and Forster, M. (2010) 'Growth, employment and inequality in Brazil, China, India and South Africa: An overview', in OECD *Tackling inequalities in Brazil, China, India and South Africa: The role of labour market and social policies*, Paris: OECD Publishing (http://dx.doi.org/10.1787/9789264088368-en).

Aten, B. and Heston, A. (2010) 'Use of country purchasing power parities for international comparisons of poverty levels: Potential and limitations', in S. Anand, P. Segal and J.E. Stiglitz (eds) *Debates on the measurement of global poverty*, Oxford: Oxford Scholarship Online.

Betts, A. (2011) *Global migration governance*, Oxford: Oxford University Press.

Cammack, P. (2004) 'What the World Bank means by poverty reduction, and why it matters', *New Political Economy*, vol 9, no 2, pp 189-211.

Chen, S. and Ravallion, M. (2008) *The developing world is poorer than we thought, but no less successful in the fight against poverty*, World Bank Policy Research Working Paper 4703 (http://econ.worldbank.org/external/default/main?pagePK =64165259&theSitePK=469372&piPK=64165421&menuPK=64166093&entity ID=000158349_20100121133109).

Cimadamore, A.D. et al (2013) 'Poverty and the Millennium Development Goals: A critical assessment and a look forward', *CROP Poverty Brief*, January (www.crop.org/ viewfile.aspx?id=422).

Davies, J.B., Sandstrom, S., Shorrocks, A. and Wolff, E.N. (2009) 'The world distribution of household wealth', in N. Yeates and C. Holden (eds) *The global social policy reader*, Bristol: Policy Press, pp 149-62.

Deacon, B. (2007) *Global social policy and governance*, London: Sage Publications.

Deacon, B. (2012) 'The Social Protection Floor', *CROP Poverty Brief*, October (www.crop. org/storypg.aspx?id=598&MenuNode=633958868628358455&zone=12).

Deacon. B. (2013) *Global social policy in the making: The foundations of the Social Protection Floor*, Bristol: Policy Press.

Dollar, D. and Kraay, A. (2004) 'Trade, growth and poverty', *The Economic Journal*, vol 114, no 493, pp F22-F49.

Dreher, A. (2006) 'The influence of globalization on taxes and social policy: An empirical analysis for OECD countries', *European Journal of Political Economy*, vol 22, pp 179-201.

Dreher, A. and Gaston, N. (2008) 'Has globalization increased inequality?', *Review of International Economics*, vol 16, no 3, pp 516-36.

ELSTAT (2013) *Living conditions in Greece*, Athens: Hellenic Statistical Authority.

Falkingham, J. and Baschieri, A. (2009) 'Gender and poverty: how misleading is the unitary model of household resources?', in N. Yeates and C. Holden (eds) *The global social policy reader*, Bristol: Policy Press, pp 123-7.

G20 (2011) *Summit of G20 heads of state and government – Final communiqué* (www. ambafrance-uk.org/Cannes-G20-summit).

Gordon, D. (2009) 'The international measurement of poverty and anti-poverty policies', in N. Yeates and C. Holden (eds) *The global social policy reader*, Bristol: Policy Press, pp 91-114.

Grimm, M., Harttgen, K., Klasen, S. and Misselhorn, M. (2006) *A Human Development Index by income groups*, Human Development Report Office Occasional Paper (http://hdr.undp.org/en/media/inequalityadjustedhdi.pdf).

Hacker, J.S. and Pierson, P. (2010) 'Winner-take-all politics: Public policy, political organization and the precipitous rise of top incomes in the United States', *Politics & Society*, vol 38, no 2, pp 152-204.

Hills, J. (2001) 'Poverty and social security', in A. Park, J. Curtice, K. Thomson, L. Jarvis and C. Bromley (eds) *British social attitudes: The 18th report*, London: Sage Publications.

ILO (International Labour Organization) (2012) *Text of the Recommendation Concerning National Floors of Social Protection*, International Labour Conference 101st Session, Provisional Record No 14A, Geneva: ILO (www.ilo.org/ilc/ILCSessions/101stSession/reports/provisional-records/WCMS_183326/lang--en/index.htm).

Lister, R. (2004) *Poverty*, Cambridge: Polity.

Marshall, K. (2008) *The World Bank: From reconstruction to development to equity*, London: Routledge.

Milanovic, B. (2009) 'Globalization and inequality', in N. Yeates and C. Holden (eds) *The global social policy reader*, Bristol: Policy Press, pp 129-47.

Milanovic, B. (2012a) 'Global inequality recalculated and updated: The effect of new PPP estimates on global inequality and 2005 estimates', *Journal of Economic Inequality*, vol 10, pp 1-18.

Milanovic, B. (2012b) 'Global inequality: From class to location, from proletarians to migrants', *Global Policy*, vol 3, no 2, pp 125-34.

Milanovic, B. and Squires, L. (2005) *Does tariff liberalization increase wage inequality? Some empirical evidence*, World Bank Policy Research Working Paper 3571, Washington, DC: The World Bank.

Neri, M.C. (2010) 'The decade of falling income inequality and formal employment generation in Brazil', in OECD *Tackling inequalities in Brazil, China, India and South Africa: The role of labour market and social policies*, Paris: OECD Publishing (http://dx.doi.org/10.1787/9789264088368-en).

OECD (Organisation for Economic Co-operation and Development) (2011) *Divided we stand: Why inequality keeps rising*, Paris: OECD Publishing (http://dx.doi.org/10.1787/9789264119536-en).

OECD (2012) *Can we still achieve the Millennium Development Goals?: From costs to policies*, Development Centre Studies, Paris: OECD Publishing (http://dx.doi.org/10.1787/9789264173248-en).

OECD (2013) *Action plan on base erosion and profit shifting*, Paris: OECD Publishing (http://dx.doi.org/10.1787/9789264202719-en).

Papadopoulos, T. and Roumpakis, A. (2012) 'The Greek welfare state in the age of austerity: Anti-social policy and the politico-economic crisis', in M. Kilkey, G. Ramia and K. Farnsworth (eds) *Social policy review 24*, Bristol: Policy Press, pp 205-30.

Papadopoulos, T. and Roumpakis, A. (2013a) 'Familistic welfare capitalism in crisis: Social reproduction and anti-social policy in Greece', *Journal of International and Comparative Social Policy*, vol 29, no 3, pp 204-24.

Papadopoulos, T. and Roumpakis, A. (2013b) 'Democracy, welfare reforms and European integration: The Greek crisis as part of the crisis of the European social model', 'Paper to the international conference on "Shifting to post-crisis welfare states in Europe? - Long term and short term perspectives", Berlin, June 4 - 5, 2013.'

Pender, J. (2001) 'From "structural adjustment" to "comprehensive development framework": Conditionality transformed?', *Third World Quarterly*, vol 22, no 3, pp 397-411.

Pogge, T. (2001) 'Priorities of global justice', *Metaphilosophy*, vol 32, no 1-2, pp 6-24.

Ravallion, M., Datt, G. and van de Walle, D. (1991) 'Quantifying absolute poverty in the developing world', *Review of Income and Wealth*, vol 37, pp 345-61.

Ridge, T. and Wright, S. (eds) (2008) *Understanding inequality, poverty and wealth: Policies and prospects*, Bristol: Policy Press.

Robinson, W. I. and Harris, J. (2000) 'Towards a global ruling class? Globalization and the transnational capitalist class', *Science & Society*, vol 64, no 1, pp 11-54.

Sen, A. (2001) *Development as freedom*, Oxford: Oxford University Press.

Townsend, P. (2009) 'Poverty, social exclusion and social polarization: The need to construct an international welfare state', in N. Yeates and C. Holden (eds) *The global social policy reader*, Bristol: Policy Press, pp 81-9.

UN (United Nations) (2012) *The Millennium Development Goals report 2012*, New York: UN (www.un.org/millenniumgoals/reports.shtml).

UN (2013a) *Millennium Development Goals* (www.un.org/millenniumgoals).

UN (2013b) *A new global partnership: Eradicate poverty and transform economies through sustainable development. The report of the High-Level Panel of Eminent Persons on the Post-2015 Development Agenda*, New York: UN.

UNDP (United Nations Development Programme) (1997) *Human development report 1997*, New York: UNDP.

UNDP (2010) *Human development report 2010*, New York: UNDP.

UNDP (2011) *Human development report 2011*, New York: UNDP.

UNDP (2013) *Multidimensional Poverty Index* (http://hdr.undp.org/en/statistics/mpi/).

UN System Task Team on the Post-2015 UN Development Agenda (2012) *Realizing the future we want for all: Report to the Secretary General*, New York: UN.

Wade, R.H. (2004) 'On the causes of increasing world poverty and inequality, or why the Matthew effect prevails', *New Political Economy*, vol 9, no 2, pp 163-88.

Wade, R.H. (2009) 'Globalization, poverty and income distribution: Does the liberal argument hold?', in N. Yeates and C. Holden (eds) *The global social policy reader*, Bristol: Policy Press, pp 115-22.

WB (World Bank) (1990) *World development report: Poverty*, Oxford: Oxford University Press.

WB (2000) *World development report 2000/2001: Attacking poverty*, Washington, DC: WB.

WB (2012) *Resilience, equity and opportunity: The World Bank 2012-2022 Social protection and labour strategy*, Washington, DC: WB.

WB (2013) *World development indicators 2013*, Washington, DC: WB (http://data.worldbank.org/products/wdi).

Webb, M.C. (2004) 'Defining the boundaries of legitimate state practice: Norms, transnational actors and the OECD's project on harmful tax competition', *Review of International Political Economy*, vol 11, no 4, pp 787-827.

Yeates, N. (2008a) 'Global inequality, poverty and wealth', in T. Ridge and S. Wright (eds) *Understanding inequality, poverty and wealth: Policies and prospects*, Bristol: Policy Press, pp 81-101.

Yeates, N. (2008b) 'Global migration policy', in N. Yeates (ed) *Understanding global social policy*, Bristol: Policy Press, pp 229-52.

three

Global and regional social governance

Bob Deacon

Overview

This chapter approaches the subject of global social policy from the point of view of its governance. Governance is a concept that allows for the recognition that a range of different actors and organisations are involved in shaping, overseeing and implementing social policies. The chapter first introduces some key concepts that help us understand the complexity of the global social governance process. It then outlines the key international organisations involved in global social governance and reviews progress in the development of global social rights, redistribution and regulation. Finally, it reviews several suggestions about how the current system of global social governance might be reformed, attending to both global and world-regional structures.

Key concepts

Complex multilateralism; global policy advocacy coalitions; global public–private partnerships; regional social policy; global social governance; global redistribution; global social regulation; global social rights

Introduction

This chapter provides an account of the institutions and actors that are engaged in the process of governing **global social policy**. This process is referred to as **global social governance**: *global* because the policy issue we are addressing is worldwide in nature, involves transnational processes and cross-border fora (see Chapter One); *social* because we are concerned with health, **social protection**, education and other social welfare issues; and *governance* because there is no one locus of elected government power, but rather a number of actors and agencies all contributing to a complex process of influence, decision making and administration. Before we examine those institutions and actors, this chapter first provides a guide to some concepts to help us understand the role of those organisations in the structures and processes of global social governance.

Conceptualising global social governance

At the outset, we have to point to the existence of the dispute within the international relations literature between those 'realists' who continue to insist that there is no such thing as *global* governance, and 'cosmopolitans' (Held and McGrew, 2002) who argue that genuinely transnational policy processes now exist in an interconnected world. For 'realists', what exists in terms of international institutions such as the United Nations (UN) and the **World Bank** (WB) are precisely that, *inter*national institutions whose policies and programmes are shaped in the main by states. Cosmopolitans, on the other hand, argue that **international organisations** and other international actors have some autonomy from states and are engaged in a genuinely transnational policy-making process. A formulation that attempts to reconcile these two perspectives is the concept of 'complex multilateralism' (O'Brien et al, 2000). This captures the extent to which states and inter-state bargaining exists alongside genuinely transnational policies and policy-making processes, whereby the professional staff and secretariats of international agencies are in dialogue with **non-state international actors**.

In addition to states and formal international organisations, a whole host of other actors and players are engaged in shaping and administering global social policy (Yeates, 1999, 2001; see also **Chapter One**, this volume). First, non-state international actors are increasingly playing an important role in world politics and global **governance**. Josselin and Wallace (2001) reviewed this literature in a volume that examined the part played by international experts, global think tanks, **transnational corporations** (TNCs), the Catholic Church, international trade unions, global **diasporas** and other transborder actors in specific policy fields. Yeates (1999, 2001) reiterated the ways in which global social policy formation and governance occur outside the realm of **international governmental organisations** (IGOs) as well as within them (see also **Chapter One** of this volume). Second, within this context have emerged a number of new multistakeholder initiatives, such as **global public–private partnerships** (PPPs) that are engaged directly with mechanisms of **global redistribution** and **global regulation**. The Global Fund to Fight AIDS, Tuberculosis and Malaria (the 'Global Fund'), for example, was established in 2002 as a PPP with a secretariat housed in the **World Health Organization** (WHO) but with the WB managing the funds as a trustee. Income is derived from donor governments and philanthropic organisations such as the Bill & Melinda Gates Foundation (BMGF) (see **Chapter Seven**, this volume).

At the global level, therefore, there are diverse actors with a stake in shaping global social policy. These actors are engaged in a struggle to define the nature of the social problems and to affect their preferred societal visions in policies. The term 'struggle' is used because there are competing and overlapping institutions and ideas about what makes effective social policy. First, the WB and, to a lesser extent, the **International Monetary Fund** (IMF) and **World Trade Organization** (WTO), are in competition for influence with the UN system. The WB's health, social protection and education policy for countries is not always the same as that of the WHO, **International Labour Organization** (ILO) or the UN Educational, Scientific and Cultural Organisation (UNESCO), respectively. While the world may be said to have one emerging Ministry of Finance in the shape of the IMF (with lots of shortcomings) and one Ministry of Trade in the shape of the WTO (which is highly contested), it has two Ministries of Health (WHO and the WB), two Ministries of Social Security (ILO and the WB) and two Ministries of Education (UNESCO and the WB). Then again, the UN social agencies (WHO, ILO, the United Nations Children's Fund [UNICEF] and UNESCO) are not always espousing the same policy as the UN Department of Economic and Social Affairs (UNDESA). Moreover, the UN Secretary-General's initiative such as the Global Compact with Business may bypass or sideline the social development policies of UNDESA. Quite apart from conflict between the UN and WB and within the UN system, there is also the **G8**, G20, **G77** and other regional groupings of countries that need to be considered. This struggle among many different global actors for the right to shape policy and for the content of that policy as well as their efforts to develop some kind of coordinated policy is what passes for a system of global social governance.

Because so many players are engaged in this complex process of global social governance, it has been argued that transnational or **global policy advocacy coalitions** (Orenstein, 2008) and **transnational knowledge networks** (Stone and Maxwell, 2005) play a major part in shaping global policy formulation. Such actors organise alliances between some of the players identified and get policy progressed more quickly. The role of global policy advocacy coalitions is discussed in **Chapter Eight** of this volume in relation to the development of global pensions and social protection policy.

A further preliminary remark is required regarding the concept of **multilevel governance** that is often used to capture the idea of layers of governance at sub-national, national, world-regional and global levels. Some have argued that it may be better to approach this issue using the concept of scale (see, for example, Stubbs 2005; see also **Chapter One** in this volume). The suggestion is that the complexity of transnational policy making cannot be captured by thinking in terms only of discrete layers or levels of government. What is important here is not only that policy making is taking place at different levels of governance, but also that key policy players operate at different levels *at any one moment*. Global actors, whether representatives of the WB or of **international non-governmental organisations** (INGOs), regional actors (for example, the European Union [EU]) and national actors all find themselves involved in activities shaping national social policy. Some actors, such as international consulting companies or international *policy entrepreneurs* are more able to access these policy spaces than some national or local organisations (Wedel, 1998). Those who are better able to travel between these policy spaces – consultants, INGO experts, policy entrepreneurs – are better placed to influence global and national social policy. Thus, national policy about poverty reduction in Tanzania is made by international WB consultants and INGO representatives acting in global, national and sub-national fora alongside consultants and non-governmental organisations (NGOs) operating in the domestic sphere (Gould, 2005).

The issue of global social governance generates intense debate between those holding different political positions and representing different interests. Marxian analysts dismiss existing global social governance as a smokescreen to manage global capitalism in the interests of global capital (Soederberg, 2006). Social democrats (Monbiot, 2003) want to reform existing global social governance to make it more effective at tackling global social problems. Some on the political right (Ohmae, 1990) dismiss existing global governance as an interference in both markets and national interests and want less of it, while others on that side of the political spectrum want an effective global governance to maintain stability and peace necessary for capital accumulation without too many concessions to social policy questions. Finally, many in the Global South (Bello, 2004) regard existing structures and processes of global social governance as skewed in favour of the interests of the Global North and want to decommission much of it (Yeates and Deacon, 2010). Here the project of world-regional social governance emerges as one possible alternative 'global' reform strategy and is discussed later in this chapter.

This chapter now proceeds to:

- elaborate on the idea of global social governance as an arena of contestation, illustrated by the example of social policy advice offered by international organisations to countries;
- outline the emergence of supranational social policies of redistribution, regulation and rights; and
- review the major arguments and proposals for global social governance reform, including an outline of the scenario of world-regional social governance.

International organisations and national social policies

The World Bank

The WB (in terms of its component bodies – the International Bank for Reconstruction and Development [IBRD] and the International Development Association [IDA]), under the guise of being *the* world's anti-poverty agency, played the major role in shaping national social policy in developing and transition countries in the 1980s and 1990s. Its earlier insistence on user charges or cost recovery, through the process of policy conditionality whereby money is lent on condition of policy change, often prevented access by people living in poverty to education and health services. Its demonstration that public spending often benefited those other than the poor was used to undermine the embryonic welfare states of Latin America, South Asia and Africa that had been built to serve the interests of the state-building middle classes. WB social policy essentially became a safety net policy for people living in poverty and fostered private commercial services for the better-off. Certainly, it advocated the privatisation of pensions throughout Latin America and Eastern Europe (Orenstein, 2008). There are some signs that the ongoing intellectual struggle inside the WB between those who still favour safety nets for the poor and private services for the better-off and those more attuned to the European story of building cross-class alliances to create a good public service for all might be tilting in favour of the latter. Indeed, one reading of the Bank's *World development report* of 2006 is that concern with the institutional and political barriers to equity is also now centre stage in the WB (Deacon, 2007). A new *Social protection and labour strategy*, published in 2012, at least pays lip service to the ILO's Social Protection Floor (SPF) (Deacon, 2013). Others continue to see pronounced **neoliberal** tenets in WB social policy (for example, Fergusson and Yeates, 2013 on youth employment; see also **Chapter Nine** of this volume in relation to education). A problem, however, for those within the WB who have struggled long and hard to reform its social policies in a more progressive direction is that they are working in an institution that does not enjoy global legitimacy. In particular, the South regards the WB as serving Northern interests (Bello, 2004). We also need to distinguish between the possibly more progressive elements within the WB and the regressive ones within the wider World Bank Group: the WB's International Finance Corporation (IFC) in particular continues to actively encourage private investment in health and education (Deacon, 2007, 2013).

International Monetary Fund (IMF)

The thrust of IMF social policy in the 1970s, 1980s and 1990s was also the 'safety net' comprising targeted subsidies, cash compensation in lieu of subsidies or improved distribution of essentials such as medicine. The IMF also insisted on these in the process of policy-conditioned structural adjustment lending. Although criticism of the IMF's structural adjustment facility led to its replacement by the poverty reduction and growth facility, critics continue to point out the contradictions between the IMF's short-term concerns with macroeconomic stability and long-term poverty reduction goals. In particular, they point out that IMF fiscal targets often lead to diminished social spending. However, in terms of the IMF's own account of its social policy prescriptions for countries, there has been a significant shift from the 'old' structural adjustment days. It now insists that in its attempts to reign in government spending, in the context of its encouragement to countries to adopt austerity measures after the global economic crisis of 2008, that it protects social spending. Generally this is still in keeping with its safety net approach preserving spending on the most vulnerable only, which means it continues to be the subject of intense criticism (Deacon, 2007, 2011, 2013; Ortiz and Cummins, 2012).

World Trade Organization (WTO)

The WTO, formed in 1995, is also a key institutional actor in global social policy, and is influencing national social policy formation in diverse and controversial ways. This is especially the case in terms of boosting global private (commercial) service providers through the General Agreement on Trade in Services (GATS) and in terms of the constraints of the Agreement on Trade-Related Aspects of Intellectual Property Rights (TRIPS) protecting drug company patents, which affects the cost of drugs in poor countries. The part played by the WTO is discussed further in this volume: in **Chapter Five** in the context of international trade and welfare, in **Chapter Seven** in the context of global health policy and in **Chapter Nine** in relation to education.

Organisation for Economic Co-operation and Development (OECD)

The Organisation for Economic Co-operation and Development (OECD), an international organisation of the richest developed countries, also plays a part in the global social governance process. The social policy advice of the OECD occupies a position somewhere between the market opening and liberalising push of the WB, IMF and WTO on the one hand, and the concern of UN social agencies on the other to protect public services. It has argued that **globalisation** creates the need for more, not less, social expenditure, and has been fairly even-handed in its advice about social policy, although Armingeon and Beyeler (2004) emphasise the neoliberal tendencies of the OECD's social policy advice provided by its Department of Economics to member countries (see also **Chapter Seven** in the context of health and **Chapter Nine** in the context of education, this volume). There is a difference of emphasis within the OECD, with the Directorate for Employment, Labour and Social Affairs (DELSA) favouring adequate public services and the Department of Financial and Enterprise Affairs encouraging private provision (Deacon and Kaasch, 2008). The OECD is proactive in advocating decent childcare services to get women into work (Mahon and McBride, 2008; Mahon, 2009) and is trying to rein in the worst excesses of tax havens.

International Labour Organization (ILO)

The ILO is the longest-established IGO concerned with social questions although mainly focused in practice on formal *workers*. It was a major player helping developing countries build state pension and social security systems for employees between 1930 and the early 1970s (Rodgers et al, 2009). Although the WB took over the global leadership role in the 1980s and 1990s in the social protection domain, arguing for and securing the rolling back of state systems in favour of privatised and individualised ones, especially in the area of pensions, the ILO fought back. It sought to expose what it regarded as the flaws in the dominant WB thinking on pensions by arguing that there was no demographic imperative leading to privatisation, that the European-type schemes were reformable and sustainable, and that the privatisation strategy was merely a cover to increase the share of private capital savings (see **Chapter Eight** for further discussion). Just as in the WB, so in the ILO there were other tendencies. The ILO's Socio-Economic Security Programme (1999-2005) had taken a broad brief to examine policies that might contribute to universal *citizen (and resident)* security in the context of global labour flexibility. This programme argued for the emergence of a new universalism 'from below', embodying, for example, universal cash income benefits conditional on a child's attendance at school or universal categorical pensions (Deacon, 2007). Although that programme ended, some of these ideas became mainstreamed within the ILO. In 2012 it promulgated an important new SPF policy for all *residents* that would provide the guarantee of income security throughout the life span and access to affordable healthcare (see **Chapter Two**). The ILO has worked hard for global policy synergy between agencies on this policy, as discussed later in this chapter.

World Health Organization (WHO)

The shadow cast by the dominant role of the WB also touched the WHO in the 1980s and 1990s, so much so that one Director-General, Gro Harlem Bruntland, attempted to rescue WHO from the margins of international influence and establish it as an agency able to compete with, or at least stand alongside, the WB as an authority on global health issues and national health policies. To do this, she believed it necessary to shift WHO discourse from a purely normative one about health for all to one that engaged with economists. Health expenditures were to be encouraged not because they were morally desirable but because they were a sound investment in human capital. However, in subsequent work on comparing healthcare systems, the WHO came under heavy criticism for ranking countries and has lost some ground to the OECD where analytical work on health services is expanding rapidly with EU support (see also **Chapter Seven**). Nevertheless it has undertaken significant work on the social determinants of health convening a Commission that produced a well-received report followed by a global conference in Rio 2011. There are signs of increased synergy between the health policies of different international organisations (Kaasch, 2013) with the WB, the OECD and the WHO increasingly arguing for free services at the point of delivery.

United Nations Educational, Scientific and Cultural Organisation (UNESCO)

One of the smallest international organisations concerned with social policy is the Paris-based UNESCO. WB versus UN social agency issues also arose with regard to education and the role of UNESCO. In the context of the Education for All (EFA) campaign with which UNESCO is centrally connected, the big question of money was in effect left to the WB to manage the fast-track initiative and the global education fund for education. It publishes an annual global monitoring report tracking the meeting of the EFA goal. UNESCO remains rather more concerned with the content of education, giving emphasis to its social and humanising purposes, and has promulgated a set of guidelines to regulate global private education. It has good links with ministers of social development in Africa, Latin America and to a lesser extent Asia, with whom it has been encouraging a South–South regional social policy dialogue (see also **Chapter Nine**).

United Nations Children's Fund (UNICEF)

UNICEF, which is funded in large part by popular donations and operates with a degree of independence from the rest of the UN system, focuses on the welfare and rights of children, and in so doing addresses a wide range of social policy issues. Its professional staff have often been in the forefront of criticisms of the residual social policy approach of the WB. For example, it was the first to argue (Cornia et al, 1987) for structural adjustment with a 'human face'. It is broadly in favour of universal child support policies. More recently it has developed its own social protection policy supportive of the ILO's SPF, and undertaken excellent work challenging the 'austerity' consensus in 2012 with publications calling for a *Recovery for all* (Ortiz and Cummins, 2012).

United Nations Development Programme (UNDP) and United Nations Department of Economic and Social Affairs (UNDESA)

For the future of social policy in developing countries, perhaps the major struggle for influence between international organisations centred in the period 2000-10 on how countries would plan to meet the **Millennium Development Goals** (MDGs) set by the UN and agreed by the WB, IMF and OECD in 2000. Planning for meeting these goals to halve poverty, get children into school and improve access to health with the support of increased aid from richer countries required countries to construct social development plans that are overseen by the UNDP. The UNDP operates in countries to support development but has far fewer resources than the WB. On the one hand, countries are required to bring these UN Development Programme (UNDP) plans into line with the WB-directed **Poverty Reduction Strategy Papers** (PRSPs), which were still largely evaluated through the lenses of its safety net approach. Also existing, on the other hand, were social policy guidance notes issued by the UN Department of Economic and Social Affairs (UNDESA) (Ortiz, 2007) to build universal and inclusive forms of provision linked to adequate job creation. However, UNDESA, as the Secretariat of the UN Economic and Social Council in New York, did not have an adequate operational capacity in countries to drive its new guidance notes, which – crucially – are not endorsed by UNDP.

Now attention turns to what UN development goals will replace the MDGs after 2015, and all UN agencies are lobbying to influence these. A fear is that concrete social goals might be replaced by vague sustainability goals.

United Nations Committee on Economic, Social and Cultural Rights (UNCESCR)

This relatively weak sub-committee of the relatively ineffective UN Economic and Social Council has responsibility for overseeing and reporting on violations by countries of the UN's 1966 International Covenant on Economic, Social and Cultural Rights. In principle, this covenant is very progressive in social policy terms, stating that parties to the covenant recognise everybody's right to social security, including social insurance, and to an adequate standard of living (see Social Watch, 2007). There are, however, no enforcement mechanisms, no means of legal redress at the global level and no individual right of appeal against any failure of governments to protect social rights (Deacon, 2007; Dean, 2008). Similar limitations apply to the more recent 1989 Convention on the Rights of the Child and the 2008 Convention on the Rights of Persons with Disabilities. However the Special Rapporteurs on Extreme Poverty and on the Right to Food combined in 2012 to make the case for a global fund for social protection (Schutte and Sepulveda, 2013).

Overview and reflection on the influence of international organisations: new actors, new thinking?

In sum, ideas about desirable national social policy argued for by the major international organisations suggested in the 1990s and early 2000s something approaching a 'war of position' between agencies and sometimes the actors within them. This struggle was essentially between those who had argued for a more selective, residual role for the state together with a larger role for private actors in health, social protection and education provision, and those who take the opposite view. This division of opinion often reflected a disagreement as to whether the reduction of poverty is a matter of targeting specific resources on the poorest, or whether it is a matter of both providing universal services and effecting major social and political-institutional change, involving a shift in power relations and a significant increase in redistribution from rich to poor (see also **Chapter Two** in this volume).

The tide *may* have begun to turn against both the residualising and privatising view towards a more universal approach to social provision. This began in the 2000s with the UN, working with sympathetic donors such as the Scandinavians and some other European countries, to undo the damage wrought by the WB over the past decades, and continues now in the 2010s with many Latin American and some African countries taking the lead, having themselves introduced new form of universal social transfers. There is certainly visible progress towards greater global social policy synergy with, for example, the ILO and WB jointly chairing a new Social Protection Inter-Agency Cooperation Board (SPIAC-B) (see also **Chapter Eight**). The EU continues to state in the context of its development agenda (European Commission, 2012) and as a global social policy player that it supports universal social protection policy, although within its own borders it has been an ally of the IMF in forcing social expenditure cuts in some EU member countries. The assumed progressive role of the EU in global social policy has certainly been questioned (Orbie and Tortell, 2009). On the one hand, the process of global social policy making has become more complicated and multi-actored, with much more South–South cooperation and less influence from the Global North. China has become a major donor in Africa supporting infrastructure development rather than social protection (Surender and Walker, 2012), seeming to place no social or human rights requirement on the countries it lends and gives to. On the other hand, the resources made available create a bit more policy space for recipient countries so they are less dependent on the IMF and WB and less influenced by them.

Finally, as suggested above, the global social policy debate has become overlaid with the global environmental debate and the global climate change debate. The Rio+20 UN meeting in 2012 was an example of this. At its best this means that some actors, such as the ILO, put the case for treating economic policy, social policy and environmental policy on a level playing field, whereas others (UNDP, WB) tend to combine a focus on environmental policy and economic policy so that concepts such as *sustained green growth* replace the concept of *sustainable growth*, and necessary discussions of how social equity and social justice might be achieved in a period of no-growth disappear (see also **Chapter Eleven**, this volume). These issues will dominate the UN post-2015 MDG agenda. One international organisation that will need to be brought much more into focus in future is the Food and Agriculture Organisation (FAO), with its concern with hunger.

Global redistribution, regulation and rights

In terms of global social policy understood as supranational social policy at the global level, the world is stumbling towards articulating a global social policy of **global redistribution**, global regulation and **global social rights**, and creating the institutions necessary for the realisation of such policies in practice.

Global redistribution

In terms of international North–South transfers, in addition to the continued overseas development aid provided by rich countries to poorer ones, we must note the birth of new Global Funds for Health (www.theglobalfund.org/en), Education (www.globalpartnership.org) and a proposal for one for Social Protection (Schutte and Sepulveda, 2013). The most well known example is the Global Fund. Poorer countries may now access limited global resources on certain criteria of social need. This fund has its critics, who suggest in the case of health that improved health outcomes needs to extend beyond pharmaceutical and technical programmes to include broad-based public health programmes. The Global Fund's accountability is also called into question (see **Chapter Seven** for further discussion of these issues). We are also witnessing the move from purely North–South support for within-country social development to the articulation of the concept of **global public goods** such as disease eradication, water provision and social stability through social protection that may need to be funded out of taxes on international air travel (Kaul et al, 2003). There have been significant moves towards some countries choosing to raise taxes on air travel and recently financial transactions, some of which will be used for these purposes, although the world still awaits a global tax authority (Aziz, 2005). The OECD in the meantime is slowly regulating tax havens to ensure transparency in TNC tax affairs that might enable governments to levy taxes that are due.

Global regulation

In terms of social regulation of the global economy, **global business** is being asked by the UN through its social compact, the Global Compact, to act in a socially responsible way. Businesses that sign up to this 'contract' are required to show that they are taking action on one or other area of labour or environmental or anti-corruption standards. There are no 'teeth' to this social compact, however, and the idea of voluntary codes rather than enforceable rules prevails for now (see **Chapters Four** and **Six**, this volume, for further discussion of this point). Neither is there a social clause in international trade deals, which would otherwise have meant that countries could refuse to trade with those not respecting international labour standards, because many in the Global South objected to a possible undermining of their **comparative advantage** and a consolidation of **trade protectionism** by the Global North (see **Chapter Five**, this volume). However, there is now a wide expectation on all countries who are members of the ILO to uphold core labour standards concerning the right to organise, the right to equal treatment and the right to no forced labour and no 'worst forms' of child labour whether they have chosen to sign up to them or not (see **Chapter Six**), although concern continues to exist about the underdevelopment of global regulatory capacities in the health, education and social care markets.

Global social rights

Despite continued controversy about aspects of global social rights and the weakness of the UN agencies, the existence of the UNCESCR and its promulgation by the UN enables others to campaign for their realisation in countries where governments have hitherto been reluctant to concede them. The UN Human Rights Declaration and the International Covenant on Social, Cultural and Human Rights remains a clear expression of a universally agreed set of social entitlements to be aspired to. The international community did also confirm its commitment to the MDGs, which are in effect a minimum set of global social standards in education, health and poverty alleviation. Of course, the global institutions to ensure these are met are not yet strong enough, and the MDGs and their post-2015 updating (See **Chapter Two**) are only benchmarks around which there will be continued struggle. The important point is that the language and discourse has changed from the dominant belief that global markets left to themselves will secure the meeting of human and social needs towards a discourse that argues the case for a global set of political institutions to secure global social justice.

Global social governance reform

The previous section has indicated that the political climate in the early 21st century differs in many ways from two decades ago, in that the question is now less *whether* there should be a global social policy than *how* such a policy should be realised. In this regard, ideas and proposals abound as to what kinds of reform are required to bring about a more coherent and effective system of global governance necessary for the development of global social policy. In recent years elements of the radical right, the radical left and the radical South would rather tear up existing institutions. The US was increasingly irritated by the need to make international policy in the shadow of the WB and UN, whose influence they would have wished to see reduced. It did withdraw funding from UNESCO when it gave associate membership to Palestine. The '50 years is enough movement' among radical NGOs called for the abolition of the Bretton Woods organisations for different reasons. Here the wish was to strengthen the UN as *the* main agent of global social governance by raising global taxes on international currency transactions through the agency of a UN-run global tax authority. The de-globalisation strand would replace long-distance trade and global markets with local production for local use that would nurture local economies and sustain ecological systems. Walden Bello (2000, p 61) had argued that 'multilateral structures entrench the power of the Northern superpowers under the guise of creating a set of rules for all.... The fewer the structures and the less clear the rules, the better for the South.' These radical reforms face considerable resistance due to outright opposition of powerful states, or because of a lack of sufficient political will or capacity among their advocates. However, a number of more limited, but nonetheless significant, reforms to the institutions and processes of global social governance are in train. Among these are moves to:

• strengthen the UN's role in economic and social policy;
• increase interorganisational cooperation, policy dialogue and synergy;
• create more social policy 'space' for the Global South;
• reform the WB; and
• construct world-regional formations with a social policy dimension.
(See **Section Five** of the *Global social policy reader* for further discussion of these and other reform proposals.)

A stronger United Nations?

Moves to strengthen the UN's role in economic and social policy were formalised in the report of the Secretary-General to the 57th session of the UN in 2002 (UN Secretary-General, 2002). It recognised (para 19) the growing role of the UN in helping to forge consensus on globally important social and economic issues, and called for the corresponding strengthening of the principal organ concerned with those issues, namely, the Economic and Social Council (ECOSOC). Some (Haq, 1998; Falk, 2002; Nayyar, 2002; Dervis, 2005) have argued differently, positing that the role of the UN in the management of the world's economic and social affairs would be strengthened by the creation of an Economic Security Council (UNESC). UNESC would operate rather like a reformed Security Council, but with a few members who could better direct global economic and social matters. More recently, Kemal Dervis, Director of the UNDP, argued (Dervis, 2005) for a UNESC with six permanent members (EU, US, Japan, China, India and Russian Federation) and eight others, two each from Asia, Latin America, Canada and the Caribbean, the Arab League, Africa and Other Europe. Voting would be weighted by **population**, gross domestic product (GDP) and financial contribution made towards global public goods. It would be the strategic governance umbrella for the WB, IMF, WTO and UN system. Others, including Johan Scholvinck, the then Director of the Division for Social Policy and Development within UNDESA, argued that it was better to concentrate reform efforts on ECOSOC, although even this would not be easy (Scholvinck, 2004).The role and function of ECOSOC was addressed in the Secretary-General's report to the UN Summit in September 2005. *In larger freedom:Towards development, security and rights for all* (UN Secretary-General, 2005) praised the work of ECOSOC to date, and asserted that a reformed council 'could start to assert leadership in driving a global development agenda' (para 179). It should 'hold annual Ministerial-level assessments of progress towards agreed development goals, particularly the MDGs.These assessments could be based on peer reviews' (para 176), and 'it should serve as a high-level development cooperation (biennial) forum' (para 177).The final agreed outcome of the summit (UN, 2005) did indeed 'recognise the need for a more effective ECOSOC as *a* (not *the*) principal body for coordination, policy review, policy dialogue and recommendations on issues of economic and social development, as well as for implementation of the international development goals agreed at the major United Nations summits and conferences, including the MDGs' (para 155; emphasis added). It went on to endorse the specific procedural recommendations of the Secretary-General.There is now, as a consequence, both an annual Ministerial Forum and a bi-annual Development Cooperation Forum as important elements of the ECOSOC process.

More significant still was the setting up of a High-Level Panel on UN System-Wide Coherence in the areas of Development, Humanitarian Assistance and the Environment. The panel reported in November 2006. Among its main points were that the UN should 'deliver as one' at country level; establish a UN Sustainable Development Board as an oversight body of core agencies; refocus UNDP's operational work on the policy coherence of UN country teams; appoint the UNDP administrator as development coordinator reporting to the Sustainable Development Board working with UNDESA's chief economist; set up a multiyear funding mechanism for 'One UN Country Programmes'; and establish a Global Leaders Forum (L27) within ECOSOC to upgrade its policy coordination and leadership role on economic, development and global public goods issues. Broadly welcomed by Northern governments and INGOs, it was criticised by the G77 for reducing the UN to a development agency and sidelining its work in trade (UN Conference on Trade and Development [UNCTAD]) and global finance. Progress has been made in terms of the 'One UN Country' policy with a number of different UN agencies in a number of pilot countries agreeing to work together on specific issues, such as HIV-AIDs (www.un.org/en/ga/deliveringasone/pdf/summaryreportweb.pdf). Less progress has been made with reform at the New York headquarters level.The subsequent Secretary-General, Ban Ki-moon, has not been a reforming Secretary-General. Complicating these proposals has been the de facto emergence since the economic crisis of 2008 of not the projected L27 but the **G20** as a self-appointed group of countries assuming global leadership, certainly on global financial issues. It has more recently, since the Seoul G20 in 2011, articulated a G20 Development Agenda with nine pillars of work overseen by groups of member countries and, most significantly, drawing on the expertise of the **UN specialised agencies** to inform its work. In the field of global social protection policy it asked the ILO and UNDP to work out how to advance progress on SPFs (Deacon, 2013). The relationship between the UN's ECOSOC, the G20 and the UN agencies remains to be addressed.

International organisation dialogue and synergy

Strengthening the role of the UN in international social and economic affairs by means of giving more power to ECOSOC might be one way of curtailing the global influence of the WB. Another approach is to call for interorganisational cooperation and policy dialogue between the WB and UN agencies. This was perhaps the most important conclusion of the ILO-sponsored World Commission on the Social Dimension of Globalisation, which reported in 2004 (ILO, 2004). Thus, 'international organizations should launch *Policy Coherence Initiatives* in which they work together on the design of more balanced and complementary policies for achieving a fair and inclusive globalization' (ILO, 2004, paras 608-11). The first of these, it said, should address the question of global growth, investment and employment creation (para 611). These proposals for policy dialogue between international organisations found reflection in the initiative of the former UN Secretary-General discussed in the last section to win agreement at the September 2005 UN Summit for ECOSOC to hold a biennial global policy forum on development issues. Progress towards a more formal collaboration between the WB, OECD, ECOSOC and other agencies became a little more apparent around joint monitoring of progress towards meeting the MDGs. In April 2002 the Joint Development Committee of the WB and IMF agreed that the WB, in 'collaboration with staff of partner agencies', would produce an annual *Global monitoring report* on progress towards meeting the MDGs. A further significant development has been the call by the G20 after the Cannes Summit of 2012 Paris for the UN agencies, the WB and IMF, to collaborate more effectively on the social aspects of globalisation. As a direct consequence, the SPIAC-B was formed chaired jointly by the ILO and WB to advance effective collaboration in supporting countries with their social protection policies (Deacon, 2013).

More policy space for the South

The reclaiming by the Global South of the right to make social policy and social development policy choices is a movement that is gaining impetus. In the 1980s and 1990s, the WB, through its policy conditions attached to loans, shaped social policy thinking in the Global South. This is now less overtly the case, and the conditions are more about the process of countries having in place *any* poverty reduction strategy. At the same time, development aid from Northern donors is now less likely to be tied to the condition that it is spent on goods and services from donor countries. More aid is going to country budgets to support their policy-making processes. The increased unconditional aid flows from China may also liberate space for Southern policy choices. UNCTAD provides one forum where some Southern governments have been able to debate an alternative developmental path from the export-orientated and privatising path laid down by the **Washington Consensus**. According to Charles Gore (2000), work within UNCTAD combined with thinking within at least two of the UN Regional Economic Commissions (ECLAC in Latin America and ESCAP in East Asia) has generated a 'Southern consensus' or a 'coming paradigm shift'. In broad terms, this implies an approach to development that involves strategic integration of a country's economy into the international economy with appropriate sequencing and sector-only opening; productive development policy, focusing on areas of comparative advantage, in addition to macroeconomic policy; building or retaining a pragmatic developmental state; and the management of the distributional consequences of development 'primarily through a production–orientated approach rather than redistributive transfers' (Gore, 2000, p 798). Since then UNCTAD has continued to pursue this goal. At the same time much more effort has been put in by the UN Research Institute on Social Development (UNRISD) in thinking through how developing countries might raise their own revenues from mineral wealth to complement donor aid funds.

Accountability of the World Bank

The question of the accountability of the WB and IMF, not only to their shareholding customers (that is, donor governments) but also to the countries they lend money to, has been a long-standing concern to elements of global **civil society**. The concerns relate to three areas: the apportionment of voting rights, the composition of the executive boards and the selection of organisation staff (Christian Aid, 2003a, 2003b). Voting rights currently largely reflect the principle of 'one dollar, one vote' rather than 'one county, one vote' (as is the case in the WTO), so that countries with more gross national income (GNI), trade flows and currency reserves get a bigger say. Reforms would centre on reducing the weight attributed to economic size and give a greater weight to the 'one country, one vote' principle. In terms of the executive boards, industrialised countries currently have an absolute majority. The EU in particular is over-represented, with EU member states currently appointing to the IMF seven out of the 24 executive directors, with the Asian countries appointing four and the African, Latin American and Arab groups appointing two each. It has been proposed, therefore, that the EU should appoint three at most, to even up the membership. Small steps have been taken to slightly increase the number of African seats. In terms of staff, the concern is the appointment of a large number of US-trained orthodox economists to the WB who tend to support particular ways of thinking about economic and social development.

World-regional social policy

Some in the Global South (Bello, 2004) regard this focus by largely Northern and European scholars and **civil society** activists on reforming the existing institutions of global social governance as essentially mistaken. The point is not so much to reform and strengthen institutions that operate in the interests of the North, but to undermine and outflank them by creating new countervailing sources of power serving the interests of the Global South more effectively. This is where the construction and strengthening of regional formations of countries that have a partly Southern protectionist purpose enters the picture. The focus should perhaps be on building several world-regional social policies of redistribution, regulation and rights. Reforming global social governance should perhaps imply building a world federation of regions, each with competence in their own locations (van Langenhove, 2011).

Several emerging trading blocks and other regional associations of countries in the South are already beginning to confront in practice the issues of the relationship between trade and labour, social and health standards and the question of how to maintain levels of taxation in the face of international competition to attract capital. In this context, the potential advantage for developing countries of building a social dimension to regional groupings of countries was reviewed by Deacon, Yeates, van Langenhove and Macovei (2010). In relation to the rest of the world, such an approach affords a degree of protection from global market forces that may erode national social entitlements and can create the possibility of such grouped countries having a louder voice in the global discourse on economic and social policy in UN and other fora. Internally, through intergovernmental agreement, world-regionalism would make possible the development of regional social *redistribution* mechanisms that can take several forms, including regionally financed funds to target particularly depressed localities or to tackle particularly significant health or food shortage issues; regional social and labour *regulations*, including standardised health and safety regulations to combat a within-region **race to the bottom**; regional social empowerment mechanisms that give citizens a voice to challenge their governments in terms of regional supranational social *rights*; and regional *intergovernmental cooperation* in social policy in terms of regional health specialisation, regional education cooperation, regional food and livelihood cooperation and regional recognition of social security entitlements.

There are signs of such a regional approach to social policy emerging in the Global South (Yeates, 2014; Deacon et al, 2010). Mercosur has developed regional labour and social security regulations and has a mutual recognition of educational qualifications. The Union of South American Nations (UNASUR) is now advancing this agenda. The African Union (AU) has agreed a social policy framework for Africa. SADC (Southern African Development Community) has approached health issues on a regional basis and its gender unit has made progress in mainstreaming these issues across the region. The Association of South East Asian Nations (ASEAN) has declared that one of its purposes is to facilitate the development of 'caring societies' and has a university scholarships and exchange programme. It is advancing slowly a regional labour market policy. SAARC (South Asian Association for Regional Cooperation) has included social issues on the agendas of its summits and in 2002 signed a regional convention for the promotion of child welfare and a regional convention on the prevention of trafficking of women and children for prostitution. Critics, however, insist that regionalism is no safe haven from neoliberal globalisation (O'Brien, 2009; Yeates, 2014).

Conclusion

This chapter has shown that the process of global social governance is best understood as a fragmented system involving contest and struggle between multiple international policy actors for the right to influence the development of global social policy and its content. Key international organisations have often been in competition with each other, with the WB being more influential than the UN agencies. Signs of more effective collaboration between these actors appear to have emerged in recent years. Several ideas for the reform of the system have been reviewed, including those to strengthen the UN and alternative scenarios to develop a more 'devolved' – world-regional – basis for global social governance.

Summary

- The system of global social governance is a mosaic of international organisations often competing with each other to shape policy, although some policy synergy between organisations is emerging.
- A large number of non-state international actors compete to influence the social policies of the formal IGOs.
- Sometimes a number of actors combine in global policy advocacy coalitions or global policy networks to drive a particular global social policy.
- Some actors are more able than others to occupy the policy spaces that open up at an international level and hence have more influence on global social policy.
- The WB has been the most influential international organisation and has influenced social policy in a residual or market-orientated direction.
- Moves to strengthen the role of the UN continue but face large obstacles from several quarters.
- The G20 is emerging as a key source of power that complicates UN reform efforts.
- Regional associations of countries have adopted supranational social policies and the strengthening of these is one possible reform direction.

Questions for discussion

- Are national governments just one among many policy actors in global social governance?
- How does the contest over social policy ideas taking place between different international organisations manifest itself?
- What are the strengths and limitations of arguments in favour of giving world-regional formations a more powerful role in global social governance and policy?

Further activities

- Search the Digest section of recent issues of *Global Social Policy* for updates under the headings 'global social governance', 'global social policies' (redistribution, regulation, rights) and 'international actors and social policy' (health, social protection, education, habitat etc). (Electronic versions of the Digest can be found at www.gsp-observatory. org – follow links to Digest.) Set yourself questions such as 'What new developments in global tax policy took place between 2013 and 2014 not mentioned in this chapter?' or 'What did the SPIAC-B do in 2014?'
- Search for examples of developing country perspectives on global social policy issues from websites such as www.focusweb.org and www.tni.org.

Further reading and resources

Deacon (2007, 2013) covers in more detail many of the points made in this chapter. Munck (2005) emphasises the role of social movements 'from below' in global social governance. The *Global social policy reader* edited by Yeates and Holden (2009) is a valuable source book. The best journals are *Global Social Policy* and *Global Governance*. Note also the *Global Institutions* Series of Books (Routledge), some of which address social policy issues.

International Labour Organization (ILO): www.ilo.org

Organisation for Economic Co-operation and Development (OECD): www.oecd.org

The World Bank: www.worldbank.org

United Nations (UN), UNDESA section: www.un.org

Global Policy Reform, UN Reform section: www.globalpolicy.org

Global Social Policy Observatory: www.gsp-observatory.org

References

Armingeon, K. and Beyeler, M. (2004) *The OECD and European welfare states*, Cheltenham: Edward Elgar.

Aziz, S. (2005) 'International taxation alternatives and global governance', *Global Governance*, vol 11, pp 131-9.

Bello, W. (2000) *Why reform of the WTO is the wrong agenda*, Bangkok: Focus on the Global South.

Bello, W. (2004) *Deglobalization: Ideas for a new world economy*, London: Zed Books.

Cornia, A., Jolly, R. and Stewart, F. (eds) (1987) *Adjustment with a human face*, Oxford: Clarendon.

Deacon, B. (2007) *Global social policy and governance*, London: Sage Publications.

Deacon, B. (2011) 'Global social policy responses to the economic crisis', in K. Farnsworth and Z. Irving (eds) *Social policy in challenging times: Economic crisis and welfare systems*, Bristol: Policy Press.

Deacon, B. (2013) *Global social policy in the making: The foundations of the Social Protection Floor*, Bristol: Policy Press.

Deacon, B. and Kaasch, A. (2008) 'Neo-liberal stalking horse or balancer of economic and social objectives', in R. Mahon and S. McBride (eds) *The OECD and global governance*, Vancouver: British Columbia Press, pp 226-41.

Deacon, B., Macovei, M., van Langenhove, L. and Yeates, N. (eds) (2010) *World regional social policies and global governance*, Basingstoke: Palgrave.

Dean, H. (2008) 'Social policy and human rights: rethinking the engagement', *Social Policy and Society*, vol 7, no 1, pp 1-12.

Dervis, K. (2005) *A better globalization: Legitimacy, governance, and reform*, Washington, DC: Center for Global Development.

European Commission (2012) *Social Protection in EU Development Cooperation*, COM (2012) 446, Brussels: European Commission.

Falk, R. (2002) 'The United Nations system: prospects for renewal', in D. Nayyar (ed) *Governing globalization*, Oxford: Oxford University Press.

Fergusson, R. and Yeates, N (2013) 'The normative and ideational foundations of international governmental organisations' discourses on global youth unemployment policies', *Policy & Politics*, doi: http://dx.doi.org/10.1332/030557312X655648

Gore, C. (2000) 'The rise and fall of the Washington Consensus as a paradigm for developing countries', *World Development*, vol 28, pp 789-804.

Gould, J. (2005) *The new conditionality: The politics of poverty reduction strategies*, London: Zed Books.

Haq, M. (1998) 'The case for an Economic Security Council', in A.J. Paolini and A.P. Jarvis (eds) *Between sovereignty and global governance*, Basingstoke: Macmillan.

Held, D. and McGrew, A. (2002) *Governing globalization*, Cambridge: Polity Press.

ILO (International Labour Organization) (2004) *A fair globalization: Creating opportunities for all. Report of the World Commission on the Social Dimension of Globalization*, Geneva: ILO.

Josselin, D. and Wallace, W. (2001) *Non-state actors in world politics*, Basingstoke: Palgrave Macmillan.

Kaasch, A. (2013) 'Contesting Contestation. Global Social Policy Prescriptions on Pensions and Health Systems', *Global Social Policy*, vol 13, pp 45-65.

Kaul, I., Conceicao, P., Goulven, K. and Mendoza, R. (2003) *Providing global public goods*, Oxford: Oxford University Press.

Mahon, R. (2009) 'The OECD's discourse on the reconciliation of work and family life', *Global Social Policy*, vol 9, pp 183-204.

Mahon, R. and McBride, S. (eds) (2008) *The OECD and trans-national governance*, Vancouver: University of British Colombia Press.

Monbiot, G. (2003) *The age of consent: A manifesto for a new world order*, London: Flamingo.

Munck, R (2005) *Globalization and Social Exclusion*, Bloomfield, C T: Kumarian Press.

Nayyar, D. (2002) *Governing globalization: Issues and institutions*, Oxford: Oxford University Press.

O'Brien R. (2009) 'No safe havens: labour, regional integration and globalization', in A. Cooper, C.W. Hughes and P. de Lombaerde (eds) (2009) *Regionalisation and global governance*, Abingdon: Routledge.

O'Brien, R., Goetz, A.M., Scholte, J. and Williams, M. (2000) *Contesting global governance: Multilateral economic institutions and global social movements*, Cambridge: Cambridge University Press.

Ohmae, K. (1990) *The borderless world*, London: Collins.

Orbie, J. and Tortell, L. (eds) (2009) *The European Union and the social dimension of globalization*, Abingdon: Routledge.

Orenstein, M. (2008) *Privatising pensions*, Princeton, NJ: Princeton University Press.

Ortiz, I. (2007) *Social policy guidance notes*, New York: United Nations Department of Economic and Social Affairs.

Ortiz, I. and Cummins, M. (eds) (2012) *A recovery for all: Rethinking socio-economic policy for children and households*, New York: United Nations Children's Fund.

Rodgers, G., Lee, E., Swepton, L. and van Daele, J. (eds) (2009) *The ILO and the quest for social justice*, Geneva: International Labour Organization.

Scholvinck, J. (2004) 'Global governance: the World Commission on the Social Dimension of Globalisation', *Social Development Review*, vol 8, pp 8-11.

Schutte, O. and Sepulveda, M. (2013) *UN Human Rights Council Briefing Note 7: Underwriting the poor: A global fund for social protection*, Geneva: UN Human Rights Council.

Social Watch (2007) *Social Watch Report 2007: In dignity and rights*, Montevideo: Social Watch

Soederberg, S. (2006) *Global governance in question*, London: Pluto Press.

Stone, D. and Maxwell, S. (2005) *Global knowledge networks and international development*, London: Routledge.

Stubbs, P. (2005) 'Stretching concepts too far? Multi-level governance, policy transfer and the politics of scale in South East Europe', *Southeast European Politics*, vol 6, no 2, pp 66-87.

Surender, R. and Walker, R. (eds) (2013) *Social policy in the developing world*, Cheltenham Edward Elgar.

UN (United Nations) Secretary-General (2002) *Strengthening the United Nations: An agenda for further change* (A/57/387), New York: UN.

UN Secretary-General (2005) *In larger freedom: Towards development and security and human rights for all* (A/59/(2005), New York: UN (www.un-ngls.org/UNreform/UBUNTU-1.pdf).

van Langenhove, L. (2011) *Building regions: The regionalization of the world order*, Farnham: Ashgate.

WB (The World Bank) (2006) *World development report 2006*, Washington, DC: WB.

Wedel, J. (1998) *Collision and collusion: The strange case of Western aid to Eastern Europe*, New York: St Martin's Press.

Yeates, N. (1999) 'Social politics and policy in an era of globalisation: critical reflections', *Social Policy and Administration*, vol 33, no 4, pp 372-93.

Yeates, N (2001) *Globalization and Social Policy*, London, Sage.

Yeates, N. (2014) 'The socialization of regionalism and the regionalization of social policy: contexts, imperatives and challenges', in A. Kaasch and P. Subbs (eds) *Global and regional social policy transformations*, Basingstoke: Palgrave Macmillan.

Yeates, N. and Deacon, B. (2010) 'Globalisation, regional integration and social policy', in B. Deacon, M. Macovei, L. Van Langenhove and N. Yeates (eds) *World-Regional Social Policy and Global Governance: new research and policy agendas in Africa, Asia, Europe and Latin America*, Routledge: Abingdon.

Yeates, N. and Holden C. (eds) (2009) *The global social policy reader*, Bristol: Policy Press.

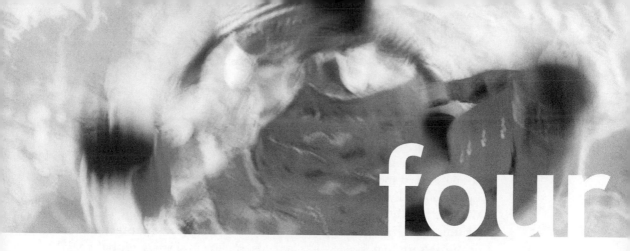

Business and global social policy

Kevin Farnsworth

Overview

The ability of business interests to shape global policy agendas has increased substantially through the period of globalisation. Transnational corporations (TNCs) have greater opportunities to relocate to more profitable business locations, target an ever-expanding customer base and take advantage of more favourable tax and trading environments. At the same time, global business interest associations, representing the biggest TNCs and national business organisations, have enjoyed increasingly privileged access to international governmental organisations (IGOs). At the same time, globalisation has given rise to new challenges and new risks. It is out of this context that modern global social policy discourse and initiatives have emerged. This chapter examines some of the key challenges presented by business activities and how business preferences have shaped global social policy formation.

Key concepts

Business power and influence; global business interest association; corporate social responsibility (CSR); corporate codes of conduct; corporate-centred social policy

Introduction

Critics of **neoliberal globalisation** have been active in voicing their concerns at the ways in which policy making at the global level in the post-war period has favoured big business. **Global business interest associations** (GBIAs) and **transnational corporations** (TNCs) have been identified as major forces that have shaped political agendas and economic capacity at the global, world-regional and national levels (see ***Box 4.1*** for further explanation of the distinction between BIAs and corporations). Various commentators from academia, **civil society**, the mass media and the business world speak of the power and dominance of 'big business' over all aspects of our lives. But what does it mean to say that business is powerful? We have already come across the notion of influence in Chapter Three in relation to the impact of **global policy actors**, such as **international organisations**, global networks and civil society in shaping **global social policy**. But the discussion so far has focused primarily on 'direct' forms of power exercised through agents or **agency power**. But here we also focus on a second form: **structural power** (see ***Box 4.2***).

Both forms of power play out in various ways to help shape global social policy formation. Business interests, broadly defined, are important to the development of global social policy in at least three key ways. First, economic priorities at the global level often dominate decisions relating to social policy formation. Second, business lobbies engage in the global social policy process. Third, global social policy has to respond to the 'risks' created by private business for citizens, as consumers and workers, and the wider physical environment. These three issues are discussed at some length in the three sections that follow.

Box 4.1: Distinguishing business and business organisations

The term 'business' is used to denote a broad set of class interests that coalesce within and between private, for-profit business organisations. 'Business' refers to business people, firms and business interest associations (organisations that represent groups of business people or firms) operating on a for-profit basis.

Business organisations may take many forms. They include both individual firms and groups of individual firms, as well as clubs and associations of business people. Business organisations vary widely in terms of their size, and can range from small, family-run firms operating on a local basis to large global corporations. The majority are legitimate legal entities but do not always adhere to the law. Many exist and operate outside of the law, in the **informal economy**. Many operate within the private commercial sphere on a for-profit basis. Many have no direct contact with consumer markets, operating to furnish the requirements of government or to supply other firms.

Box 4.2: Business power – structure and agency

Structural power, as it relates to the power of businesses, stems from the control over present and future economic investment (Lindblom, 1977). Investment decisions have long-lasting and far-reaching consequences for governments and citizens, directly influencing future tax revenues, growth, employment and consumption. Governments and citizens depend on sustained business investment, but they have little or no control over it. The only thing they can do is induce investment through policies that either encourage investment or at least do not undermine it.

Agency perspectives stress the importance of direct political engagement to an understanding of business power. Business people may become politically active and seek election; others may be nominated to public decision-making bodies. Business organisations also use the media and other resources to win popular support and make direct representation to policy makers and decision makers through their lobbying activities.

Economic priorities within global policy

The first reason business is important to an understanding of global social policy relates to the economic sphere. Private business investment is, within market economies, essential to national economic growth. As Przeworski and Wallerstein (1988, p 12) put it, business investment decisions 'determine the future possibilities of production, employment and consumption for all.' Despite the importance of private investment to jobs, wages and government revenues, business investment decisions are private and based on the long-term strategies of individual companies. For this reason, national governments promote policies that fit with business priorities because they are compelled to create and sustain the conditions that maximise business incentives to invest (Offe and Ronge, 1984). Governments respond to business demands, not simply because business interests form powerful political lobbies, but because they depend on business investment, growth and healthy corporate profits in order to extract taxes on companies and workers. High levels of unemployment and falling corporate tax revenues also have a negative impact on citizens as workers and taxpayers, and are therefore unlikely to convert into widespread electoral success. The fact that the interests of politicians and trade unions are tied to the decisions of companies, over which they have little or no control, places corporations in a position of power. All they can do is try to *induce and incentivise* businesses to invest by implementing public policies that service the needs and/or preferences of TNCs. Marxist and elite pluralist commentators refer to this particular form of power as *structural power*, the ability to influence without having to resort to political engagement.

International governmental organisations (IGOs) experience the structural power of business in slightly different ways. They do not directly depend on business investment for their funding and they do not depend on the electoral support of a mass electorate. Nonetheless, *the economic* often takes priority over *the social* because of the constitution and institutional make-up of these organisations. The various IGOs were established in order to help coordinate economic cooperation and growth as well as political stability. The key arguments ever since have been about the best way to create and maintain growth, and whether particular social policies are compatible or incompatible with these models of growth.

While they do not directly depend on national taxation structures and citizens' votes (at least if we exclude the European Parliament), IGOs do depend on the political and financial support they obtain from member states. As the chapters of this volume make clear, IGOs do not operate independently of governments. They were set up by national governments that continue to play key roles in their **governance** and policy-making procedures. In many instances, national government representatives, including ministers and heads of state, sit on and/or make representation to, key policy committees, and the net result is to privilege economic concerns at the international level. The most important decisions have implications for national budgets and, as such, decisions tend to bring together ministers that represent economic interests and, by extension, business interests (Wade, 2002). The key players and interests are, for Joseph Stiglitz (2002, p 19), former Chief Economist of the **World Bank** (WB), clear:

> At the IMF, it is the finance ministers and the central bank governors. At the WTO, it is the trade ministers. Each of these ministries is closely aligned with particular constituencies within their countries. The trade ministers reflect the concerns of the business community.

The structural power of business is also reinforced in another way, through ideology. When one particular set of ideas, or ideology, become dominant, they become, in the words of Gramsci, hegemonic. The dominant ideological perspective in recent years has been neoliberalism (Cox, 1983). Neoliberal ideas are not in line with all business perspectives, but some of the policies that are associated with neoliberalism – privatisation, deregulated markets, and flat or regressive taxation structures – are in line with the dominant global business perspective (see Farnsworth, 2004a, 2004b, 2005).

The effect of the above on global policy making is that agreements have tended to develop most rapidly, most fully, and with greatest agreement within the economic sphere. As Tony Evans (2005) points out, this is the case even in the area of human rights where property rights, coupled with basic political rights, have taken precedence over social rights such as freedom from poverty and access to basic healthcare and **social protection**. Even within the European Union (EU), economic cooperation has extended far deeper than cooperation on social policy, and economic priorities have continued to dominate policy concerns (see *Box 4.3*).

To summarise, a combination of embedded institutional priorities and ideological bias, coupled with lobbying and pressure from member states, has meant that IGOs, especially the **World Trade Organization** (WTO), WB and **International Monetary Fund** (IMF), tend 'naturally [to] see the world through the eyes of the financial community' (Stiglitz, 2002, p 21). And they do so, not because of the direct lobbying of business interests, although this is also important, but because of institutional bias that exists within the IGOs themselves.

Box 4.3: The EU – prioritising economic over social policy

The primacy of economic policy above social policy was illustrated well by the post-2008 global economic crisis. The IMF and EU have responded to the crisis in various and often contradictory ways, at times calling for the expansion of social policy and at times for drastic cuts. The key reason for the contradiction is only loosely related to the needs of citizens. It has been far more closely linked to the needs of the economy. The IMF heaped heavy praise on the UK in 2011 following the UK government's announcement of unprecedented cuts in budgets, up to 25 per cent in some departments. By 2013 it was clear that these cuts had had heavily depressed growth, almost plunging the UK into its third recession since 2009. As a result, the IMF criticised the government for cutting too deeply, and argued for an expansion in government-backed investment. A similar prioritisation of economy has steered the responses to several Eurozone economies including Greece, Portugal and Ireland. All three have had to engage in deep cuts in order to qualify for assistance from the European Central Bank and the IMF. The problem of 'conditionality' has been discussed at length in terms of its impact on developing economies, but new forms of conditionality have recently been imposed on a number of developed economies most notably, Greece and Ireland.

Business as a political actor

The second reason business is important to a greater understanding of global social policy relates to the power and political engagement of business agents at the global and world-regional level. Business interests have generally been adept at exploiting new opportunities to engage with policy makers at the global level, and IGOs have been equally keen to engage with business interests. TNCs and GBIAs have, since the 1980s, been provided with increasing opportunities to engage with IGOs. Consultative mechanisms have developed that have enhanced the role of business in global agenda setting and policy making, alongside other **civil society organisations** (Yeates, 2001). Whereas IGOs have gone out of their way to incorporate business representatives within various committees and other decision-making bodies, labour and citizen groups have not been afforded the same advantages (Korten, 1997; Tesner, 2000; O'Brien, 2002; Stiglitz, 2002, 2005; Utting, 2006). Stiglitz has pointed to a revolving door between senior business people and the WB and IMF. The effect has been to create, according to Sklair (2001), a transnational capitalist class.

The creation of new channels and formalised linkages between IGOs and business organisations since the 1990s has also amplified the voices of GBIAs. *Table 4.1* presents a summary overview of the different kinds of GBIAs and the mechanisms that facilitate their access to various IGOs. The International Organisation of Employers is the recognised voice of business for the **International Labour Organization** (ILO). The International Chamber of Commerce (ICC) has a firm and enduring link to the United Nations (UN) (Korten, 1997; Tesner, 2000). Business Europe has emerged as the key business organisation in EU deliberations. The Business and Interest Advisory Committee (BIAC) represents business at the Organisation for Economic Co-operation and Development (OECD). And more broadly, business interests have been successful in networking across borders and forging links sympathetic elites within IGOs (Sklair, 2001), including through the Transatlantic Business Alliance and, most importantly, the World Economic Forum (WEF), which brings together the most senior business people and political figures from across the world. Indeed, the strength of the WEF has been in its ability to attract support from across the political spectrum with a common interest in building strong economies. IGOs have also actively engaged with business representatives and have fostered stronger networks with business organisations in order to both 'legitimate' their policy positions, and in order to discover more about what businesses 'need' from effective global social policy (Ollila, 2003). Other chapters in this volume highlight some other ways in which these institutional linkages have been forged: **Chapter Seven**, for example, discusses how business actors have been drawn into global health policy as institutional partners in the Global Fund; **Chapter Nine** does similarly in the context of education.

Table 4.1: Global business interest associations and their links with IGOs

Global business interest association	Membership	Key institutional links
Business and Industry Advisory Committee to the OECD (BIAC)	The largest business organisation representing business interests within the OECD countries.	Consulted on major OECD policies. Its main role is to put business arguments to OECD committees and member states.
International Chambers of Commerce (ICC)	Drawn from various trade organisations and companies from all sectors in over 130 countries throughout the world.	Has direct access to the most important political and economic institutions, including the OECD, WB, IMF and UN, where it promotes 'open international trade and investment ... and the market economy'. Has a particularly close relationship with the UN.
European Round Table (ERT)	Represents CEOs from around 45 leading EU companies. Membership is by invitation, and only the most powerful and largest corporations are allowed to join. As a result, it commands a huge amount of attention from Europe's decision makers.	Consulted regularly by institutions within the EU. It often coordinates its lobbying efforts with UNICE.
Union of Industrial and Employers' Confederations of Europe (UNICE)	Membership consists of 33 employers' federations from 25 European countries.	The official voice of industry in the EU and partner in the EU's Social Dialogue. It commonly attempts to influence policy at the EU level, but also acts to provide a steer to national employers' federations within member states. Often coordinates its efforts with the ERT.
European Association of Craft, Small and Medium-Sized Enterprises (UEAPME)	Represents the interests of small and medium-sized employers within the EU. It has a relatively small membership drawn from SME trade associations from each of the EU member states.	Lobbies on a range of issues that directly impact on SMEs within the EU. Sits alongside UNICE within the EU's Social Dialogue.

Beyond these linkages, there has been a general move towards partnership working within a number of global institutions that has tended to prioritise business partnerships as solutions to various economic and social problems. The emphasis on such partnerships has gotten in the way of adequate critical reflection and analysis of the behaviour of TNCs in particular (Utting, 2006, Zammit, 2006).

Global business interest associations and social policy

Although TNCs have played a key role in the formation of global policy on the **liberalisation** of services and other issues, their voice is limited to a relatively narrow range of issues and their presence on the international stage tends to be less formalised than the position occupied by GBIAs, which represent the collective voice of business at the international level. The membership of GBIAs is made up of firms and national business organisations from all sectors. Because they purport to speak for general business interests, GBIAs, rather than specialised or narrow sectoral interests, tend to have better access to IGOs, are better funded and are a more consistent presence in international policy debate.

For GBIAs, social policy is justified only if it contributes in some way to economic stability and growth, or at least does not undermine it; and it is affordable only if it exists in an environment populated by profitable and successful firms (see Farnsworth, 2005; Human Rights Council, 2008). As BIAC stated in 2009 in their submission to OECD ministers on the global jobs crisis:

> Governments must ensure that labour market and social policy frameworks support business activity in order that more jobs can be retained and new ones created. Labour Ministers must be engaged in the overall recovery efforts.... Public policy, including reactive and countercyclical emergency responses, must support enterprises. Governments must continue to adopt appropriate labour policies and structural change that will support enterprise creation, entrepreneurship and innovation. (BIAC, 2009)

What this tends to translate into is strong business lobbying against public policies that impose costs on businesses and for policies that facilitate business activities and promote higher productivity. This is not to suggest that GBIAs have lobbied hard against all social policies; their approach to social policy has been more instrumental and selective than this. The campaign for lower taxes and regulations has tended to minimise the need to engage in drawn-out battles over social policy because lower corporate taxation either places a brake on public policy generally or it shifts the cost burden towards citizens.

GBIAs have lobbied hard where the interests of business (or the specific interests of their particular membership) are threatened. Thus, while in some areas it is difficult to detect a singularly clear and coherent business perspective, GBIAs have tended to speak with a relatively coherent voice when they have lobbied against social policies that are perceived to create disincentives to work. Business has also argued that governments need to act to increase labour market skills whilst tackling workplace sickness and the propensity towards early retirement. The strength of such arguments varies, however, according to the economic cycle. In 2011, for instance, in the wake of the 'Great Recession', BIAC was sounding a more positive note about social policy:

> Social policies continue to play an important role in providing support to individuals who face employment transition or continue to be unemployed and to companies to sustain jobs. If well-designed and implemented effectively, they can be a powerful tool to complement labour market policies in supporting employment creation and the successful move of unemployed workers back into the labour market. "Active" social policies should provide incentives to work, and must be inclusive in reaching all groups, especially the most vulnerable including youth, as well as older, disabled, and low skilled workers. (BIAC, 2011a)

It is no surprise that, in the face of a major financial crisis and global economic downturn, business interests should be more positive about government and social policy. As social historians have pointed out, major economic crises in the past have softened business attitudes to social policy (see, for instance, Swenson, 2002). The key is that social policies can help to boost economic growth and help to manage the effects of economic crisis; thus, BIAC (2011) stated that social policies should be 'designed in a way that encourages entrepreneurial activity, innovation, higher productivity, enterprise creation, and competitive business environments.' It went on to state that they should be 'effectively linked with active labour market policies', 'support labour market flexibility' and be targeted towards the poorest.

GBIAs have also lobbied hard to ensure that governments pay particular attention to the needs and concerns of employers in formulating social policy, especially regarding skills, flexibility and adaptability within the labour force (see, for example, BIAC, 2002, 2007). Human capital formation policies, such as education and training provision, have therefore been prioritised and vigorously defended as key strategies to improve business competitiveness through more business-centred schooling and university provision, and state-sponsored training and re-training in order to increase employability, work readiness and availability, wage affordability and personal responsibility have been promoted. This is even more important during difficult economic times. BIAC argued in its joint statement with the International Organisation for Employers to **G20** Labour Ministers in 2011 that education budgets should be increased and that governments should foster greater partnerships between education and training providers and businesses and other stakeholders

(BIAC, 2011). Income maintenance programmes have also been defended in instances where they are necessary to the management of economic booms and slumps and/or changing labour markets. More generally, however, high social security costs and accompanying administrative burdens are argued to undermine profitability and increase unemployment levels in the long run. Strict qualifying conditions, time limitations, the retention of work incentives and conditionality based on the acceptance of employment are, in this context, viewed as essential (BIAC, 1998, 2011a, 2013). Similarly, sufficiently wide gaps between benefits and the lowest pay rates in order to maintain work incentives were considered to be crucial in some of the earliest statements on social protection by BIAC (OECD, 1981, p 87). What is different today is that GBIAs are more vocal in their support of state measures to increase work incentives through the use of 'activation' measures (based on compulsion) and in-work benefits (BIAC, 2011b).

In the case of pensions, GBIAs have tended to advocate greater private provision and have argued for more flexibility in the age of retirement (BIAC, 1998; **Chapter Eight**, this volume). Whether in pensions or other forms of social protection, the key for business is that employers should be able to shed surplus labour with relative ease, but retain workers as economic conditions dictate (see **Chapter Six**).

With regard to the provision of services, the state is viewed by business as an important guarantor of certain minimum social standards, and in some instances, funding, but with the exception of schooling, greater private involvement has been actively encouraged (BIAC, 1996, 2011b). Each of the major global business organisations considers state-funded and state-regulated, but not necessarily state-provided, schooling to be essential. The approach of GBIAs to education varies by the level of learning, however. A far greater role for the state is envisaged for lower-level schooling than for the further and higher education sectors, within which an expanded role for the private sector is encouraged (see **Chapter Nine**, this volume).

More generally, GBIAs tend to favour **targeted provision**, funded and delivered by a mixture of public and private. In those areas dominated by the state and with strong public support, for instance, healthcare, the expansion of private insurance has been advocated. In pensions, GBIAs have defended state provision, provided it is underpinned by robust occupational and private provision (BIAC, 1998). In both instances, a mixed-economy approach is favoured. On the question of the method and impact of funding, GBIAs generally favour provision that is funded by employees or consumers and pays little attention to social equity issues. Redistribution, where it occurs, should be horizontal, across individuals' lifetimes, rather than vertical, from rich to poor – whether nationally or internationally (see **Chapter Two** of this volume for further discussion).

To summarise, what emerges from this analysis is a relatively coherent, if instrumental, business position on social policy that, on the face of it, neither favours nor opposes the idea of the welfare state. The bottom line assertions of GBIAs on social policy are relatively robust even over time. Certain social policies, and certain ways of organising and/or delivering social policies, can bring major benefits to businesses and such provision receives support from business. In this respect, the views of business are broadly in line with the views of IGOs, and the two have moved closer together over time, in part because of the lobbying efforts of GBIAs and in part because of the structural dimensions that promote a particular kind of global social policy.

Corporate risk and harm

The third reason business is important to a greater understanding of global social policy formation is quite independent of the political pressures exerted by GBIAs. It stems from the fact that businesses impose huge risks and harms on societies that IGOs have to respond to. The concept of corporate harm has developed rapidly in recent years, having its roots within the criminology literature where it refers to a range of activities that are detrimental to human welfare but not necessarily illegal (Tombs and Whyte, 2003; Hillyard et al, 2004). The development of this concept was in part a reaction to the focus of criminologists on the crimes of the poor to the neglect of the crimes of the rich and powerful. The concept of harm includes the following categories that relate directly to corporations:

- physical harm, such as is caused by exposure to environmental pollutants, hazardous products or by unsafe working conditions;
- financial/economic harm, such as poverty wages and financial losses that are the result of, for example, fraud, price fixing or corporate tax avoidance;
- emotional and psychological harm, such as anomie and depression resulting from poor working environments.

Manufacturing processes, employment practices, sales and marketing strategies can all lead to harm and even death. The range of harms and case studies are highlighted in *Table 4.2*. The processes of **neoliberal globalisation** have only extended these risks. The ability to shift investment from one location to another not only places pressure on governments to reduce regulations and corporate taxation in order to attract their investment, it also facilitates the greater level of exploitation of workers in those countries and undermines workers within countries that have lost investment (for a discussion, see Monshipouri et al, 2003).

Corporate harm is also a result of regulatory deficits: it occurs where regulations fail to keep up with new risks presented by changes in commodity or labour markets or where these regulations are not implemented. One of

Table 4.2: Globalisation and corporate harm

Example of corporate harm	Case studies/further reading
TNCs accused of exploiting weak labour regulations, especially in developing countries, paying poverty wages and exploiting employees, including young women and children. Existing social protection and revenues are placed under pressure from outward investment.	No Sweat (www.nosweat.org.uk) alleges widespread exploitation within factories making clothing for Nike, The Gap and Walmart. ActionAid have campaigned since the 1990s to expose the exploitation of workers in developing countries in a range of industries from farming to clothing manufacturing by the UKs four largest supermarkets (Tesco, Asda, Sainsbury's and Safeway/Morrisons) and accused them of using their increasing purchasing power to drive down the price of goods sourced from developing countries, which in turn has driven down the wages and conditions of work within those countries (www.actionaid.org.uk). Apple, one of the most successful companies in the world, has been accused of contracting with companies that are alleged to employ child labourers and force workers to do overtime. Apple state that 'Our Supplier Code of Conduct limits work weeks to 60'[a] despite the fact that the statutory limit in China is 49 hours per week.[b]
TNCs accused of investing in and/or colluding with undemocratic regimes that systematically torture and kill opposition groups, including trade unionists.	Amnesty International has suggested that Columbia is the most dangerous country to be a member of a trade union. It has reported death threats and assassinations of trade unionists in Columbia, including eight trade union leaders from four separate Coca Cola bottling plants between 1994 and 2002.[c] In Nigeria in the mid-1990s, opponents to land grabs and environmental destruction by the oil industry were arrested and later executed by the government. This led to long-running campaign to boycott Shell Oil, one of the major oil companies operating in that region.
Corporations accused of the unethical or illegal pursuit of new markets, including: bribing government officials in order to gain access to markets selling inappropriate products, or of marketing them in inappropriate ways, to the detriment of human health and welfare denying access to essential commodities for the poorest and most vulnerable.	BAE systems was accused in 2007 of giving multimillion pound bribes to the Saudi Arabian government in order to secure major arms deals (*The Guardian*, 7 June 2007, 'BAE accused of secretly paying £1bn to Saudi Prince'). Nestlé has been accused of consistently flouting global regulations on the marketing of baby milk formula, and this has led to one of the longest corporate boycotts against a single company in history (Richter, 2001). A lack of access to clean water directly contributes to the deaths of some 105 million babies each year, according to UNICEF (2001) (see also www.babymilkaction.org). Unilever is accused of promoting racism through the sale of 'fair and lovely' skin lightening products in India and the Middle East.[d] Water privatisation in a number of countries has led to large price increases and cuts in supply to the poor. Pharmaceutical companies are accused of denying access to essential drugs to those within developing countries. Agribusiness is accused of continuing to market pesticides in some states that have been banned over safety concerns in other countries and of using international patents and GM (genetically modified) technologies to assert greater control over crop production.

Example of corporate harm	Case studies/further reading
Corporations accused of profiteering and risk taking at the expense of human life and physical environments.	BP has been accused of negligence leading to environmental devastation in a number of 'accidents': a fractured BP oil pipeline in Alaska and an explosion in 2007 in which 15 people were killed in an oil plant in Texas City, both owned by BP. According to investigations by the Congressional Committee on Energy and Commerce, and the Chemical Safety Board, both accidents were caused by cost-cutting measures.[e] In Bhopal, India, in 1983, four separate safety devices in a factory producing pesticides failed because of corporate negligence resulting in a major gas explosion. According to official estimates, some 2,000 people died immediately, but others suggests a death toll of around 7,000 is more accurate, with a further 20,000 people dying later from exposure. Many babies have subsequently been born with birth defects. A Greenpeace study conducted in 2004 found that soil and water supplies in Bhopal remain heavily contaminated. Union Carbide, a US firm that owned the plant, had neglected to properly maintain it in anticipation of selling it, was ordered by a local court to pay US$470 million in compensation to the victims, an inadequate amount that, in any case, didn't find its way to most of the victims. The chief executive officer (CEO) of the company was arrested and charged with manslaughter, although he fled to the US and has never faced trial. In 2001, Union Carbide was taken over by Dow Chemicals, the largest chemical company in the world, which denies it has any outstanding liabilities in Bhopal.
TNCs are accused of undermining public services through harmful tax evasion and avoidance practices.	The Tax Justice Network states that the total cost of tax evasion globally is worth in excess of US$3 trillion. The estimate for the UK is that £70 billion is lost in tax evasion per year, most of it in corporate tax avoidance. Tax Research UK estimates that the cost of tax avoidance by the 700 biggest companies was around £12 billion in 2010 (www.tuc.org.uk/economy/tuc-14238-f0.cfm).

Notes: a See www.apple.com/supplierresponsibility/labor-and-human-rights.html; b See www.chinalaborwatch.org/news/new-459.html; c http://us.oneworld.net/external/?url=http%3A%2F%2Fnews.amnesty.org%2Findex%2FENGAMR230172007; d www.theguardian.com/world/shortcuts/2013/aug/14/indias-dark-obsession-fair-skin; e www.theguardian.com/business/2007/mar/20/oilandpetrol.news

the major concerns here is that the rapid growth of international markets since the early 1980s has outstripped regulatory reach. This has been illustrated in the increasing examples of corporate harm that international regulations appear unable to address, the most prescient example being the global economic crisis. Corporations can also undermine the efforts by IGOs to promote better social conditions or tackle harm. As the Head of the **World Health Organization** (WHO) put it in June 2013:

> Efforts to prevent non–communicable diseases go against the business interests of powerful economic operators.... It is not just Big Tobacco anymore. Public health must also contend with Big Food, Big Soda, and Big Alcohol. All of these industries fear

regulation, and protect themselves by using the same tactics.... This is formidable opposition. Market power readily translates into political power. Few Governments prioritize health over big business. As we learned from experience with the tobacco industry, a powerful corporation can sell the public just about anything.... Let me remind you. Not one single country has managed to turn around its obesity epidemic in all age groups. This is not a failure of individual will-power. This is a failure of political will to take on big business. (Margaret Chan, WHO Director-General, 2013; see www.un.org/apps/news/story. asp?NewsID=45129#.Uf-yshb3C2w)

Now that we have discussed the importance of business to global social policy formation, the following sections highlight the ways in which these factors have helped to create business-centred global social policy.

International governmental organisations and business-centred social policy

Despite these advances made by business in terms of its impact on policy outcomes, its power influence is by no means uniform across all areas and all institutions. Different states and different organisations have in place different institutional arrangements and traditions that reduce or amplify the power of business to influence policy making. The power and influence of business also varies over time, with the rise and fall of 'rival' interests (see also **Chapter Six** in this volume). During the 1980s in particular, **business power** was largely structural; global business lacked the organisational capacity and institutional access. Thus, global policy tended to promote what was 'assumed' to be in the interests of business, and as a general rule, it tended to favour those parts of business that stood to gain most from the expansion of the global economy, namely, large TNCs keen to take advantage of cheaper and more docile labour or new market opportunities. As noted earlier, agency power of business gained in importance from the early 1990s with the creation of new institutional channels into global social policy making. The success of business power in global social policy making is evidenced by global regulations: it was able to lever its power to shape global rules dealing with access to markets and investment, ownership, the right to free movement of capital and certain aspects of tax policy, for example, with regards to **double taxation** arrangements, all of which developed rapidly from the early 1980s, while initiatives to regulate corporate behaviour practices have been fewer in number and weaker in substance. We return to these global social regulatory mechanisms later.

The recent history of global social policy making has suggested a cementing of business-centred social policy. Prior to 2008 the EU, historically a defender of more comprehensive social policies, had already undergone a decisive shift towards a business agenda. Since 2000 its Lisbon Agenda has aimed to push its members towards making improvements to education and training provision, cutting regulations and red tape on corporations, increasing work incentives, cutting non-wage labour costs and completing the internal market in services, with the aim of making Europe 'the most competitive and dynamic knowledge-based economy in the world' by 2010 (EC, 2004, p 1). In order to help increase competitiveness in services, the EU has also pushed member states to privatise telecoms, energy, rail transport, waste and postal services. The 2005 Directive on Services in the Internal Market (the so-called Balkestein Directive) laid down a number of rules governing the opening up of competition in a range of services, including those that make up the welfare state. While it does not force states to privatise welfare services, it lays down certain requirements that governments must open up markets to EU competition that have already been privatised. The concern is that the momentum towards the marketisation of all services in Europe will be difficult to halt (Andruccioli, 2007; Balanya et al, 2003; see also **Chapter Five**, this volume). The EU's strategies for dealing with the economic crisis, especially since 2010, appear to have reinforced neoliberal economic strategies. Since 2008, the European Central Bank has further reinforced the primacy of the economic above the social. While the US government has pursued macro economic expansion and the extension of social policies (see Béland and Waddan, 2011), intervention to stave off economic collapse, and have urged caution in imposing deep cuts in public expenditure, the EU has promoted deep cuts in social policy in a number of member states (Farnsworth and Irving, 2011).

The OECD has also changed its approach to social policy since the early 1990s. In 1994, it presented an archetypal **Washington Consensus**-style solution to unemployment: tackle inflation, increase wage and employee flexibility, eliminate 'impediments to the creation and expansion of enterprises', relax regulations on employment, increase employee skills and reform social protection systems to ensure that they do not impinge on labour markets (OECD, 1994). By 1999, however, the OECD was promoting an altogether more interventionist and positive model of social policy, which 'can ensure that those who lose their jobs are insured against loss of all their income during the period while they search for a new job' and can 'assist displaced workers to readjust to the new labour market opportunities' (OECD, 1999, p 77). However, it went on to argue that 'well administered' social provision can 'reduce resistance to change and new working practices' and enhance 'the attractiveness of the country concerned as a business location' (OECD, 1999, p 77). Although it concluded that 'one effect of globalisation could be to increase the demand for social protection', it went on to suggest that governments, under financial pressures, should make 'more effective use of the networks and skills of non-government organisations' including 'outsourcing some activities ... to the private and not-for-profit sector' in order to 'benefit from cost-efficiencies and competitive tendering' (OECD, 1999, p 126).

By 2005, the OECD was acknowledging that 'however essential economic growth is to improving people's lives, it has not been sufficient to solve all social problems' and that 'despite greater prosperity, a substantial portion of the **population** in every OECD country continues to face ... risks of disadvantage in childhood, of exclusion from work in prime age, of isolation and limited self-sufficiency in old age' (OECD, 2005a). In order to address these problems, the OECD has also promoted 'active social policies that seek to change the conditions in which individuals develop, rather than limiting themselves to ameliorating the distress these conditions cause' (OECD, 2005a, p 6). In this way, active social policies 'hold the promise of reducing the negative effects of social protection systems on economic growth that have long dominated public discussions about the welfare state' (OECD, 2005a, p 13). The private financing of social policy, meanwhile, is defended because it 'may help individuals face the true price of social protection, and thereby reduce the risk of excess provision' (OECD, 2005a, p 43). This view was mirrored by Social Policy Ministers meeting at the OECD in 2005, the substance of whose Final Communiqué restated the primacy of economic growth as a de facto social policy (OECD, 2005b). Its most recent communiqué on social policy, released in 2011, also emphasised the importance of social policy to social cohesion and sustainable growth in the wake of the Great Recession.

The OECD has continued to focus more squarely on equality of opportunity rather than outcome. However, in this area there also appears to be some movement. In 2005 the OECD warned against vertical redistributive taxation because 'better-off voters may reject continuing tax increases and climbing tax rates may deter investment and work effort' (OECD, 2005a, p 6), favouring instead horizontal redistribution over the course the lifetime. The OECD clearly remains ambivalent on the subject of redistribution, but in 2011 it hinted at the need to put in place more progressive taxation systems by stating that:

> There is also a need to review whether existing tax provisions are optimal in the light of equity considerations and current revenue requirements. (OECD, 2011, p 40)

WB and IMF discourse on social policy has also changed since the 1990s, becoming more positive about the impact of social provision and embracing the need for state intervention in social welfare provided it results in more positive investment climates and promises greater returns for business. The WB, for instance, has promoted private sector pensions alongside contributory state pensions schemes and has continued to do so during the crisis, cautioning states against a return to state **pay-as-you-go** (PAYG) systems as a way of dealing with those forced to retire early (see **Chapter Eight**, this volume; see also Deacon, 2011, p 95). The WB has also continued to promote market liberalisation with particular effectiveness through its private sector development strategies. Its private finance arms – the International Finance Corporation (IFC) and its Multilateral Investment Guarantee Agency – promote private sector financing and involvement in education and healthcare. Despite the change in terminology and structures, the WB's **Poverty Reduction Strategy Papers** (PRSPs) are as prescriptive in terms of opening up markets and forcing privatisation deals as were the previous structural adjustment programmes (Mehrotra and Delamonica, 2005; see also **Chapter Two** in this volume). The IMF, meanwhile, pursued a largely neoliberal line leading up to the post-2008 crisis, since when it has softened its approach to social policy although it has continued to prioritise economic above social interests (see above). Its message has also, at times, been contradictory. It enthusiastically endorsed deep cuts in social spending in the UK in 2011 but heavily criticised them later, in 2013, when it became clear they were having a negative impact on growth.[1]

Tackling corporate harm: corporate social responsibility and corporate codes of conduct

This final section of this chapter focuses on **corporate social responsibility** (CSR) as an example of how global social policy has responded to the growing problem of corporate harm. Since the 1990s, for various reasons, including a lack of political strength and will, IGOs have looked to alternative methods of controlling corporate behaviour. One such method includes CSR. Broadly defined, CSR describes a range of business initiatives and policies that contribute positively to the welfare of a company's stakeholders, whether employees, consumers or their communities, while maintaining the interests of another set of corporate stakeholders – its shareholders. Such initiatives may be pushed by business interests, national governments, non-governmental organisations (NGOs) and international organisations. As Robert O'Brien points out in Chapter Six of this volume, CSR garners support, albeit in varying degrees, from a range of business actors, IGOs, national governments and parts of civil society, but it also attracts a strong degree of scepticism from its critics. Part of the reason for the scepticism is that business interests appear to be more enthusiastic about CSR when it offers an antidote to greater regulation.

Today the majority of the world's largest companies audit and actively publicise a range of 'positive' activities that they engage in. Such activities are often distinct from their main production or sales activities. Many have whole departments dedicated to engaging in and promoting their positive and responsible engagement with various stakeholders. Many corporations have also established **corporate codes of conduct**, both as a response to negative publicity and the fear of the imposition of mandatory regulations being introduced (Haufler, 2000). GBIAs have encouraged companies to promote themselves as socially responsible organisations in order to foster 'peaceful conditions, legal certainty and good human relations' (ICC, 2002, p 10) and 'credibility and trust amongst stakeholders' (ERT, 2001, p 16). In 2006, BusinessEurope, the European Association of Craft, Small and Medium-sized Enterprises (UEAPME) and the European Commission established the CSR Alliance in order to publicise and promote 'the value of *voluntary* business engagement and the difference it can make' (emphasis added; see www.businesseurope.eu/content/default.asp?PageID=606).

This emphasis on voluntarism is important in making sense of business strategies. Indeed, GBIA interest in CSR has been informed at least in part by the desire to resist formal global regulations (see, for example, ERT, 2001; ICC, 2002, 2009). For global business, enforceable regulations fail to adequately take into account 'the vast differences in circumstances, objectives, operating methods and resources of individual companies' (ICC, 2013).

There are also signs that GBIAs have changed their declared positions with regard to CSR and human rights. In the past, the key business organisations in Europe have argued that CSR initiatives risk distracting companies from their core task of 'creating prosperity' (UNICE [now BusinessEurope], 2001) and the ERT have argued that basic standards should remain the responsibility of individual governments, and if they fall short, governments, not corporations, are to be blamed (ERT, 2001). Today GBIAs have become more pragmatic when it comes to CSR as it has become more established and something that businesses can live with, precisely because organised business interests have been able to prevent the firming up of regulations on all but the most harmful of business activities. The International Organization of Employers focus on helping businesses to understand the (minimal) legal regulations on businesses while the ERT appear to view the debate on CSR as peripheral to core business concerns. From discussing CSR widely in the 1990s and early 2000s, the ERT lacked a basic position on CSR by the 2010s.

It is against this backcloth that a number of global voluntary or self-regulatory initiatives have evolved that lay down minimum standards for corporations to voluntarily sign up to have emerged. The UN's Global Compact is an example of one such initiative (***Box 4.4***). Although it is relatively comprehensive (see ***Table 4.3***), it has won support from companies precisely because it is voluntary and it provides good opportunities for corporations to associate themselves, or their products, with the UN's positive 'brand'. This has been referred to this process as 'bluewashing', referring to the process by which companies hide their irresponsible acts behind the blue of the UN's logo (Friends of the Earth, 2012). As a result, the Global Compact has grown rapidly since its establishment in 1999 to include around 7,000 companies by 2013 (see www.unglobalcompact.org).

The Global Compact has been criticised on the basis that it lacks 'teeth' and relies too heavily on consumers and NGOs to monitor, highlight and respond to abuses (see **Chapter Six** for further discussion). It has also been criticised for being far less critical of its business 'partners' than it is of governments (Utting and Zammit, 2006).

Box 4.4: Aim of the UN Global Compact

The stated aim of the Global Compact is to 'advance responsible corporate citizenship so that business can be part of the solution to the challenges of globalisation. In this way, the private sector – in partnership with other social actors – can help realize the Secretary-General's vision: a more sustainable and inclusive global economy. (UN, 2007)

The Global Compact has responded to such criticism by 'delisting' companies from its database that have failed to report on progress towards implementing the Compact goals.[2]

Other IGOs have also entered the field of CSR. The OECD, EU and ILO have all drawn up guidelines on good corporate behaviour, especially for multinational companies (MNCs) operating abroad (see ***Table 4.3***). All of these, however, are merely recommendations – they have no legal basis – and all the major developments until now have repeatedly stressed their voluntary basis. This is partly because of the resistance of governments for reasons of national sovereignty, but it is also because governments have been heavily lobbied by corporations keen to resist global regulation and eager to preserve their **competitive advantage**.

Table 4.3: OECD guidelines for multinational enterprises and the UN Global Compact

OECD guidelines for multinational enterprises	UN Global Compact
The common aim of the governments adhering to the guidelines is to encourage the positive contributions that multinational enterprises can make to economic, environmental and social progress and to minimise the difficulties to which their various operations may give rise. Two key principles underpin the guidelines: they are voluntary but apply worldwide. The guidelines: • call on enterprises to take full account of established policies in the countries in which they operate; • recommend disclosure on all matters regarding the enterprise such as its performance and ownership, and encourages communication in areas where reporting standards are still emerging, such as social, environmental and risk reporting; • rule out child and forced labour, discrimination and encourage employee representation and constructive negotiations; • encourage enterprises to raise their performance in protecting the environment; • stress the importance of combating bribery; • recommend that enterprises, when dealing with consumers, act in accordance with fair business, marketing and advertising practices, respect consumer privacy, and take all reasonable steps to ensure the safety and quality of goods or services provided; • promote the diffusion by multinational enterprises of the fruits of research and development activities among the countries where they operate, thereby contributing to the innovative capacities of host countries; • emphasise the importance of an open and competitive business climate; • call on enterprises to respect both the letter and spirit of tax laws and to cooperate with tax authorities.	Principle 1: Businesses should support and respect the protection of internationally proclaimed human rights; and Principle 2: make sure that they are not complicit in human rights abuses. Principle 3: Businesses should uphold the freedom of association and the effective recognition of the right to collective bargaining; Principle 4: the elimination of all forms of forced and compulsory labour; Principle 5: the effective abolition of child labour; and Principle 6: the elimination of discrimination in respect of employment and occupation. Principle 7: Businesses should support a precautionary approach to environmental challenges; Principle 8: undertake initiatives to promote greater environmental responsibility; and Principle 9: encourage the development and diffusion of environmentally friendly technologies. Principle 10: Businesses should work against corruption in all its forms, including extortion and bribery.

Sources: OECD (2000, 2008); www.unglobalcompact.org

Given these limitations, the potential for voluntary agreements positively to influence corporate behaviour is likely to depend on the companies themselves. While some commentators argue that corporations are inherently harmful (Bakan, 2004), others adopt the position that the extent to which business organisations are harmful depends on a number of variables: the regulatory regime in which they operate; the ownership of the firm (whether it is a publicly floated company and faces shareholder pressure to boost sales and profits or whether it is a private business following its own internal logic); prevailing sector standards and practices; the national regulations imposed by the host country; the relative strength of trade unions and other activist groups; and the extent of public scrutiny.

Some companies and 'philanthropists' (most notably, the Bill & Melinda Gates Foundation [BMGF], Warren Buffet and George Soros), have established multimillion pound trusts to fund various 'good' causes of their choice and some (such as the BMGF) are involved in global welfare provision (the Global Fund; see **Chapter Seven**). Although the rise of **global philanthropy** has to be viewed alongside the growth in the number of super-rich business elites and the fact that charitable giving in many nations reduces overall corporate and personal tax liabilities, since the 1990s there has been a clear trend towards the establishment of more globally minded foundations and their involvement in global social policy formation and provision. Estimates of the value of philanthropic giving and spending by private foundations range from US$22.2 billion (OECD, 2009) and US$56 billion (Hudson Institute, 2012). Of this, the BMGF spent US$3 billion, constituting 15 per cent of total private development aid funding (HoC, 2012). The kind of activities that big business foundations support also varies. The BMGF, along with other large foundations including the Ford and Rockefeller foundations, focus on development issues, and overwhelmingly in the area of health (HoC, 2012). Other, more recent foundations, including the Omidyar Network, established by the founder of eBay, seek to marry philanthropy with enterprise through '**philanthrocapitalism**' by making grants available to for-profit companies operating in areas that may deliver social gains (HoC, 2012).

While such initiatives may be important, the limitations of such initiatives are all too clear. Voluntary engagement in funding 'good causes' may bring net benefits, but not if the profits on which such philanthropy are based on excessive profits based on poor employment practices, inflated prices or tax avoidance measures. There is also a problem of accountability, where philanthropic foundations are accountable to their boards rather than taxpayers more generally. This latter point is important since corporate giving often attracts tax relief. Foundations are also accused of undermining their own positive projects by investing in companies that behave irresponsibly.[3]

Even where corporations assert their ethical credentials, they are rather selective in their choice of 'good' causes. Company policies on the environment and instances of company giving tend to be highlighted most enthusiastically; in contrast, the employment conditions of those that help to make or sell their products are seldom discussed. Moreover, firms have located ways of dealing with the ethical concerns of certain consumers without necessarily changing their behaviour. Rather than impose similarly high standards on their complete product range, some larger corporations have introduced new product ranges, or have bought out successful 'ethical' brands, which they sell alongside existing less 'ethical' lines. Cadbury, for instance, took over Green & Black's organic and fairly traded chocolate brand

UNIVERSITY OF WINCHESTER
LIBRARY

in 2005 before it was itself taken over by Kraft in 2010. The Body Shop, which had been established as an ethical brand critical of testing perfumes on animals, was taken over by L'Oréal, in 2006, a global cosmetic company heavily criticised by animal rights activists for experimenting on animals. The companies themselves capture both the 'ethical' consumer and the more price conscious consumer.

Such problems have led some commentators to argue for the abandonment of voluntary CSR measures and the move towards stronger regulation. The UN Universal Declaration on Human Rights (1948) states that every individual *and institution* has a responsibility to promote human rights. The UN and various NGOs have also, in recent years, thrown their weight behind a number of new initiatives designed to impose legal duties on corporations to uphold human rights. The UN's Committee on Economic, Social and Cultural Rights (UNCESCR) has sought to encourage, with increasing urgency, states to hold their own corporations accountable for their activities in other nations (Ruggie, 2007, p 15). In 2003, a UN sub-committee on human rights proposed that corporations should be legally bound to uphold and protect human rights. Although this move failed, it resulted in the appointment of a Special Representative to the UN on business and human rights and, in 2008, the UN's Human Rights Council supported a proposed new framework on human rights which would emphasise the role of states in protecting against human rights abuses by corporations and would require corporations to respect human rights and act with due diligence in this regard (Human Rights Council, 2008).

Conclusion

It is impossible to understand the direction and purpose of global social policy without considering the direct and indirect role of business interests. Global social policy is corporate-centred: instead of being kept at arm's length, business has been increasingly integrated into global social policy making, and economic priorities are as deeply embedded in global social policy discourse as they were two decades ago (see also Utting, 2006). A truly progressive future for global social policy may be limited by moves to engage more closely with business. The kind of voluntary agreements that are supported by GBIAs and IGOs are unlikely to resolve the gaps in corporate regulation that would help to protect citizens and their environments. It is also unlikely that they will be able to proceed much further while still retaining the support of business. It is possible, of course, for IGOs to go beyond business wishes, but this would require engagement with more powerful rival interests and the support of national governments. Unless IGOs help to boost the power of rival groups, including global civic actors and social movements, by affording them access to global social policy making on an equal footing with business, corporate values and interests rather than social democratic ones are likely to remain at the heart of global social policy making.

Summary

- The power of corporations has increased in this current period of globalisation. Structural power has increased as a result of greater investment options combined with the institutionally embedded economic growth priorities of IGOs. Agency power has grown as a result of the increased political opportunities offered for business organisation and mobilisation at a global level.
- Greater corporate power has resulted in a range of harms on populations and the environment. Concerned citizens have mobilised nationally and transnationally to increase knowledge and awareness of corporate harms and hold corporations to account.
- IGOs have opened up to international business lobbies. Business interests are represented in global business interest associations at the global level. These have lobbied for social policies to be steered towards their needs and interests. Economic priorities continue to dominate global policy decisions.
- Global social policy has to respond to the 'risks' created by private business for citizens, as consumers and workers, and the wider physical environment. Corporate social responsibility has been one such response that has met with varying success.
- Global social policy has shifted closer towards business interests over the past two decades.

Questions for discussion

- What are the dangers of the globalisation of production and/or sales for citizens and their environments?
- What are the limitations of current global initiatives to ensure that corporations behave more responsibly?
- What evidence is there for the development of a corporate-centred global social policy?

Further activities

- Research an example of alleged corporate harm (for example, Bhopal or baby milk formula). Examine the allegations made against the TNCs involved and how they have responded to them. Investigate how successful opposition groups have been in forcing policy changes and/or how successful the companies involved have been in dealing with allegations against them.

- Compare the CSR policies of a selection of the largest global companies listed in the *Fortune 500*. Investigate the similarities and differences in strategy and approach to CSR within various companies. How do strategies within the same company vary with location? What might account for these different strategies/approaches?

Further reading and resources

Bakan's (2004) *The corporation* accompanies the documentary by the same name. It is one of the most engaging and comprehensive books on the evolution and power of the corporation in the US. Balanya et al (2003) is (to date) the most thorough and well-referenced of research studies into the power and organisation of business interests within the EU. It is indispensible for those interested in how corporations became a powerful voice on the European stage. Tesner (2000) is an interesting study of the evolving relationship between global business and the UN since its establishment. It argues that both interests increasingly depend on each other and documents how the two have become closer since the 1990s.

Business & Human Rights Resource Centre 'tracks the positive and negative impact of over 4,000 companies worldwide': www.business-humanrights.org Corporate Watch documents alleged corporate abuses: www.corporatewatch.org

Corporate European Observatory (publishers of *Europe Inc*): www.corporateeurope.org

Business and Industry Advisory Committee to the OECD, one of the most important international business organisations: www.biac.org

Multinational Monitor publishes research into the harmful activities of global corporations: www.multinationalmonitor.org

Notes

[1] In 2010, shortly after the UK government had announced record cuts in public expenditure, the IMF stated that, 'The government's strong and credible multi-year fiscal deficit reduction plan ... reduces the risk of a costly loss of confidence in public finances and supports a balanced recovery.' In 2013, in what was widely interpreted as a thinly veiled criticism of the UK government's policies, the IMF was 'recommending a range of other policies besides fiscal policies that would also be supportive of the economy. Our view is that there is no single silver bullet' (www.imf.org/external/np/tr/2013/tr052213.htm).

[2] See www.guardian.co.uk/sustainable-business/cleaning-up-un-global-compact-green-wash

[3] See www.latimes.com/news/la-na-gatesx07jan07,0,2533850.story#axzz2i PNKcAXC

References

Andruccioli, P. (2007) *Public services in Europe: From privatisation to participation*, Amsterdam: Transnational Institute (www.tni.org/detail_page.phtml?&act_id=16816).

Bakan, J. (2004) *The corporation*, New York: Free Press.

Balanya, B. et al (2000) *Europe Inc: Regional and global restructuring and the rise of corporate power*, London: Pluto Press.

Béland, D. and Wadden, A. (2011) 'Social policy and the recent economic crisis in Canada and the United States' in K. Farnsworth and Z. Irving (eds) (2011) *Social policy in challenging times*, Bristol: Policy Press, pp 231-249.

BIAC (Business and Industry Advisory Committee to the OECD) (1996) *Discussion paper by A. Sommer: Productivity to the rescue of social protection*, Paris: BIAC.

BIAC (1998) *Meeting of the Employment, Labour and Social Affairs Committee at Ministerial Level on Social Policy*, Paris: BIAC.

BIAC (2002) *Employment and learning challenges for the 21st century*, Paris: BIAC.

BIAC (2007) *Innovation for growth OECD council meeting at ministerial level*, (15-16 May), Paris: BIAC.

BIAC (2009) *Business Statement to the G8 Social Summit*, March 29, 2009, Rome, Italy. Paris: Business Industry Advisory Committee to the OECD.

BIAC (2011a) *OECD meeting of social policy ministers building a fairer future: The role for social policy BIAC discussion note introduction economic crisis and beyond: Social policies for the recovery*, Paris: Business Industry Advisory Committee to the OECD, pp 1-7.

BIAC (2011b) *BIAC submission to the 50th anniversary OECD council meeting at ministerial Level (MCM) fostering a pro-growth policy agenda*, Paris: BIAC.

BIAC (2011c) *Final communiqué of the ministerial meeting on OECD social policy: building a fairer future: The role of social policy*, Paris: BIAC.

BIAC (2013) *Delivering Confidence for Private Sector-Led Growth and Job Creation*, pp 1-13, Paris: BIAC.

Cox, R. (1983) 'Gramsci, Hegemony and International Relations: An Essay in Method', *Cambridge Studies in International Relations*, vol 12, no 2, pp 162-75.

Deacon, B. (2011) 'Global social policy responses to the economic crisis', in K. Farnsworth and Z. Irving (eds) (2011) *Social policy in challenging times*, Bristol: Policy Press, pp 81-100.

EC (2004) *Facing the challenge: The Lisbon Strategy for Growth and Employment*, Brussels: EC.

ERT (European Round Table) (2001) *ERT position on corporate social responsibility and response to Commission Green Paper 'Promoting a European framework for corporate social responsibility'*, Brussels: ERT of Industrialists.

Evans, T. (2005) *The politics of human rights: A global perspective*, London: Pluto Press.

Farnsworth, K. (2004a) 'Anti globalisation, anti capitalism and the democratic state', in G. Taylor and M. Todd (eds) *Democracy and participation: Popular protest and new social movements*, London: Merlin Press, pp 55-77.

Farnsworth, K. (2004b) *Corporate power and social policy in global context: British welfare under the influence?*, Bristol: Policy Press.

Farnsworth, K. (2005) 'International class conflict and social policy', *Social Policy and Society*, vol 4, no 2, pp 217-26.

Farnsworth, K. and Irving, Z. (eds) (2011) *Social policy in challenging times*, Bristol: Policy Press.

Friends of the Earth (2012) 'Reclaim the UN from Corporate Capture', London (www.globalpolicy.org/component/content/article/222-un/51824-reclaim-the-un-from-corporate-capture.html)

Haufler, V. (2000) 'Private sector international regimes', in R.A. Higgott, G.R.D. Underhill and A. Bieler (eds) *Non-state actors and authority in the global system*, London: Routledge, pp 121-37.

Hillyard, P., Pantazis, C., Tombs, S. and Gordon, D. (2004) *Beyond criminology: Taking harm seriously*, London: Pluto Press.

HoC (2012) The International Development Committee, *Private Foundations – Thirteenth Report of Session 2010–12, Volume I: Report*, together with formal minutes, oral and written evidence, London: House of Commons.

Hudson Institute (2012) 'The index of global philanthropy and remittances', Hudson Institute (www.hudson.org/files/documents/8. The Insider 4.27.06.doc)

Human Rights Council (2008) *Protect, Respect and Remedy: a Framework for Business and Human Rights*, Report of the Special Representative of the Secretary-General on the issue of human rights and transnational corporations and other business enterprises, New York: UN Human Rights Council (www.reports-and-materials.org/Ruggie-report-7-Apr-2008.pdf).

ICC (International Chamber of Commerce) (2002) 'Business in society: making a positive and responsible contribution' (www.iccwbo.org/uploadedFiles/ICC/static/B_in_Society_Booklet.pdf).

ICC (2009) 'The Business Case for Corporate Responsibility', Paris: ICC

ICC (2013) 'Business in society: Making a positive and responsible contribution', Paris: ICC (www.iccwbo.org/products-and-services/trade-facilitation/9-steps-to-responsible-business-conduct/).

Korten, D.C. (1997) 'The United Nations and the corporate agenda' (www.unc.edu/depts/diplomat/AD_Issues/amdipl_5/korten.html).

Lindblom, C.E. (1977) *Politics and markets*, New York: Basic Books.

Mehrotra, S. and Delamonica, E. (2005) 'The private sector and privatization in social services: is the Washington Consensus "dead"?', *Global Social Policy*, vol 5, no 2, pp 141-74.

Mitchell, A. (1998) 'Human rights: one more challenge for the petroleum industry', in A. Mitchell (ed) *Companies in a world of conflict: NGOs, sanctions and corporate responsibility*, London: Earthscan, pp 227-52.

Monshipouri, M., Welch, C.E. and Kennedy, E.T. (2003) 'Multinational corporations and the ethics of global responsibility: Problems and possibilities', *Human Rights Quarterly*, vol 25, pp 965-89.

O'Brien, R. (2002) 'Organizational politics, multilateral economic organizations and social policy', *Global Social Policy*, vol 2, no 2, pp 141-61.

OECD (Organisation for Economic Co-operation and Development) (1981) *The welfare state in Crisis: An account of the Conference on Social Policies in the 1980s*, Paris: OECD.

OECD (1994) *Jobs study: Facts, analysis, strategies*, Paris: OECD.

OECD (1999) *A caring world: A new social policy agenda*, Paris: OECD.

OECD (2000) *The OECD guidelines for multinational enterprises*, Paris: OECD (www.oecd.org/dataoecd/56/36/1922428.pdf).

OECD (2005a) *Extending opportunities: How active social policy can benefit us all*, Paris: OECD.

OECD (2005b) *Meeting of OECD Social Affairs Ministers, 2005. Extending opportunities: How active social policy can benefit us all. Final Communiqué*, Paris: OECD.

OECD (2009) *Development aid: Grants by private voluntary agencies – Net disbursements at current prices and exchange rates*, Paris: OECD.

OECD (2011) 'An Overview of Growing Income Inequalities in OECD Countries: Main Findings' in 'Divided We Stand: Why Inequality Keeps Rising. Paris: OECD.

Offe, C. and Ronge, V. (1984) 'Theses on the theory of the state', in C. Offe (ed) *Contradictions of the welfare state*, London: Hutchinson, pp 119-29.

Ollila, E. (2003) 'Health-related public–private partnerships and the United Nations', in B. Deacon, E. Ollila, K. Koivusalo and P. Stubbs (eds) *Global social governance*, Helsinki: Globalisation and Social Policy Programme, pp 36-76.

Przeworski, A. and M. Wallerstein (1988) 'Structural Dependence of the State on Capital', *American Political Science Review*, vol 82, no 1, pp 11-29.

Richter, J. (2001) *Holding corporations accountable: Corporate conduct, international codes and citizen action*, London: Zed Books.

Ruggie, J. (2007) 'Business and human rights: Mapping international standards of responsibility and accountability for corporate acts', Report of the Special Representative of the Secretary-General (SRSG) on the issue of human rights and transnational corporations and other business enterprises, Paris: United Nations.

Sklair, L. (2001) *The transnational capitalist class*, Oxford: Blackwell.

Stiglitz, J. (2002) *Globalization and its discontents*, London: Norton House.

Stiglitz, J. (2005) 'More instruments and broader goals: moving towards the post-Washington Consensus', in UN University-World Institute for Development Economics Research (ed) *WIDER perspectives on global development*, Houndmills: Palgrave Macmillan, pp 16-48.

Swenson, P.A. (2002) *Capitalists against markets: The making of labour markets and the welfare states in the United States and Sweden*, Oxford: Oxford University Press.

Tesner, S. (2000) *The United Nations and business: A partnership recovered*, London: Macmillan.

Tombs, S. and Whyte, D. (eds) (2003) *Unmasking the crimes of the powerful: Scrutinising states and corporations*, London: Peter Lang.

UN (United Nations) (2007) 'United Nations Global Compact' (www.unglobalcompact.org/ParticipantsAndStakeholders/index.html).

UN (2008) *The ten principles of the UN Global Compact* (www.unglobalcompact.org/AboutTheGC/TheTenPrinciples/index.html).

UNICE (Union of Industrial and Employers' Confederations of Europe) (2001) *Corporate social responsibility: UNICE position*, Brussels: UNICE.

UNICEF (United Nations Children's Fund) (2001) *The state of the world's children*, Paris: United Nations.

Utting, P. (ed) (2006) *Reclaiming development agendas: Knowledge, power and international policy making*, Basingstoke: Palgrave.

Utting, P. and J. C. Marques (2010) *Business, Politics and Public Policy*, London: Palgrave Macmillan.

Utting, P. and Zammit, A. (2006) *Appraising UN-Business Partnerships*, Geneva: UNRISD. (http://kms1.isn.ethz.ch/serviceengine/Files/ISN/45947/ipublicationdocument_singledocument/daecdf4e-e4d3-4613-921e-c84b40e0646d/en/001.pdf)

Wade, R.H. (2002) 'US hegemony and the World Bank: The fight over people and ideas', *Review of International Political Economy*, vol 9, no 2, pp 215-43.

Yeates, N. (2001) *Globalization and social policy*, London: Sage Publications.

Zammit, A. (2003) *Development at risk: Rethinking UN-business partnerships*, Geneva, South Centre and the United Nations Research Institute for Social Development (UNRISD).

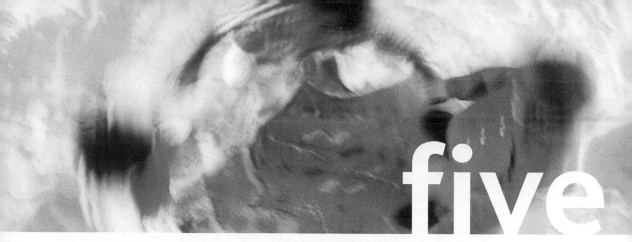

five

International trade and welfare

Chris Holden

Overview

International trade is a core element of economic 'globalisation', and its regulation in the interests of social welfare is a central concern of global social policy. This chapter examines a number of key perspectives and debates about the relationship between international trade and welfare. While economists generally favour 'free' trade, in practice international trade has been characterised by bargaining between states of varying degrees of power. Despite fears of a 'race to the bottom' in welfare provision engendered by economic competition, welfare states provide a key mechanism by which the risks and gains from trade can be more evenly distributed and inequalities reduced. Nevertheless, the emergence of international trade in welfare services has important implications for social policy and has emerged as a key issue in global social policy debates.

Key concepts
Trade negotiations; protectionism; liberalisation; displacement; global standards

Introduction

Trade is the earliest and most basic form of economic relationship between people of different communities and countries. International trade in the period after the Second World War laid the basis for the kind of economic integration we now associate with '**globalisation**'. This chapter aims to explain the significance of international trade to current debates within

global social policy. It reviews how the international trading system and its **governance** has developed in the post-war period, what forms trade policy making takes, and how trade relates to the welfare state, welfare services and 'welfare' more generally. It begins with a discussion of the different ways that economists and social policy analysts think about welfare, and why trade is important for social policy. It then explains how the trading system has developed in the post-war period, before looking in detail at policy-making processes and institutions. The role of the **World Trade Organization** (WTO) and the centrality of bargaining between states are explained. The final two sections examine in detail the social policy implications of international trade. While the penultimate section discusses the relationship of the welfare state to international trade in general, the final section looks at the development of such trade in welfare services themselves. These issues have become even more important since the global economic crisis that began in 2007-08 but, as we shall see, the relationship between international trade and welfare can be a complex one.

Economics, trade and welfare

The development of capitalism as an economic system has been intimately entwined with the development of national states. States have played a crucial role in facilitating the development of capitalism through providing a system of law and contract that guarantees the rights of property owners and sets a framework within which exchange can take place, as well as legitimising and regulating a common currency. Of course, trade across the borders created by these states has taken place as long as those borders have been in place, but the existence of national institutions, governments and currencies has meant that such trade is necessarily *inter*national, that is, it takes place between countries as well as between specific individuals or firms. Governments have therefore usually tried to regulate this international trade to some extent, from the mercantilism of early capitalism (when the goal was seen as making the nation rich by accumulating as large a trade surplus as possible), to the trade barriers (and negotiations aimed at reducing them) still prevalent today. However, ever since the 19th century the most orthodox economists have operated on the premise that 'free trade' is good and therefore desirable and the **protection** of domestic industries against foreign competition (often referred to as 'protectionism') is bad and to be discouraged (see *Box 5.1*).

Box 5.1: Trade protection

Trade 'protection' entails the use of certain mechanisms such as tariffs and quotas in order to protect the interests of owners and workers in domestic industries from foreign competition. Tariffs are taxes that are levied on goods entering a country. Since the cost of these has to be passed on to consumers, the foreign goods end up being more expensive than would otherwise be the case. Quotas are restrictions on the amount of a given category of foreign goods that is permitted to be imported, thus limiting competition with domestically produced goods of the same type. Governments have also developed other more sophisticated forms of protection, such as 'voluntary export restraint', where one government agrees to 'voluntarily' limit its exports to another country, often as a result of political pressure placed on it by the government of that country. More recently, various forms of government intervention in the domestic economy, such as subsidies and regulatory mechanisms, have been identified as sometimes offering 'unfair' advantages to domestic firms. Including such domestic intervention in trade talks has proved particularly controversial, as it may have implications for the way welfare services are provided, since these are usually government-funded and/or regulated. For some, 'fairtrade' and other initiatives to socially regulate the terms of trade also fall under the rubric of protectionism.

This commitment to free trade is based on the idea that if 'artificial' barriers to trade were removed, this would ensure that countries could import those goods made more cheaply elsewhere, leading to the optimum utilisation of the world's resources, in much the same way that markets are seen to produce the most efficient allocation of resources within countries. This idea is underpinned by the concept of **comparative advantage**, that is, that every country should specialise in those industries in which it has a comparative cost advantage over other countries. Although trade theory has subsequently been modified significantly, including through the development of the concept of **competitive advantage** (which recognises that the competitive position of specific industries in different countries is affected by historical, cultural and even political factors, as well as purely economic ones), this basic premise still informs the thinking of most economists (see Gilpin, 2001, pp 196–233, for a concise overview of these theoretical developments). Although economists often speak of free trade maximising the economic 'welfare' of societies, what they are usually referring to is economic growth, measured in relation to gross domestic product (GDP), rather than the broader and deeper concepts of welfare favoured by social policy analysts.

Economists therefore expect free trade to lead to greater efficiency and therefore greater wealth for society than protection. While this is clearly an important goal, from the point of view of social policy analysts, there are two problems with this approach. The first is that, although free trade may lead to society as a whole becoming richer over time, this tells us nothing about the distribution of that wealth. Social policy is centrally concerned with questions of income and wealth distribution, and the intervention of the government may be required to bring about more equal outcomes. The second related problem is that there are both 'winners' and 'losers' from the play of market forces. While the benefits of more open trade policy may be distributed quite widely across society (via cheaper or better quality products, for example), the 'losers' are sometimes highly concentrated and visible. What happens to these people is also the remit of social policy. Given that in the current period of economic 'globalisation' the losers may not just vary between economic sectors within a country but also between countries, affecting millions of people in both rich and poor countries, international trade is a key issue for global social policy.

These issues can be illustrated in relation to the least developed countries, where even when there has been economic growth it has not necessarily increased aggregate employment. This was the case in a number of African countries between 2000 and 2007, where the economy often experienced significant growth, but an over-reliance on the export of a few basic commodities (such as agricultural goods or raw materials) led to only weak employment growth (ILO, 2011). This over-reliance on a small number of commodities for export also makes growth volatile and economies extremely vulnerable to changes in the world market, such as global price fluctuations. The **International Labour Organization** (ILO) identifies 'jobs-rich' growth as being more likely to occur where economies are more diversified and can benefit from significant exports of manufactured goods. This, however, 'does not result automatically from trade and financial **liberalisation** and deregulation'; rather, it requires governments to actively pursue a coherent set of policies (ILO, 2011, p xii).

In East Asia, where governments have focused more on manufacturing and have strategically pursued **export-oriented policies**, this has often led to dramatic economic growth, but inequality has also grown substantially. Those in favour of free trade usually point to the gains provided by economic growth, and it certainly appears to be the case that absolute poverty (as measured by the **World Bank**, WB) has declined considerably in East Asia (see **Chapter Two**). Yet at the same time, inequality has increased as some people have got richer much more quickly than others, with young people and women much more likely to be unemployed (UNDP, 2006). According to the United Nations Development Programme (UNDP) (2006), the vast foreign exchange reserves accumulated by these countries have not been sufficiently invested in health and education, or used to redistribute income to compensate the poor.

These problems are brought into particularly sharp relief because, in common with many areas of economic and social policy, the free trade agenda at the global level has been driven by a strongly **neoliberal** ideology since the 1980s. The contours of this ideology are well known, and involve a belief that markets are nearly always better than state intervention and that (sometimes extreme) inequalities are an acceptable outcome of increased capitalist growth. In the domestic arena, this approach favours the privatisation of state-owned industries and a minimalist approach to welfare, where the welfare state is seen as at best a necessary evil that distorts economies, damages incentives and imposes costs on otherwise efficient businesses. In the global arena, the neoliberal approach assumes that **liberalisation** of trade and a minimisation of the regulatory functions of the state will usually be positive, regardless of the short or long-term social costs.

In contrast to this 'free trade' approach, proponents of 'fairtrade' focus on the inequalities and exploitative relationships that are often produced by the trading system, arguing that trade should take whatever form most benefits the poorest and least developed countries. Fairtrade initiatives sometimes take the form of consumer campaigns, whereby consumers are encouraged to buy goods from accredited suppliers that have ensured adequate working conditions and pay rates for workers, or to boycott companies that have been identified as engaging in particularly exploitative practices (see **Chapter Six**). Supporters of fairtrade and 'trade justice' also run political campaigns aimed at exposing the way the system seems to be stacked in favour of the richest and most powerful countries, and point to the ways in which trade relationships in practice often fall short of free trade ideology. As we shall see in the next section, the reality of the modern trading system is a far cry from neoliberal prescriptions, and is characterised by extensive protection and bargaining between states.

Development of the trading system

The world economy has only rarely been characterised by anything close to free trade. The development of international trade between emerging capitalist economies first took the form of 'mercantalism', whereby governments tried to get rich by exporting more goods than they imported. However, in keeping with the free trade views of the classical economists, in which foreign exchange reserves are regarded as merely a means to pay for imports, the second half of the 19th century was characterised by a more 'hands-off' or 'laissez-faire' approach. Yet by the end of the century, protectionism had begun to increase again. In the period between the two world wars of the 20th century, governments resorted to 'beggar-thy-neighbour' policies of protection in a cycle that both responded to and deepened the economic depression of that time. The political and economic settlement that followed the Second World War was thus based partly on the recognition that protectionism in the inter-war period had damaged growth for all countries, and partly on the need to bind the capitalist economies of the West together in the face of economic and military competition from the expanded Soviet bloc. In Western Europe, the desire to avoid another European war and cohere the capitalist countries against the perceived threat from the East led to the creation of the European Economic Community in 1957 (which formed the basis for what we now call the European Union [EU]).

While the post-war settlement led to the creation of the **International Monetary Fund** (IMF) and the WB in the financial sphere, the allied countries were unable to agree on the creation of an international trade organisation until the World Trade Organization (WTO) was set up in 1995. The WTO is based on the system of negotiated trade agreements that formed the basis for the lowering of trade barriers up until that time, known as the General Agreement on Tarrifs and Trade (GATT). GATT and other subsequent trade agreements, such as the General Agreement on Trade in Services (GATS) discussed below, are now administered through the WTO, but continue to be negotiated in a similar way. GATT and other agreements work on the basis of 'negotiating rounds', that is, a series of protracted negotiations between governments, the aim of which is to progressively lower trade barriers between countries. These rounds are based on 'reciprocity', that is, a quid pro quo process in which governments agree to concessions to each other that lead to an incremental reduction in protection. Since the WTO has 159 members and the aim is a general reduction in protection, agreements are facilitated by the principle of 'non-discrimination', which has two components, the 'most favoured nation' (MFN) rule and the 'national treatment' rule (Hoekman and Kostecki, 2001, p 29). The MFN rule requires that a product made in one member country be treated no less favourably than a like good made in any other country. Thus by immediately treating all member nations in the same manner as the country afforded best treatment relating to a specific product, the gains of tariff reduction are generalised to all member countries. The national treatment rule requires that foreign goods, once they have passed customs, be treated no less favourably than like or directly competitive goods produced domestically in terms of internal taxes or regulations.

On this basis, barriers to trade in goods were significantly lowered as the result of a series of negotiating rounds, each of which usually took years to accomplish. The last of these prior to the current Doha round of negotiations, the Uruguay round, was held between 1986 and 1993. The most significant outcomes of the Uruguay round were the agreement to create the WTO and the agreement of a number of further treaties in addition to the GATT, the most important of which are the GATS and the Agreement on Trade-Related Intellectual Property Rights (TRIPS). These new agreements substantially expand the scope of **trade negotiations** so that they now cover services as well as manufactured goods, and incorporate issues relating to intellectual property rights, investment and domestic regulation as well as tariffs and quotas. Both GATS and TRIPS have extremely important implications for social policy, particularly for healthcare and education. TRIPS is discussed further in **Chapter Seven** in the context of global health policy, while GATS is discussed in more detail in the final section of this chapter.

One of the key outcomes of this process of relative trade liberalisation in the post-war period has been a substantial growth in trade as a proportion of world output. Thus for most countries, and for the world economy as a whole, trade has grown at a faster rate than GDP. This means that trade has been one of the most important engines of the increasing integration of national economies, what has come to be known as economic 'globalisation'. However, it is difficult to entirely separate trade from other aspects of economic integration. Economic globalisation is typically thought of as also encompassing two other key aspects, **foreign direct investment** (FDI) and the globalisation of financial markets. Trade is integrated with financial markets because most countries still have their own national currencies (the obvious exception being the Euro countries), which must be exchanged with each other for trade to take place. Since the collapse of the post-war **Bretton Woods** monetary system in the 1970s, which was based on a fixed **exchange rate system** overseen by the IMF, most countries have been subject to floating exchange rates, which has rendered their currencies a prime object of financial speculation. Similarly, since the 1980s FDI has been growing at an even faster rate than trade. This means that more and more firms are becoming **transnational corporations** (TNCs) and choosing to invest in other countries, rather than simply producing their goods at home and exporting them to other countries. So dominant have TNCs become in the world economy that intrafirm trade (trade between different national branches of the same TNC) now accounts for up to a third of total world trade (Lanz and Miroudot, 2011, p 12). This intrafirm trade has important implications for social policy and power in the world economy, since it allows firms to, for example, minimise the taxes they pay to governments by manipulating the prices of goods traded within the firm so that they can declare their profits where taxes are lowest.

Global institutions and policy processes

The creation of the WTO formalised and extended the structure of the global trading system that had been developed over a period of 50 years (Hoekman and Kostecki, 2001, pp 49-53). The organisation now has 159 member countries, with a number of others engaged in accession negotiations. It facilitates the implementation and operation of the **multilateral** trade agreements, provides a forum for government negotiations, administers a dispute settlement mechanism, provides surveillance of national and regional trade policies and cooperates with the WB and IMF with a view to achieving greater coherence in global economic policy making. It is headed by a Ministerial Conference of all members that meets at least once every two years, but between these meetings it is run by a General Council of Officials that meets about 12 times a year. Three subsidiary councils deal with trade in goods, trade in services and intellectual property rights, and it has a number of other committees and working parties.

Although the trading system remains one characterised principally by bargaining between states, the primary function of the WTO is to facilitate the creation of a *rules-based* international trading system. The organisation's reliance on its member states means that its secretariat is relatively small, with only about 500 staff. However, the secretariat stands at the centre of a network of perhaps 5,000 people who work on trade matters in its member governments' trade and other ministries, central banks, and so on (Hoekman and Kostecki, 2001, pp 54-5). Developing countries therefore find themselves at a particular disadvantage when it comes to participating fully in WTO activities, since they often do not have the resources to devote to these matters that developed countries do. Many developing countries do not have officials based permanently at the WTO in Geneva, and when they do, they might have only one or two people to cover all the activities of the WTO as well as of the other **international organisations** based in Geneva (Hoekman and Kostecki, 2001, pp 54, 396).

Trade negotiations take the form of bargaining between formally independent and equal states, based on the principle of 'one member, one vote', yet it is clear that the economic, political and military power of these states varies considerably, and that this disparity is a key factor in influencing the outcomes of trade negotiations. The WTO attempts to work by 'consensus', but consensus is often arrived at in informal meetings in the so-called 'Green Room', which are dominated by the US and the EU (Woods and Narlikar, 2001, pp 573; Jones, 2009). Developed countries also have access to a far higher level of technical advice in what are highly complicated negotiations, and sometimes bring various forms of informal pressure to bear on developing countries (Jawara et al, 2004). This differential power often translates into differential outcomes from the negotiations, and it was to deal with the perception that previous trade rounds had served the interests of developed countries more than developing ones that the Doha round was declared the 'development round'. The Doha round began in 2001 following the failure of an earlier attempt to develop a new round in Seattle in 1999. This earlier round had failed as a result of a combination of domestic US politics, the failure of the negotiators to reach agreement on agricultural issues and the opposition of a broad coalition of **civil society** groups (Yeates, 2001, pp 150-1).

The main negotiating difficulty in the Doha round related to agricultural protection by developed countries, particularly the EU and the US, which involved a combination of high tariffs on imports, domestic subsidies and export subsidies. Such policies have for many years prevented a number of developing countries from realising their comparative advantage in agricultural production, by artificially raising the price of developing country goods sold in developed country markets and lowering the price of developed country goods sold in developing countries. Agreement on terms deleterious to the interests of developing countries was prevented in the Doha round by the creation of the **G20** on agriculture (not to be confused with the G20 group of major economies), a WTO negotiating bloc led by Brazil, India and China, which demonstrated an unprecedented level of cohesiveness (Narlikar and Tussie, 2004). Successful negotiation in trade rounds often depends on a group of countries being able to form a coalition of this kind, but developing countries have in the past often had trouble in sustaining them. Nevertheless, the developed countries signalled that they were only likely to give way if they achieved significant concessions allowing them to gain greater access to the manufacturing and service sectors of developing countries, and have pressed for the removal of regulations that restrict investment by Western corporations in those countries. These difficulties meant that the Doha round had been unable to reach resolution at the time of writing.

Although we have focused on the WTO so far in this chapter, world-regional trade agreements and formations, such as the EU and the North American Free Trade Agreement (NAFTA), are also important aspects of global economic governance and have taken on renewed significance since the stalling of the Doha round (see also **Chapters Three** and **Six**, this volume). The EU is the most developed regional initiative of this type; starting as a customs union (in which members eliminate all trade restrictions against each other and adopt a common external tariff), its goal is now full economic union (in which labour and capital as well as goods and services are free to move and there is a common monetary policy with a single currency), and it has its own supranational political institutions in the form of the European Commission and Parliament. Most other regions of the world also have some form of regional trade agreement, some of which are developing social policies, but none of them is as advanced as the EU, which also aims at a degree of harmonisation of social policies (Yeates, 2014; Yeates and Deacon, 2006; Deacon et al, 2010). The level of economic and political integration brought about by the EU means that, in contrast to other regional trade organisations, the EU negotiates within the WTO on behalf of its member countries. However, the EU has not reached the point of full political union and the problems of maintaining a single currency across a number of different countries were brought into sharp relief by the global economic crisis that started in 2007-08 (Papadopoulos and Roumpakis, 2012).

The difficulties in concluding the Doha round have also tended to lead to more **bilateralism** on the part of the US and the EU, as well as more negotiations between and across regional formations, leading to a much more complex picture of overlapping agreements. While these new agreements have sometimes included social provisions, such as minimum labour standards, they have often provided an opportunity for high-income countries to conclude agreements with low or middle-income countries that go beyond what is contained in WTO agreements (Yeates et al, 2009). These have included more stringent intellectual property protection, such as so-called 'TRIPS-plus' provisions (see **Chapter Seven**), and investment protection for transnational corporations. Bilateral negotiations tend to shift the balance of power even more in the favour of the high-income countries than multilateral ones carried out through the WTO, since they preclude the alliances that can be formed within the latter (Yeates et al, 2009). The proliferation of bilateral treaties also leads to a far more complex and messy system of trade and investment governance, to some extent undermining the **multilateral system** of rules the WTO has attempted to establish (Yeates et al, 2009; Adlung, 2010). Particularly important in this regard is the huge growth in the number of **bilateral investment treaties** (BITs), whereby governments agree to a range of obligations such as 'fair and equitable treatment' and national treatment for foreign companies investing within their borders (Adlung, 2010, p 236). Such treaties represent a shift towards investment obligations, rather than simply those concerning trade, and tend to be organised in overlapping hub and spoke systems around particular high-income countries. They often shift power in favour of TNCs by allowing them to initiate disputes directly with governments, something not possible in the WTO where only governments can initiate disputes. BITs often involve an obligation for governments to compensate companies that are deemed to have had their property expropriated in some way, and consequently may make it harder for governments to reverse past policies of privatisation or to expand the public sector (Adlung, 2010, p 237).

These trade and investment agreements are not without opposition. **Civil society organisations** (CSOs) and social movements have made key interventions in the political process surrounding global trade and investment talks. CSOs have vigorously campaigned on a national and transnational basis against the perceived negative effects of the WTO and other agreements, including both the health issues related to TRIPS and GATS and the wider issues of development and inequality related to trade more generally. They form an important **transnational advocacy coalition** seeking to promote fairer terms of international trade, and, to the extent that they have been able to shape the process, they are to be regarded as key players in the global governance of trade. WTO negotiations have often become the focus of 'anti' or 'alter' globalisation protests, most famously at Seattle in 1999, following which the Seattle round was abandoned, but at other sites and locations since then (Mac Sheoin and Yeates, 2007). Trade justice campaigners who form a key part of this movement often argue, with substantial justification, that the now developed countries invariably used selective trade barriers when they were building their own industries, to protect them from competition until they were established, but want to deprive developing countries of the same mechanisms. The WTO has also suffered from a lack of transparency, and campaigners question the way that social policies made at the national level sometimes seem to be undermined by trade agreements made at the international level (see, for example, the discussion in the final section of this chapter concerning GATS). The WTO has attempted to respond to this attention from social movements by developing a more transparent and consultative approach (O'Brien et al, 2000; Woods and Narlikar, 2001), although many of its critics argue that it has not yet gone far enough (Bello, 2002; Marceau and Hurley, 2012).

Before we examine the implications of the growth of trade in welfare services themselves, we consider in some depth the relationship between the welfare state and trade more generally.

The welfare state and trade

The relationship between the welfare state and international trade (and the global economy more widely) is not a straightforward one. It has often been argued that economic globalisation is undermining the welfare state, since the competition it creates between countries leads to a **race to the bottom** in welfare provision, as governments pare back the costs imposed on businesses to the minimum. Trade openness is seen as one element in this process, since if labour and other production costs are cheaper elsewhere, businesses will choose to locate in those areas and export their goods from there. The relatively well-paid workers of high income countries may then experience both downward pressure on their wages and unemployment as whole sectors of business become uncompetitive (see **Chapter Six** of this volume). While this may present an opportunity for developing countries to grow their own businesses, these are often (initially at least) confined to particular, low-skilled, sectors of the economy. The disadvantages that developing countries experience in a whole range of business sectors, including lack of access to capital, technology and skills, may mean that trade openness is perceived as acting in the interests of those countries that are already rich, whatever the fate of particular groups of workers in those countries. Where production does shift to developing countries, the owners are often TNCs based in the developed countries that take advantage of lower wages while retaining control over technical knowledge and capital. Those developing countries that have moved from predominantly low-skilled production to more skilled capital-intensive production, such as in East Asia, have often done so by using selective trade barriers alongside an aggressive **export-oriented policy** in the industrial sphere.

Furthermore, it is often argued that in order to remain competitive, developing countries need to continue to suppress wages and other conditions for their own workers, with the result that trade openness not only damages jobs in the advanced economies, but legitimises poor working conditions and even child labour in developing countries. One response to this is for trade unions and others in high income countries to try to tie labour standards to trade agreements, so that developing countries competing with high income countries are forced to agree to certain minimum standards. Indeed, attempts have been made to try to pursue such labour standards agreements through the WTO itself. These have failed for various reasons, including the perception by developing country governments that this is a form of 'back door' protectionism by rich countries (see also **Chapter Six**).

There is in fact a range of factors in addition to trade (and other aspects of economic globalisation) that have been identified as contributing to unemployment in the advanced capitalist countries, the foremost of which is technological advance (Gilpin, 2001, p 204). Both technological advances and greater trade openness have a particular impact on low-skilled, low-waged workers. Trade-displaced workers in developed countries have tended to be older and less educated than typical workers, to have worked in only one industry, to take longer than average to find a new job and to be paid less in their new job than in the one they held previously (*The Economist*, 2006). This has led to the widespread realisation on the part of governments in these countries that they cannot compete in the world economy on the basis of low wages, but only on the basis of high skills. A highly skilled workforce is likely to attract investment in industries that pay high wages, thus maintaining prosperity. Education and training has thus become a central plank of social policy in countries like Britain, as well as in East Asia. Unlike some parts of the welfare state, such as social security, education is seen as a productive investment in competitiveness rather than a drain on resources, as well as a way of enhancing social inclusion and social mobility (Holden, 1999). However, the high level of mobility of both data and people facilitated by technological development means that even the highly skilled will be competing in a global labour market. The rapidity of technological and economic change has led governments to emphasise 'lifelong learning' rather than see education as a 'one-off' event taking place early in life (see **Chapter Nine**).

However, the relationship between trade openness and the welfare state, and human welfare more generally, is by no means a straightforward or obvious one. While increased trade often leads to the **displacement** of particular industries and groups of workers, its effect on overall growth can be a positive one. Jobs may not be so much destroyed, as moved from one sector of the economy to another, while the result for consumers is usually that the goods and services they buy are cheaper than they otherwise would be. This may seem like scant consolation for those whose lives are disrupted, and it is often the case that those who lose out have difficulty in finding jobs elsewhere because, for example, their skills are redundant. It is commonly accepted that while the benefits of more open trade are widely diffused, the costs can sometimes be very concentrated, making it a difficult and highly contested political issue. Yet the consequences of protectionism may be that citizens pay to maintain inefficient producers.

The role of the welfare state in all this is crucial. Welfare states have played a key role in capitalist economies ever since they were created in *facilitating* economic change. It is in the nature of capitalist economies, even conceived of as bounded national entities (which they rarely ever have been), that readjustments constantly take place between and within businesses and industrial sectors. These adjustments are usually the outcome of the play of market forces rather than the decisions of governments. The welfare state has played a key role in allowing these adjustments to take place without the disastrous impact on workers that they would otherwise have. While unemployment benefits and other forms of income maintenance have provided an income for workers that substitutes for their wages while they are unemployed, education, retraining and job search services have facilitated their return to work. A number of authors have argued that welfare states have played the same role for workers within the world economy, providing protection from the potential impact of more openness to international trade.

An early example of this work is that by Cameron (1978), which showed that the size of the public sector tends to be positively correlated with a country's openness to trade. A number of smaller European countries in particular have had both greater exposure to the world economy, as a result of the limited size of their domestic economies, and more extensive welfare states. Welfare benefits, active labour market policies and public sector employment have all, therefore, compensated workers for the actual or potential losses from international competition and provided a form of 'insurance' against their greater vulnerability to external economic shocks (see Katzenstein, 1985; Rodrik, 1997, 1998; Garrett, 1998). Iversen (2001) has disputed this correlation between open economies and the growth of the welfare state, arguing instead that it is insecurities produced by 'deindustrialisation' that explains this welfare state growth. Whatever the causal relationship between trade openness and the growth of welfare states, however, it is clear that welfare states can play a key role in allowing economic adjustments to take place while protecting workers from at least some of the associated costs.

Rieger and Liebfried (2003) draw an explicit inverse link between trade protection and the welfare state, arguing that the welfare state has facilitated open trade by substituting for protectionism. The US, for example, has relied on protectionism as a means of shielding certain industries (and therefore workers) from foreign competition, but has a much less developed welfare state than most other economically advanced countries. Given the weaker welfare state in the US, some state benefits have even been tied explicitly to trade. Trade Adjustment Assistance (TAA) was introduced by President Kennedy in 1962 to build support for tariff cuts, and was expanded as part of the NAFTA in 1993 and again in 2002 when President Bush asked Congress for special negotiating authority on trade (*The Economist*, 2006). For those who successfully apply to be recognised as having lost their jobs as a result of trade competition, TAA provides up to two years of unemployment benefits while workers retrain (four times longer than for ordinary workers), temporary subsidies to help pay for medical insurance and, for those over 50, a temporary wage subsidy for those who get a new job that pays less than their previous one. However, while gains from trade for the US economy as a whole have been estimated at US$1 trillion a year, the country spends only US$1 billion a year on support for trade-displaced workers (*The Economist*, 2006).

Nevertheless, there are problems with targeting benefits specifically at those displaced by international trade. Given that the (positive and negative) effects of trade are often diffuse, it is not always easy to identify who has been affected, or whether trade is the cause of any particular outcome. The US targets benefits in this way because its welfare state is less developed than those in Europe, and because its political system encourages bargaining on policy choices in order to get specific measures, such as trade liberalisation, passed. Although the EU has created a Globalisation Adjustment Fund as 'a sign of solidarity from those who benefit from openness to the few who face the sudden shock of losing their job' (EC, 2008), European welfare states have tended to be more extensive and less based on targeting than in the US. This more **institutionalised** and comprehensive form of welfare support makes more sense in a (global) market economy where the gains from growth are diffuse and, even though the losses may be more concentrated, the risks are shared.

Such arguments demonstrate the key role that the welfare state has played in allowing capitalist economies to operate effectively while shielding workers from the worst risks of markets and redistributing the gains from growth. They provide a sound justification for the maintenance and strengthening of welfare states within the context of the current world economy, and a corrective to claims that welfare states are incompatible with globalised markets and must 'inevitably' whither away in the face of global economic forces. Indeed, the global economic crisis that began in 2007-08 demonstrated just how unstable the world economy can be and, despite the actions of some governments in responding to the crisis through austerity policies that pare back welfare states (Farnsworth and Irving, 2011), strong **social protection** is all the more necessary in a period of increased vulnerability to external shocks. However, while this is fine for the developed countries, what of developing countries where welfare states have not yet been built but where the desire and potential for economic growth are great? These countries often have a clear comparative advantage in low-skilled, low-waged, labour-intensive production. Such countries have often resisted agreements on labour standards, such as the insertion of a social clause into WTO or other trade agreements, fearing that they might lose one of their few advantages.

Developments in China and elsewhere indicate that welfare provision tends to grow as economies grow, and despite the findings of the UNDP (2006) discussed above, a number of newly industrialised East Asian countries have begun to develop extensive welfare states. Welfare development in some East Asian countries actually speeded up *after* the financial crisis of 1997, indicating once again the role that welfare states can play in both protecting people from the worst effects of economic crises and facilitating economic adjustment. Yet reasons of cost, the influence of the international financial institutions, and the desire for economic growth among governments may all militate against more than minimal welfare development in the poorest countries with the worst labour conditions. For governments in the developed countries, the more their competitors in developing countries seem to undercut their own working conditions and welfare provisions, the more they may feel the pressure to scale these back.

Mishra (1999) has suggested one way of addressing this (although he overstates the current 'race to the bottom' in welfare provision). This would involve the agreement at the international level of social standards that are related to the level of economic development of each country, so that those with the most developed economies would have the most developed welfare states. According to Mishra (1999, p 119), this link with economic development 'would provide an automatic "social escalator", in that as societies develop economically, their social standard of living rises in tandem', making for 'an upward harmonization in social standards'. Echoing the emphasis the WTO places on a rules-based global economy, Mishra (1999, p 122) concludes that these social standards 'must not be allowed to become a part of the competitive game but must form a part of the *rules* of the game' (original emphasis). Allied with greater **global redistribution** to help fund welfare provision in developing countries, an agreement on this basis could properly integrate social concerns into the almost exclusively economic (and neoliberal) concerns of the WTO as it is currently constituted. This would not only provide a **multilateral** basis for extending the welfare achievements of the advanced capitalist countries to developing countries, but would also in itself help to overcome the suspicion of and resistance to international trade present in both developed and developing countries, by recognising the social costs of economic adjustment and allowing for the social redistribution of the gains from economic growth (both nationally and globally). However, such a system would have to set a 'floor' of minimum standards, rather than a 'ceiling' of maximum standards, in order to avoid the institutionalisation of differentiated (that is, unequal) social standards to the detriment of those living in developing countries, which would undermine the principle of equality and human dignity irrespective of where one happens to live in the world. The ILO's Social Protection Floors (SPF) initiative (discussed in **Chapter Two**) does not go as far as Mishra's proposals, but is an important step forwards in terms of global agreement on minimum social standards.

Trade in welfare services

As the world economy has become more integrated, international trade in services has grown alongside international trade in goods. And as governments have increasingly contracted out many welfare services to the private (commercial) sector instead of providing them directly through state agencies, trade in welfare services such as health and education has also grown. What constitutes 'trade' in services is less straightforward than that in goods, since while goods can be produced in one country and then exported to be consumed in another, services usually have to be consumed as they are produced. It is therefore difficult to separate 'trade' in services from FDI, for example, or from the **migration** of professionals. The most significant WTO agreement relating to welfare services is the GATS, which identifies four 'modes of supply' in services (see ***Box 5.2***).

Box 5.2: Services – 'modes of supply'

The WTO's GATS identifies four modes of supply for services, all of which apply to welfare services. *Cross-border trade* takes place where services are traded across borders without the need for the movement of people. This may take the form of the shipment of laboratory samples for healthcare diagnosis, for example, or clinical consultation done via traditional mail channels, but it is advances in communications technologies that have led to a significant increase in this form of trade. The internet enables providers of diagnostic health services or education services, for example, to reside in one country while the consumers reside in another. *Consumption abroad* refers to the movement of the consumer of a service to another country where the service is provided, such as when patients travel abroad to have an operation in another country or students travel abroad to study. *Commercial presence* involves foreign direct investment in the establishment of business outlets such as hospitals, schools or universities. *Movement of natural persons* refers to the movement abroad of practitioners such as healthcare workers or teachers. It may arise from labour demand and supply imbalances between countries, or from the search by practitioners for better wages or working conditions.

Where services are included in the GATS, governments must adhere to the non-discriminatory principles of MFN and national treatment discussed above. This has raised a number of concerns about the extent to which welfare services such as health and education may be affected by the GATS, since it suggests that where governments allow foreign private providers to operate in their country they cannot discriminate between them and must treat them in the same way as domestic (including public) ones. However, governments must agree to include specific services in the GATS before they are required to meet the full obligations of the agreement, a process known as 'scheduling'. Relatively few commitments on health services have so far been scheduled, although significant commitments have been made on health insurance (Yeates, 2005; Adlung, 2010). However, since such commitments are made as a result of negotiations, the fear is that the specific concerns of social policy may be subordinated to wider trade goals, leading to welfare services being inappropriately included as a result of a 'trade-off' by trade negotiators designed to secure an overall agreement.

Public services appear to be protected by Article I.3 of the GATS, which exempts those services that are 'supplied in the exercise of governmental authority' and that are 'supplied neither on a commercial basis, nor in competition with one or more service sectors'. However, critics have pointed to the manner in which domestic reform processes that encourage private provision and competition, such as those in the UK National Health Service (NHS), may render even publicly provided welfare services vulnerable to the claim that they *are* supplied on a commercial basis and in competition with other providers (Price et al, 1999; Holden, 2003). Once commitments have been made under the GATS, they are extremely difficult to reverse, and therefore lock governments into decisions and tend to consolidate market-based public service reforms already made at national level.

Concerns have also been expressed about the rights of member states to regulate their welfare services under GATS in the manner of their choosing in order to pursue social policy goals. While a number of the provisions of the GATS appear to protect the right of member states to regulate services as they wish, closer inspection reveals a series of ambiguities and causes for concern. The GATS involves requirements related to regulation that could be interpreted as being 'top-down', that is, as applying to *all* services regardless of whether they have been scheduled (Sexton, 2001, p 8). Developments in the WTO have tended to take the view that domestic regulations should take the form that is 'least burdensome' to trade (Pollock and Price, 2000), which may not necessarily be the form that governments decide best allows them to meet their social policy goals. Furthermore, where international trade does take place in education, health and welfare services, it raises a range of new regulatory issues that can only effectively be addressed through international agreements focused on the goals of social policy (social equity, minimum standards of quality, and so on), rather than simply the goal of increasing trade (Holden, 2009; see also **Chapter Nine**, this volume, on trade in education services).

One of the difficulties of these discussions about the impact of GATS on welfare services is that, while such impacts may come to be quite profound, there is little evidence of them having any direct effect so far. This combination of the potentially significant effects GATS may have on welfare services in the future and a context where these effects have not yet become evident has often led discussion of them to be speculative and highly contested. Two important observations can be made in this regard. First, the very ambiguity of some of the GATS provisions is in itself problematic. What these provisions will come to mean in practice for welfare services is dependent partly on negotiations that have not yet taken place or reached agreement and partly on future precedents that will be decided through the WTO's disputes settlement mechanism, where trade officials rather than social policy experts take the decisions. Second, concrete examples relating to areas of policy other than service provision can be given that demonstrate the capacity for WTO, regional and bilateral agreements to have important impacts on public policy, especially in health. One policy area where this has particularly been the case is tobacco control (see ***Box 5.3***). Similarly, the TRIPS agreement may have a profound effect on access to medicines in developing countries, as discussed in **Chapter Seven**. Furthermore, while we have focused on the GATS when discussing the potential impact of trade agreements on welfare services, agreements at the regional level may have a more profound effect on these services in the short term. For example, both NAFTA and the Association of South East Asian Nations' (ASEAN) Framework Agreement on Services contain similar provisions to the GATS, and in 2011 the EU adopted a new directive clarifying the rights of patients to seek cross-border healthcare in Europe (Legido-Quigley et al, 2011).

Box 5.3: Tobacco control and trade and investment agreements

Transnational tobacco companies have initiated trade and investment disputes with governments, or lobbied other governments to do so on their behalf, on a number of occasions.

- In 1990 the US government initiated a GATT dispute with Thailand following lobbying by US transnational tobacco companies, in an attempt to force the removal of Thailand's ban on imports of foreign cigarettes and overturn a ban on tobacco advertising. The GATT panel ruled that Thailand must lift its import ban, but that it could keep advertising restrictions as long as these were applied in a non-discriminatory way. Transnational tobacco companies were thus allowed to enter the Thai market and then engaged in aggressive marketing practices in order to increase sales of their cigarettes.

- In 2010, Indonesia initiated a WTO dispute against the US, arguing that its newly imposed ban on flavoured cigarettes discriminated against Indonesian clove cigarettes because it exempted US-manufactured menthol cigarettes. The WTO ruled against the US, requiring the country to change its law.

- In 2010, the transnational tobacco company Philip Morris initiated a dispute with the government of Uruguay under the terms of the Switzerland–Uruguay Bilateral Investment Treaty, arguing that its intellectual property rights had been violated. Philip Morris claimed that Uruguay's increase in the size of health warnings on cigarette packs, to 80 per cent of the total size of the pack, unnecessarily restricted the use of its trademarks.

- In 2011, Philip Morris initiated a dispute with the Australian government under the terms of the Australia–Hong Kong Bilateral Investment Treaty, arguing that

> Australia's introduction of plain packaging legislation for cigarettes violated the company's intellectual property rights by restricting the use of its trademarks.
> - In 2012, the Ukraine, Honduras and the Dominican Republic all initiated a WTO dispute against Australia, arguing that its introduction of plain packaging legislation for cigarettes violated tobacco companies' intellectual property rights under the TRIPS agreement. Transnational tobacco companies are paying the legal costs of the three governments that initiated the dispute.
> Note: See WHO (2012) for a more detailed examination of the impact of trade and investment agreements on tobacco control.

Conclusion

International trade has played a key role in the development of economic globalisation, laying the basis for the economic integration that also includes extensive FDI and global financial flows. Yet we have seen that trade has rarely been genuinely 'free', and that governments use various forms of economic protection to pursue domestic political, social and economic goals. Despite the increasing importance of the WTO, the world trade system is therefore characterised by bargaining between states that have varying levels of power and influence. While international trade and economic globalisation more generally may exert pressure on them, welfare states have played a crucial role in allowing market economies to adjust. Strong welfare states, that provide high levels of social protection and universal access to health and education services, have the potential to coexist with international trade in a way that allows economies to grow, while sharing both the risks and the gains of trade in a fairer way. International trade provides a means by which, in the right circumstances, developing economies can grow, but the outcomes both domestically and globally can involve huge inequalities. There is an extremely strong case, therefore, for trade negotiations to be conducted in a way that genuinely serves the needs of the poorest and least developed countries. International agreement could also lay the basis for the development of welfare states in developing countries that would match the development of their economies, avoiding any 'race to the bottom' in welfare provision and labour conditions. However, given the emergence of international markets in welfare services themselves, we need to clarify when such services should be exempt from trade negotiations and agreements, and allow national governments and their citizens adequate scope to determine the goals of their social policies and the manner in which they are to be pursued.

Summary

- Economists generally support free trade as leading to an increase in wealth production, while social policy analysts are also concerned with the inequality of outcomes and the distribution of risks.
- The modern world trading system is overseen by the WTO, whose job is to facilitate a rules-based system. However, outcomes are still largely the result of bargaining between states that have varying levels of power and influence, and increasing numbers of regional and bilateral agreements threaten to undermine the WTO's multilateral system.
- Multilateral, regional and bilateral trade and investment agreements increasingly have a direct impact on social policy. These international agreements have been criticised as subordinating wider social goals to narrow economic ones.
- Welfare states play a crucial role in allowing economic adjustment to take place in capitalist economies. International agreement could provide the basis for social welfare provision to be written into the 'rules' governing trade at the global level.
- Civil society is increasingly engaged with the trade agenda. Improvements could be made to the transparency and accountability of international institutions such as the WTO. At the same time, the limits of WTO influence over governments' social policies need to be clarified.

Questions for discussion

- Why does genuinely 'free' trade very rarely exist?
- Why do economic considerations seem to dominate over social ones in organisations such as the WTO?
- What are the challenges for social policy of the development of international markets in welfare services?

Further activities

- Take the interactive training modules on the WTO website at www.wto.org/english/res_e/d_learn_e/d_learn_e.htm
- Using the websites listed below, compare the different ways that trade issues are presented by the WTO and the Trade Justice Movement (TJM). What kinds of activities are organised by the TJM and its member organisations?

Further reading and resources

O'Brien and Williams (2013) and Held et al (1999) both provide good detailed introductions to the global economy, including trade issues. Farnsworth and Irving (2011) provide analyses of the impact of the 2007-08 global financial crisis on social provision in various countries. Yeates (2001) and Mishra (1999) provide good introductions to social policy and globalisation that complement this volume, and pay particular attention to trade issues. Smith et al (2009) analyse trends in health services trade as an example of how welfare services can be traded across borders. For a discussion of how GATS relates to social security, see Yeates (2005).

World Trade Organization: www.wto.org

United Nations Conference on Trade and Development (UNCTAD): **www.unctad.org**

Trade Justice Movement (TJM): www.tjm.org.uk

References

Adlung, R. (2010) 'Trade in healthcare and health insurance services: WTO/GATS as a supporting actor(?)', *Intereconomics*, vol 45, no 4, pp 227-38.

Bello, W. (2002) 'Lack of transparency in the WTO', *Development Dialogue*, no 1, pp 117-23.

Cameron, D.R. (1978) 'The expansion of the public economy: a comparative analysis', *American Political Science Review*, vol 72, no 4, pp 1243-61.

Deacon, B., Macovei, M.C., van Langenhove, L. and Yeates, N. (2009) *World-regional social policy and global governance: New research and policy agendas in Africa, Asia, Europe and Latin America*, London: Routledge.

EC (European Commission) (2008) 'European Globalisation Adjustment Fund' (http://ec.europa.eu/social/main.jsp?catId=326&furtherPubs=yes&langId=en).

Economist, The (2006) 'In the shadow of prosperity. Briefing: trade's victims', vol 382, no 8512, pp 28-30.

Farnsworth, K. and Irving, Z. (eds) (2011) *Social policy in challenging times: Economic crisis and welfare systems*, Bristol: Policy Press.

Garrett, G. (1998) *Partisan politics in the global economy*, Cambridge: Cambridge University Press.

Gilpin, R. (2001) *Global political economy: Understanding the international economic order*, Princeton, NJ: Princeton University Press.

Held, D., McGrew, A., Goldblatt, D. and Perraton, J. (1999) *Global transformations: Politics, economics and culture*, Cambridge: Polity Press.

Hoekman, B.M. and Kostecki, M.M. (2001) *The political economy of the world trading system: The WTO and beyond*, Oxford: Oxford University Press.

Holden, C. (1999) 'Globalization, social exclusion and Labour's new work ethic', *Critical Social Policy*, vol 19, no 4, pp 529-38.

Holden, C. (2003) 'Actors and motives in the internationalization of health businesses', *Business and Politics*, vol 5, no 3, pp 287-301.

Holden, C. (2009) 'Regulation, accountability and trade in health services', in E. Mordini (ed) *Ethics and health in the global village: Bioethics, globalization and human rights*, Rome: CIC Edizioni Internazionali.

ILO (International Labour Organization) (2011) *Growth, employment and decent work in the least developed countries*, Report of the ILO for the Fourth UN Conference on the Least Developed Countries, Geneva: ILO.

Iversen, T. (2001) 'The dynamics of welfare state expansion: trade openness, de-industrialization, and partisan politics', in P. Pierson (ed) *The new politics of the welfare state*, Oxford: Oxford University Press, pp 45-79.

Jawara, F., Kwa, A. and Sharma, S. (2004) *Behind the scenes at the WTO: The real world of international trade negotiations/Lessons of Cancun*, London: Zed Books.

Jones, K. (2009) 'Green room politics and the WTO's crisis of representation', *Progress in Development Studies*, vol 9, no 4, pp 349-57.

Katzenstein, P.J. (1985) *Small states in world markets*, Ithaca, NY: Cornell University Press.

Lanz, R. and Miroudot, S. (2011) *Intra-firm trade: Patterns, determinants and policy implications*, OECD Trade Policy Papers, no 114, Paris: OECD Publishing (http://dx.doi.org/10.1787/5kg9p39lrwnn-en).

Legido-Quigley, H., Passarani, I., Knai, C., Busse, R., Palm, W., Wismar, M. and McKee, M. (2011) 'Cross-border healthcare in Europe: clarifying patients' rights', *British Medical Journal*, vol 342, pp 364-7.

Mac Sheoin, T. and Yeates, N. (2007) 'Division and dissent in the anti-globalisation movement', in S. Dasgupta and R. Kiely (eds) *Globalisation and after*, New Delhi: Sage Publications, pp 360-91.

Marceau, G. and Hurley, M. (2012) 'Transparency and public participation in the WTO: a report card on WTO transparency mechanisms', *Trade, Law and Development*, vol 4, no 1, pp 19-44.

Mishra, R. (1999) *Globalization and the welfare state*, Cheltenham: Edward Elgar.

Narlikar, A. and Tussie, D. (2004) 'The G20 at the Cancun ministerial: developing countries and their evolving coalitions in the WTO', *The World Economy*, vol 27, no 7, pp 947-66.

O'Brien, R. and Williams, M. (2013) *Global political economy: Evolution and dynamics*, New York: Palgrave.

O'Brien, R., Goetz, A.M., Scholte, J.A. and Williams, M. (2000) *Contesting global governance: Multilateral economic institutions and global social movements*, Cambridge: Cambridge University Press.

Papadopoulos, T. and Roumpakis, A. (2012) 'The Greek welfare state in the age of austerity: anti-social policy and the politico-economic crisis', in M. Kilkey, G. Ramia and K. Farnsworth (eds) *Social policy review 24*, Bristol: Policy Press.

Pollock, A. and Price, D. (2000) 'Rewriting the regulations: how the World Trade Organization could accelerate privatization in healthcare systems', *The Lancet*, vol 356, pp 1995-2000.

Price, D., Pollock, A.M. and Shaoul, J. (1999) 'How the World Trade Organization is shaping domestic policies in health care', *The Lancet*, vol 354, pp 1889-91.

Rieger, E. and Leibfried, S. (2003) *Limits to globalization*, Cambridge: Polity Press.

Rodrik, D. (1997) *Has globalization gone too far?*, Washington, DC: Institute for International Economics.

Rodrik, D. (1998) 'Why do more open economies have larger governments?', *Journal of Political Economy*, vol 106, pp 997-1932.

Sexton, S. (2001) *Trading health care away? GATS, public services and privatisation*, Briefing 23, Sturminster Newton: The Corner House.

Smith, R., Chanda, R. and Tangcharoensathien, V. (2009) 'Trade in health-related services', *The Lancet*, vol 373, no 9663, pp 593-601.

UNDP (United Nations Development Programme) (2006) *Trade on human terms: Transforming trade for human development in Asia and the Pacific, Asia–Pacific Human Development Report 2006*, New Delhi: Macmillan and UNDP.

WHO (World Health Organization) (2012) *Confronting the tobacco epidemic in a new era of trade and investment Liberalization*, Geneva: WHO.

Woods, N. and Narlikar, A. (2001) 'Governance and the limits of accountability: the WTO, the IMF, and the World Bank', *International Social Science Journal*, vol 53, no 170, pp 569-83.

Yeates, N. (2001) *Globalization and social policy*, London: Sage Publications.

Yeates, N. (2005) 'The General Agreement on Trade in Services: what's in it for social security?', *International Social Security Review*, vol 58, no 1, pp 3-22.

Yeates, N. (2009) 'The evolving context of world regional social policy', in B. Deacon, M.C. Macovei, L. van Langenhove and N. Yeates (eds) *World-regional social policy and global governance: New research and policy agendas in Africa, Asia, Europe and Latin America*, London: Routledge.

Yeates, N. and Deacon, B. (2006) *Globalism, regionalism and social policy: Framing the debate*, United Nations University Centre for Comparative Regional Integration Studies (UNU-CRIS) Working Paper 0-2006/6, Bruges: UNU-CRIS.

Part II

Policy domains and issues

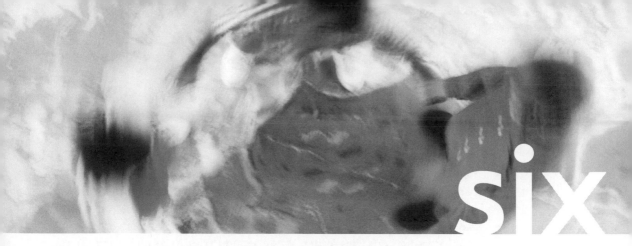

six

Global labour policy

Robert O'Brien

Overview

This chapter examines the collection of actors, ideologies and policies that compose global labour policy. Although international labour policy has been guided by the presence of a dedicated international organisation (the International Labour Organization [ILO]) for almost 100, years this chapter argues that global labour policy is created by a much larger number of public and private authorities. Key public actors are states and international organisations, while private actors include civic associations and transnational corporations (TNCs). The competition and struggle over global labour policy is illustrated in debates surrounding international enforcement of labour standards and corporate self-regulation. These debates pit a number of state and non-state actors against each other as they espouse a variety of ideological positions from neoliberalism to social democracy and from nationalism to cosmopolitanism. The United Nations (UN)-sponsored Global Compact is an example of how states, corporations and civic associations might come together to bolster global labour rights and standards. However, the potential effectiveness of that initiative is limited by its reliance on voluntarism.

Key concepts

Core labour standards; comparative advantage; self-regulation; cosmopolitanism; nationalism

Introduction

The inhabitants of Western countries happily consume products from around the world. They drink coffee from Ethiopia, eat bananas from Columbia, use computers from China, wear clothes from Cambodia, walk on carpets from Pakistan, talk to customer service representatives in India, display flowers from Kenya and show off diamonds from Africa. These patterns of trade and consumption influence working conditions in both importing and exporting countries. When Western industries need cheap labour for domestic production and service provision, they often turn from importing products to importing people. Examples include the UK importing health workers from Africa, the US relying on Mexican labour for agricultural and service work, Canada's importation of Filipinas to work as nannies, Arab Gulf states importing Indian construction workers and Western Europe importing East European women to work in the sex trade. This movement of workers also affects labour conditions in both the importing and exporting countries.

As products and services move across borders, labour issues and policies increasingly have a transnational impact. New patterns of consumption, production and movement have internationalised labour policy. Whereas domestic regulation of working conditions was seen to be sufficient in an era when most production and consumption was nationally based, increasing global exchanges reduce the influence of such regulation. Because of the **globalisation** of communication, the conditions of work generated by global production and exchange have also appeared in public debate and generated political pressure for action. Thus, stories of child labour in the Pakistan carpet industry, forced labour in the West African diamond industry, sweatshop labour in China, dangerous and exploitative working conditions for **migrants** and undocumented workers in the US and European Union (EU) have generated demands for new forms of regulation of working conditions on a transnational basis. The demand is that rules ensuring basic rights should reach across national boundaries to include workers around the world.

This chapter unfolds in four sections. The first provides a brief overview of global working conditions so that readers get a sense of the challenges in this field. The second examines the key actors in global labour policy: civic actors, states, **international organisations** and TNCs. In the third section two policy issues are investigated: enforcement of core labour standards and corporate self-regulation. The competing perspectives on enforceable labour standards are highlighted, and the promise and perils of self-regulation are considered. The fourth section examines one particular policy arrangement, the Global Compact, as an example of the problems of dealing with global labour standards. The chapter concludes by arguing that the debate around securing labour standards and decent working conditions is likely to continue well into the future.

Global labour conditions

The world faces immense challenges in the field of employment and labour rights. For example, there are approximately:

- 15,000 people punished for legitimate trade union activity each year (ranging from dismissal to murder) (ITUC, 2007)
- 6,300 people die daily as a result of occupational accidents or work-related diseases – more than 2.3 million deaths per year (ILO, 2013a)
- 20.9 million people are trapped in forced labour (ILO, 2012)
- 202 million will experience unemployment in 2013 (Rushe, 2013)
- 215 million child labourers (ILO, 2013b)
- 2.47 billion people living on $2 or less a day (WB, 2013)
- 80 per cent of the world's **population** lacking access to adequate social security provision (ISSA, 2013).

In addition to these startling figures, the past two decades have witnessed a decrease in secure employment and the growth of insecure and informal forms of employment (ILO, 2002a). The term 'informal sector' was coined in the 1970s to refer to that sector of the economy where workers are highly vulnerable to exploitation because they are not protected or recognised under legal regulatory frameworks. Examples of sectors that make wide use of informal workers are: street vendors, rubbish and rag pickers, domestic workers, home workers, sex and entertainment workers and agricultural workers. Most new work in many developing countries is in the informal sector. Much of the growth of global production has involved outsourcing of production and labour, much of it women working at home (Carr et al, 2000). Many jobs in the developed world are also being made more flexible, insecure and precarious. The problem with the growth of such employment is that the workers in these jobs are usually denied workers' rights and access to social security benefits, pensions and healthcare. Such workers are often marginalised from society, creating the emergence of a large group of disenfranchised and alienated people. Guy Standing (2011) has labelled this global insecure class the 'precariat'.

Perhaps the most desperate situation faced by workers is encountered by those in conditions of forced or unfree labour. The ILO (1930, Article 2.1) defines forced labour as 'all work or service that is exacted from any person under the menace of any penalty and for which the said person has not offered himself voluntarily.' People can be coerced into work by the state, companies or individuals. Forced labour is more than simply working in poor conditions for low wages. It involves the additional violation of workers' freedoms such as restricting the movement of workers, withholding wages or identity documents (such as passports), threatening or inflicting physical and sexual violence or demanding work to service fraudulent or exorbitant debts. Crucially, workers are not allowed to leave their employment relations because of debt or coercion. The ILO estimates that 55 per cent of forced labourers are women and girls, while a quarter are children (ILO, 2013c). Women and children are the majority of those caught up in human trafficking and the sexual exploitation of forced labourers.

Forced labourers are incorporated into the global economy in numerous ways (Phillips, 2013). Some are trafficked across borders in the global sex industry. Others may live in virtual slavery in rural areas engaged in producing commodities such as soybeans, cotton, sugar and coffee for export. Alternatively, forced labourers may be working at home in large cities producing sections of clothing or manufactured goods that are incorporated into textile and manufacturing exports. As a result, the problem of forced labour reaches every part of the globe.

With the advent of global information technologies, the poor state of working conditions around the world is increasingly apparent, moving the issue of global labour policy higher up the international agenda.

Actors in global labour policy

Labour policy that crosses international borders differs from national labour policy because it attempts to regulate relations between sovereign national political communities. This adds an extra layer of complexity to labour policy that tends to be highly charged, even in the domestic context. Labour policy is often a source of intense conflict because its content can influence the profit levels of corporations and the wage levels of individuals. In addition, political opposition to labour rights is generated by the fact that organised workers can influence political order and power. Labour groups are also political actors, and their increased activity can threaten governments or political parties. For example, labour groups played a key role in undermining authoritarian leaders in states such as Poland, Brazil and South Africa. This section examines the activities of key actors engaged in influencing global labour policy: civic associations, international organisations, states and TNCs. Key policy issues are highlighted in the following section.

Civic actors

The demand for transnational or global labour policies comes in the first place from workers themselves. A wide range of workers, from unionised workers in developed states to informal sectors in developing countries, have mobilised on a national and transnational basis to oppose economic exploitation and to demand improvements to their working conditions and their lives. These mobilisations, whether or not explicitly invoking or opposing 'globalisation', are a classic example of processes of 'globalisation from below' and of a transnational advocacy coalition (see **Chapters One** and **Three**, this volume).

Unionised workers are represented at the international level by their own associations. The most prominent union association is the International Trade Union Confederation (ITUC, formerly the International Confederation of Free Trade Unions [ICFTU] and the World Confederation of Labour). While the old ICFTU was subject to withering criticism for its conservatism (Greenfield, 1998), later developments suggest a more progressive agenda that moves beyond male unionists in developed states to include women and people in developing countries (O'Brien, 2000). For example, the ITUC has run campaigns promoting decent work, the ethical production of sporting goods for events such as the Olympics, World Cup and Commonwealth Games, the achievement of the **Millennium Development Goals** (MDGs), AIDS prevention, the banning of child labour and the advancement of worker rights in the activity of the **World Trade Organization** (WTO), **International Monetary Fund** (IMF) and World Bank (WB) (see www. ituc-csi.org).

In addition to the ITUC, workers in unions in particular industries have their own sector representatives called global union federations (GUFs). For example, automobile unions are affiliated to the International Metalworkers' Federation, public servant unions can be members of Public Services International, and miners can belong to the International Federation of Chemical, Energy, Mine and General Workers' Unions. Some of these GUFs have negotiated global framework agreements with TNCs. The framework agreements set out the basic union rights and health and safety principles and conditions that will apply in TNCs all over the world. They also provide for a review mechanism to monitor the company's implementation of the principles. While global framework agreements advance workers' rights, only about 100 currently exist (Global Unions, 2013).

Most of the world's workers do not have unions or political parties to take care of their interests. Although these 'unprotected' workers (Harrod, 1987) face more obstacles than their protected counterparts, they still attempt to influence global labour policy. For example, small farmers and peasants from many parts of the world have coalesced around the group Via Campesina. Via Campesina describes itself as 'an international movement that coordinates peasant organisations of small and middle-scale producers, agricultural workers, rural women, and indigenous communities from Asia, Africa, America, and Europe' (see www.viacampesina.org). It advances farmers' interests by advocating for landless populations and small farmers while resisting the spread of **free trade agreements**, genetically modified organisms and national and transnational agribusinesses that undermine peasant incomes. Via Campesina has been active in the World Social Forums and has engaged institutions such as the WTO, WB and the Food and Agriculture Organization (FAO) as well as regional integration projects. The goal is to create the conditions in the global political economy for small-scale farmers to pursue their livelihoods free from the threat of economic and social extinction that is posed by large agricultural businesses. Large agricultural businesses, sometimes in the form of **multinational corporations** (MNCs), often have the market power to drive smaller-scale producers out of business.

In many developing countries, the vast majority of the population works as unprotected workers in the informal sector. Transnational cooperation between such groups is very difficult, since they often lack the resources to form even local or national institutions. However, there are instances of informal sector workers whose organisations become stable enough that they can develop an international presence and serve as an example to workers in other countries. One of the most prominent of these is the Self Employed Women's Association in India (www.sewa.org). In addition to affiliating with the established international union association ITUC, the Self Employed Women's Association is building its own international networks. It has become involved in working with Homenet (which organises home-based workers) and Streetnet (an organisation of street vendors). Another example of informal sector transnational organising is the Global Alliance of Waste Pickers (http://globalrec.org). It brings together people who collect, sort and recycle waste. They often work in unhealthy and unsafe conditions in rubbish dumps and on the streets of large cities in developing countries.

One significant way in which unprotected workers have been making transnational contacts and advances has been with the cooperation of consumer groups. The movement for ethical trade links consumers in advanced industrialised countries with workers and farmers in developing countries. In its broadest sense, ethical trade encompasses two elements (Blowfield, 1999). The first is a concern with how companies make their product. This involves pressuring companies to ensure that the production process respects key human rights and environmental standards. Examples include companies that adopt codes of conduct guaranteeing respect for workers' rights or banning child labour. The second element is the fairtrade movement, which seeks to increase the financial return to poor producers as a method of improving sustainable development (see **Chapter Five**). Major fairtrade initiatives have taken place with products such as coffee and chocolate. Both of these initiatives are designed to give workers in developing countries more autonomy in their working lives by supporting human rights or transferring wealth. This requires the formation of new transnational communities joining Southern producers with Northern consumers.

States in the global division of labour

The first stop for workers seeking protection in the global economy is their national state. However, states are differentially located in the **global division of labour**. As a result, they define their interests in different ways and take varying approaches to global labour policies. One crucial difference is between states with advanced industrialised economies and developing countries that are trying to industrialise. Advanced industrialised economies such as those in Western Europe, Japan, the US, Canada and Australia share a number of characteristics. They are relatively wealthy states, they are home to a majority of the world's TNCs, they produce many high-value-added products, wages are relatively high, they have advanced service, manufacturing and agricultural industries and they have ageing populations. In contrast, many developing countries are struggling to industrialise, have large informal sectors, relatively low wages, widespread poverty and young and growing populations, and are very dependent on investment from TNCs and overseas investors for economic growth.

States are locked into global competition with one another for investment and economic growth. However, they engage in different competitive strategies (Palan and Abbott, 2000). Relatively wealthy countries with high education levels can afford to pay relatively high wages to retain skilled workers because the value of their products produces large profits. Poorer countries may pursue other routes to maintain economic activity. Some countries will send their citizens abroad to find work that can support families at home. The remittances, or money, that these individuals send home can be greater than the official development aid the countries receive. In 2011 migrants sent back US$70 billion to India, US$66 billion to China, US$24 billion to the Philippines, US$24 billion to Mexico, US$21 billion to Nigeria and US$18 billion to Egypt (WB, 2012). Rather than sending people abroad to earn money, an alternative strategy is to attract capital into a country through the creation of **export processing zones**. These zones often suspend features of domestic regulation such as labour standards and taxation as incentives to lure foreign TNCs to set up shop. The lack of labour standards in these zones can lead to very poor and dangerous working conditions. Other states may rely on exporting their natural resources to generate wealth. These resources can range from those highly prized in the international market, such as oil, to those that attract paltry returns, such as coffee or bananas.

The differences in resources and intense competition for economic growth encourage states to have differing interests with regards to global labour policies. The poorest countries, most desperate for investment, will be most likely to curb labour protection in order to attract investment. Since labour is inexpensive in these countries, there will be an effort to attract investment into industries that use a large amount of labour. A classic example is the textile industry. In order to keep that investment, countries may be reluctant to do anything that increases the cost of labour. In contrast, wealthier countries have industries where labour costs are a smaller percentage of the total cost of production. This means they are better able to afford the costs of labour standards. Poorer countries will also press for labour mobility so that their citizens can work abroad. They will also have an interest in trying to protect their citizens when they are working abroad. In contrast, wealthier countries will want to be more selective about allowing labour to move between states, and may not be as concerned about the fate of migrant workers. Thus, we can hypothesise that wealthier countries will be more interested in global labour standards and poorer countries more interested in labour mobility and access to developed states markets. Both sets of countries will use the doctrine of **state sovereignty** as a justification for resisting compulsory labour regulations.

These general divisions are complicated by the fact that even advanced states are in global competition and limited as to the amount of labour protection they deliver. Advanced industrialised countries also point to the need to deregulate labour markets and have more flexible forms of labour available for their industries (McBride and Williams, 2001). The threat of TNCs moving production to lower wage jurisdictions threatens workers with unemployment. Competition from low-wage producers limits the wages that corporations from a wealthy country will be willing to give their workers. The movement of migrant labour also serves to check the wage demands and puts pressure on working conditions in developed states. This occurs because migrant workers often work for longer hours and less pay than domestic workers due to their desperation for employment.

Thus states find themselves in a balancing act. They must position themselves in the global competition for development and economic growth, but they must also respond to domestic and international pressure by workers for safe working conditions and fair remuneration.

International organisations

A number of international organisations have become involved in the effort to create global labour policy. They can be divided into three groups: those whose primary concern is labour issues; those primarily concerned with freeing the movement of trade and services; and those primarily focused on finance. Although each of these groups of institutions is engaged in labour issues, they have had a limited impact on advancing labour protection in the global economy.

The first category of institutions, those primarily focused on labour issues, is dominated by the **International Labour Organization** (ILO). This is the oldest arm of the United Nations (UN) system, originating in the Treaty of Versailles (1919), which led to the creation of the League of Nations. The ILO promotes labour standards in its member states through its Conventions and Recommendations. Conventions are statements of principle that member states are asked to ratify, while Recommendations outline administrative matters that carry less weight. The ILO has no coercive power and relies on the power of its argument to influence state behaviour. It also provides technical support to governments, employers and worker organisations that wish to improve working conditions. The organisation's primary task is to improve the living and working conditions of the world's population.

By the mid-1990s, advocates of international labour standards, such as trade unions and social democratic parties, had become discouraged about the possibility of the ILO being an institution that could bring significant improvement. The problem lay with the inability of the ILO to ensure enforcement of its Conventions. Labour rights advocates shifted their attention to having labour standards written into trade agreements and institutions such as the newly formed WTO. The ILO's response to this marginalisation was to focus attention on its role in defending labour rights through the creation of a new political instrument. In 1998, the ILO adopted the Declaration on Fundamental Principles and Rights at Work. It committed all member states to respect and promote ILO Conventions in four key areas: freedom of association and collective bargaining; the elimination of forced or compulsory labour; the abolition of child labour; and the elimination of discrimination in employment. Whether countries had ratified particular ILO Conventions or not, they became bound by this Declaration.

A second component of the ILO's attempt to come to grips with globalisation was recognition of the diversity of work relationships in the global economy. This involved a shift away from focusing on the standard employment relationship of a male unionised worker in a factory to considering the variety of employment patterns in the economy, which included precarious employment such as casual labour, work in the informal sector, various types of home work and contract work. The method for making this shift was twofold. One involved the introduction of a new theme and work programme – decent work (ILO, 2002a). The other was the introduction of new Conventions such as the Homeworking Convention. The shift to a rhetoric of 'decent work' was designed to take account of the large range of labour-related issues beyond the employer–trade union relationship. 'Decent work' covers issues such as fair incomes, employment security, **social protection**, social integration, freedom to express views and organise, and equality of opportunity and treatment for all women and men. It allows the ILO to address issues of informal employment as well as broad policy debates around social security and public policy.

A third initiative is the ILO's attempt to reinsert itself into debates about the impact and future of globalisation. The primary tool for accomplishing this objective was the 2002 creation of the World Commission on the Social Dimension of Globalisation. The Commission was composed of 26 high-profile people from different parts of the world involved in government, business, labour and academic fields. The Commission published its report, entitled *A fair globalisation: Creating opportunities for all*, in 2004. While not challenging the general trend of existing globalisation, it highlighted problems in current global economic **governance** and called for changes to ensure more equitable development (ILO, 2004). From a political point of view, the Commission's goal was to raise issues of equity and fairness in the global governance agenda. Similar to the UN's MDGs, the ILO Commission was an effort to shift the economic agenda and to focus attention on poverty and development.

A fourth area of activity is the ILO's attempt to regain a prominent role in the architecture of international organisations. The ILO, similar to other international organisations working in the social field, has been greatly overshadowed by international financial and trade organisations such as the IMF, WB and WTO. Even though these were all taking initiatives that had a direct impact on labour markets, the ILO was not a player in the formulation or implementation of those institutions' policies. In response to this lack of communication and feeling pressure from **civil society** groups, the ILO established formal inter-institutional channels of communication with the financial institutions and attempts to participate in their activities. In terms of policy, the ILO is attempting to influence other organisations' views on labour-related subjects. For example, it has tried to influence the content of **Poverty Reduction Strategy Papers** (PRSPs), which are used by the IMF and WB to demonstrate that their lending goes through a process of consultation with recipients.

A more recent fifth initiative has been the ILO's advocacy of a Social Protection Floor (SPF). This is designed to encourage countries to implement a basic or minimum level of social provision, and consists of a series of services and social transfers. Basic services that should be provided include water and sanitation, food and nutrition, health, education and information about saving and other social services. Social transfers require the allocation of cash or in-kind provisions to ensure a minimum income for vulnerable populations such as the poor, children, the sick and the old (SPF, 2012). The implementation of a SPF would improve the welfare of workers and provide them with greater options for an improved quality of life. However, success of the initiative requires cooperation from the WB to advocate universal social programmes and the IMF to allow countries fiscal space to fund those programmes (see Deacon 2012, and **Chapters Two** and **Eight** for further discussion of the SPF).

Ideologically, the ILO challenges the international financial institutions (IFIs) because it suggests that macroeconomic stabilisation plans undertaken in the absence of proper labour market institutions risk failure (ILO, 2004). It also disagrees with IFI policies that blame labour rigidity for unemployment. The ILO argues that 'rather than create rigidities, the labour institutions that are built upon the realisation of these fundamental principles and rights at work can be key to negotiating flexibility' (ILO, 2000). The ILO review of early PRSP consultations also raised three concerns about the degree and significance of **civil society** participation in the 'pro-poor' policies of the IMF and WB (ILO, 2002b). First, insufficient attention was being given to social equity issues. Second, trade unions, ministries of labour and even employers' organisations had difficulty participating in the process because it was dominated by trade and finance ministries. And third, labour market issues, social protection and other elements of decent work were often absent from poverty reduction policies.

Other institutions that influence labour conditions are those that focus on trade and services **liberalisation**, such as the WTO at the **multilateral** level and world-regional trade agreements (see also **Chapters Three** and **Five**, this volume). The establishment of the WTO in 1995 led workers' rights activists to demand the inclusion of labour standards in its enforcement mandate. The WTO hosts a relatively robust legal structure that puts immense pressure on states to implement its decisions. Disillusionment with the weakness of the ILO led campaigners to lobby their states and the WTO to enforce labour standards. This campaign proved unsuccessful because of opposition from TNCs, **neoliberal** states in the developed world and many developing countries.

At the world-regional level, a new wave of expanded trade and investment agreements swept the world in the 1980s and continued into the 21st century. These agreements raised the issue of whether or not labour standards and broader social rights should be part of the economic packages. **Chapter**

Three of this volume examines some of the responses by different regional associations of countries in terms of social policy generally. In terms of labour, the response varied greatly between regions, although the tendency was for labour standards to have a minor place. Indeed, one could build a regional integration typology based on provisions for labour rights and mobility. This would have the EU, with some common labour rights and representation, at one end of the spectrum, the North American Free Trade Agreement (NAFTA) simply urging states to enforce their own legislation in the middle and the Association of South East Asian Nations (ASEAN), with a tendency to deal with labour issues only under the heading of human resources, at the other end. Assessing the implications of world-regional economic agreements requires two steps. First, the provision or non-provision of labour issues within and around the agreements needs to be judged. Second, these provisions need to be compared with the institutional arrangements for other interests, such as investors. Labour groups continue to struggle to advance basic standards and rights, but the regional level, with the exception of the EU, has not proved to have been particularly fruitful (O'Brien, 2008).

IFIs are a third group of institutions having an impact on labour policy. They disperse finance to countries either for the purpose of dealing with a financial crisis or assisting with development. The two most prominent institutions are the IMF and WB. These institutions become involved in labour policy because their loans come with conditions. In some cases, those conditions include restructuring domestic labour markets. A prominent strain of thought at the WB and IMF is that the competitiveness of developing countries would be increased if labour was more flexible and wages were lower. This view is sometimes articulated in the policy advice given to member states. For example, a WB-sponsored report on Mexico suggested that its labour laws be revised to increase flexibility because the labour code was 'at best, outdated (part of it dates back to 1917), at worst, an impediment rather than a tool for workers' (Oliver et al, 2001). A Letter of Intent between the IMF and Ecuador outlines how the government's 'economic transformation law' will facilitate the introduction of temporary contracts to increase labour market flexibility and boost employment (Government of Ecuador, 2000).

In response to criticisms of the impact on labour, the IFIs have modified their procedures and policies. They have taken steps to regularise (but not formalise) their contact with trade unions at the international level. Every two years, leaders of the IMF and WB meet with those of the ITUC and GUFs, and smaller yearly thematic meetings are conducted. Indeed, as the WB pursues development strategies that touch on numerous domestic governance issues, it has become impossible to argue that advocacy of core labour standards should be ignored. In September 2003, the WB's private sector lending arm, the International Finance Corporation (IFC), announced that its loan recipients would soon have to abide by all the core labour standards. In January 2004, the IFC made approval of a loan to a free trade zone operator in Haiti conditional on the employer recognising its workers' rights to freedom of association and collective bargaining (ICFTU, 2004). In 2006 the IFC's 'Performance Standard 2: Labor and Working Conditions' (PS2) stipulated that all borrowing companies had to ensure that their operations were in compliance with core labour standards (IFC, 2006). Trade unions have reported positive results in countries and with firms that are already sympathetic to labour, but inaction from previously hostile states and firms (ITUC, 2011). In 2007 the WB introduced labour standards into its Standard Bidding Document for Procurement of Works with suggested clauses for contractors bidding on projects. This initiative followed several years of negotiating with international trade unions and in the wake of scandalous labour conditions on several WB projects in Chad/Cameroon and Indonesia. The WB proposed that all multilateral development banks integrate core labour standards into the general conditions required for major construction projects. This idea was accepted and the new harmonised contracts were adopted in June 2010 (ITUC, 2011).

At the same time that progress was being made in having the WB demand contractors and projects respect core labour standards, another part of the Bank recommended the dismantling of labour regulation in member states. The WB publication *Doing business* made its first appearance in 2004 with a mandate of identifying regulation that constrained business activity (WB, 2004, p viii). Labour regulation from Portugal to Zimbabwe was alleged to be too restrictive, out of date with modern business practices, contributing to unemployment, restricting economic growth, and postponing research and development (WB, 2004, pp 29–39). Trade unions argued that Bank and IMF officials were using the report to undermine national labour regulation (Bakvis, 2006; ITUC, 2007). Although changes have been made to the labour sections of the report, the 2013 *Doing business* edition continued the trend of praising countries that reduced protection for workers. This led to the General Secretary of the ITUC calling for labour issues to be left out of the *Doing business* reports altogether (ITUC, 2012).

For its part, the IMF supports the policy of core labour standards, but continues to push labour market deregulation wherever it can. A review of IMF conditionality in the field of labour deregulation (as evidenced by Letters of Intent and loan contracts) between 1988 and 2000 has demonstrated that it is most stringent on weak states and less stringent on stronger states (Caraway et al, 2012). In those states where organised labour is relatively strong, labour market conditionality is weaker than in those countries where organised labour is relatively weak. In the language of the

IFIs, the IMF imposes labour market conditionality not in those states where labour markets are most rigid (where organised labour is strongest), but in those states where labour is least able to defend its interests. This suggests that the IMF is committed to liberalising labour markets and undermining labour power, limited only by the strength of the labour movement in borrowing countries.

The IMF continues to provide a wide range of advice on labour issues and labour market policies. The European debt crisis that began in 2010 has allowed the IMF to become particularly active in Greece and Portugal. Within the general prescriptions for structural adjustment the Fund examines a number of labour issues. It highlights the problem of unemployment, particularly youth unemployment, and suggests some targeted social protection and active labour market initiatives (such as wage subsidies). However, depending on the country, the Fund also recommends reductions in minimum wages, lowering labour taxes (reducing social security contributions through wages), transformation of collective bargaining, privatisation and deregulation of particular industries, and reduction of the public sector wage bill (IMF, 2012).

Labour issues are a subject of considerable debate in a series of different international organisations. However, the struggle to forge a global labour policy that improves workers' conditions has not been very successful. This has caused some campaigners to turn their attention away from the state and inter-state organisations to the activity of corporations and the harms they cause (see ***Box 6.1***).

Box 6.1: Deadly factories

On 10 May 1993, the worst-ever factory fire occurred in a toy plant just outside Bangkok in Thailand (ICFTU, 1994). There were 188 fatalities. Of these, 174 were women and girls, many of whom were as young as 13. Over 460 other people were injured in the fire. These injuries were due to people jumping from upper floors, being trampled in the panic or suffering from smoke inhalation or burns. The factory violated many basic health and safety standards: it lacked fire exits and sprinkler systems; hallways and stairwells were used to store flammable materials; and locked doors and barred windows made it impossible for some workers to escape. The mainly young female workforce had not been able to pressure the employer into providing a safe place to work.

The factory was owned by Kader Industrial Company based in Hong Kong. Among its many activities, Kadar manufactures toys for Western companies such as Arco, Kenner, Gund, Hasbro, J.C. Penny, Toys-R-Us, Fisher-Price and Tyco. The responsibility for allowing the conditions that fuelled the fire begins with the company itself and reaches all the way to Western consumers. The company failed in its duty to provide a safe working environment for its employees, the Thai government failed in its duty to enforce safety standards, Western retailers failed in their duty to ensure that sub-contractors produced products in a safe environment, and Western governments ignored the issue of safety in the production of imported products. Western consumers were indirectly implicated because their demand for ever-cheaper toy prices encourages producers to save costs by cutting back on expenses such as health and safety regulation.

Twenty years later, not much had changed. In November 2012 a Bangladeshi factory making clothing for Western retailers such as Walmart and Sears caught fire, killing 112 people. The fire broke out in the evening as the mainly female workforce was putting in overtime to fill orders for international brands. The factory was in violation of safety codes and some managers demanded the workers stay at their sewing machines as the alarm sounded (Manik and Yardley, 2012). As horrific as this fire was, worse was yet to come. On 9 May 2013, ten times the number of workers (over 1,000) were killed in the collapse of the Rana Plaza building that housed two factories in Dhaka, Bangladesh. A subsequent investigation revealed that three fifths of Bangladeshi factories making clothing for Western brands were vulnerable to collapse as owners sought to cut corners in the pursuit of profits and Western markets (Burke, 2013).

Transnational corporations

The world's largest TNCs are larger and richer economic actors than many states. Because of this enormous economic influence, the decisions corporations make about where they will locate their production or the types of working practices they engage in have immense implications for global labour standards. Given the lack of success international organisations have had in advancing labour rights, civic actors have increasingly targeted corporations to advance labour rights. The response by most corporate leaders to an upsurge in public interest in labour standards and labour rights has been to argue that such concerns are best addressed through self–regulation. The role of corporations will be addressed in more depth in the section on self–regulation below.

Policy issues in global labour policy

This section examines two linked policy issues in global labour policy. The first is whether there should be a common set of basic labour rights that covers all workers and is enforced worldwide through the activity of states and international organisations. A second issue is whether international labour rights would be advanced by encouraging TNCs to engage in self-regulation.

International enforcement of core labour standards

One key policy issue is whether or not there should be international enforcement of core labour standards. There are a series of theoretical and practical arguments both for and against having states or international organisations impose penalties on states that violate core labour standards. The concept of core labour standards originates in a series of ILO Conventions (87, 98, 29, 105, 100, 111, 138). These were designed to protect the most important and basic of workers' rights: freedom of association, the right to collective bargaining, abolition of forced labour, prevention of discrimination in employment and a minimum age for employment. These rights are seen as enabling rights: the provision of these rights should enable workers to struggle for other rights. The core labour standards do not provide for specific wage levels or safety standards, but they do provide workers with the tools to organise and bargain over working conditions.

As mentioned above, all states are committed to core labour standards through the ILO's Fundamental Declaration. However, many states do not respect these standards. The question is whether some mechanism should be put in place to punish states that consistently violate labour rights. For example, the WTO could be used to sanction states that did not protect labour standards in the same way that it is used to enforce respect for intellectual property rights. Violating states could be hit with economic sanctions from other states.

The debate over global enforcement of core labour standards divides groups favouring rival economic programmes and having different views over the role of state sovereignty. Those against having an enforcement mechanism for core labour standards tend to take a neoliberal approach to labour conditions and often advocate state sovereignty over international regulation. The neoliberal ideology has guided much economic globalisation since the 1980s. In this view, labour is a commodity (something that is bought and sold), freedom of expression and association for workers is not essential or even desirable for economic growth, and poverty will be resolved by market rather than state mechanisms. The appropriate payment for work is determined by the market and the only real solution to poor working conditions is economic growth.

Neoliberals often point to the doctrine of **comparative advantage** (see also **Chapter Five**) to bolster their case against enforcement of labour standards. They argue that countries with a large pool of cheap labour should use that as an economic advantage and attract businesses that want to use such labour in their production. This allows poor countries to industrialise and begin the path to economic development. Thus, a difference in labour standards and working conditions between countries is seen to be both natural and beneficial. Opponents of labour standard enforcement also often cite the doctrine of **state sovereignty**. Under this doctrine, governments only have a responsibility to their own citizens and are uninterested in the fate of people living in other countries. This suggests that states will engage in a variety of labour practices to advance national interests, and that they will not be concerned about working conditions in other countries.

In contrast, those in favour of global enforcement of core labour standards tend to have a social democratic economic philosophy and a **cosmopolitan approach** to human rights. The social democratic approach to labour rights is captured in the core assumptions of the ILO's 1944 Declaration of Philadelphia. This Declaration declared that labour is not a commodity; freedom of expression and of association are essential to sustained progress; poverty anywhere constitutes a danger to prosperity everywhere; and the war against want must be vigorously pursued. In this view, labour is composed of human beings who deserve protection from economic exploitation. Failure to deliver this protection is not only immoral, but will lead to political conflict and even warfare between states.

The doctrine of state sovereignty is challenged by the concept of **cosmopolitanism**. Cosmopolitanism posits that all people are part of a universal human community. Even through people are divided into national political communities by birth, they have moral obligations to all human beings by virtue of a common humanity. Ethical obligations transcend state borders. Thus economic activity and rule making must take into account their impact on foreigners as wells as national citizens. A cosmopolitan approach to global labour issues would stress two points. First, all people enjoy rights to basic labour standards. And second, people in wealthier countries have an obligation to ensure that their economic activity does not contribute to labour abuses in other countries.

The arena where the enforcement of core labour standards became most prominent in the 1990s was the negotiations surrounding the founding of the WTO and agenda setting in its early years. The establishment of the WTO in 1995 led workers' rights activists to demand the inclusion of labour standards in its enforcement mandate. This campaign proved unsuccessful due to the opposition of TNCs, neoliberal states in the developed world and many developing countries (O'Brien et al, 2000, pp 67–108). Developing countries feared that labour standards would be used as an excuse for protectionism in developed states. They were concerned that wealthier states would use labour standards to undermine their comparative advantage. While the effort to have the WTO deal with labour standards failed, it did result in the ILO refocusing its efforts (see above) and the initiation of new policies such as **corporate codes of conduct** and the Global Compact (see below).

State enforcement of core labour standards remains on the agenda. The negotiation of regional trade agreements usually features a debate about whether trade agreements should contain labour elements. Pressure for some enforcement of labour rights is generated by coverage of labour abuses and the influx of cheap consumer goods into industrialised states from countries that fail to respect core labour standards. Nevertheless, the failure to actually agree on a state-based enforcement mechanism has led to considerable discussion of corporate self-regulation as a method for improving global labour standards.

Self-regulation

Self-regulation is where corporations set and monitor their own rules. This can take place either through the actions of an individual corporation or through the activities of business associations in a particular sector. The concept and practice of **corporate social responsibility** (CSR) has been the primary rejoinder to those arguing for state-based international labour regulation (see also **Chapter Four**). The European Commission provides a useful definition of CSR as a concept 'whereby companies integrate social and environmental concerns in their business operations and in their interaction with stakeholders on a voluntary basis' (Greenwood, 2003, p 56). It has also come to be known as 'the triple bottom line' or 'corporate citizenship', signifying the responsibility of companies to create wealth, pursue sustainable development and enhance the lives of their employees and the communities in which they locate. As Chris Thomas, a corporate reputation consultant, writes, 'CSR is a prudent adaptation to changing circumstances: countering the increased ability of stakeholders to scrutinise corporate activities and motives with openness and complementary action' (Thomas, 2003). CSR policies have been put into practice by many firms, including many of those caught in sweatshop scandals.

While TNCs and business organisations suggest that CSR will advance social rights, critics contend that CSR has been developed as a substitute and diversion for action (Justice, 2002). For example, one analyst argues that 'in plain terms, business "talks the talk" *so as not to* "walk the walk"' (Rowe, 2005, p 144; original emphasis). In this view, CSR is a public relations ploy. The main targets are average consumers who may have encountered anti-corporate campaigns but are not particularly engaged with the issue and therefore largely ignorant of the ongoing situation on the company's factory floors. The goal is 'to solve guilty consumer consciousness' rather than to improve working conditions (Brooks, 2005, p 134).

In response to scepticism over in-house company codes of conduct, many TNCs have been forced to support a number of third party or joint corporate–non-governmental organisation (NGO) initiatives. In addition to numerous partnerships between firms and NGOs, the most prominent response has been the creation of a number of multi-stakeholder initiatives in the US and Western Europe such as the Fair Labour Association (FLA) and the Ethical Trade Initiative (ETI), industry-based initiatives such as the Worldwide Responsible Apparel Production and the emergence of third party certification providers such as Social Accountability International. All of these attempt to avoid traditional state-based regulation. For example, the FLA was created after sweatshop scandals in the US in the early 1990s raised industry fears that Congress would pass tougher regulation (Jenkins, 2002). Voluntary initiatives claim to support labour standards through a mix of cooperation between key actors, learning networks, 'enlightened company self-interest', benchmarking, internal and external monitoring and enforcement through market sanctions (O'Rourke, 2003).

Numerous organisations have sprung up to support the corporate response to labour and social issues. In Chapter Four, Kevin Farnsworth reviewed the ways in which **global business interest associations**, such as the Business and Interest Advisory Committee (BIAC), International Chamber of Commerce (ICC) and European Round Table (ERT), have been involved in promoting corporate responses on these issues within **global social policy** making. In the UK, there are the following organisations: Business in the Community (the UK member of CSR Europe), Common Purpose, the Institute of Business Ethics and the Prince of Wales International Business Leaders Forum (Greenwood, 2003). Most major TNCs belong to more than one such organisation in addition to having their own CSR committees. These initiatives are supported by academics within corporate-funded business schools that advocate CSR and carry out research to improve its practice and effectiveness. The vast majority of their focus is on how TNCs can use CSR to respond to anti-corporate activism, protect corporate reputations and brand names and encourage a 'business-friendly' regulatory environment.

In adopting CSR, corporations draw on both liberal economic and cultural/nationalist arguments that suggest that movement to enforceable labour standards may hurt development. Many neoclassical economists argue that regulation and codes of conduct reduce wealth and therefore harm the very workers labour activists are attempting to help. In 2000, a letter signed by over 250 economists was sent to US university presidents at a time when the FLA and the Worker Rights Consortium (WRC) were quickly gaining university memberships. According to these economists, the codes of conduct promoted by the FLA and WRC would cause employment in the developing world to shift away from the poorest workers. They also argued that regulation was unnecessary as TNCs already pay higher wages than the 'prevailing market wage' (Wells, 2004). The economists' intervention offered comfort to TNCs trying to avoid meaningful codes of conduct, much less effective regulation. Echoing arguments made by some developing country leaders (such as Mahathir Mohamad, former Prime Minister of Malaysia), corporations have been able to argue that their hands-off approach to labour issues respects national sovereignty and cultural diversity. For example, some members of the Toy Manufacturers of America, when faced with demands to live up to the ILO's universal standards to avoid a repeat of the Kadar toy factory disaster (see *Box 6.1*), argued that they did not want to be seen as imposing 'Western values' on non-Western cultures (Justice, 2002).

A key element of CSR engagement is the emphasis on partnerships between firms and their NGO opponents. The concept of partnership has 'become an orthodox public affairs strategy' (Greenwood, 2003, p 54). From a public relations perspective, it is an attempt to protect brands plagued by mistrust by associating with NGOs that enjoy a higher level of trust (Hatcher, 2003). This strategy has come to be known as 'greenwashing' in relation to partnerships between environmental NGOs and TNCs. More recently, anti-corporate activists have coined the term 'bluewashing' to describe partnerships between TNCs and the UN, such as the Global Compact (see below). Some examples of partnerships between TNCs and/or employers' associations and NGOs linked to labour rights include: Gap and the National Labour Committee; the Fairtrade Foundation and Sainsbury's; the Co-operative Wholesale Society, World Federation of Sporting Goods Industry and Save the Children; and the FLA and the ETI.

Although there are literally hundreds of corporate codes of conduct in existence, there is increasing doubt about whether this will resolve the labour standards issue. Numerous studies have documented the serious weaknesses of these private regulatory approaches, and it is increasingly apparent that they do not serve as an effective substitute for traditional labour regulation (Bruno and Karliner, 2002; Christian Aid, 2004; Rowe, 2005). Self- and voluntary regulation of labour standards is not successful in national markets and is even less likely to succeed transnationally. An extreme example of the divergence between intentions stated in codes of conduct and practices on the ground is provided in *Box 6.2*.

Box 6.2: Codes versus practice

Statement from the Code of Conduct of Chiquita (famous for selling bananas):

Chiquita believes in doing business with suppliers and other business partners who demonstrate high standards of ethical business conduct. Our ultimate goal is to direct all of our business to suppliers that demonstrate their compliance with the social responsibilities included in our Code of Conduct and that operate in an ethical and lawful manner. (Chiquita, 2004)

Statement from lawyers suing Chiquita for activities in Columbia:

Advocates for the families of 173 people murdered in the banana-growing regions of Colombia filed suit today against Chiquita Brands International, in Federal District Court in Washington, DC. The families allege that Chiquita paid millions of dollars, and tried to ship thousands of machine guns to the Autodefensas Unidas de Colombia, or AUC. The AUC is a violent, right-wing terrorist organisation supported by the Colombian army, and was designated a 'terrorist organisation' in 2001 by the Bush Administration. Its units are often described as "death squads". (Iradvocates, 2007)

The Global Compact

The Global Compact is an example of an attempt to bring together states, civic associations and corporations to build better global labour policy. It was launched by the Secretary-General of the UN and asks corporations to incorporate 10 principles drawn from the Universal Declaration of Human Rights, the ILO's Declaration on Fundamental Principles and Rights at Work, the Rio Principles on Environment and Development and the UN Convention Against Corruption into their corporate practices. It does not monitor corporate practice and nor does it assess corporate performance. It is designed to identify and disseminate good practice. It asks leaders of some of the world's most prominent corporations to publicly commit themselves to good labour and environmental practices.

The Global Compact simultaneously addresses the concerns of some corporate, state and civic associations. From a developing country point of view, the initiative is tolerable because it is aimed at influencing the policy of TNCs rather than restricting state policy or punishing developing states for poor labour conditions. This is preferable to the WTO enforcing standards because it removes the threat of Northern protectionism. From the corporate viewpoint, it is tolerable because regulations are voluntary and allow continued expansion of the global economy and accumulation of profits. TNCs can claim to be good corporate citizens without being bound by compulsory regulation. For some civic actors, it represents a limited advance in enshrining some principles of social protection. It is a small step that might lead to more binding forms of regulation.

The Global Compact has severe shortcomings and many critics. Many of the companies participating in the venture are those that have been attacked as abusers of environmental and human rights or accused of engaging in the super-exploitation of workers. The list includes Shell, Nike, Disney and Rio Tinto. Each of these companies has been, or is subject to, boycotts or anti-corporate campaigns by civic associations. One can question the degree to which such companies will actually change their stripes. Domestically, reliance only on voluntary regulation of corporate behaviour is unacceptable. Why would such activity at the global level prove any more satisfying? The ILO has hundreds of Conventions, but sees many abused because of a lack of enforcement powers. How would this initiative be any different? Another problem is that the selection of participating civic associations in the Global Compact was very narrow and not reflective of the wider community. The UN selected civic groups based on its judgement of who would be the most likely to cooperate. Reaction from many other groups has been very critical. The initiative has been condemned because it threatens the integrity of the UN, as corporations attempt to 'bluewash' their record by association with the UN (TRAC, 2000). The Global Compact is accused of allowing corporations to claim higher ethical credentials while continuing to inflict serious harm on populations and environments, safe in the knowledge that such actions are likely to go unnoticed or unpunished (ActionAid, 2007).

This example of the Global Compact is informative for our efforts to understand global labour policy for three reasons. First, it illustrates that the concerns of civic actors about the damaging aspects of globalisation on labour are being taken seriously by other actors in the system. The UN is responding to public unease about the costs of globalisation. This initiative follows public demonstrations against institutions such as the WTO and IMF. The UN Secretary-General is trying to put a more humane face on globalisation so that the process will continue, but in a less brutal manner. The goal is to restrain competition that is based on the abuse of labour and environmental standards so that the public will not fight the liberal rules under which globalisation is taking place. Corporations are also being forced to respond to civic pressure by setting up codes of conduct and projecting the image of moral behaviour.

Second, it highlights the failure of existing global governance arrangements to deal adequately with global labour issues. We already have an institution that is designed to bolster labour standards – the ILO. However, the ineffectiveness of the ILO has forced labour activists to turn to the enforcement mechanisms found in the WTO to support labour standards. Many developing states oppose dealing with labour standards because they fear that developed states might increase their protectionism through the device of labour standards. Those groups in **civil society** trying to improve labour standards find themselves blocked at the WTO and faced with a weak ILO. Existing global governance mechanisms seem unable to improve social standards. Thus, initiatives such as the Global Compact are being devised in an urgent attempt to resolve difficult dilemmas.

Finally, the Global Compact illustrates just how difficult it is to create global labour policy. The cost of freer markets is creating more public resistance, but many states and corporations resist instruments that would require better labour, environmental or social standards. Agreements that secure widespread corporate and state support are unlikely to satisfy the social interests that are pressing for protection. For the time being, social interests may have to accept incremental steps towards reforming institutions and policies at the global level.

Conclusion

The world faces several challenging issues in the field of global labour policy. Unemployment is widespread, poverty is extensive and basic labour rights are often lacking. One strategy to deal with these issues is to focus attention on core labour rights in the hope that securing these rights will allow workers to mobilise and attain other rights. However, states have pursued very different policies towards labour, and have struggled to reach agreement in the international arena. The lack of state action to protect labour rights and to improve working conditions has created a regulatory vacuum. Social groups such as labour unions and ethically motivated consumers continue to press for fair labour standards. Many TNCs have responded to these concerns by introducing codes of conduct and arguing that corporate self-regulation is the best path for improving labour conditions around the world. Critics doubt that self-regulation will improve standards.

The UN's Global Compact initiative is an example of an attempt by state, corporate and civic leaders to advance labour rights and standards by highlighting desirable labour practices. However, the voluntary nature of the Global Compact and many other international initiatives raises doubts about their effectiveness. With consumers demanding ever-cheaper products and corporations competing to supply mass consumer goods at low cost, it is likely that pressure on working conditions and wages will continue. It is also likely that workers and citizens will continue the struggle to advance a more humane global labour policy.

Summary

- The majority of the world's working population lacks the protection of core labour standards and access to social security.
- A wide range of actors, from civic associations to international organisations and TNCs, attempt to influence global labour policy.
- State enforcement of labour standards at the global level remains a controversial topic.
- Increasing attention has been paid to corporate self-regulation to bolster labour standards, but there is considerable scepticism about whether it can deliver.
- The Global Compact is an example of a voluntary initiative supported by particular civic associations, corporations and states to improve global labour standards.

Questions for discussion

- What are the key challenges for workers in a global economy?
- Why would some states oppose core labour standards?
- Should core labour standards be enforced on a global basis?

Further activities

- Visit the Fairtrade website (www.fairtrade.net) to get a sense of the extent and scope of fairtrade practices. Have you ever bought any fairtrade products? What are the benefits and shortcomings of such products? How do they improve working conditions?
- Visit www.guardian.co.uk/news/datablog/2013/feb/05/remittances-around-world-visualised. Examine the graph that shows the flow of remittances around the world. Can you detect any patterns? Do any of these flows come as a surprise to you?
- Examine the news stories from the LabourStart website (www.labourstart.org). Did you realise that all this activity was taking place? How many of these stories had you heard of in the papers you read or news that you watch? How might the issues raised by them be addressed by global policy?

Further reading and resources

A wide range of labour issues is addressed in the open access online publication *Global Labour Journal* (http://digitalcommons.mcmaster.ca/globallabour).

Dimitris and Boswell (2007) provide a recent overview of the impact of global governance mechanisms on labour and the attempt of labour unions to influence global governance.

The World Commission on the Social Dimensions of Globalisation (ILO, 2004), examines how social standards could be improved and globalisation made into a fairer process.

International Labour Organization (ILO): www.ilo.org

United Nations (UN) Global Compact: www.unglobalcompact.org

International Trade Union Confederation: www.ituc-csi.org

United Students Against Sweatshops: usas.org

References

ActionAid (2007) 'Critique of the Global Compact' (www.actionaid.org/pages. aspx?PageID=34&ItemID=282).

Bakvis, P. (2006) *How the World Bank and IMF use the Doing business report to promote labour market deregulation in developing countries*, Washington, DC: International Confederation of Trade Unions (library.fes.de/pdf-files/gurn/00171.pdf).

Blowfield, M. (1999) 'Ethical trade: a review of developments and issues', *Third World Quarterly*, vol 20, no 4, pp 753-70.

Brooks, E. (2005) 'Transnational campaigns against child labour', in J. Bandy and J. Smith (eds) *Coalitions across borders: Transnational protest and the neoliberal order*, Lanham, MD: Rowman & Littlefield, pp 212-39.

Bruno, K. and Karliner, J. (2002) *Earthsummit.biz: The corporate takeover of sustainable development*, Oakland, CA: Food First Books.

Burke, J. (2013) 'Majority of Bangladesh garment factories vulnerable to collapse', *The Guardian*, Monday 3 June (www.guardian.co.uk/world/2013/jun/03/bangladesh-garment-factories-vulnerable-collapse?INTCMP=SRCH).

Caraway, T., Rickard, S.J. and Anner, M. (2012) 'International negotiations and domestic politics: The case of the IMF labor market conditionality', *International Organization*, vol 66, Winter, pp 27-61.

Carr, M., Chen, M.A. and Tate, J. (2000) 'Globalization and home-based workers', *Feminist Economics*, vol 6, no 3, pp 123-42.

Chiquita (2004) 'Introduction to "Code of conduct: living by our core values"' (www.chiquita.com).

Christian Aid (2004) *Behind the mask: The real face of corporate social responsibility*, London: Christian Aid.

Deacon, B. (2012) 'The Social Protection Floor', *CROP Poverty Brief*, October (www.crop.org/storypg.aspx?id=598&MenuNode=633958868628358455&zone=12).

Dimitris, S. and Boswell, T. (2007) *Globalization and labor: Democratizing global governance*, Lanham, MD: Rowman & Littlefield.

Global Unions (2013) 'Framework agreements' (www.global-unions.org/framework-agreements.html).

Government of Ecuador (2000) *Memorandum of economic policies of the Government of Ecuador for 2000*, Ministry of Finance and Public Credit (ed), Washington, DC: International Monetary Fund.

Greenfield, G. (1998) 'The ICFTU and the politics of compromise', in E. Wood (ed) *Rising from the ashes: Labour in the era of global capitalism*, New York: Monthly Review, pp 180-9.

Greenwood, J. (2003) 'Trade associations, change and the new activism', in S. John and S. Thomson (eds) *New activism and the corporate response*, New York: Palgrave Macmillan.

Harrod, J. (1987) *Power, production and the unprotected worker*, New York: Columbia University Press.

Hatcher, M. (2003) 'Public affairs challenges for multinational corporations', in S. John and S. Thomson (eds) *New activism and the corporate response*, New York: Palgrave, pp 96-144.

ICFTU (International Confederation of Trade Unions) (1994) *From the ashes: A toy factory fire in Thailand*, Brussels: ICFTU.

ICFTU (2004) 'World Bank's IFC approves Haiti/Dominican Republic loan, with union rights conditions', Press Release, 20 January, Brussels: ICFTU.

IFC (International Finance Corporation) (2006) *Performance standards and guidance notes: 2006 edition*, Washington, DC: IFC (www.ifc.org).

ILO (International Labour Organization) (1930) *CO 29 Forced Labour Convention*, Geneva: ILO.

ILO (2000) *Organization, bargaining and dialogue for development in a globalizing world*, GB.279/WP/SDG/2, Working Party on Social Dimensions of Globalization, Geneva: ILO.

ILO (2002a) *Decent work and the informal economy*, Geneva: ILO.

ILO (2002b) *Poverty Reduction Strategy Papers (PRSPs): An assessment of the ILO's experience*, Committee on Employment and Social Policy, Geneva: ILO.

ILO (2004) *A fair globalization: Creating opportunities for all*, Geneva: ILO.

ILO (2012) 'Summary of the ILO 2012 global estimate of forced labour' (www.ilo.org/sapfl/Informationresources/ILOPublications/WCMS_181953/lang--en/index.htm).

ILO (2013a) 'Safety and health at work' (www.ilo.org/global/topics/safety-and-health-at-work/lang--de/index.htm).

ILO (2013b) 'Child labour' (www.ilo.org/global/topics/child-labour/lang--de/index.htm#a3).

ILO (2013c) 'Questions and answers on forced labour' (www.ilo.org/global/about-the-ilo/newsroom/comment-analysis/WCMS_181922/lang--en/index.htm).

IMF (International Monetary Fund) (2012) 'The IMF's advice on labor market issues', Factsheet, 7 October, Washington, DC: IMF (www.imf.org/external/np/exr/facts/labor.htm).

Iradvocates (International Rights Advocates) (2007) 'Victims' advocates sue banana giant', Press release, 7 June (www.iradvocates.org).

ISSA (International Social Security Association) (2013) 'About social security', Geneva: ISSA (www.issa.int/Topics/About-social-security).

ITUC (International Trade Union Confederation) (2007) *Annual survey of violation of trade union rights*, Brussels: ITUC (http://survey07.ituc-csi.org).

ITUC (2011) *Labour standards in World Bank Group Lending Lessons Learned and next steps*, Brussels: ITUC (www.ituc-csi.org/labour-standards-in-world-bank.html).

ITUC (2012) 'World Bank's doing business 2013: Unfounded claims about deregulation', News (www.ituc-csi.org/world-bank-s-doing-business-2013.html).

Jenkins, R. (2002) 'The political economy of codes of conduct', in R. Jenkins, R. Pearson and G. Seyfang (eds) *Corporate responsibility and labour rights: Codes of conduct in the global economy*, London: Earthscan, pp 13-30.

Justice, D. (2002) 'The international trade union movement and the new codes of conduct', in R. Jenkins, R. Pearson and G. Seyfang (eds) *Corporate responsibility and labour rights: Codes of conduct in the global economy*, London: Earthscan.

McBride, S. and Williams, R. (2001) 'Globalization, the restructuring of labour markets and policy convergence', *Global Social Policy*, vol 1, no 3, pp 281-309.

Manik, U. and Yardley, J. (2012) 'Bangladesh finds gross negligence in factory fire', *New York Times*, 18 December (www.nytimes.com/2012/12/18/world/asia/bangladesh-factory-fire-caused-by-gross-negligence.html).

O'Brien, R. (2000) 'Workers and world order: the tentative transformation of the international union movement', *Review of International Studies*, vol 26, no 4, pp 533-55.

O'Brien, R. (2008) 'No safe havens: labour, regional integration and globalization', in A. Cooper, C. Hughes and P. Lombaerde (eds) *Regionalisation and global governance: The taming of globalisation?*, London: Routledge, pp 142-56.

O'Brien, R., Goetz, A.M., Scholte, J.A. and Williams, M. (2000) *Contesting global governance: Multilateral economic institutions and global social movements*, Cambridge: Cambridge University Press.

Oliver, L., Nguyen, V. and Giugale, M. (2001) *Mexico: A comprehensive development agenda for the new era*, Washington, DC: The World Bank.

O'Rourke, D. (2003) 'Outsourcing regulation: analyzing nongovernmental systems of labor standards and monitoring', *Policy Studies Journal*, vol 31, no 1, pp 1-29.

Palan, R. and Abbott, J. (2000) *State strategies in the global economy*, London: Continuum.

Phillips, N. (2013) 'Unfree Labour and Adverse Incorporation in the Global Economy: Comparative Perspectives from Brazil and India', *Economy and Society*, vol 42, no 2, 96.

Rushe, D. (2013) 'World unemployment figures set to rise in 2013, claims UN labour agency', *The Guardian*, 22 January (www.guardian.co.uk/business/2013/jan/22/ilo-unemployment-numbers-rise-2013).

Rowe, J.K. (2005) 'Corporate social responsibility as business strategy', in R. Lipschutz and J.K. Rowe (eds) *Globalization, governmentality and global politics: Regulation for the rest of us?*, London: Routledge, pp 122-60.

SPF (Social Protection Floor) (2012) 'About the Social Protection Floor' (www.socialprotectionfloor-gateway.org/4.htm).

Standing, G. (2011) *The precariat: The new dangerous class*, New York: Bloomsbury Academic.

Thomas, C. (2003) 'Cyberactivism and corporations: new strategies for new media', in S. John and S. Thomson (eds) *New activism and the corporate response*, New York: Palgrave Macmillan.

TRAC (Transnational Resource and Action Center) (2000) *Tangled up in blue: Corporate partnerships at the United Nations*, Oakland, CA: TRAC (www.corpwatch.org).

WB (The World Bank) (2004) *Doing business in 2004: Understanding regulation*, Washington, DC: WB.

WB (2012) 'Remittances to developing countries will pass $400 billion in 2012', *Migration and Development Brief 19*, Washington, DC: WB (http://web.worldbank.org/WBSITE/EXTERNAL/TOPICS/0,,contentMDK:21924020~pagePK:5105988~piPK:360975~theSitePK:214971,00.html).

WB (2013) 'Poverty overview' (http://web.worldbank.org/WBSITE/EXTERNAL/TOPICS/EXTPOVERTY/EXTPA/0,,contentMDK:20040961~menuPK:435040~pagePK:148956~piPK:216618~theSitePK:430367~isCURL:Y,00.html).

Wells, D. (2004) 'How ethical are ethical purchasing policies?', *Journal of Academic Ethics*, vol 2, no 1, pp 119-40.

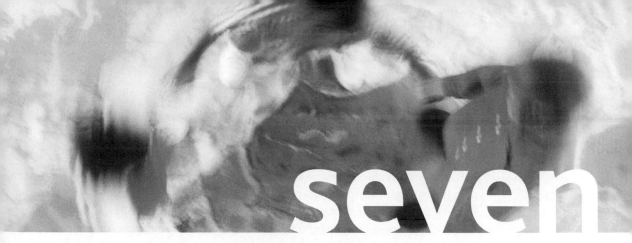

seven

Global health policies

Meri Koivusalo and Eeva Ollila

Overview

This chapter explains why health is of major significance for global social policy. It identifies a range of global health policy issues and sets these in the context of global health inequalities. It outlines the governance of global health policies in terms of the legal basis for action, institutions, actors and global policies. Three key contemporary global health policy agendas and challenges are discussed: health systems and the interplay between disease-based programmes and health systems development; addressing inequalities and health in policy fields other than health policy; and pharmaceutical policies and the challenge of prioritising health and health policy needs in the context of global health policy.

Keywords

Health, health policy, governance, health inequalities, determinants of health

Introduction

Health is a major issue for global social policy. Gross social inequalities in health and global poverty of the kind outlined in Chapter Two of this volume undermine health as a universal human right in the 1948 United Nations (UN) Declaration of Human Rights. In addition, major public health threats, such as major epidemics and global pandemics, are amplified by globalisation. The movement of people and goods around the world increases the risk that a localised outbreak of a disease cannot be contained and that it will spread rapidly around the world, affecting many millions, even billions, of people. It is increasingly argued that national policy measures require global regulation and coordinated action in order to gain sufficient policy space for comprehensive health responses to emerge and develop. This is especially the case to protect national health policies from the adverse effects of powerful multinational industries or from being encroached on by policy priorities emanating from trade and industrial policies. As this chapter explains, a range of global health policy measures have developed to address existing global health inequalities through mechanisms of global solidarity (for example, to address child mortality and particular diseases, such as HIV/AIDS, tuberculosis and malaria) and global regulation (for example, to reduce the potential harms to health from corporate practices or products, or to mitigate their effects).

In this chapter, global health policy is defined as policies and practices of global actors, structures and measures pertaining to these different aspects of health and health policy. It also concerns the ways in which national health policies and the determinants of health (**Box 7.1**) are shaped by global actors and global processes.

Box 7.1: Determinants of health

The health of individuals is not only a product of genetic inheritance and constitutional factors, the functioning of health systems or lifestyle choices – our capacity to stay healthy is affected by a range of public policies and wider social conditions. These socioeconomic, cultural and environmental conditions are traditionally articulated as *determinants of health*. Social determinants of health describe in particular those determinants of health that contribute to inequalities in health (WHO, 2008) (see also *Figure 7.1*).

Overview of global health inequalities and policy issues

Table 7.1 highlights the extent of international variations in mortality rates for adults and children aged under-five. *Table 7.2* shows the significance of communicable (infectious) diseases for low-income countries. About half the world's **population** is at risk of malaria, and in 2010 an estimated 216 million cases of malaria led to approximately 655,000 deaths, 86 per cent of which were children under the age of five (WHO, 2012a). Non-communicable diseases (NCDs) are also of major importance to the global **burden of disease** (*Table 7.2*).

Figure 7.1: Determinants of health

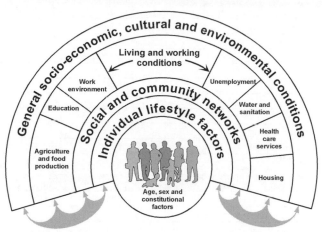

Source: Dahlgren and Whitehead (1991)

Table 7.1: International variations in child and adult mortality rates

Country	Adult mortality[a] (2009)		Under-five mortality[b] (2011)
	Male	Female	
Sweden	74	47	3
Italy	77	41	4
Japan	86	42	3
United Kingdom	95	58	5
Cuba	120	78	6
United States	134	78	8
Chile	116	59	9
Malaysia	175	95	7
Sri Lanka	275	82	12
Russian Federation	391	144	12
Vietnam	173	107	22
Argentina	160	88	14
Ukraine	395	148	10
Mexico	157	88	16
China	142	87	15
Bangladesh	246	222	46
India	250	169	61
Kenya	358	282	73
Uganda	539	348	90
Afghanistan	440	352	101

Notes: a Adult mortality rate is the probability of dying aged 15-60 (per 1,000 population); b Under-five mortality is the probability of dying before the age of five (per 1,000 population).

Source: WHO World Health Statistics (2013) (http://apps.who.int/gho/data/node.main.1)

Table 7.2: Mortality by causes of death, 10 main causes

Low-income countries	Deaths in millions	% of deaths
Lower respiratory infections	1.05	11.3
Diarrhoeal diseases	0.76	8.2
HIV/AIDS	0.72	7.8
Ischaemic heart disease	0.57	6.1
Malaria	0.48	5.2
Stroke and other cerebrovascular disease	0.45	4.9
Tuberculosis	0.40	4.3
Prematurity and low birth weight	0.30	3.2
Birth asphyxia and birth trauma	0.27	2.9
Neonatal infections	0.24	2.6

Middle-income countries	Deaths in millions	% of deaths
Ischaemic heart disease	5.27	13.7
Stroke and other cerebrovascular disease	4.91	12.8
Chronic obstructive pulmonary disease	2.79	7.2
Lower respiratory infections	2.07	5.4
Diarrhoeal diseases	1.68	4.4
HIV/AIDS	1.03	2.7
Road traffic accidents	0.94	2.4
Tuberculosis	0.93	2.4
Diabetes mellitus	0.87	2.3
Hypertensive heart disease	0.83	2.2

High-income countries	Deaths in millions	% of deaths
Ischaemic heart disease	1.42	15.6
Stroke and other cerebrovascular disease	0.79	8.7
Trachea, bronchus, lung cancers	0.54	5.9
Alzheimer and other dementias	0.37	4.1
Lower respiratory infections	0.35	3.8
Chronic obstructive pulmonary disease	0.32	3.5
Colon and rectum cancers	0.30	3.3
Diabetes mellitus	0.24	2.6
Hypertensive heart disease	0.21	2.3
Breast cancer	0.17	1.9

World	Deaths in millions	% of deaths
Ischaemic heart disease	7.25	12.8
Stroke and other cerebrovascular disease	6.15	10.8
Lower respiratory infections	3.46	6.1
Chronic obstructive pulmonary disease	3.28	5.8
Diarrhoeal diseases	2.46	4.3
HIV/AIDS	1.78	3.1
Trachea, bronchus, lung cancers	1.39	2.4
Tuberculosis	1.34	2.4
Diabetes mellitus	1.26	2.2
Road traffic accidents	1.21	2.1

Source: WHO (2011)

Infectious diseases, such as respiratory tract infections, malaria, tuberculosis and HIV/AIDS, have been particularly important for global health as these can cause *epidemics* and *global pandemics*. This is a matter of *global health security* in the context of biological warfare, but of equal if not greater concern in this regard are the potential of emerging and new sources of pandemics, in particular, of influenza-type viruses (for example, the H5N1 [bird flu] and H1N1 [swine flu] viruses), which have a high capacity to spread.

Unequal access to healthcare is a major element in global health inequalities. This is recognised in the **Millennium Development Goals** (MDGs), where MDG 4 refers to child mortality, MDG 5 refers to maternal health, while MDG 6 refers to HIV/AIDs, malaria and other diseases. These MDGs, in particular the goal relating to maternal and child mortality, are a reflection of the extent of *global health inequalities* (see *Tables 7.1* and *7.2*). Policy attention has increasingly focused on developing common strategies to improve access to healthcare and to strengthen health systems as part of achieving the aims of global health policies. This focus on health *systems* is important for health, as well as for the reduction of poverty and inequality, as the high costs of illness and access to healthcare can drive people further into poverty. It is reflected both in a focus on *universal health coverage* as well as on the *right to health* as critical components of access to preventative and curative treatments (WHO, 2010a; UN, 2012a).

A key element of this is addressing shortages in the health workforce. Over the last decade there has been increasing recognition of the need for global action on human resources for health, and in particular on health worker **migration** as a result of the growing scale of outward migration from low-income countries that face a growing burden of disease and the most acute shortages of health workers (WHO, 2006b). In 2010 a global code of conduct was agreed that aimed to ensure that the international recruitment of health work forces is undertaken on an ethical basis. The code encourages member states to 'strive to create a self-sufficient health workforce and work towards establishing effective health workforce planning that will reduce their need to recruit migrant health personnel' (WHO, 2010b). Written into the code's provisions are reporting and monitoring mechanisms. However, it is argued that the code's effectiveness is limited because it is voluntary and lacks the means of enforcement (see Yeates and Pillinger, 2013).

Some health determinants are influenced by globalisation, priorities of multinational industries and global economic integration, and it has been argued that in order to ensure adequate 'policy space' for health at a national level, a more substantial degree of global cooperation and action is needed (Koivusalo et al, 2013). For example, efforts to *regulate* consumption may require global cooperation and support. In the area of tobacco control, governments have coordinated action at a global level. The Framework

Convention on Tobacco Control (FCTC) is a key global instrument to control tobacco use and to limit pressure from the tobacco industry in the interests of health. Global policies have been important in shaping the ways in which governments are able to pursue policies to ensure everyone has *access to medicines*, including by lowering the price of medicines.

Global health governance

World Health Organization

Responsibility for global health, health policy making and standard setting has traditionally been invested in the **World Health Organization** (WHO), a **UN specialised agency**. Given that the WHO came into existence as a result of international cooperation over cholera epidemics and the International Sanitary Conferences, it is not surprising that its work started with a disease–based focus on international health (Siddiqi, 1995; Koivusalo and Ollila, 1997). However, the WHO has a mandate to go substantially beyond infectious diseases and epidemics. Its 1948 Constitution bestows obligations on governments to promote health, and recognises health as a human right (see *Box 7.2*). Rights to health also feature in the UN's human rights agenda and agreements (Koivusalo and Ollila, 2008). The interplay between global and national legislation is evident in a number of areas. In the area of *essential medicines*, for example, the right to health can be legally enforceable through the courts (Hogerzeil et al, 2006).

Box 7.2: Constitution of the World Health Organization

THE STATES, Parties to this Constitution declare, in conformity with the Charter of the United Nations, that the following principles are basic to the happiness, harmonious relations and security of all peoples:

Health is a state of complete physical, mental and social well-being and not merely the absence of disease or infirmity.

The enjoyment of the highest attainable standard of health is one of the fundamental rights of every human being without distinction of race, religion, political belief, economic or social condition.

The health of all peoples is fundamental to the attainment of peace and security and is dependent upon the fullest co-operation of individuals and States.

The achievement of any State in the promotion and protection of health is of value to all.

Unequal development in different countries in the promotion of health and control of disease, especially communicable disease, is a common danger.

Healthy development of the child is of basic importance; the ability to live harmoniously in a changing total environment is essential to such development.

The extension to all peoples of the benefits of medical, psychological and related knowledge is essential to the fullest attainment of health. Informed opinion and active co-operation on the part of the public are of the utmost importance in the improvement of the health of the people.

Governments have a responsibility for the health of their peoples which can be fulfilled only by the provision of adequate health and social measures.

ACCEPTING THESE PRINCIPLES, and for the purpose of co-operation among themselves and with others to promote and protect the health of all peoples, the Contracting Parties agree to the present Constitution and hereby establish the World Health Organization as a specialized agency within the terms of Article 57 of the Charter of the United Nations.

The WHO is mandated to operate as a global regulatory and normative health agency. It is accountable to national ministries of health, which represent member states in the World Health Assembly (WHA). A large share of its activity relates to technical standards and diagnostic criteria in health, and undertaking reference work. The WHO also issues 'soft' guidance and guidelines that provide a basis for benchmarking and the setting of national policy priorities. The strongest, and perhaps most contested, form of its global regulatory focus and guidance is its ability to negotiate conventions. To date, it has done so only in the context of tobacco (the FCTC).

International Health Regulations (IHR) are a binding instrument of international law that seeks to prevent the outbreak of acute public health problems and emergencies that have a strong potential to spread worldwide. Other WHO normative policy measures include the International Code on Marketing of Breast Milk Substitutes (1981) and more recently, the Global Code of Conduct on the International Recruitment of Health Personnel (WHO, 2010b). In 1963 WHO, along with the Food and Agriculture Organisation (FAO), established the Codex Alimentarius Commission 'to develop harmonised international food standards, guidelines and codes of practice to protect health of the consumers and ensure fair practices in the food trade' (see www.codexalimentarius.org). The Codex Alimentarius is the international reference for the **World Trade Organization** (WTO) Agreement on Application of Sanitary and Phytosanitary Measures. WHO also works closely with the **International Labour Organization** (ILO) on occupational health standards and health-related aspects of **social protection**.

WHO's financing comes from contributions by the member states' health ministries. It receives additional resources from national development aid budgets and other development-related sources. Although WHO's core funding has been in decline in real terms, the share of extra-budgetary resources for its total budget has increased significantly, from about 25 per cent of total resources in the 1970s to 75 per cent in 2006-07 and remaining at 24 per cent for the programme budget in 2012-13 (WHO, 2006a, 2011). This has meant that while voting powers within WHO lie with ministries of health, they have less power to control which WHO activities are funded through external development-oriented funds. Development financing has been important to the WHO in supporting disease-based measures, joint disease and research programmes on tropical diseases and technical assistance for developing countries, for example, in relation to essential medicines. WHO is not a development agency, and its influence over development policy is limited to providing technical assistance and **global policy** guidance.

A challenge for the WHO is how to balance the need for country-level technical support, global disease-based action programmes and the more regulatory aspects of its work. One issue WHO has faced is that its normative role as the global knowledge-based and standard-setting agency in health is frequently contested. This is an issue about the ways in which WHO relates to **civil society** and various interest groups. Critics have drawn attention to problems in the way that WHO engages with corporate actors with strong interests in influencing the process of health decision making and standard setting (Ollila, 2003; Richter, 2004; Beigbeder, 2005). There have been particular concerns about the extent of lobbying of WHO and the potential conflict of interest involved in proposed partnerships with multinational industries. This became an issue, for example, in relation to WHO action with respect to the influenza A/H1N1 pandemic (Godlee, 2010). The tobacco industry's efforts to thwart the health promotion aims of the WHO as an organisation and its activities in the area of tobacco control, including on the FCTC, has been documented by Zeltner (2001) and Collin et al (2009). Conflicts of interests have also been a concern in relation to WHO's reliance on pharmaceutical companies' donations in the area of 'neglected diseases' (WHO, 2012b). The concern is that this may compromise how WHO deals with global regulatory issues in relation to pharmaceutical policies.

UN funds, programmes, measures, priorities and processes in global health policy

Health issues feature in various UN funds and programmes, including:

- The UN Children's Fund (UNICEF): UNICEF hosts the Convention on the Rights of the Child (1989). The Convention has formed the core of UNICEF's work, but UNICEF also monitors the status of the world's children more broadly. Its *State of the children* report has been influential in comparing countries' performance across a range of children's issues and in raising children's issues in global health policy. UNICEF has recently renewed its focus on the health impacts of economic policies, and has cooperated with the ILO on wider social protection matters (see, for example, Patel, 2009; Ortiz and Cummins, 2011). UNICEF is tangibly involved in service delivery: it supports childhood immunisation programmes and provides services to procure supplies for children.
- The UN Population Fund (UNFPA) has worked with **reproductive rights** and family planning. Commitments made at the Cairo Conference on Population and Development (1994) and the Beijing Conference on Women (1995) have provided a framework for action and have remained a major reference point for global policy making since (see also **Chapter Eleven**, this volume).
- The Joint UN Programme on HIV/AIDS (UNAIDS), founded in 1994, coordinates the UN's activities around HIV/AIDS. It is co-sponsored by 10 UN agencies and the **World Bank** (WB). Its work has been important for realising a stronger global focus and response to the HIV/AIDS epidemic.

While the UN MDGs contain three health-related goals, the narrow focus on MDGs has been problematic for advocacy initiatives seeking to progress more systemic approaches to health policy. In response to this criticism, there is now a greater focus on strengthening health systems to achieve **universal health coverage** and/or population health as a goal in the new (post-2015) **Sustainable Development Goals** (SDGs) (the successor to the MDGs). There is expected to be just one comprehensive goal for health in the SDGs (WHO, 2012c, 2013). They are also expected to inscribe a commitment that reflects the need to focus on the broader determinants of health. This is recognised as a progressive move, but there are concerns that this may undermine a focus on acute health needs and the unfinished agenda of MDGs. There is also a concern that very narrow definitions of universal health coverage come to prevail.

UN high-level meetings and special sessions of the UN General Assembly have become more important for health policy making in recent years. The UN Special Session (2001) and High-Level Meeting (2011a) have been

UNIVERSITY OF WINCHESTER LIBRARY

important in achieving support for HIV/AIDS policies. The UN high-level meeting on NCDs (UN, 2011b) and the UN General Assembly that passed a resolution in support of the universal coverage of healthcare (UN, 2012a) have also both been important in global health policy. Political declarations and statements such as these are often considered to be of limited value, but they nonetheless provide legitimacy and language for approved policies and priorities that shape future action, including resourcing.

Global financial and trade policy institutions

International financial institutions' (IFIs) loans to governments have been important influences on what financial resources are available for global health as well as the extent of public financing that governments can allocate for health. The WB's guidance on macroeconomic policies, broader public sector reforms and poverty reduction strategy measures place certain parameters on options for national health policy and the resources available to fund them. The WB is also involved in health issues as part of its population, health and nutrition agenda, which initially began as a lending programme to fund **population control** measures (Wolfson, 1983; WB, 2007; see also **Chapter Eleven** of this volume).

The WB became a major transnational policy actor in global health policies after publishing its landmark report, *Investing in health*, in 1993 (WB, 1993). At that time, it emphasised health reforms, such as introducing user cost sharing and making more use of the private commercial sector and non-governmental organisations (NGOs) in health service provision. On the other hand, the WB's analysis of the economics of tobacco control proved an important source of support during WHO negotiations over the FCTC.

The relevance of the **International Monetary Fund** (IMF) for health arises from its mandate to ensure the stability of the international monetary system and its role in providing loans to governments in times of economic crisis. Health issues are therefore included in IMF policy advice to governments regarding economic reforms, terms of lending and debt repayment and aid allocation. The capacity of governments to provide additional budgeting resources for health is influenced by IMF and WB policy advice. WB-promoted policies on user cost sharing and health financing have also been either part of the IMF's lending negotiations with governments or consequential to overall requirements to reform public budgets in return for loans.

The international trade agenda has been significant for global health policy. The three main organisations here are the World Trade Organization (WTO) (**multilateral trade negotiations**, which incorporate, for example, health services), the World Intellectual Property Organisation (WIPO) (which promotes the development and harmonisation of intellectual property laws, standards and practices, affecting, for example, health research and pharmaceutical policies), and the UN Conference on Trade and Development (UNCTAD) (whose relevance to health arises from its focus on trade and development). Trade-related aspects of intellectual property rights have been the most explicitly discussed issue in the field of global health, though the WTO dispute settlement mechanism has been applied to a variety of health issues, including several cases on tobacco and alcohol (see also **Chapter Five**, this volume). The Agreement on the Application of Sanitary and Phytosanitary Measures has direct relevance for public health measures and standard setting within countries as well as global standard setting efforts as part of Codex Alimentarius process. The WTO's General Agreement on Trade in Services (GATS) has implications for health services (Fidler et al, 2003; Luff, 2003; see also **Chapter Five**, this volume).

Since the stalling of multilateral trade negotiations in the mid-2000s, trade negotiations are increasingly undertaken in the form of bilateral or plurilateral agreements between governments. These agreements use WTO agreements as a basis for negotiation. Investment treaties are of growing importance. There are fears that these will weaken the ability to challenge multinational industries because they empower corporations to challenge governments, as the tobacco firm Philip Morris has done with respect to Australia's policy on tobacco control (Gleeson and Friel, 2013).

Role of other intergovernmental organisations, non-governmental organisations and the private sector

Over the last three decades the Organisation for Economic Co-operation and Development (OECD) has become an increasingly important actor shaping OECD member states' health policies and public sector and regulatory reforms. OECD members include mostly high-income countries. The OECD's ability to influence policy makers through policy networks has been of particular interest as, unlike the WB, it has no direct financial power or normative global mandate (see also **Chapter Nine** in respect of the OECD's influence in global education policy). The OECD's work on comparative data on health systems has been important. It has also worked directly on health sector reforms in OECD countries (OECD, 1992, 1994). Another channel for OECD influence on health policies is its Development Advisory Committee (DAC), which is important in the context of international development policies among aid agencies.

Global health-related public–private partnerships (GHPPPs) are crucial to policy making and feature prominently in global campaign agendas in health. GHPPPs tend to be issue- or disease-specific 'vertical' programmes.

However, they have been criticised for not being coordinated with national health systems and wider international development policies seeking to strengthen health systems, and for instituting conflicting aims and diverting limited public funds towards the corporate sector (Ollila, 2003; Richter, 2004; Beigbeder, 2005; Buse and Harmer, 2007). They are said to be more agile in relation to new financing options and mechanisms. Part of UNITAID's financing comes from airline taxes (UNITAID, 2012). GHPPPs can also bring together different actors across non-governmental and public sector agencies for product development purposes, as has been the case for Drugs for Neglected Diseases Initiative.

While large service providers are not necessarily the most prominent in agenda setting at the global level, **international non-governmental organisations** (INGOs) such as Médecins Sans Frontières (MSF), play an active role in agenda setting and service provision at the local level. The People's Health Movement (PHM) has been perhaps the main **civil society** *movement* engaged with health policies, globally and nationally. It participates in the World Health Assembly (WHA) and global conferences, and compiles the alternative *World health report* (PHM et al, 2005, 2008, 2011). The International Baby Food Action Network has contributed substantially to the development of global guidelines on the advertising of infant foods (Koivusalo and Ollila, 1997; Richter, 2004). Many national and international NGOs have campaigned around the contested interface between health and trade priorities (Koivusalo and Mackintosh, 2011).

Private foundations, such as the Rockefeller Foundation and the Population Council, have traditionally played an active role in global health. The rise of **'philanthrocapitalism'** in recent years, as discussed in **Chapter Four**, is also seen in health. In particular, the global health programme of the Bill & Melinda Gates Foundation (BMGF) has taken global health philanthropy to another level because of the volume of funds it raises and its influence on global health policy (Edwards, 2008). The magnitude of funds that BMGF is able to mobilise overshadows that of many 'traditional' donors. BMGF funds research and development, government programmes, NGOs, lobbying activities, international PPPs and intergovernmental organisations, such as WHO, as well as research and follow-up on global health financing initiatives, such as the Health Metrics Institute (McCoy et al, 2009; BMGF, 2011). BMGF has gone beyond charitable work to increasingly regard the donations it makes as an investment entailing ongoing engagement with what the money is spent on and how it is managed. According to BMGF, its funding for global health in 2010 was US$1,485,337 and in 2011 US$1,977,507 (BMGF, 2011). This is more than the WHO receives from member state contributions, and almost half of WHO's total budget for 2012-13, which was US$3,959,000 (WHO 2011).

Finally, global NGOs also include representative associations for health professionals and health service-related industries, such as the International Federation of Pharmaceutical Manufacturers and Associations representing the pharmaceutical industry. They have been prominent in matters where there are large health-related industry interests (for example, pharmaceuticals) or where there are large health-related interests, which would limit markets or the marketing of products (for example, the tobacco, alcohol and infant food industries).

Global health policy agendas

Health for All, primary healthcare and the balance between universal and selective targets

The WHO's role in global health first took shape during major campaigns to eradicate diseases through 'vertical' programmes. The successful eradication of smallpox supported vertical programmes, which were implemented from global to local level as separate programmes with a focus on a single disease or a narrow group of interventions. However, the failure of the malaria programme was a catalyst leading to greater emphasis on strengthening health systems and broader health policies in the context of the Alma Ata Declaration (see *Box 7.3*), an emphasis on primary healthcare and the use of appropriate technology, such as access to essential medicines.

Box 7.3: Alma Ata Declaration

In 1978, the WHO and UNICEF organised an international conference on primary healthcare in Alma Ata in the Soviet Union (now Kazakhstan) that resulted in the Declaration of Alma Ata (WHO and UNICEF, 1978). Below are extracts from the Declaration:

The Conference strongly reaffirms that health, which is a state of complete physical, mental and social wellbeing, and not merely the absence of disease or infirmity, is a fundamental human right and that the attainment of the highest possible level of health is a most important world-wide social goal whose realisation requires the action of many other social and economic sectors in addition to the health sector.

The existing gross inequality in the health status of the people particularly between developed and developing countries as well as within countries is politically, socially and economically unacceptable and, is therefore, of common concern too all countries.

> Governments have a responsibility for the health of their people that can be fulfilled only by the provision of adequate health and social measures. A main social target of governments, international organizations and the whole world community in the coming decades should be the attainment by all peoples of the world by the year 2000 of a level of health that will permit them to lead a socially and economically productive life. Primary healthcare is the key to attaining this target as part of development in the spirit of social justice.
>
> The full text is available at www.who.int/hpr/NPH/docs/declaration_almaata.pdf
>
> Source: WHO and UNICEF (1978, points I, II and V)

There are several points of note about the Alma Ata Declaration. First, it reflects the ideals of justice and equality, taking as its point of departure that health is a fundamental human right. Second, it sets out a clear global agenda, in health as well as social justice and equality more widely. While it points to global health inequalities, the underlying issue of global economic inequalities is not too far from the surface (elsewhere in the Declaration it points to a new international economic order as necessary to address these health inequalities). The implementation of the Declaration has, however, been less than rigorous.

Despite being one of the architects of the Alma Ata conference, UNICEF has advocated strongly in favour of a selectivist approach to healthcare, in contrast to the more **comprehensive healthcare** approach advocated by WHO in the context of a primary healthcare approach and global strategy on Health for All (HFA) by the year 2000 (Koivusalo and Ollila, 1997). WHO faced difficulties in shifting away from a disease-based focus, and the Alma Ata Declaration and HFA strategy further declined after the election of Gro Harlem Bruntlandt as Director-General of WHO in 1998. However, the primary healthcare approach returned as a WHO strategy after the change of directorship in 2003, and it has been supported by Director-General Chan (2006-17).

In the 1990s, the importance of HIV/AIDS, malaria and tuberculosis rose on global policy agendas and gave rise to initiatives founded on 'vertical' programme structures. The role of HIV/AIDS as a global epidemic was further enhanced as infectious diseases were identified as a security threat for industrialised countries (Ollila, 2005), and as the existence (but non-accessibility) of HIV/AIDS drugs for the majority of the HIV-infected population made HIV/AIDS a human rights issue. Increased campaigning around HIV/AIDS, tuberculosis and malaria led to new initiatives for global health and access to medicines, including the establishment of new financing mechanisms of the Global Fund and UNITAID for these purposes. In similar vein, a focus on vaccines and vaccine development led to the establishment of **GAVI** (see *Box 7.4*).

Box 7.4: The Global Fund, UNITAID and GAVI

The Global Fund to fight HIV/AIDS, malaria and tuberculosis is a PPP mechanism to fund access to treatment of these three diseases in low-income countries (see www.theglobalfund.org/en). It provides some financing for health systems. Questions about the role of the Global Fund as well as how it should be financed have been raised, with a view to ensuring more funding for other necessary areas as well as for the functioning of health systems. Financing of the Global Fund comes predominantly from governments, with a minor share coming from the private sector.

UNITAID was established in 2006 by the governments of Brazil, Chile, France, Norway and the UK as the International Drug Purchasing Facility. It aims to 'increase treatment coverage for HIV/AIDS, malaria and TB through market solutions' in the context of developing countries (see www.unitaid.eu/en), aiming to increase access to drugs and diagnostics programmes. Approximately half of its funding comes from a small airline levy in several countries, with the remaining funds coming from governments and the Bill & Melinda Gates Foundation (BMGF).

The aim and purpose of GAVI (formally, GAVIalliance) is to support access to vaccines and accelerate access to new vaccines. It has a specific focus on research and development (R&D) in relation to access to new vaccines (see www.gavialliance. org/index.aspx). Its origins lies in a WHO programme to expand immunisation as well in WHO and UNICEF work to support immunisation programmes. It was established with the support of BMGF in Davos 2000. On its board are representatives from governments (five from recipient and five from donor countries), industry, WHO, UNICEF, the WB, BMGF, NGOs as well as a substantial number of independent individuals.

The Global Fund, UNITAID and GAVI and their specific focus for action all reflect the increased emphasis on development and access to new technologies as a key feature for global health. They have also been main beneficiaries of the increase in financing for global health from donor governments as well as from private foundations, such as BMGF.

The WB's launch of its *World development report* (WB, 1993) coincided with sharply increased lending for health from the late 1980s, and foretold the growing dominance of the WB in shaping global health agendas in the years to come. In many ways, the Bank health reform agenda was a continuation of its earlier prioritisation of **selective healthcare**, but now with an additional emphasis on cost-effective health interventions targeted on the poorest, the introduction of user charges and the promotion of non-governmental providers of healthcare services (Koivusalo and Ollila, 1997; Kim et al, 2000). Although the WB's effects on **healthcare reforms** were seen and felt most keenly in developing countries, there had been growing concerns by the OECD countries over healthcare costs and, consequently, they too had sought to implement these kinds of healthcare reforms under the auspices of the OECD (1992, 1994).

In the early 2000s, a second stage of healthcare reforms placed increased emphasis on targeting public services and provision for the poorest, increasing the scope for market involvement and contracting services to NGOs (see, for example, WB, 2001/02). The poor performance in lending on health, population and nutrition, persisting health challenges, an influx of financing and an increased focus on HIV/AIDS, malaria and tuberculosis came to be reflected in the new WB sector strategy (WB, 2007). However, the wider context was one of declining influence of the Bank in global health policy making as the WHO regained the initiative. The WHO *World health report* (2010a) on financing for health as well as leadership by Director-General Chan have contributed a much more prominent WHO engagement with **health systems** and the promotion of universal coverage and health systems strengthening. This was taken further by a UN General Assembly resolution (UN, 2012a).

Just as in the 1970s when the failure of the malaria eradication programme gave support to a focus on HFA policies and primary healthcare, so the disease-based initiatives and new global actors in the 2000s have come to recognise and support the role of comprehensive health systems in achieving the goals of global health policies as well as support calls for more effective global coordination. The failing state of health systems in many countries has led to concern over 'medicines without doctors' because of a lack of sufficient health professionals and personnel in many countries (Ooms et al, 2007; Yeates, 2008; Yeates and Pillinger, forthcoming). The negotiation of the Global Code of Practice on the International Recruitment of Health Personnel can be seen as a global response to the crisis and lack of adequate health workforce in many countries (WHO, 2010b).

The UN General Assembly resolution on universal health coverage (UN, 2012) can be seen as a significant contribution to the evolving debate on healthcare reforms and policy in that it emphasises social equity in access to healthcare and universal coverage. This agenda is also actively promoted within the post-2015 sustainable development goals agenda, while universal health coverage has backing from the ILO and UNICEF in the context of the Global Social Protection Floor (SPF) initiative and social insurance (in particular, health insurance) (ILO, 2007; see also **Chapters Two** and **Eight** in this volume).

As the WHO inclined during the 1990s more towards the views of the WB, the WB and OECD had come to recognise the value of **universal healthcare** and a long-term focus to ensure the pooling of risks and resources within health systems as a means of ensuring solidarity and sustainable financing (Docteur and Oxley, 2003; Gottret and Schieber, 2007). It is expected that WB policies on health will further change in the coming years as its President Jim Yong Kim (a past critic of the WB) supports the principles and aims of Alma Ata Declaration and HFA strategy (Kim, 2013). Furthermore, the principles and priorities of the Alma Ata Declaration and primary healthcare approach have found their way into three different policy initiatives: Universal Health Coverage (UHC), **Health in All Policies** (HIAP) and **Social determinants of health** (SDH).

Emerging agendas in global health

The emerging agendas on SDH and HIAP policies address diverse challenges. SDH is based on an understanding that there is an unjustifiable gap in health between rich and poor people that needs to be addressed through action and a focus on SDH. It is therefore not only concerned with improving health, but with improving socially equitable access to healthcare and the reduction of health inequalities. SDH rose on the global agenda as result of the work of the WHO Commission on the Social Determinants of Health. The Commission report entitled *Closing the gap* was explicit on the need for international monitoring and action (WHO, 2008), and was followed up by a political declaration on the social determinants of health endorsed by the WHA (2012). SDH was also reflected in the UN Resolution on Universal Coverage (UN, 2012a).

The agenda for addressing SDH is also directly linked with a greater emphasis on social equity in the context of HIAP policies. These policies draw legitimacy from three main strands (Leppo et al, 2013). First is the HFA strategy with its focus on intersectoral action (Sihto et al, 2006). Second are commitments and obligations made by governments with respect to health-related rights and population health as part of the WHO Constitution (see **Box 7.1**), human rights related obligations or other related commitments, such as European Union (EU) Treaty commitments with respect to maintaining a high level of health protection in all policies.

Third are declarations, such as the Ottawa Charter in 1986, the Rio Political Declaration 2011 and the Helsinki Statement 2013.

Addressing the impacts of policies in other sectors have been particularly important in the context of efforts to prevent NCDs, which have become more important since the UN High-Level Summit in 2011 (UN, 2011b). The UN High-Level Meeting on NCDs progressed the issues further in the context of the UN's global health agenda, but it is unclear to date whether the proposed measures for tackling intersectoral issues, such as multisectoral action together with industry and NGOs, will be able to deliver results at a national level. This is because it is at a national level that industrial lobbying to oppose broader policy measures is encountered (Moodie et al, 2013; see also *Box 7.5*). While the agenda on NCDs is currently focused on preventive measures, it is likely that the emphasis will shift to include access and treatment-related issues (see Hogerzeil et al, 2013). A key issue for future global action on NCDs is whether it will remain part of a broader health system and policy framework or whether it becomes articulated as an independent strand of work with demands for new separate institutions and disease-based GHPPPs.

Tobacco control policies remain a disputed area (see **Chapter Five**). The WTO's dispute settlement body has dealt with a number of cases on tobacco (and alcohol) with concerns emerging about the role that the new generation of investment agreements may play in limiting government measures in tobacco control (see WHO, 2012d). Similar concerns remain with respect to alcohol, the promotion of healthier diets and pharmaceutical policies (for further discussion, see Koivusalo et al, 2013).

Box 7.5: Confronting industry interests in global health policy

'The challenges for Health in All policies are effectively addressed by WHO', said Director-General Dr Margaret Chan in her opening speech for the WHO Conference on Health Promotion in Helsinki:

> In the 1980s, when we talked about multisectoral collaboration for health, we meant working together with friendly sister sectors. Like education, housing, nutrition, and water supply and sanitation. When the health and education sectors collaborate, when health works with water supply and sanitation, conflicts of interest are rarely an issue.
>
> Today, getting people to lead healthy lifestyles and adopt healthy behaviours faces opposition from forces that are not so friendly. Not at all. Efforts to prevent non-communicable diseases go against the business interests of powerful economic operators. In my view, this is one of the biggest challenges facing health promotion.

As the new publication makes clear, it is not just Big Tobacco anymore. Public health must also contend with Big Food, Big Soda, and Big Alcohol. All of these industries fear regulation, and protect themselves by using the same tactics.

Research has documented these tactics well. They include front groups, lobbies, promises of self-regulation, lawsuits, and industry-funded research that confuses the evidence and keeps the public in doubt.

Tactics also include gifts, grants, and contributions to worthy causes that cast these industries as respectable corporate citizens in the eyes of politicians and the public. They include arguments that place the responsibility for harm to health on individuals, and portray government actions as interference in personal liberties and free choice.

This is formidable opposition. Market power readily translates into political power. Few governments prioritize health over big business. As we learned from experience with the tobacco industry, a powerful corporation can sell the public just about anything.

Source: Margaret Chan, address at the 8th Global Conference on Health Promotion, 10 June 2013 (www.who.int/dg/speeches/2013/health_promotion_20130610/en)

Addressing global regulatory challenges: pharmaceutical policies and access to medicines

Pharmaceutical drugs have been long-standing issues on global health policy agendas. The underlying concerns have remained essentially the same: financial and physical access to pharmaceuticals, and proper quality, information and use of pharmaceutical drugs (Koivusalo and Ollila, 1997; Koivusalo, 2010). In the 1990s the traditional emphasis on the rational use of pharmaceuticals changed towards an emphasis on access to medicines more generally for two reasons: first, the concern over HIV/AIDS and the availability of new drugs for the treatment of HIV/AIDS for all; and second, increased consideration of pharmaceutical drugs as a key trade issue in the WTO Trade-Related Aspects of Intellectual Property Rights (TRIPS) agreement and in bilateral trade negotiations.

In the field of health the initial focus was on access to medicines, and in particular, access to HIV/AIDS medicines, in developing countries. Emphasis of the right to have access to pharmaceuticals has brought a more universal rights–based discourse to global health policy and has challenged corporations' commercial rights. At the same time, this has contributed to shifting the focus of global health policy towards single-disease and vertical approaches, giving rights to access pharmaceutical drugs for some diseases while neglecting others.

The TRIPS agreement changed process patents, which allowed production of the same end product through another process, to product patents that did not allow it. It also established the terms for trademark protection, and provided certain flexibilities allowing governments to issue compulsory licensing on defined grounds so as to allow production for government use or competition in production. The interpretation of whether and when governments could use these flexibilities became a matter for contention before the Doha negotiations. The Doha Declaration on Public Health and TRIPS Agreement (2001) was a major watershed in global health as it confirmed that TRIPS should be interpreted in a way that supports public health priorities. However, despite the Doha Declaration, the issue of access to medicines remains contested ground. This is in part due to the increasing role of bilateral trade agreements, which have introduced new provisions that exceed those of the TRIPS agreement.

Inadequate investment in R&D for diseases that affect developing countries was first raised as an issue by the WHO Commission on Innovation, Intellectual Property Rights and Public Health (WHO, 2006c). Since then, it has come to be reflected in global health policies more generally, as evidenced in the establishment of the intergovernmental working group and global strategy and plan of action on public health, innovation and intellectual property rights (WHA, 2008). The global plan of action provided a basis to further focus on the financing and coordination of research, and in particular how to ensure that sufficient investment in R&D takes place *and* that this produces affordable products to meet health needs in areas where current incentives have failed to do so (such as in R&D for antibiotics and diseases primarily affecting poorer countries) (see WHO, 2006c and 2012e for more discussion).

Another aspect of global regulatory challenges in pharmaceutical policies is that of 'spurious, falsely labelled, falsified or counterfeited' medicines. This affects both highly priced patented medicines and generic medicines, which are off-patent. The issue is how to enhance regulatory capacities in poor countries and to ensure that international trade-related measures to address the problem of such medicines do not limit the scope for generic drugs competition or hamper access to affordable medicines in poorer countries.

A particular challenge in the context of pharmaceutical policies has been the lack of consideration given specifically to *health*, and a focus on the differences between rich and poor countries. However, the regulatory challenges in the sector as well as concerns over affordability are in many respects similar across countries, even if these remain more serious for poorer developing countries (for more discussion, see OECD, 2008; Koivusalo, 2010a, 2010b; WHO, 2012e).

Conclusion

There is a discernable global dimension to health policy. The biomedical and clinical aspects of health have provided a more universal basis for common dialogue and action. A set of commonly agreed global commitments and a legal framework exist in health, albeit in a rather limited form. The Alma Ata Declaration and primary healthcare strategy is an example of an intergovernmental strategy approved, although less than optimally implemented. On the other hand, healthcare reforms represent a more technical and expert-driven agenda under the influence of international agencies that may not be formally agreed to or comprehensively debated in the context of global health policies and the WHO. The global health agenda on access to medicines is influenced by NGOs as well as by global trade and industrial policies.

The politics of global health policy making and agenda setting is fraught with competing outlooks, interests and prospects. A key challenge for global health **governance** and health policies is to ensure that health policy priorities – rather than trade, financial or industrial policy priorities – remain at the top of the agenda. There are grounds for optimism on this front: the need to address the social determinants of health and the linkages between health, poverty and social inequalities are now more recognised. Health and health-related rights are likely to have an increasing role in global health policy debates in the years to come. Finally, to address SDH and to ensure access to healthcare for all, in accordance with HFA and UHC, global health policies need to take account of a need to focus much more on the redistribution of resources both between and within countries. This includes understanding better the distributive outcomes of different models of health systems financing within and between different societies.

Summary

- WHO has a normative and regulatory role in global health policy. It has institutional responsibilities for controlling the international spread of disease. International financial institutions, aid agencies and private foundations also have discernable impacts on global health financing in ways that can impinge on WHO's mandate.
- Beyond WHO, many other international organisations, private foundations, global funds, initiatives, networks and PPPs are involved with measures to support access to treatment and research on specific issues, in particular, HIV/AIDS, malaria and tuberculosis and vaccines.

- Global health policy agendas currently include a focus on social equity in their new emphasis on ensuring universal health coverage (UHC) and addressing the SDH. The need to focus on policies in other sectors and an emphasis on HIAP policies have become increasingly important as a result of the increasing significance of NCDs for the global disease burden.
- Multinational industries have a history of seeking to influence global health policies, in particular, in the field of pharmaceutical policies and control of tobacco, alcohol and nutrition.
- Global health policies, guidelines and agreements, such as the FCTC, are important in ensuring individual countries can regulate in the interests of health.

Questions for discussion

- What different factors determine global health inequalities?
- What are the key principles and values underlying WHO's HFA strategy?
- What are the key issues to be addressed in global health policy in the coming years?

Further activities

- Investigate the ways in which global health agendas are reflected in policy in your country of choice.
- Referring to the issues raised in this chapter and in Chapter Four on global business and Chapter Five on international trade in this volume, how do global trade and industry actors shape global policies affecting healthcare? Among the issues you could focus on are access to medicines or plans to tackle obesity, malnutrition and hunger.
- Consult the websites of national or international NGOs involved in trade, environmental and social justice campaigns. To what extent are they raising health as an issue of *global* concern rather than one of *national* or *local* concern? And what are the global policies, measures and practices they are highlighting that need to be changed?

Further reading and resources

For further information and discussion about global health policy and governance, see Benatar and Brock (2011) with a focus on global health ethics, Youde (2012) and Buse et al (2009) on global governance and Davies (2010) on the politics of global health. On WHO, see Lee (2008). For volumes and chapters dealing with issues of globalisation, aid policies, health and healthcare more generally, see Lee et al (2002), Mackintosh and Koivusalo (2005), Koivusalo et al (2009) and Unger et al (2010).

The following journals regularly carry articles and features on global health policy: *Bulletin of the World Health Organization* (www.who.int/bulletin/en/index.html);

Globalization and Health (www.globalizationandhealth.com – some materials are open access); *Global Social Policy*; and *Global Public Health*.

Global health statistics are readily available from WHO and UN websites. These include the annual flagship reports of UN organisations and the *World health statistics* report. The UN website also provides human rights-related materials. Other materials and information on human rights and Special Rapporteurs reports are available at: www.ohchr.org/EN/Issues/Health/Pages/SRRightHealthIndex.aspx

Global policy documents can be obtained directly from international organisations' web pages. Recommended reading are the report of the Commission on Social Determinants of Health (WHO, 2008), *World health reports* (WHO, 2005, 2006b, 2007, 2008b, 2010a), and the reports of the Commission on Innovation, Intellectual Property and Public Health (WHO, 2006c) and the Consultative Working Group on Research and Development: coordination and financing (WHO 2012e).

Among the global NGOs that have a focus on health and development are the People's Health Movement (www.phm.org), which also monitors global health policies, and Global Health Watch, which has authored three alternative world health reports (www.ghwatch.org).

References

Beigbeder, Y. (2004) *International public health. Patients' rights vs the protection of patents*, Burlington, VT: Ashgate.

Benatar, S. and Brock, G. (eds) (2011) *Global health and global health ethics*, Cambridge: Cambridge University Press.

BMGF (Bill and Melinda Gates Foundation) (2011) *Annual report 2011*, Seattle: BMGF (www.gatesfoundation.org/~/media/GFO/Documents/Annual%20 Reports/2011Gates%20Foundation%20Annual%20Report.pdf).

Buse, K. and Harmer, A. (2007) 'Seven habits of highly effective global public– private partnerships: practice and potential', *Social Science and Medicine*, vol 64, no 2, pp 259-71.

Buse, K. and Walt, G. (2009) 'The World Health Organization and global public/private partnerships: in search of "good" global health governance', in N. Yeates and C. Holden (eds) *The global social policy reader*, Bristol: Policy Press, pp 195-217.

Buse K., Hein W. and Dragr N. (eds) (2009) *Making sense of global health governance: a policy perspective*, Basingstoke: Palgrave MacMillan.

Collin, J., Lee, K. and Bissel, K. (2009) 'The Framework Convention on Tobacco Control: the politics of global governance', in N. Yeates and C. Holden (eds) *The global social policy reader*, Bristol: Policy Press, pp 239-51.

Davies, S.E. (2010) *Global politics of health*, Cambridge and Malden: Polity Press.

Docteur, E. and Oxley, H. (2003) *Health care systems. Lessons from the reform experience*, OECD/ELSA/WD/HEA, OECD Health Working Paper no 9, Paris: OECD.

Doha WTO (World Trade Organization) Ministerial Declaration (2001*) Declaration on the TRIPS Agreement and Public Health*, WT/MIN(01)/DEC/2 (www.wto.org/english/tratop_e/trips_e/ta_docs_e/3_wtmin01dec2_e.pdf).

Edwards, M. (2008) *Just another emperor*, Young Foundation, Demos (www.futurepositive.org/edwards_WEB.pdf).

Fidler, D., Correa, C. and Aginam, O. (2003) *Legal review of the General Agreement on Trade in Services (GATS) from a health policy perspective*, Geneva: WHO.

Gleeson, D. and Friel, S. (2013) 'Emerging threats to public health from regional trade agreements', *Lancet*, vol 381, pp 1507-9.

Godlee, F. (2010) 'Conflicts of interest and pandemic flu', *British Medical Journal*, vol 340, c2947.

Gottret, B. and Schieber, G. (2007) *Health financing revisited. A practitioner's guide*, Washington, DC: The World Bank (http://siteresources.worldbank.org/ INTHSD/Resources/topics/Health-Financing/HFRFull.pdf).

Hogerzeil, H., Samson, M., Casasnovas, J.V. and Rahmani-Ocora, L. (2006) 'Is access to essential medicines as part of the fulfilment of the right to health enforceable through the courts?', *The Lancet*, vol 368, issue 9532, pp 305-11.

Hogerzeil, H.V., Liberman, E.J., Wirtz, V.J., Kishore, S.P., Selvaraj, S., Kiddell-Monroe, R., Mwangi-Powell, F.N. and von Schoen-Angerer, T. (2013) 'Promotion of access to essential medicines for non-communicable diseases: practical implications of the UN political declaration', *The Lancet*, vol 381, no 9867, pp 680-9.

ILO (International Labour Organization) (2007) *Social health protection. An ILO strategy towards universal access to health care: Issues in social protection*, Discussion Paper 19, Geneva: ILO.

Kim, J.Y. (2013) 'Poverty, health and the human future', Speech at the World Health Assembly, 21 May (www.worldbank.org/en/news/speech/2013/05/21/world-bank-group-president-jim-yong-kim-speech-at-world-health-assembly).

Kim, J.Y., Shakow, A., Bayona, J., Rhatigan, J. and Ruben Celis, E. (2000) 'Sickness amidst recovery: Public debt and private suffering in Peru', in J.Y. Kim, J.V. Millen, A. Irwin and J. Gershman (eds) *Dying for growth. Global inequality and the health of the poor*, Monroe, ME: Common Courage Press, pp 127-53.

Koivusalo, M. (2010a) 'Common interests and the shaping of global pharmaceutical policies', *Ethics & International Relations*, vol 24, no 4, pp 395-414.

Koivusalo, M. (2010b) 'Trade and health – the ethics of global rights, regulation and redistribution', in S. Benatar and G. Brock (eds) *Global health ethics*, Cambridge University Press, pp 143-54.

Koivusalo, M. and Mackintosh, M. (2011) 'Commercial influence and global nongovernmental public action in health and pharmaceutical policies', *International Journal of Health Services*, vol 41, pp 539-63.

Koivusalo, M. and Ollila, E. (1997) *Making a healthy world. Agencies, actors and policies in international health*, London: Zed Books.

Koivualso, M. and Ollila, E. (2008) 'Global health policy', in N. Yeates (ed) *Understanding global social policy*, Bristol: Policy Press, pp 149-77.

Koivusalo, M., Labonte, R. and Schrecker, T. (2009) 'Globalization and policy space for health and social determinants of health', in R. Labonte, T. Schrecker, C. Packer and V. Runnels (eds) *Globalization and health: Pathways, evidence and policy*, New York and London: Routledge, pp 105-30.

Koivusalo, M., Labonte, R., Wilpulpolprasert, S. and Kanchanachitra, C. (2013) 'Globalization and policy space for health and a HiAP approach', in K. Leppo, E. Ollila, S. Pena, M. Wismar and S. Cook (eds) *Health in all policies. Seizing opportunities, implementing policies*, Helsinki: Ministry of Social Affairs and Health, pp 81-101.

Lee, K. (2008) *The World Health Organization*, New York and Abingdon: Routledge.

Lee, K., Buse, K. and Fustukian, S. (eds) (2002) *Health policy in a globalising world*, Cambridge: Cambridge University Press.

Leppo, K., Ollila, E., Pena, S., Wismar, M. and Cook, S. (eds) (2013) *Health in All policies. Seizing opportunities, implementing policies*, Helsinki: Ministry of Social Affairs and Health.

Luff, D. (2003) 'Regulation of health services and international trade law', in A. Mattoo and P. Sauve (eds) *Domestic regulation and service trade liberalisation*, New York: The World Bank and Oxford University Press, pp 191-220.

Mackintosh, M. and Koivusalo, M. (eds) (2005) *Commercialisation of health care*, Basingstoke: Palgrave Macmillan.

McCoy, D., Kembhavi, G., Patel, J. and Luintel, A. (2009) 'The Bill and Melinda Gates Foundation's grant-making programme for global health', *The Lancet*, vol 373, no 9675, pp 1645-53.

Moodie, R., Stuckler, D., Montero, C., Sheron, N., Neal, B., Thamarangsi, T., Lincoln, P. and Casswell, S. (2013) 'Profits and pandemics: prevention of harmful effects of tobacco, alcohol, and ultra-processed food and drink industries', *The Lancet*, vol 381, pp 670-9.

OECD (Organisation for Economic Co-operation and Development) (1992) *The reform of health care. Comparative analysis of seven OECD countries*, Paris: OECD.

OECD (1994) *The reform of health care systems. A review of seventeen OECD countries*, OECD Health Policy Studies, Paris: OECD.

OECD (2008) *Pharmaceutical pricing policies in a global market*, Paris: OECD.

Ollila, E. (2003) 'Health-related public–private partnerships and the United Nations', in *Global social governance. Themes and prospects, elements for discussion*, Helsinki: Ministry for Foreign Affairs of Finland (www.gaspp.org).

Ollila, E. (2005) 'Global health priorities – priorities of the wealthy?', *Globalization and Health*, vol 1, no 1, p 6 (www.globalizationandhealth.com/ content/1/1/6).

Ooms, G., van Damme, W. and Temmerman, M. (2007) 'Medicines without doctors. Why the global fund must fund salaries of health workers to expand AIDS treatment', *PLOSmedicine*, vol 4, no 4, pp 605-8.

Ortiz, I. and Cummins, M. (2011) *A recovery for all: Rethinking socio-economic policies for children and poor households*, New York: UNICEF.

Patel, M. (2009) 'Children and the economic crisis in East Asia', *Global Social Policy*, April, vol 1, Suppl.

PHM (People's Health Movement) et al (2005) *Global health watch 2005-2006*, London: Zed Books.

PHM et al (2008) *Global health watch 2: An alternative world health report*, London: Zed Books.

PHM et al (2011) *Global health watch 3: An alternative world health report*, London: Zed Books.

Richter, J. (2004) *Public–private partnerships and international health policy-making. How can public interests be safeguarded?*, Helsinki: Ministry for Foreign Affairs of Finland.

Siddiqi, J. (1995) *World health and world politics*, London: C. Hurst & Co.

Sihto, M., Ollila, E. and Koivusalo, M. (2006) 'Principles and challenges of health in all policies', in T. Stahl, M. Wismar, E. Ollila, E. Lahtinen and K. Leppo (eds) *Health in all policies. Prospects and potentials*, Helsinki: Ministry for Social Affairs and Health.

Unger, J.-P., de Paepe, P., Sen, K. and Soors, W. (2010) *International health and aid policies. The need for alternatives*, Cambridge: Cambridge University Press.

UN (United Nations) (1948) *Universal Declaration of Human Rights*, New York: UN (www.un.org/Overview/rights.html).

UN (1989) *Convention of the Rights of the Child*, New York: UN (www.ohchr.org/EN/ProfessionalInterest/Pages/CRC.aspx).

UN (2001) *Declaration of Commitment on HIV/AIDS. United Nations General Assembly Special Session on HIV/AIDS*, 25-27 June (www.unaids.org/en/media/unaids/contentassets/dataimport/publications/irc-pub03/aidsdeclaration_en.pdf).

UN (2011a) *Political declaration on HIV/AIDS: Intensifying our efforts to eliminate HIV and AIDS*, 8 July, General Assembly A/RES/65/277 (www.unaids.org/en/media/unaids/contentassets/documents/document/2011/06/20110610_UN_A-RES-65-277_en.pdf).

UN (2011b) *Political declaration of the High-level Meeting of the General Assembly on the prevention and control of non-communicable diseases*, General Assembly, 16 September, A/66/L.1 (www.un.org/ga/search/view_doc.asp?symbol=A/66/L.1).

UN (2012) *Global health and foreign policy*, General Assembly A/67/L.36 (www.un.org/ga/search/view_doc.asp?symbol=A/67/L.36).

UNITAID (2013) *Innovative financing* (www.unitaid.eu/en/how/innovative-financing).

WB (The World Bank) (1993) *World development report*, Washington, DC: WB.

WB (2001/02) *World development report*, Washington, DC: WB.

WB (2007) *Healthy development. The World Bank strategy for health, nutrition and population: Results*, Washington, DC: WB.

WHA (World Health Assembly) (2008) *Global strategy and plan of action on public health, innovation and intellectual property*, Resolution WHA 61.21, 24 May (http://apps.who.int/gb/ebwha/pdf_files/A61/A61_R21-en.pdf).

WHA (2012) *Outcome of the World Conference on Social Determinants of Health*, WHA 65.8, 26 May, Geneva: WHO (www.who.int/sdhconference/background/A65_R8-en.pdf).

WHO (2005) *World health report: Make every mother and child count*, Geneva: WHO.

WHO (2006a) *Programme budget 2006-2007 update*, 7 December, WHO EBPBAC5/5, Geneva: WHO.

WHO (2006b) *World health report: Working together for health*, Geneva: WHO.

WHO (2006c) *Public health, innovation and intellectual property rights. Commission on Intellectual Property Rights, Innovation and Public Health, Final report*, Geneva: WHO (www.who.int/intellectualproperty/en).

WHO (2007) *World health report: A safer future: global public health security for the 21st century*, Geneva: WHO.

WHO (2008a) *Closing the gap. Report of the Commission on Social Determinants of Health*, Geneva: WHO (www.who.int/social_determinants/en).

WHO (2008b) *World Health Report. Primary Health Care (Now more than never)*, Geneva: WHO.

WHO (2010a) *World health report: Health systems financing: The path to universal coverage*, Geneva: WHO

WHO (2010b) *Global code of practice on the international recruitment of health personnel*, World Health Assembly Resolution 63.16, May (www.who.int/hrh/migration/code/code_en.pdf).

WHO (2011) *Programme budget 2012-2013*, Geneva: WHO (http://whqlibdoc.who.int/pb/2012-2013/PB_2012%E2%80%932013_eng.pdf).

WHO (2012a) *World health statistics*, Geneva: WHO (www.who.int/gho/publications/world_health_statistics/2012/en/index.html).

WHO (2012b) *Accelerating work to overcome the global impact of neglected tropical diseases. A roadmap for implementation*, Geneva: WHO (http://whqlibdoc.who.int/hq/2012/WHO_HTM_NTD_2012.1_eng.pdf).

WHO (2012c) *Positioning health in the post-2015 Development Agenda*, WHO Discussion Paper, October, Geneva: WHO: Geneva (www.who.int/topics/millennium_development_goals/post2015/WHOdiscussionpaper_October2012.pdf).

WHO (2012d) *Confronting the tobacco epidemic in a new era of trade and investment liberalization*, Geneva: WHO (http://whqlibdoc.who.int/publications/2012/9789241503723_eng.pdf).

WHO (2012e) *Research and development to meet health needs in developing countries: Strengthening global financing and coordination*, Report of the Consultative Expert Working Group on Research and Development Financing and Coordination, Geneva: WHO.

WHO (2013) *Health in the post-2015 development agenda*, Report by the Secretariat, A 66/47, 1 May, Geneva: WHO (http://apps.who.int/gb/ebwha/pdf_files/WHA66/A66_47-en.pdf).

WHO and UNICEF (1978) *Declaration of Alma Ata*, Geneva: WHO (www.who.int/hpr/NPH/docs/declaration_almaata.pdf).

Wolfson, M. (1983) *Profiles in population assistance. A comparative review of the principal donor agencies*, Development Centre Studies, Paris: OECD.

Yeates, N. (2008) 'Global migration policy', in N. Yeates (ed) *Understanding global social policy*, Bristol: Policy Press, pp 229-52.

Yeates, N. and Pillinger, J. (2013) *Human Resources for Health Migration: global policy responses, initiatives and emerging issues*, Milton Keynes: Open University. Available at: http://oro.open.ac.uk/39072

Youde, J. (2012) *Global health governance*, Cambridge: Polity Press.

Zeltner, T., Kessler, D.A., Martiny, A. and Randera, F. (2000) *Tobacco companies' strategies to undermine tobacco control activities at the World Health Organization*, Geneva: WHO.

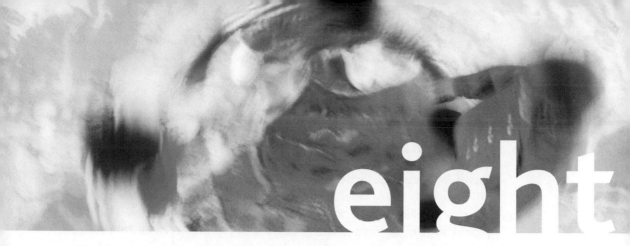

eight

Global pensions and social protection policy

Mitchell A. Orenstein and Bob Deacon

Overview

This chapter provides an overview of global pensions policy in the context of social protection policy, and shows that global policy actors have had an increasing influence on country reform decisions. Awareness of the impact of global social protection policy grew with the rise of a transnational campaign for new pension reforms led by the World Bank (WB) since 1994. Through this campaign, the WB successfully supplanted the International Labour Organization (ILO) as the dominant force in global pensions policy. A WB-led coalition of global policy actors helped to launch and implement the new pension reforms in more than 30 countries worldwide. Yet the transnational campaign for pension privatisation ground to a halt in 2005. Since that time, a number of countries have dismantled or reduced the size of their private pension systems. The future of global pensions policy remains uncertain, but there is a growing emphasis on minimum pensions in the context of a 'social floor' for global social policy. From 2007 an alternative transnational campaign for a global social floor restored the influence of the ILO on global policy and national debates. Tension, however, remains between the WB and ILO's approaches to social protection and pensions policy.

Key concepts

Transnational policy campaign; global policy actors; new pension reforms; funded pension systems; pay-as-you-go (PAYG) pension systems; notional defined contribution pension systems; social pensions, Social Protection Floor (SPF)

Introduction

This chapter provides an overview of *global pensions policy* within the context of a wider **social protection** policy, and shows that it has become increasingly central to decision making in countries around the world. Whereas only a few years ago social policy scholars would have regarded the idea of a global pensions policy or a global social protection policy as a pipe dream, today it is a reality. Awareness of the impact of global pensions policy in particular grew with the rise of a transnational campaign for new pension reforms led by the WB since 1994. Through this campaign, the WB successfully supplanted the ILO as the dominant force in global pensions policy, a position held by the ILO since the end of the Second World War (Charlton and McKinnon, 2002, p 1178; see also Deacon, 1997). This chapter provides historical background on the ILO's global pensions policy and the rise of the WB-led transnational campaign for the pension reforms. It demonstrates the extent to which key ideas about pension reform have 'travelled' or diffused internationally. It shows that **global policy actors** have a major impact on pensions policies of countries in all regions of the world, and provides several country examples. The chapter describes how the WB campaign ran out of steam faced with evidence of the reforms' shortcomings in the context of a global economic crisis that undermined private **pension funds**. In its place arose the campaign for a global social floor focused on a minimum social pension. This was to give the ILO once again potentially more influence over national policies.

World Bank pension reform phenomenon

Awareness of global pensions policy grew with the dramatic emergence of a transnational policy campaign for new pension reforms led by the WB. This campaign was launched in 1994 with the publication of a major WB report, *Averting the old age crisis* (WB, 1994). This advocated new pension reforms worldwide to cope with an emerging demographic 'crisis' in 'developed' and soon in many 'developing' countries as well: **population ageing** (see also James, 1998; James and Brooks, 2001). While most **pay-as-you-go** (PAYG) or **social security**-type pension systems were established under more favourable demographic conditions, economic development, improved medical care and falling birth rates have reduced the proportion of contributing workers to pension beneficiaries in many countries, particularly in Europe. Many developing countries, including China with its one-child policy, will face these issues in coming years. The PAYG pension systems common in most countries of the world use current revenues from current workers to pay current pension beneficiaries. As people live longer and have fewer children, PAYG pension systems suffer from growing fiscal pressure. To support a growing proportion of older people living longer and longer in retirement, the WB report argues that either payroll tax rates must rise, pension ages must increase or benefit levels must fall. A fourth possibility introduced in the report is to fully or partially replace PAYG pension systems with ones based on private, individual, pension savings accounts. Pre-funding seeks to ameliorate the budget crisis of PAYG systems by providing benefits from an individual's own mandatory (and often state-subsidised or tax-preferred) savings. Pension privatisation is controversial because it revolutionises the structure of pension systems.

The reform model advocated by the WB recommends a 'multipillar' structure for pension provision that includes a redistributive state pension pillar comprising either a minimum flat or means-tested benefit or a reduced PAYG pension system, a second funded pillar based on privately managed pension savings accounts, and a third voluntary pillar of occupational pensions. In this model, pension systems have two sorts of objectives: to provide a safety net for most older people and to provide an income-related benefit that enables people to maintain their standard of living in retirement. The WB report argued that private savings accounts are a superior method of providing income-related benefits since private sector managers can achieve higher rates of return on investment than state social security administrations. Individual accounts, however, cannot provide the redistribution that is often achieved in state PAYG systems, so must be coupled with some other method to protect those with low earnings or short or interrupted working histories. In addition, the report argued that private pension funds provide an important source of capital for investment in emerging market economies. Creating such funds can spur economic growth and increase standards of living across the board. A further argument for the new pension reforms has been that handing the management of pension funds over to private sector companies relieves beneficiaries from reliance on inefficient and sometimes corrupt state administration. While PAYG pension systems have been well managed in most developed countries, some developing countries have faced significant problems with the administration of their state-managed systems.

Critics have easily disputed most claims made on behalf of pension privatisation. First, they have argued that pension funds do not create new capital for investment, since savings in **individual pension funds** are likely to be offset by reductions in government and individual savings in other areas. Thus, the introduction of private, individual accounts merely reallocates personal savings (Barr and Diamond, 2006, p 30). Second, critics have questioned the high administrative fees typically charged on individual pension savings accounts, arguing that these often substantially reduce investment returns, making these programmes a boon for private investment companies rather than small investors (Minns, 2001; Gill et al, 2005). Third, critics have pointed out that reform of PAYG pension systems remains a more effective way of achieving the most important pension system objectives (Fultz, 2004; Barr, 2005). Many of these critiques are rooted in the social democratic perspective underpinning the earlier PAYG model pension systems.

Debates have also focused attention on the political roots of pension privatisation, spread in part by a transnational coalition of global policy actors as part of a loosely coordinated campaign, or what Tarrow (2005) calls a 'campaign coalition'. Scholars analysing the adoption of the new pension reforms in Latin America, Central and Eastern Europe (CEE) and elsewhere have become more attuned to the role of global policy actors in social policy. Müller (2003) has argued that global policy actors are more influential in countries with high indebtedness, which makes them more exposed to global policy advice. Madrid (2003) shows that the presence of a WB pension advisory mission makes countries on average 20 per cent more likely to adopt new pension reforms. Weyland (2004) assembled a team of experts to investigate the role of global policy actors in pension and health policy in Latin America, reaching a variety of conclusions (Brooks, 2004; Demarco, 2004; Nelson, 2004; Pinheiro, 2004). Brooks (2005) found little quantitative evidence of international influence on pension policies, but suggested that qualitative research may be better at isolating WB influence. Indeed, many country case studies show the influence of global policy actors in particular countries' pension reforms since the 1990s. In Brazil, global actors introduced **notional defined contribution pensions**, which introduce individual accounts to a PAYG system (Pinheiro, 2004). In CEE, global policy actors were often the first to put new pension reforms on the policy agenda, and spent years supporting policy implementation (Orenstein, 2000, 2008). A broad scholarly literature has thus emerged that suggests that global policy actors have taken a major role in pensions policy worldwide, particularly in middle-income developing countries.

Historical background: the International Labour Organization and post-war global pensions policy

While interest in global pensions policy rose with the WB's intervention, the phenomenon is not new (Orenstein, 2003). An effort to create a global pensions policy began towards the end of the Second World War as allied leaders considered ways to better regulate the world economic system with a view towards preventing the outbreak of another war. Political leaders such as US Franklin Delano Roosevelt had become convinced that global depression, inflation and poverty were contributing factors to the rise of

Nazism in Germany and other extremist political movements. In order to prevent the outbreak of war in the future, the allies established a set of international financial institutions to better regulate the world economy. A top-level conference in 1943 put the ILO in charge of developing a post-war social policy order. This new social policy encouraged all countries to implement state-administered pensions and unemployment insurance, public health systems and social assistance in the interest of social peace. The ILO's Declaration of Philadelphia became the blueprint for this new **global social policy** order. The ILO vigorously pursued this agenda worldwide by advising countries on social policy development, organising high-profile regional conferences and spreading this new vision of social policy, including state-managed, PAYG pension insurance. Prior to the Second World War, countries in Europe, North America and Latin America had already established national pension systems. These were revised according to the new ILO model. After the war, state-managed PAYG pension systems quickly became standard practice worldwide. ILO dominance of global pensions policy waned with the decline of trade unions in developed Western countries and the rise of **neoliberal economic policy** in the 1980s (Gillion et al, 2000). However, it took a number of years for a serious challenge to the ILO pensions agenda to arise.

Rise of the privatising pension reforms

The first neoliberal experiment in pensions policy took place in Chile in the early 1980s. Chile, under military dictator General Augusto Pinochet, undertook radical economic reforms led by the so-called 'Chicago boys', a group of young economists trained at leading US universities. The University of Chicago, in particular, had established a training programme for young Chilean economists in the 1950s with US government support that turned out a cadre of neoliberal economists who returned to work at the Catholic University of Santiago (Valdes, 1995). Pinochet called on these economists to undertake various reforms in Chile, including a pension reform that replaced the previous PAYG pension system with one based on individual pension savings accounts. The Chilean model of pension reforms became celebrated in neoliberal economic circles. While the Chilean model of pension reforms excited much interest in other countries in Latin America (Brooks, 2004; Weyland, 2004), its association with the Pinochet regime tarnished its reputation in other countries, particularly among the political left.

After a period of poor economic performance in the mid-1980s, Chile's economy began to improve dramatically, and other Latin American countries began seriously to consider the new pension reform model in Chile. At the same time, major **international organisations** such as the WB, Inter-

American Development Bank (IDB) (de Oliveira, 1994), United Nations (UN) Economic Council for Latin America and others began to support these reforms (Müller, 2003). They were joined by Chilean reformers and pension fund managers, who organised international conferences to promote the Chilean reforms and acted as consultants throughout Latin America and beyond (Brooks, 2004). In 1994, the WB published *Averting the old age crisis*, signalling its full support for the pension privatisation campaign and presenting a new, more flexible template for including private pension savings accounts as part of national pension systems.

Backed by comprehensive research and powerful figures in the international economics community, *Averting the old age crisis* quickly became a template for WB policy advice; its authorship team became the core of WB pension advisory efforts worldwide. *Averting the old age crisis* was commissioned by the then WB Chief Economist, Larry Summers, and placed under the control of Research Director, Nancy Birdsall. The lead author was economist Estelle James. The WB successfully recruited other organisations as partners in its efforts. In particular, it enjoyed the support of regional development banks such as IDB and the Asian Development Bank (ADB). Second, it developed a strong relationship with the United States Agency for International Development (USAID), the US bilateral aid agency that saw the new pension reforms as part of its fiscal sector reform strategy for CEE transition states (Snelbecker, 2005). The Organisation for Economic Co-operation and Development (OECD) also supported efforts to promote the new pension reforms among and beyond its member states.

Starting in the early 1990s, new pension reforms inspired by the Chilean model and the WB's multipillar model spread to more than 30 countries around the world. Most of these countries have been concentrated in two regions of the world: Latin America and CEE. In Africa, Nigeria became the first adopter in 2004 (Casey, 2011), and South Africa was in the process of considering these reforms in 2007 (Republic of South Africa National Treasury, 2007). Taiwan's adoption of the new pension reforms in 2004 signalled increasing prevalence of these reforms in Asia as well.

Table 8.1 shows all countries worldwide that had adopted the new pension reforms by the end of 2004. It divides these countries' reforms into three categories: substitutive, mixed and parallel. **Substitutive reforms** are those that fully replace social security-type systems with ones based on individual, **funded pension** savings accounts. In substitutive reforms, the previous PAYG pension system is phased out; all new labour force entrants make **contributions** to individual pension savings accounts only; and those with accumulated credits under the old system may have the opportunity to switch to the new system and to have their previous contributions credited in some manner. Those nearest to retirement typically stay with the PAYG

Table 8.1: New pension reforms worldwide by type

Substitutive	Mixed	Parallel
Chile 1981	Sweden 1994	UK 1986
Bolivia 1997	China 1998	Peru 1993
Mexico 1997	Hungary 1998	Argentina 1994
El Salvador 1998	Poland 1999	Colombia 1994
Kazakhstan 1998	Costa Rica 2001	Uruguay 1996
Dominican Republic 2001	Latvia 2001	Estonia 2001
Nicaragua 2001	Bulgaria 2002	Lithuania 2002
Kosovo 2001	Croatia 2002	
Nigeria 2004	Macedonia 2002	
Taiwan 2004	Russia 2002	
	Slovakia 2003	
	Romania 2004	
	Uzbekistan 2004	

Sources: Orenstein (2000), Madrid (2003), Müller (2003), Palacios (2003), Fultz (2004), Becker et al (2005), Holzmann and Hinz (2005), Orifowomo (2006) and WB, IDB and USAID websites.

system, which is phased out over time. **Mixed reforms**, the most common type in CEE states, partially replace the former social security–type system with individual accounts. Under mixed systems, popular in CEE, participants contribute to both a scaled-down, PAYG pension system and to an individual account and gain benefits from both systems over time. **Parallel reforms** maintain both systems side by side and allow individuals a choice of which system to participate in. Participants may opt to stay with the PAYG system or choose to devote some portion of their contribution to an individual pension savings account. Substitutive reforms are often the most radical, while parallel reforms are likely to result in smaller private pension systems.

The new pension reforms spread from Chile, first to Latin America and then, with extensive support from global policy actors led by the WB and USAID, to CEE starting in 1998. Britain and Sweden implemented new pension reforms without substantial external policy advice. Many African, Asian and Middle Eastern countries began to seriously consider and adopt new pension reforms in the late 1990s and 2000s, facilitated by the **World Bank** Institute organising numerous seminars to promote new pension reform ideas (interview with Gustavo Demarco, World Bank Institute, 2004) in these regions. While the new pension reforms had initially been viewed as a regional trend affecting Latin America and CEE, it has recently become clear that this trend has global scope and implications.

Methods of policy diffusion

How did global policy actors help to spread the new pension reforms to more than 30 countries worldwide? Global policy actors face substantial challenges in influencing state pensions policy since they do not hold any formal veto power (Tsebelis, 2002) over domestic policy. Therefore, global policy actors are forced to use more indirect methods of influence. These are typically broken down into two broad categories: coercion and persuasion. Coercive methods include loan or membership **conditionalities** that enable global policy actors to create conditions under which a country may or may not gain access to certain resources or opportunities. For instance, international financial institutions often use conditions for the release of loans to influence domestic policy, including that on pensions. Persuasive methods include the exercise of ideational or normative influence by creating new problem definitions, new measures of pension system crisis, new policy solutions, and seek to convince domestic policy makers of the benefits of new ways of looking at things (Barnett and Finnemore, 2004). Persuasion may be particularly effective when global policy actors can rely on like-minded domestic partners (Chwieroth, 2007).

While scholars have debated the relative influence of coercion and persuasion (Kelley, 2004), both methods are often used in combination (Johnson, 2008), and often combine in ways that are difficult to disentangle (Epstein, 2008). This makes Jacoby's (2004) typology of global policy actor **influence mechanisms** particularly relevant (see also Tarrow, 2005). Jacoby finds that global policy actors tend to use four different mechanisms of influence. The first is 'inspiration', in which global policy actors seek to influence state bodies through the development and promotion of reform ideas. The second is 'subsidy', in which global policy actors offer support conditional on the enactment of reform. The third is 'partnership', in which global policy actors support the political fortunes of domestic political allies. The fourth is 'substitution', in which global policy actors seek to enforce their preferred solution without cooperation from domestic actors. Inspiration, subsidy and partnership are common means by which global policy actors have supported the new pension reforms.

Global pension policy advocates have typically used several methods to advance their pension reform agenda. First, they develop pension policy ideas, metrics, problem definitions and solutions. Second, they seek to spread these ideas through publications, conferences and seminars. Third, they identify local partners with whom they can work and provide resources to these actors to advance their agendas. Fourth, they fund government reform teams planning new pension reforms. Fifth, they provide technical assistance to government reform teams. And sixth, they provide long-term assistance with reform implementation. These mechanisms are illustrated in case studies of reform presented below.

Country examples

Kazakhstan exemplifies a case in which the WB and USAID helped to place the new pension reforms on the policy agenda through persuasion of governmental leaders, used loan conditionalities to keep reforms on track and later provided long-term assistance with reform implementation. Kazakhstan began to consider the new pension reforms in 1996, when Central Bank chief Grigori Marchenko attended a WB-sponsored seminar and heard a speech by José Piñera, Chilean former Labour Minister and father of the Chilean reforms. Marchenko returned to Almaty resolved to cancel the reform programme he had already begun planning and implement the new pension reforms in Kazakhstan (interview with author, July 1998). He persuaded the President of Kazakhstan to create a reform team to plan the new pension reforms, which completed its work in 1997. With USAID and WB assistance, Kazakhstan prepared reform legislation and led a public relations campaign to sell these reforms to a population sceptical of privatisation and investment companies. The Kazakh Parliament approved these reforms under threat of dissolution by the President in 1998. The WB ultimately lent US$300 million to Kazakhstan to finance the transition to the new system, while USAID provided extensive technical assistance for the establishment of the pension system over a period of eight years (see Orenstein, 2000).

The case of Hungary also demonstrates the critical role the WB and USAID played in putting the new pension reforms on the agenda and pushing them through despite substantial domestic opposition. Hungary began to consider the new pension reforms in 1995, after socialist Lajos Bokros was appointed Finance Minister and began to pursue a controversial set of liberal economic reforms called the 'Bokros Plan'. Bokros appointed a small working group on pension reform to begin work within the Ministry of Finance. This group received substantial financial and intellectual backing from the WB and USAID. It advanced a fully elaborated proposal for the new pension reforms in Hungary in 1996. After a deadlock between the Ministries of Finance and Labour was broken with the appointment of a new Finance Minister, Hungary decided to move ahead with a more limited version of the Ministry of Finance's new pension reform proposals. The WB and USAID again provided tremendous technical and financial support for this project. The WB took the unusual step of seconding two of its top pensions advisers to the inter-ministerial working group on pension reform in Hungary. These advisers engaged in day-to-day discussions about the planning of the new pension reforms with government officials and helped to design a comprehensive strategy for reform adoption in Hungary, including public opinion polls, public relations campaigns, access to top advisers worldwide and help in drafting reform legislation. After a variety of consultations and negotiations with domestic interest groups, the reform was passed in Hungary in 1998. USAID continued to provide support for pension fund regulators in Hungary for many years after the reform (Snelbecker, 2005).

China provides an additional example of the extent of the ideational influence of global policy actors. China reformed its pension system in 1997 under the influence of WB advice. Although the implementation of these reforms has been troubled, with some provincial administrations inadequately or not funding individual accounts (China Economic Research and Advisory Programme, 2005, p 1), China appears to be committed to continuing down the path of the new pension reforms. While China had been considering reforms to its pension system throughout the 1990s, its subsequent development was heavily influenced by a WB report conducted in 1995 and led by Ramgopal Agarwala (Piggott and Bei, 2007, p 15). This report, which advocated a multipillar pension system for China along the lines of *Averting the old age crisis*, was debated by top Chinese policy makers and then adopted in Circular No 26 of 1997, which created a second, **funded pension** pillar in China (Piggott and Bei, 2007, p 19). While China has also taken advice from a variety of other global policy actors, including the ILO, the influence of the WB has been paramount. The ADB has supported the development of a multipillar pension model in China by funding a pilot programme for **funded pension** systems in Liaoning in 2001 (Piggott and Bei, 2007, p 13). While China has clearly taken its own decisions on the future shape of social security, its thinking has been shaped by the WB. Progress on further reforms and reform implementation has occurred with the assistance of a variety of global policy actors working as part of a coordinated campaign.

Peru was the first Latin American country to follow Chile in adopting the new pension reforms. Peru's adoption of its reform decree in December 1992, prior to the publication of *Averting the old age crisis*, has sometimes been seen as evidence that the new pension reform trend took place without the assistance of global policy actors. However, Chilean economic advisers, particularly Chilean former Labour Minister José Piñera, were deeply influential in Peru. Piñera is credited with convincing Peruvian President Alberto Fujimori to adopt the new pension reform decree (Rofman, 2007, p 3). Because of the strong influence of the Chilean model, the Peruvian reforms were similar in many ways, although workers were allowed to continue to opt into the state system if they preferred. Peru's pension system suffers from a low rate of coverage, below 12 per cent of the total labour force. The WB was not involved in the design of the pension system in Peru, although it did help to support pension system work in Peru through a 1992 **Structural Adjustment Loan** and a 1992 **Financial Sector Adjustment Loan**. A 1996 Pension Reform Adjustment Loan was a vehicle for persuading Peru to adopt some important adjustments to its pension system, creating more monitoring, auditing and equal treatment of workers in both pension systems (Rofman, 2007, p 10). The Peruvian experience shows that even in the small number of developing countries in Latin America that considered reform prior to 1994, the WB played an important supporting role in reform implementation and redesign.

The transnational privatisation campaign grinds to a halt

Despite all the resources and triumphs of the transnational campaign for pension privatisation between 1994 and 2005, pension privatisation suddenly ground to a halt worldwide in 2005 (Orenstein, 2011). Why? Between 2005 and 2010, no further countries privatised their pensions systems. And after the global financial crisis of 2008, a number of reforming countries dismantled or reduced the size of their private pension pillars (Drahokoupil and Domonkos, 2012). Scholars have offered two explanations for the decline of the pension privatisation campaign: first, fiscal pressures forced countries to reconsider the difficulties of paying for the transition costs to the new system, and second, ideas in transnational expert communities and international organisations suddenly changed. Both explanations have some validity and together can account for the sudden halt to pension privatisation and subsequent developments that have seen a reshaping of advice in global pensions policy. Transition costs were always the Achilles heal of pension privatisation. Transitioning from a PAYG pension system to one based on individual accounts means that governments have to continue paying current retirees while 'socking away' money in individual accounts. Governments were initially forced to borrow all the money they divert to individual accounts. Over time, pension privatisation was intended to reduce fiscal pressure on states, but in the short run, it increases it substantially. The borrowing often amounts to between 1 to 3 per cent of national gross domestic product (GDP) per annum, and in times of economic crisis, this borrowing can be unsustainable.

Indeed, during the global financial crisis, countries began to reconsider pension privatisation from two perspectives: first, they questioned whether they were able to sustain the borrowing needed to finance the transition to the new system, and second, they considered confiscating balances in individual accounts in order to pay down government debt. Only two countries (to date) have confiscated balances in individual accounts and closed down their pension systems – Argentina and Hungary. Many more scaled back the contribution rate to the private system, which reduced the amount of government borrowing.

However, the global financial crisis started in 2008, and the global pause in pension privatisation started in 2005. Clearly, fiscal crisis was not the only factor: 2005 were good times for the global economy. Why then? Analysis of transnational pension policy discourse provides a persuasive explanation: 2005 was a critical year for pension privatisation discourse globally for at least three reasons. First, 2005 was the year in which US President George W. Bush's efforts to privatise the US social security system failed. Second, 2005 was the year in which the Chilean system discussed above was re-reformed under progressive Chilean President Michelle Bachelet. Third, 2005 was the year in which several new WB publications caused it to back away from its strong support for the pension privatisation campaign.

After US President Bush's re-election in 2004, he promised that pension privatisation would be the main domestic initiative of his presidency. He undertook a number of steps to initiate pension privatisation in the US that, however, failed in 2005. Pension privatisation in the US met enormous resistance from well-organised advocacy groups for pensioners, from Nobel-winning *New York Times* correspondent Paul Krugman, and from individual voters. As the debate wore on, pension privatisation became deeply unpopular among normal US citizens, forcing even Republican Party law makers to reject the issue for fear of losing re-election, making it impossible to pass privatisation in the US Congress. As one of the leading states identified with the campaign for pension privatisation worldwide, thanks to its identification with the '**Washington Consensus**' WB, the failure of this reform in the US may have sent a strong signal worldwide.

At the same time, one of the leading countries in pension privatisation, Chile, was reconsidering its pension reforms. The new leftist President of Chile, Michelle Bachelet, a prominent rights advocate, initiated a sharp critique of pension privatisation in Chile, calling it bad for women and for the poor. The reforms she advocated increased the minimum pension in Chile dramatically by initiating a 'Solidarity' pension. This meant that, for many people, the guaranteed minimum pension they would receive would vastly exceed the amount generated by their individual savings, rendering these savings meaningless. The overturning of pension privatisation in a key model country, Chile, may also have shaped global pension policy discourse.

Finally, pension privatisation discourse changed within the WB in 2005 with the publication of several reports that criticised aspects of previous WB pensions policy. Debates had occurred within the Bank since Chief Economist Joseph Stiglitz famously opposed the WB's work on pension reform and organised a conference in 1999 to present his paper on '10 myths' of pension system design (Orszag and Stiglitz, 2001). However, in 2005 and 2006, three books published by the WB took aim at aspects of the Bank's work on the new pension reforms. Gill et al (2005) criticised the high fees charged in Latin American pension savings accounts, and questioned whether the new pension reforms had been adequately designed (Kay and Sinha, 2008). Barr (2005) advocated reforms to PAYG pension systems rather than the introduction of funded individual accounts. The WB's Independent Evaluation Group (WB, 2006) also issued a report critical of the Bank's pension work, suggesting that it had foisted the new pension reforms on countries with insufficient financial and administrative preconditions, creating potential for disaster. As a result, the WB consensus on pension privatisation frayed (Matijascic and Kay, 2006, pp 20-1). Consequently, neither the WB nor other global policy actors should be regarded as monoliths connected with a stable, single-policy approach.

Shifts in global pensions discourse can be timed exactly to the halt in pension privatisation worldwide. The global financial crisis of 2008 deepened a crisis in pension privatisation, forcing a number of reforming countries to scale down their privatised pensions systems and even to confiscate balances to pay off government debt. But there is strong evidence that this crisis originated with ideas and global pensions policy discourse.

Emerging discourse in global pensions and social protection policy: towards a social floor?

Global pensions discourse among experts, advocates and international organisations has a powerful impact on policy in multiple states. The transnational campaign for pension privatisation, which caused more than 30 countries worldwide to privatise their pension systems, demonstrated this clearly. So did the sudden halt to the pension privatisation campaign in 2005. Ideas matter, and it is through the transfer of ideas that global pensions policy had its greatest impact. Given the impact of the global financial crisis and the events described above, where is global pensions policy heading today? Unlike the mid-1990s, when a neoliberal discourse dominated policy around the world, today no one decisive force is shaping policy in every country. Instead, a multiplicity of trends has emerged.

One significant trend is the campaign for a global 'social floor'. This approach seeks to move away from the debate over privatisation to emphasise a factor common to all pension systems: the minimum pension. Advocates of PAYG and privatised pensions can both agree that minimum pensions are important and have advised countries to focus on improving minimum pensions. Most workers today in developing countries still do not benefit from a pension at all. The 'social floor' advocates argue that this is the most pressing question to address, not the controversial issue of privatisation. Interestingly, this campaign has been led in part by the ILO, indicating that that organisation may regain some of its prior prominence in global pensions discourse.

This **transnational advocacy** campaign got seriously under way in 2007. Michael Cichon, Director of the ILO Social Security Department, convened a meeting in the ILO Turin Training Centre of people from the UN Department of Economic and Social Affairs (UNDESA), UN Children's Fund (UNICEF), Help Age International and others under the banner of 'Building a coalition for a global social floor'. The founding document (Coalition for a Global Social Floor, 2007) asserted that the 'Coalition for a global social floor aims to become an alliance of organizations united in the common pursuit of a more fair globalization and the right to social security for all, driven by the conviction that a global social floor is achievable and essential to fast-track poverty reduction.' Initially, it suggested that the coalition would simply have an informal Steering Committee that would be hosted by the UN, ILO, UNICEF or other UN agency, in the spirit of One-UN. The 2007 meeting accepted this idea, and there were side meetings held at the Doha Financing for Development Conference in 2008, at the UN Commission on Social Development events, and so on. However, events were to unfold in a slightly different way to that envisaged. It was the global economic crisis of 2008, combined with the fortuitous circumstance of the ILO happening to hold the rotating chair of the High-Level Panel on Programmes of the UN's Chief Executive Board (UNCEB) that triggered this. A meeting of the UNCEB was held in Paris later in April 2009, which generated the UNCEB issue paper, *The global financial crisis and its impact on the work of the UN system.* The report called for work towards a global Social Protection Floor (SPF) that should ensure 'access to basic social services, shelter, and empowerment and protection of the poor and vulnerable' (UNCEB, 2009, p 31). The ILO and **World Health Organization** (WHO) would lead on this policy, supported by a host of other agencies, including UNICEF and UNDESA. The global SPF had become UN policy, at least in terms of the UNCEB. In effect the transnational campaign goals became formal UN policy, and so the informal coalition meetings that had been envisaged became formal interagency meetings lead by the ILO and WHO.

Between 2008 and 2012 work progressed on several fronts at once to enshrine the concept of the SPF as formal ILO policy, as **G20** policy and even as a policy that the WB would enable countries to establish (Deacon, 2013). The ILO recommendation on SPF (ILO, 2012a) advises countries that they establish four guarantees, one of which is access to adequate income in old age, the social pension. The aforementioned Michelle Bachelet, President of Chile, who had worked to establish a social pension in Chile, was invited by the ILO to chair a commission that resulted in the Bachelet report, advocating adoption of the SPF policy (ILO, 2012b). Chile, instrumental in the earlier campaign by the WB to privatise pensions worldwide, would now be instrumental in the campaign to establish a global social minimum pension policy. The global financial crisis not only contributed to the weakening of the earlier campaign for private pensions, but now also boosted the efforts to establish social pensions. The ILO's complete social security strategy (ILO, 2012a) combines working for the SPF (the horizontal extension of social protection) and for improved PAYG social security pensions and other benefits for those with contributory benefits (the vertical extension of social security).

This is not to conclude that the ILO has won and that the Bank has lost in global influence. First, it is too early to tell what will be the impact in countries of the new SPF policy. Second, tensions about the SPF policy remain between the ILO's newly named Social Protection Department headed from 2013 by Isabel Ortiz and the WB's Social Protection and Labour Department headed by Arup Banjeri.

At the same time, it is important to note that to some extent the pension privatisation campaign remains alive. The Czech Republic and Malawi privatised their pension systems in 2011, although the Czech reforms showed some lessons had been drawn from previous experiences. The Czech privatised system is smaller than others in CEE and was made optional from the beginning; a 'parallel'-type system, rather than the 'mixed' systems implemented in most CEE countries. Britain has implemented a new NEST (National Employment Savings Trust) pension system that is also voluntary, with automatic enrolment. This encourages workers to sign up, but also enables them to opt out of a private, individual account. It seems that countries have moved away from mandatory private accounts to systems that encourage private savings. Time will tell how far national pensions reforms commit to instituting a SPF, and how important private pensions savings will be within in the overall system of pension provision and social protection more widely.

Towards a global social protection policy synergy?

One of the outcomes of the intense global discussions about social security policy in the period leading up to the adoption of the SPF Recommendation was the call by the G20, engineered by the ILO, for greater synergy between the work and policies of the several international agencies working in the social protection field. This resulted in the establishment in 2012 of the Social Protection Inter-Agency Cooperation Board (SPIAC-B) to be chaired jointly by the ILO and the WB, but with, initially, the ILO providing the Secretariat out of its New York office. The first meeting of SPIAC-B took place on 2-3 July 2012 in New York. Several **international non-governmental organisations** (INGOs) that had been involved in the campaign for a global social floor were invited. These included the International Council on Social Welfare (ICSW), Help Age International and Save the Children. Many UN agencies such as the UN Development Programme (UNDP), Food and Agriculture Organisation (FAO), UNICEF and WHO were present. The minutes of the meeting report the discussion on the link between the SPIAC-B and the SPF. The clarification was offered in the following terms (ILO, 2012c):

> Social Protection Floors are part of comprehensive social protection systems (eg as in ILO two-dimensional strategy for the extension of social security); while the SPF addresses the horizontal dimension (basic levels of social protection), the SPIAC-B provides a broader and more inclusive mechanism for sharing of information and coordination between partners, addressing social protection systems as a whole (including the vertical dimension).

Time will tell if there is a genuine synergy between the ILO and WB on global social protection and pension policy, or whether SPIAC-B becomes a forum in which struggles over policy ideas between these two organisations continue to be waged (see Fergusson and Yeates, 2013, for a discussion of this tension in inter-institutional policy networks in the context of global youth employment policy).

Conclusion

Pension reform is often thought to be a quintessential example of national policy making. Yet, as this chapter shows, global pensions policy discourse has had a tremendous effect on welfare states worldwide since the 1940s. After the Second World War, the UN organisation advocated on behalf of the victorious powers that developed welfare states, including state PAYG pension systems, were essential to maintain the peace. That consensus broke down in the 1970s, and the 1980s saw the rise of a neoliberal policy discourse that rejected this Keynesian compromise. Pension privatisation began in 1981 in Chile and turned into a transnational campaign in the 1990s with the support of the WB and other international actors. More than 30 countries worldwide privatised their pension systems until this trend abruptly stopped in 2005. Scholars have identified both fiscal and ideational reasons for this collapse of the pension privatisation trend. While the global financial crisis of 2008 forced countries to cut back their commitments to private pension savings accounts, the timing of the halt suggests that ideas were the root cause.

Global pension policy discourse changed dramatically in 2005, with the failed debate over pension privatisation in the US, the re-reform of the Chilean system in 2006, and the publication of critical WB reports in 2005 and 2006, before the global financial crisis broke out. The emergence of the new transnational campaign for a SPF including social pensions was also driven by ideas, but ideas whose time had come with the global economic crisis of 2008.

Although the policy process for the diffusion of pension privatisation and the global SPF has been mostly top-down, a bottom-up perspective helps to understand the formulation of global pensions policy. While social movements, NGOs and other social actors have been deeply involved in national pensions debates, they had been notably absent from cross-border discourse in the initial global debates about pension privatisation. However, following the criticisms that had been made of pension privatisation by individual experts, independent **civil society** actors and INGOs became more engaged in the global pensions discourse as it has subsequently taken place. This suggests that bottom-up influences can be important in setting global policy agendas. But under what conditions can social movements define global actor policies? This constitutes an important topic for comparative policy research. The experience of global pensions policy suggests that such opportunities are available, but that only a small number of organisations have the resources and inclination to undertake global policy campaigns. As this chapter has shown, ideas have a powerful impact on global pensions and social protection policy, and although historically this has been a decidedly elitist area of global social policy making, advocacy movements and campaigning groups have shown they can exert a significant role in shaping global pensions and social protection policy discourses.

Summary

- Global policy actors have a renewed importance in setting pensions and social protection policy in countries around the world.
- The campaign for the privatising of pensions is a good example of what authors such as Woods (2006) calls a global governance network or coalition.
- While global pensions policy originated with the ILO after the Second World War, the privatising pension reform campaign of the WB replaced ILO dominance over global pensions policy and sparked a growing awareness of the international influences on pension system design.

- Evidence presented here has shown that global policy actors have exerted effective influence over country reform adoption across many continents.
- Global policy actors use a mix of influence mechanisms to achieve their goals, including norms creation, persuasion and economic incentives. While global policy actor influence has its limits and these reforms require willing domestic partners in order to proceed, global policy actors have been a determining factor in the spread of new pension reforms to more than 30 countries worldwide.
- The privatising of pensions slowed down and indeed halted in the mid-2000s. In its wake emerged a new transnational advocacy campaign for a global social floor including social pensions. This won wide support from the UN, G20 and even the WB.
- It is too early to tell if the re-emergence of the ILO, which has been central to the global SPF campaign, will have brought a new balance of influence between the WB and the ILO and a new global social protection policy synergy.

Questions for discussion

- What were the WB's pension reforms, and how did they differ from PAYG pension systems?
- Are domestic politics and economics or global policy actor influence more important in explaining the adoption of the WB's pension reforms and the global SPF policy?
- What is the new apparent global consensus on the SPF and social pensions?

Further reading and resources

Brooks (2005) and Müller (2003) are recommended if you wish to follow up the issues explored in this chapter. For further reading on the ways that policy ideas 'travel' around the world, see Weyland (2005). See Deacon (2013) for further details about the global SPF.

World Bank pensions: www.worldbank.org/pensions

OECD private pensions: www.oecd.org/department/0,2688,en_2649_34853_1_1_1_1_1,00.html

ILO Social Protection Department: www.ilo.org/secsoc/lang--en/index.htm

References

Barnett, M. and Finnemore, M. (2004) *Rules for the world: International organizations in global politics*, Ithaca, NY: Cornell University Press.

Barr, N. (ed) (2005) *Labor markets and social policy in Central and Eastern Europe: The accession and beyond*, Washington, DC: The World Bank.

Barr, N. and Diamond, P (2006) 'The economics of pensions', *Oxford Review of Economic Policy*, vol 22, no 1, pp 15-39.

Brooks, S.M. (2004) 'International financial institutions and the diffusion of foreign models for social security reform in Latin America', in K. Weyland (ed) *Learning from foreign models in Latin American policy reform*, Washington, DC and Baltimore, MD: Woodrow Wilson Center and Johns Hopkins University Press.

Brooks, S.M. (2005) 'Interdependent and domestic foundations of policy change: the diffusion of pension privatization around the world', *International Studies Quarterly*, vol 49, no 2, pp 273-94.

Casey, B. (2011) 'Pensions in Nigeria: The performance of the new system of individual accounts', *International Social Security Review*, vol 64, no 1, pp 1-14.

Charlton, R. and McKinnon, R. (2002) 'International organizations, pension system reform and alternative agendas: bringing older people back in?', *Journal of International Development*, vol 14, no 8, pp 1175-86.

China Economic Research and Advisory Programme (2005) 'Social security reform in China: issues and options', Unpublished manuscript (http://econ.lse.ac.uk/staff/nb/Barr_SocialSecurityStudy2005.pdf).

Chwieroth, J. (2007) 'Neoliberal economists and capital account liberalization in emerging markets', *International Organization*, vol 61, no 2, pp 443-63.

Coalition for a Global Social Floor (2007), mimeo. Geneva, ILO.

de Oliveira, F. (ed) (1994) *Social security systems in Latin America*, Washington, DC: Inter-American Development Bank.

Deacon, B. (1997) *Global social policy: International organizations and the future of welfare*, London: Sage Publications.

Deacon, B (2007) *Global Social Policy and Governance*. London: Sage Publications.

Deacon, B. (2013) *Global social policy in the making: The foundations of the Social Protection Floor*, Bristol: Policy Press.

Demarco, G. (2004) 'The Argentine pension system reform and international lessons', in Kurt Weyland (ed) *Learning from foreign models in Latin American policy reform*, Washington, DC and Baltimore, MD: Woodrow Wilson Center and Johns Hopkins University Press.

Drahokoupil, J. and Domonkos, S. (2012) 'Averting the funding gap crisis: East European pension reforms since 2008', *Global Social Policy*, vol 12, no 3, pp 283-99.

Epstein, R. (2008) 'Transnational actors and bank privatization', in M.A. Orenstein, S. Bloom and N. Lindstrom (eds) *Transnational actors in Central and East European transitions*, Pittsburgh, PA: University of Pittsburgh Press, pp 98-117.

Fergusson, R. and Yeates, N. (2013) 'Business, as usual: the policy priorities of the World Bank's discourses on youth unemployment, and the global financial crisis', *Journal of International and Comparative Social Policy*, vol 29, no 1, pp 64-78.

Fultz, E. (2004) 'Pension reform in the EU accession countries: challenges, achievements, and pitfalls', *International Social Security Review*, vol 57, no 2, pp 3-24.

Gill, I.S., Packard, T. and Yermo, J. (2005) *Keeping the promise of social security in Latin America*, Washington, DC and Stanford, CA: The World Bank and Stanford University Press.

ILO (2012a) *The strategy of the International Labour Organization: Social security for all; Building Social Protection Floors and comprehensive social security systems*, Geneva: ILO.

ILO (2012b) *Recommendation concerning national floors of social protection (Social Protection Floors Recommendation), 2012 (No 202)*, International Labour Conference, Geneva: ILO.

ILO (2012c) First Social Protection Inter-Agency Cooperation Board Meeting, www.ilo. org/wcmsp5/groups/public/---dgreports/---nylo/documents/genericdocument/ wcms_226913.pdf

Jacoby, W. (2004) *The enlargement of the European Union and NATO: Ordering from the menu in Central Europe*, Cambridge: Cambridge University Press.

James, E. (1998) 'The political economy of social security reform: a cross-country review', *Annals of Public and Comparative Economics*, vol 69, no 4, pp 451-82.

James, E. and Brooks, S.M. (2001) 'The political economy of structural pension reform', in R. Holzmann and J.E. Stiglitz (eds) *New ideas about old age security: Toward sustainable pension systems in the 21st century*, Washington, DC: The World Bank.

Johnson, J. (2008) 'Two-track diffusion and Central Bank embeddedness: The politics of Euro adoption in Hungary and the Czech Republic', in M.A. Orenstein, S. Bloom and N. Lindstrom (eds) *Transnational actors in Central and East European transitions*, Pittsburgh, PA: University of Pittsburgh Press, pp 77-97.

Kay, S.J. and Sinha, T. (2008) 'Overview', in S.J. Kay and T. Sinha, *Lessons from pension reform in the Americas*, Oxford: Oxford University Press, pp 6-21.

Kelley, J. (2004) *Ethnic politics in Europe: The power of norms and incentives*, Princeton, NJ: Princeton University Press.

Madrid, R.L. (2003) *Retiring the state: The politics of pension privatization in Latin America and beyond*, Stanford, CA: Stanford University Press.

Matijascic, M. and Kay, S. (2006) 'Social security at the crossroads: Toward effective pension reform in Latin America', *International Social Security Review,* vol 59, no 1, pp 3-26.

Minns, R. (2001) *The Cold War in welfare: Stock markets versus pensions*, London: Verso.

Müller, K. (2003) *Privatising old-age security: Latin America and Eastern Europe compared*, Aldershot: Edward Elgar.

Nelson, J.M. (2004) 'External models, international influence, and the politics of social sector reforms', in K. Weyland (ed) *Learning from foreign models in Latin American policy reform*, Washington, DC and Baltimore, MD: Woodrow Wilson Center and Johns Hopkins University Press.

Orenstein, M.A. (2000) *How politics and institutions affect pension reform in three post-Communist countries*, World Bank Policy Research Working Paper 2310, Washington, DC: The World Bank.

Orenstein, M.A. (2003) 'Mapping the diffusion of pension innovation', in R. Holzmann, M. Orenstein and M. Rutkowski (eds) *Pension reform in Europe: Process and progress*, Washington, DC: The World Bank.

Orenstein, M.A. (2008) *Privatizing pensions: The transnational campaign for social security reform*, Princeton, NJ: Princeton University Press.

Orenstein, M.A. (2011) 'Pension privatization in crisis: Death or rebirth of a global policy trend', *International Social Security Review*, vol 64, no 3, pp 65-80.

Orszag, P.R. and Stiglitz, J.E. (2001) 'Rethinking pension reform: ten myths about social security systems', in R. Holzmann and J.E. Stiglitz (eds) *New ideas about old age security: Toward sustainable pension systems in the 21st century*, Washington, DC: The World Bank.

Piggott, J. and Bei, L. (2007) *Pension reform and the development of pension systems: An evaluation of World Bank assistance*, Background Paper: China Country Study, Washington, DC: Independent Evaluation Group, The World Bank.

Pinheiro, V.C. (2004) 'The politics of social security reform in Brazil', in K. Weyland (ed) *Learning from foreign models in Latin American policy reform*, Washington, DC and Baltimore, MD: Woodrow Wilson Center and Johns Hopkins University Press.

Republic of South Africa National Treasury (2007) *South security and retirement reform: Second discussion paper*, Pretoria: Republic of South Africa.

Rofman, R. (2007) *Pension reform and the development of pension systems: An evaluation of World Bank assistance*, Background Paper: Peru Country Study, Washington, DC: Independent Evaluation Group, The World Bank.

Snelbecker, D. (2005) 'Pension reform in Eastern Europe and Eurasia: experiences and lessons learned', Paper prepared for USAID Workshop for Practitioners on Tax and Pension Reform, Washington, DC, 27-29 June.

Tarrow, S. (2005) *The new transnational activism*, Cambridge: Cambridge University Press.

Tsebelis, G. (2002) *Veto players: How political institutions work*, New York and Princeton, NJ: Russell Sage Foundation and Princeton University Press.

UNCEB (United Nations Chief Executives Board) (1999) *The global financial crisis and its impact on the work of the UN system*, UNCEB Issue Paper.

Valdes, J.G. (1995) *Pinochet's economists: The Chicago School in Chile*, Cambridge: Cambridge University Press.

WB (The World Bank) (1994) *Averting the old age crisis: Policies to protect the old and promote growth*, Oxford: Oxford University Press.

WB (2006) *Pension reform and the development of pension systems: An evaluation of World Bank assistance*, Independent Evaluation Group Report, Washington, DC: WB.

Weyland, K. (2004) 'Learning from foreign models in Latin American policy reform: an introduction', in K. Weyland (ed) *Learning from foreign models in Latin American policy reform*, Washington, DC and Baltimore, MD: Woodrow Wilson Center and Johns Hopkins University Press.

Weyland, K. (2005) 'Theories of policy diffusion: lessons from Latin American pension reform', *World Politics*, vol 57, no 2, pp 262-95.

Woods, N. (2006) *The globalizers: The IMF, The World Bank and their borrowers*, Ithaca, NY: Cornell University Press.

Global education policies

Roger Dale and Susan Robertson

Overview

This chapter points out that existing 'conceptual grammars' of education, based on the primacy and centrality of national education systems, are inadequate in an era of globalisation. Globalisation has changed the structures, processes, scales and actors involved in education policy. These arguments are developed through the analysis of four educational trajectories: the first focuses on the fate of the first attempt to 'globalise' education policy, the United Nations (UN) Declaration of Human Rights. Second, the Organisation for Economic Co-operation and Development's (OECD) PISA (Programme for International Student Assessment), a contemporary example of how the purposes of education systems are being reframed through the setting of benchmarks and targets. The third trajectory, the growth of traded education services, illustrates how education has become a commodity within the global trading system. Fourth, the emergence of public–private partnerships (PPPs) on education highlight the ongoing processes of the privatisation of public services.

Key concepts
Conceptual grammar; competitive comparison; multilateralism

Introduction

Globalisation not only transforms the nature, content and framing of policies, but also significantly penetrates national education systems themselves as the means of producing and realising education policy. In this chapter we take globalisation to mean the formulation and transmission by a range of transnational and national, public and private, organisations and agencies, of (largely economic) discourses and institutions, that are not directly prescriptive of national education policies, but which refashion the **governance** and goals of education policy, and frame its meanings and possibilities.

Globalisation thus affects not just the goals and outcomes of education, but also the processes and institutions, and the scales and actors, involved in its making. This requires the use of a new **conceptual grammar**, to replace that based on notions of the nature and capacities of national states, what counts as education, and the associated discourses and contestation about the outcomes of policy decisions and actions. Many of the driving ideas in national education 'policy' had their origins in the assumption that national/sub-national governments had the capacity to act in ways that could directly and indirectly alter the behaviours of people and institutions, and hence improve the levels of wellbeing of communities and societies. This grammar had its roots in policies and processes tied to the national state, for it was at this scale that questions of political authority, legitimation and rule were settled. However, the fact that education systems are still 'national' in the sense that decisions are still taken at national level does not necessarily imply that that is where the power over those decisions lies. Indeed, that existing forms and models of education continue *apparently* more or less unchanged does not alter the fact that their meanings have changed, and that new forms, located at different scales, are coming to exist beside them.

Over the past two decades there have been important changes in the scales (supranational, regional, sub-national, as well as national), and actors (such as non-multilateral, international and non–governmental organisations [INGOs], education consultants, global education firms, venture philanthropists) engaged in framing, advancing and materialising education policies. Not only does the globalising of education policy involve these actors' extension across national territorial boundaries on the one hand, but also the reassembling and transformation of units deep inside national territorial states (such as within education ministries) into global ones on the other.

These processes are clearly evident in the four policy trajectories examined in this chapter. These are:

• the nature and consequences of the changing roles of the major **international organisations** (UN Educational, Scientific and Cultural Organisation [UNESCO], the **World Bank** Group, the OECD) in education, particularly around education for development and what is widely referred to as Education for All (EFA);

- the expansion of an ambitious and far-reaching programme of globalisation of education policy, the OECD's Programme for International Student Assessment (PISA);
- the growth of international student mobility in higher education as a tradeable commodity negotiated through trade agreements at national, regional and global scales (for example, the **World Trade Organization**'s [WTO] General Agreement on Trade in Services [GATS]); and
- the promotion of privatisation of education discourses and projects by the World Bank Group, particularly under the umbrella of PPPs.

These four global education policies reveal a great deal about processes associated with the production of global education policy and practices particularly as they point to the significant redistribution of the labour of education, vertically and horizontally, within and across scales. Taken together, they also raise important questions about sources of authority, legitimacy and accountability, and especially where and how such policies might be contested in national and transnational spaces by those with a stake in education and democracy.

From national education systems to global (post-national) learning regimes

The major shift originating in what we now recognise as the globalisation of education policy came at the end of the Second World War, with the breakdown of the empires and colonies that European countries had set up across the world in the previous half millennium. This had two significant consequences. One was that there was widespread acknowledgement of the *collective* responsibility of the world for ensuring the human rights of all inhabitants of the planet. This is most clearly inscribed in the UN Charter and most clearly instantiated in the creation of a UN body with responsibility – on a global scale a – for education, in the form of UNESCO. Education as a 'human right' was also enshrined in the 1948 Declaration of Human Rights, which all UN countries are signatories to. The Universal Declaration (see *Box 9.1*) stated not only that everyone has the right to education, but that education should also be free of charge. What is proving to be more controversial is the role the private sector might play, and most recently, the role of for-profit firms on delivering education as a public good.

The second consequence was that a large number of new nations had emerged following the end of the Second World War, now with formal responsibility for their own education policy. This was seen by the former colonial powers, but also by the US and Russia, as an opportunity to maintain and increase their spheres of interest internationally. They did this largely through conceptualising the problem for the newly emergent states as one of 'modernisation' to be addressed by 'new' countries pursuing those same stages of development that had been followed by their former European masters. Importantly, it was argued that these 'stages of growth' (Rostow, 1960) could be accelerated, with education playing an important role. It was this broad global understanding of the key problems for developing countries' education policy that informed early attempts to contribute to, and inform, education policy in 'underdeveloped countries'. Of crucial and lasting significance here was the identification of what came to be known as **human capital theory** (see Schultz, 1971). This theory suggested that the key variable that distinguished more successful economies – such as (the then West) Germany and Japan – from those that weren't, was their investment in education. This later became known as the human capital theory of economic growth (Schultz, 1971). Education as development thus essentially followed the same dual objectives – making citizens, and making economies, as had informed the growth of Europe in the 19th and 20th centuries. These two very different understandings of 'education' in global education policy, the one broadly humanitarian, the other deeply economic, were to become the basis of a division that has persisted across the decades since.

> **Box 9.1: Universal Declaration of Human Rights (1948), Article 26:**
>
> - Everyone has the right to education. Education shall be free, at least in the elementary and fundamental stages. Elementary education shall be compulsory. Technical and professional education shall be made generally available and higher education shall be equally accessible to all on the basis of merit.
> - Education shall be directed to the full development of the human personality and to the strengthening of respect for human rights and fundamental freedoms. It shall promote understanding, tolerance and friendship among all nations, racial or religious groups, and shall further the activities of the United Nations for the maintenance of peace.
> - Parents have a prior right to choose the kind of education that shall be given to their children.

By the early 1980s, however, as national economies ceased to be nationally located or controlled, and the nature of the state itself was changing under the precepts of **new public management** (NPM) (Hood, 1991), which weakened states' ability to direct and develop policy at national level, it became taken for granted that a narrower view of education, now as learning, should prevail, and that education systems should become an engine for global competitiveness through the development of 'lifelong learners' for 'knowledge-based' economies. The NPM/**neoliberal** projects rolled out in the 1980s featured:

- the unpicking of the state's protectionist policies to enable the freer movement of finance, trade and labour across national boundaries (referred to as 'deregulation'), for instance, the removal of barriers to transnational education providers;
- the implementation of competition policies across the public and private sectors aimed at creating efficiencies in how education was managed, for instance, competitive tendering for the provision of educational services;
- the privatisation of a range of former state activity, for instance, examination boards in England, such as Edexel (Pearson);
- the rescaling of state activity (involving a dual process of decentralisation and recentralisation), for instance, 'free schools' in England, reflecting the character and needs of their local communities.

The special status of state activities as 'public services' either no longer applied, or needed to be radically rethought. And while the outcomes of neoliberalism as a political project differed from country to country, their broad form and the basis of how these interventions were being legitimated, did not. Markets and competition, and the role of the private sector in new and old areas of service delivery (Ball, 2007), were all promoted by key **international non-governmental organisations** (INGOs), such as the World Bank (WB), the OECD and WTO. These outcomes were also presented as being 'in the national interest', as central to global economic competitiveness, as a means for arresting poverty and slowing economic growth, and the basis for building knowledge-based economies. Thus, by the beginning of the 21st century, not only had a narrower understanding of education as 'learning', come to frame global and national education policy agendas, but also new combinations of agents/agencies increasingly dominated the form, shape and outcomes of policy in the education sector. In the remainder of this chapter we elaborate on the four major global policy trajectories that exemplify this shift.

Globalisation of education through 'development'

What might be seen as the first step towards the 'globalisation of education policy' occurred with the promulgation of the UN Declaration of Human Rights (see *Box 9.1*). This was accompanied by the creation of a UN organisation set up specifically to address 'universal' 'social' issues, in the form of UNESCO. In essence, UNESCO might be seen as the repository of the post–Second World War understanding of the need for encoding a shared basis for common humanity: '… to contribute to the building of peace, the eradication of poverty, sustainable development and intercultural dialogue through education, the sciences, culture, communication and information' (see www.unesco.org/new/en/unesco/about-us/who-we-are/introducing-unesco), and to move towards 'attaining quality education for all and lifelong learning, addressing emerging social and ethical challenges, fostering cultural diversity, a culture of peace and building inclusive knowledge societies through information and communication' (UNESCO, 2007).

However, the Cold War period saw both the Western and Soviet blocs seeking to influence newly emerging nations, typically by offering bilateral aid rather than contributing to the kind of **multilateral** projects that UNESCO fostered, for the new states to join them. This greatly reduced the possibility of the kind of 'international community' that UNESCO sought to represent, but which, in the words of the former UN Rapporteur on Education, Katerina Tomasevski, '… has yet to be created' (2007, p 6). And while UNESCO has '… persistently attempt(ed) to subjugate functional approaches to learning to a more humanistic vision … its history has been one of continuous struggle to manage politicisation, offer global programs on a small budget and maintain its centrality within a broader, evolving system of multilateralism' (Mundy, 2007b, p 238).

During this period, there was clear recognition that the 'underdeveloped' countries needed assistance, but the optimum form of that assistance was widely perceived to have been identified by the discipline of development economics. So, while the phenomenon of 'education for development' has persisted in various forms since the era of decolonisation in 1950s, the failure of **modernisation theory**, and the educational 'aid' distributed in support of it by NGOs and donor countries, has been both increasingly visible and attention drawn to it. It is important to note, however, that education featured only at the margins of the debates about how to bring about 'development', largely as these debates continued to be dominated by different strands of development economics theory (for an excellent account of the nature and consequences of this perspective, and its consequences for the role of education in development, see McGrath, 2010).

From the end of the Cold War, and associated with the wider changes in the global economy, there were increasing levels of activity by international organisations, and by the WB in particular. The WB's activities in education began in 1960, and from having hardly any investments in education in the early 1960s, by 1965 it was spending about the same amount as UNESCO on education; by 2010 it was spending 16 times as much as UNESCO (Klees, 2010). Significant changes in both the goals and the modalities of 'aid' resulted from this that amount to the emergence of new forms of globalisation of education tied to an increasingly neoliberal agenda. It was during the 1980s that many observers argue that the WB replaced UNESCO as the lead agency for education (Jones, 1992). It was also during this time that the WB began producing a series of education strategy papers that have increasingly set global education policy (Klees, 2010).

The first example of this was the shift to aid policies informed by the so-called '**Washington Consensus**' (Williamson, 1993), based around a set of key ideas: that of privatisation, **liberalisation**, deregulation and fiscal discipline, to be implemented through Structural Adjustment Programmes (SAPs). SAPs favoured the use of **conditionalities** to implement free market policies, but were strongly criticised, particularly in low-income countries. Nevertheless, various strands of **post–Washington Consensus** policies emerged that included support for education as a means to produce human capital that in turn was the basis of economic growth. Washington Consensus policies also spawned marketisation and privatisation policies in education. At the global level, the OECD, WB and WTO also joined forces to create a vision for an education services sector that would in turn be part of a 'global education industry', with emphasis now placed on 'free' trade in educational goods and services (Robertson et al, 2002). In this new formulation, aid could be replaced by trade as a means of building capacity.

While the WB's goals continued to be on economic growth and poverty reduction in developing countries, UNESCO continued to focus on peace and security through education, science and culture. The guiding principle for UNESCO is human rights, and it is this that underpinned efforts to advance a major initiative that came to be known as Education for All (EFA) (see *Box 9.2*). EFA policy and programmes were first launched in 1990, to be followed later by the **Millennium Development Goals** (MDGs) in 2000 aimed at ensuring that by 2015 all children were able to access basic education.

Box 9.2: Education for All

The Education for All (EFA) movement is a global commitment to provide quality basic education for all children, youth and adults. At the World Education Forum (Dakar, 2000), 164 governments pledged to achieve EFA and identified six goals to be met by 2015. Governments, development agencies, civil society and the private sector are working together to reach the EFA goals.

The Dakar Framework for Action mandated UNESCO to coordinate these partners, in cooperation with the four other convenors of the Dakar Forum (UN Development

UNIVERSITY OF WINCHESTER
LIBRARY

Programme [UNDP], UN Population Fund [UNFPA], UN Children's Fund [UNICEF] and WB). As the leading agency, UNESCO focuses its activities on five key areas: policy dialogue, monitoring, advocacy, mobilisation of funding and capacity development.

In order to sustain the political commitment to EFA and to accelerate progress towards the 2015 targets, UNESCO has established several coordination mechanisms managed by UNESCO's EFA Global Partnerships team. Following a major review of EFA coordination in 2010-11, UNESCO reformed the global EFA coordination architecture.

Source: www.unesco.org/new/en/education/themes/leading-the-international-agenda/education-for-all

The EFA initiative, led by UNESCO, WB and a combination of other UN agencies (see Chabbott, 1998), represents the most significant move towards a human rights–based globalisation of education policy. It was promulgated at a meeting in Jomtien, Thailand, in 1990, where delegates from 155 countries adopted a World Declaration on Education for All, reaffirming the notion of education as a fundamental human right and urging countries to intensify efforts to address the basic learning needs of all.

However, these goals were not met by 2000, and at the World Education Forum (WEF held in Dakar, 2000), governments, development agencies, **civil society** and the private sector agreed to work together to reach the EFA goals. The Dakar Framework for Action mandated UNESCO to coordinate these partners. However, while the leaders of the world economy continue to 'need' the kind of legitimation provided by UNESCO: '… the G8 dominated international community wants and needs the legitimation of an EFA campaign, and UNESCO is still the most plausible and universal "performer" of the EFA/universal right to education skit [sic]' (Mundy, 2007b, p 38), its ability to do that was clearly in question, since:

> … when UNESCO left Dakar intending to lead and direct the global EFA movement, it was quickly disabused of the notion that it could assign tasks to other multilaterals, to governments, or to NGOs and civil society [but] when it … tried to form a collaborative to foster joint action on EFA, it was chastised for being insipid and uninspired. (Pigozzi, 2007, p 241)

In the event, it became clear that UNESCO did not have the capacity to deliver the goals, and the lead role was effectively taken over by the WB, which had, at the time, also expanded its remit by more generally identifying itself as 'the Knowledge Bank', a significant shift towards 'globalising' educational development. This was taken a further step forward with the launch of the MDGs at the UN Millennium Summit in 2000, one of which was devoted to the ensuring access to primary school for all children by 2015 (a goal that seems unlikely to be achieved).

The shift from EFA to MDGs can be seen as a shift from a 'multilateral' agency approach (Mundy 2002) to a 'global agency' approach. The MDGs came to form the framework through which the efforts of the world community would be channelled and implemented to achieve significant and measurable improvements in people's lives by the year 2015. More fundamentally, they represented the confluence of a number of different streams, raising the profile and recognition of the importance of poverty in numerous ways. Most recently, a major driving force for the MDGs has been via the Learning Metrics Task Force, a joint project between UNESCO's Statistical Office and the US-based Brookings Institute, whose main objective is '… to catalyze a shift in the global conversation on education from a focus on access to access *plus* learning'[1] which brings it much closer into line with the increasing global emphasis on the measurement of educational outputs.

This very brief discussion of the relationships between globalisation and education, as exemplified by the case of education for development, has indicated that the power, reach and resources of global institutions with strong alignments with powerful states and global capital have been far more influential in shaping what is to count as education for development, with the consequent subsumption of the goals of education for social cohesion and as a human right in favour of a narrower conception of learning as the key goal of education. The EFA agenda was essentially bifurcated into UNESCO's emphasis on education as a human right, and education as economic investment, especially following the WB's increasing interest in education. These tensions were played out as EFA developed, with the WB effectively taking over leadership of the project from UNESCO, and its agendas coming to dominate, with 'the institutionalization of a standard model for educational reform and educational investment' Mundy (2002, p 493), and its ability to impose its discourse (see also Klees, 2012).

Nevertheless, UNESCO continues to play an important role in EFA, in particular through its stewardship and publication of the annual 'EFA Global Monitoring Report' which since 2002 has tracked and reported the progress of the EFA towards achieving the Dakar goals. The GMR report 'identifies effective policy reforms and best practice in all areas relating to EFA, draws attention to emerging challenges and seeks to promote international cooperation in favour of education', and each annual report focuses on a particular issue (www.unesco.org/new/en/education/themes/leang-the-international-agenda/efareport/reports/). See *Box 9.3*.

Box 9.3: Education for All Global Monitoring Report 2012

Goal 2: Universal primary education
Highlights

- On current trends the target of universal primary education will be missed. The number of out-of-school children of primary school age fell from 108 million in 1999 to 61 million in 2010.
- The rate of decline was rapid between 1999 and 2004, but then started slowing, and progress has stalled since 2008. Sub-Saharan Africa, where the number of children out of school increased by 1.6 million between 2008 and 2010, accounts for half of the world's total.
- The number of countries with a primary net enrolment ratio of over 97 per cent increased from 37 to 55 out of 124 countries between 1999 and 2010. Just five years before 2015, 29 countries have a net enrolment ratio of less than 85 per cent, and so are very unlikely to achieve the goal by the deadline.
- Children of official school starting age who did not enter school by 2010 will not be able to complete the primary cycle by 2015. In 2010, out of 98 countries with data there were 16 countries with a net intake rate below 50 per cent and 71 countries below 80 per cent.
- Drop-out remains a problem in low-income countries, where on average 59 per cent of those starting school reached the last grade in 2009. The problem is particularly acute for those children starting late.

Source: Education for All Global Monitoring Report, UNESCO, 2012, p 72

OECD's Programme of International Student Assessment

The clearest challenge to a nationally based conceptual grammar of education policy is to be found in the OECD's PISA. Formally, this is '... an international study which aims to *evaluate education systems worldwide* by testing the skills and knowledge of 15-year-old students' (OECD, 2006; emphasis added). It claims to involve 400,000 students in 57 countries, making up 90 per cent of the world economy, with nationally representative samples representing 20 million 15-year-olds from 30 OECD and 27 partner countries (note that these are non-members of the OECD, and may generally be less prosperous countries); in any case, their presence in the programme very much enhances its 'global' coverage (OECD, 2006). It is thus a huge and ambitious project that in many ways may be seen to represent the apogee of the relationship between globalisation – 90 per cent of the world economy – and education, in the countries taking part, and coordinated and promoted by an organisation, OECD, with global scope and interest, and a mandate to achieve the highest sustainable level of economic growth, and to contribute to the development of the world economy.

In approaching PISA as an example of the operation of international organisations in education, it is important to note that the basis of their interventions is not so much providing *responses* to the new challenges of 'globalisation' to national governments, but in *framing* and *defining the nature of* those new challenges. That is, they specify and formulate the nature of the problems faced by national systems through the nature of the advice and suggestions they provide. In the case of PISA, they do this by 'evaluat(ing) education *systems*' by testing the competences of 15-year-old students in the areas of literacy, science and mathematics.

PISA rests on two basic principles. The first is a focus on students' competences, that is, on what students are able to *do* with the knowledge they accumulate. The second is in making national education systems comparable in terms of a single metric, which in turn is then used to order and hierarchically rank countries' education systems against each other. As Martens argues, '... [international organisations] gain power by setting standards *independent of the original motives states had for delegating them the task of objective evaluation....* If IOs [international organisations] successfully reveal and promote the linkage between certain they might reframe the national understanding of a topic and alter its domestic evaluation' (Martens, 2007, pp 47, 49; emphasis added).

PISA illustrates the importance of an approach to education policy that is global in that:

- it cannot be seen as the worldwide extension of any existing national policy (such as we find in studies of '**policy transfer**', or '**policy borrowing**', for instance); indeed, it contains features that are scarcely found in any national policy; and
- it sets a common *global* benchmark for all its member states, no matter how different their socioeconomic position, current education policies or cultural background.

And it is this that becomes a common basis for holding national education systems to account globally. More than this, the international comparability puts countries into a relationship of **competitive comparison** with each other, on the basis of their 'success' on PISA tests (see Breakspear, 2012, for evidence of the forms of importance countries attach to rankings as a stimulus to change).

PISA does not so much *prescribe* any particular policy as provide a common framework of analysis that any policies might be expected to take into account. In this sense it is most usefully seen as a 'meta-policy', that is, it is a policy that frames the possibilities and expectations of, and sets limits to, what can count as policy. However, this does not mean that PISA somehow escapes, or overrides, existing differences between national conceptions of education. Nevertheless, the nature of such a common base cannot be neutral, or indeed be able to treat all existing systems in the same way; since being developed and carried out by the OECD, PISA is not ideologically neutral, but rather evaluates education from an economic perspective and promotes, according to this paradigm, related learning techniques. From this viewpoint, PISA is much closer to the pre-existing Anglo-American understanding of education than to that of continental Europe (Martens and Niemann, 2010, p 1).

The editors of a recent book on PISA and its effects express these views more trenchantly, seeing PISA as:

> ... well on its way to being institutionalized as the main engine in the global accountability regime, which measures, classifies and ranks students, educators and school systems from diverse cultures and countries using the same standardized benchmarks. The OECD, in turn, begins assuming a new institutional role as arbiter of global educational governance, simultaneously acting as diagnostician, judge and policy advisor to the world's school systems.

They see PISA as:

> ... advancing a new mode of global educational governance in which state sovereignty over educational matters is replaced by the influence of large-scale international organizations, and in which the very meaning of public education is being recast from a project aimed at forming citizens and nurturing social solidarity to a project driven by economic demands and labour market orientations. (Meyer and Benavot, 2012, pp 9, 10)

One important mechanism through which PISA works is that it shifts the burden of education accountability to *outputs* (such as achievement levels) rather than *inputs* (such as funding or curriculum). It therefore defines what counts as evidence (the scores of 15-year-olds on tests of mathematics, literacy and science), irrespective of national locations. This makes it truly transnational, and the forms of governance it promotes both acknowledge and respond to this mission. PISA is not directly concerned with what is taught in a country's schools. Rather, it is '... as a tool of expectation management [that] PISA fosters a transformation of what had been ill-defined issues (eg curriculum contents) into seemingly well-defined attainment goals. It delivers, at the same time, a parameter for holding schooling accountable – for delivering according to the expectations embedded into its questionnaires' (Hopmann, 2008, p 425).

However, it is also important we consider how PISA has been received and interpreted by its members, and ask about its impact on national education policies and practices. A recent study by Breakspear (2012), of the 'normative impact' of PISA, suggests that PISA 'on the ground' becomes essentially a 'problem framing' discourse that is differently interpreted as it comes into contact with historically grounded national education systems. This suggests that the acceptance of/adherence to PISA's common problematic, the discursive framing of educational quality via accountability, is more prominent in PISA's aims than in its outcomes as delivered in and through national education systems. For most respondents, the most significant aspect in bringing about change was that (rather than being rationally persuaded by the programme) it was '... the overall international rank (that) had led to/inspired changes in 19 countries/economies and partially led to change in a further 11 countries/economies' (Breakspear, 2012, p 11). The most frequently mentioned specific country targets and motivations for change were improving relative rank and specific scores (which amount to improving adherence to the proxy [PISA] results), rather than the substance of educational quality. The results also identified national policy makers as the most significant stakeholder group (which may not be surprising, since national policy makers were clearly the intended recipients of the PISA message), and while '... a range of policies and initiatives had been undertaken in light of PISA, it was also emphasised that such policy initiatives often displayed a low level of policy coherence overall' (Breakspear, 2012, p 7).

One interesting finding was the low level of attention paid in most participating countries to the place and importance of PISA's most directly educationally relevant element, its emphasis on *competences*, that is, what young people can do with what they have learned, rather than the 'amount' that they have learned (Breakspear, 2012). Breakspear concludes by suggesting that while '... the extent of influence varies across countries/economies ... in some of these contexts, PISA may come to increasingly shape, define and evaluate the key goals of the national/federal education system ... and set the agenda for policy debate at the national and state levels' (Breakspear, 2012, p 27), while more broadly 'the analysis ... reveals the emerging role and influence of the OECD as an international education monitor and policy actor' (2012, p 28).

More broadly, Carvalho suggests that '... PISA objects and texts are reinterpreted, made acceptable and efficient for specific socio-cognitive contexts, and each context may exhibit different abilities and knowledge resources and circumstances with which to do so' (Carvalho, 2012, p 183). For instance, 'national' policy actors may use PISA as a form of domestic policy legitimation, or as a means of defusing discussion by presenting policy as based on robust evidence. Nevertheless, commitment to PISA signals adherence of a nation to reform agendas (Steiner-Khamsi, 2004, p 76), and makes participating countries eligible to join the club of competitive nations. However, even such tactical and strategic adoptions of PISA mean that it becomes a new part of national education landscapes.

So we might see as the main relevant consequences of PISA for the globalisation of education policy as meaning:

- that governance is more significant than policy content/intent;
- that beyond the very different ways in which it has been received it retains at its core a tool of quantitative comparison that promises to improve educational evaluation – and through this the means to influence national education systems;
- while its specific focus is the outputs rather than the outcomes, and the objectives rather than the purposes of national education systems, its influence may go beyond this; and
- it stands as a paradigm case of the globalisation of education policy.

International trade in education services

To casual observers, describing education is a key export in a nation's 'trade' sounds odd. After all, education is widely viewed as a public good rather than a tradeable services sector. Yet from the early 1980s, a number of countries – notably the UK, Australia and New Zealand – began to view their (largely higher) education institutions as able to directly contribute to the economy through the recruitment of full fee-paying international students (Welch, 2000). This shift in how education was viewed and valued can be traced to the growing dominance of neoliberal ideologies referred to above, that were beginning to permeate, reshape and drive policy sectors more generally. It was also fuelled by an emerging middle class in Asia, their desire for higher education qualifications, and a view that English as a language was an asset for future employment. By the late 1980s, countries such as Australia and New Zealand began to position themselves more strategically to capture more of this market, and in some cases to market or export their educational services more aggressively. Indeed, for by the early 1990s, the export of education services had risen to become a greater foreign exchange earner than the wine industry in New Zealand.

The US, of course, had always attracted a significant number of students into graduate programmes. However, these students were attracted to the US because of the generous scholarship programmes, particularly in the sciences, mathematics and engineering. In the face of growing competition from Australia, New Zealand and the UK, their share of this market had begun to wane. Welch (2002, p 442) argues that whereas the US accounted for 40 per cent of all international students in the early 1990s, by the late 1990s this proportion had shrunk to 32 per cent.

At the global level, the idea that education might be a tradeable service was given impetus by a growing view within the US Department of Trade, and among influential lobby groups such as the US Coalition of Service Industries, that education might be regarded as part of a services sector, and that a growing services sector would compensate for the US' declining share in the production of goods (Kelsey, 2008). These views were critical to shaping the GATS that was launched by the WTO in 1995. The WTO replaced the General Agreement on Tariffs and Trade (GATT) that had guided international negotiations and agreements through the post-Second World War period. In contrast to GATT, where the negotiations took place over plurilateral codes, the WTO had a much stronger capacity to enforce rules as the member countries (153 in 2013) commit themselves to all of the codes already negotiated (see also **Chapter Five**, this volume).

For the US, their interest in a strengthened global agreement that was binding is that it meant protecting the supply of international students in their science, technology and engineering programmes. The US had become dependent on these students for their research and development (R&D) activity, for a significant percentage of students, particularly from China, remained in the US following completion of their studies (Robertson and Keeling, 2008). However, sending countries such as China were themselves looking to limit the outflow of students, which they saw as a form of 'brain drain'. This meant limiting outflow by restrictions on exit visas.

GATS represented a significant, and controversial, global policy for the education sector. First, while our discussion here refers to higher education, *all* sectors of education (from early years learning to schooling and higher education) were to be included in negotiations and obligations. Second, WTO membership meant a commitment to the progressive liberalisation of the economy – in this case – to opening up education sectors to other countries and their trade departments. Third, four 'modes' were included in the negotiations on education as a tradeable services sector: *cross-border supply*, meaning providing services such as testing or distance education over national borders; *consumption abroad*, such as enabling students to study abroad; *commercial presence*, enabling a foreign investor to establish a commercial presence (such as a foreign university); and *presence of natural persons*, such as the ability to move labour (such as academics) beween countries (Robertson et al, 2002, p 486). In short, these modes were an attempt to bind a country into long-standing decisions that were difficult to withdraw from. The controversial elements of this global policy were that it reinforced the view that education was now a tradeable good, and that it enabled those countries that were well positioned in the market to both extend and protect their interests. It also meant that the negotiations around education would be undertaken by the trade ministries of the member countries, and not education ministries, many of whom did not operate at a federal level (such as Canada and the US).

The WTO negotiations around education services were difficult and protracted, and by 2003, they had largely stalled because of pivotal opposition by protestors. However, this did not mean those countries and the interested providers simply stopped pushing ahead on liberalising education sectors and opening them to more commercial interests and foreign investors. Rather, these have been pursued through parallel tracks of regional, sub-national and bilateral agreements and unilateral sanctions. For instance, in 2006 the European Union (EU) launched a services agreement among its member countries opening up their education sectors to trade and mobility. After 2003 the number of bilateral agreements multiplied – largely as these negotiations took place away from the eyes of the global campaigners opposing the WTO and other powerful multilateral agencies.

Nor has opposition at the global level slowed the expansion of trade in education, which has increasingly taken in not just university studies but also technical and further education. And indeed, the sectors have come to depend on the revenues that these flows generate. In the UK, for instance, around 8 per cent of the overall funding for universities comes from international students. The significance of what this means to the economy of a country such as Australia is captured in the following statement issued in an Australian Reserve Bank Bulletin in 2008: 'Australia's education services exports have continued to grow in importance this decade. Since 1982, education services exports have grown at an average annual rate of around 14 per cent in volume terms, with their share in the value of total exports increasing from less than 1 per cent to almost 6 per cent in 2007…. Indeed, education exports are now Australia's largest export, behind only coal and iron ore' (Reserve Bank of Australia, 2008). The estimated value of education to the Australian economy was calculated to be in the order of AUS$18 billion in 2009/10.

By 2012, the OECD's Education at a Glance reported a five-fold increase in the number of students studying abroad, from 0.8 million in 1975 to a phenomenal 4.1 million in 2010 (OECD, 2012, p 46). Of this percentage,

52 per cent of the students studying abroad were from Asia, and in absolute terms, the largest numbers came from India, China and Korea, while the destination countries for 77 per cent of the students studied in OECD countries, or as some like to say, the rich countries club. The effect of policies aimed at increasing the flow of international students means that *particular* local and national economies have been economically invigorated, while the colour and character of parts of institutions and cities have changed. Cities such as Vancouver, Sydney, London and Auckland, and more recently Singapore and Hong Kong, have seen their institutional profiles, built environments and cultural milieus transformed and not without significant local resentment. Yet their dependence on international students as a source of income will, over the longer run, be challenged as countries like Malaysia, Singapore and China increase their share of the international student market.

Globalising public–private partnerships in education

In this final policy trajectory we introduce a relatively recent, but potentially very far-reaching, policy that has been reshaping the governance of education sectors, that of public–private partnerships (PPPs). These new governance tools have largely replaced privatisation policies and programmes more generally associated with the Washington Consensus. However, in reality they continue to pursue similar goals and outcomes.

At the broadest of levels, they can be defined as '… cooperative institutional arrangement between public and private sector actors … where they jointly develop products and services and share risks, costs and resources which are connected to these products' (Hodge et al, 2010, p 4). In the education sector, policies promoting PPPs have resulted in a range of combinations of state/private/civil society engagements. The most common forms include state-funded vouchers for places in privately run (for-profit and not-for profit) schools; per pupil grants for privately run schools, such as charter schools and academies; privately run management of schools and school districts; and building and maintaining school infrastructures that are then rented back to the public sector on a long-term basis. The claim is that these kinds of arrangements can promote greater competition and therefore efficiencies in education systems; increase the quality of learner outcomes; and enable governments to avail themselves of greater budgetary flexibility, particularly as teacher contracts are open to individual negotiation rather than being mediated through unions (Barrera-Osorio et al, 2012). Opponents of PPPs argue these policies both foster greater privatisation in the education system, and are also part of a rapidly growing corporate industry in the education sector (Ball, 2009, 2012; Greve, 2010).

The significance of PPPs, and the changing relationship between the public and the private sectors in education governance, rests on two things: (1) the fact that many of the developed economies have sought to develop their services sectors as a basis for trade, and in the face of a declining share in the production of goods through manufacturing; and (2) the emergence of neoliberal policies in the 1980s, which argued (and still do) that state-driven Keynesian policies tend to create monopolies that crowd out the private sector from those areas where competition would generate efficiencies, greater risk taking and innovation. For neoliberals, the appropriate role for the state was to create and preserve an institutional framework that ensured the conditions for the market to work efficiently (Harvey, 2005, p 2), even in the areas for which it was held responsible.

The key point about the more recent iteration of increasing the role of the private sector in education sectors (from schooling to higher education) is that it enables for-profit firms to operate in the sector, including in areas of core business. This includes (1) the management of school districts (Ball, 2007; Scott and DiMartino, 2009); (2) the delivery of education provision, such as through charter schools, school vouchers (cf Lubienski, 2013) or low-fee private schools (Tooley, 2013); and (3) deals done with commercial firms around exclusive rights regarding textbooks, testing services, tutoring, quality assurance and inspection services, and so on (cf Scott and DiMartino, 2009; Hentschke et al, 2010). The education sector has also attracted the attention of global private equity firms with investments in reform initiatives and online platforms servicing schools and higher education institutions, such as ImagineK12, Macmillan New Ventures and Rethink Education (Leventhal and Tang, 2013). And while these ventures tend to be more national in their focus, the tendency has been for them to look for economies of scale through extending out globally into new markets (Ball, 2007, 2012).

Not surprisingly, for-profit firms tend to view education itself as simply another sector from which to make a profit, and the students and their family as consumers of education. This is, of course, not uncontroversial in that education continues to be viewed by many within civil society as both a public good and a human right, and therefore a sector that should not be tied to the vagaries of the market, the business world and profit making.

Despite their controversial status, PPPs have become a favoured policy by the large international agencies within the UN system, including: UNESCO, UNICEF, the World Bank Group (especially the International Bank for Reconstruction and Development [IBRD] and the International Finance Corporation [IFC]); the OECD and the World Economic Forum; and bilateral aid donors, such as the Department for International Development (DFID), the US Agency for International Development (USAID) and Danida (cf Kirkemann and Appelquist, 2008). By the late 1990s, all had begun to focus on partnerships, arguing that if countries were going to achieve the MDGs they would need to advance a new development paradigm (Dunning, 2006). Partnerships also featured in the 10 principles of the Global Compact launched by UN Director, Kofi Annan, in 1999 (Cammack, 2006; Bull, 2010). Under Annan, new emphasis was placed on the market and entrepreneurship as a means of resolving longer-standing financial constraints facing the UN system; thus '... PPPs were ... a means to make corporations pull in the same direction as states and multilateral organizations' (Bull, 2010, p 248). And while these partnerships had multiple purposes, they shared a common goal: to combine the efforts of states, multilateral organisations and the private sector in pursuit of commonly accepted goals.

Major corporations were invited to adopt the Global Compact as part of their social responsibility commitments, in cooperation with the UN (Bull, 2010). In 2004, the UN launched its PPP programme (Bull and McNeil, 2007). And while these partnerships had multiple purposes, they also shared the same common goal: to combine the efforts of states, multilateral organisations and the private sector (such as the for-profits, NGOs), in pursuit of commonly accepted goals. In doing so, Bull and McNeil (2007, p 1) argue, PPPs transformed the **multilateral system**.

Arguably, however, the most powerful pressure for PPPs as a global education policy has come from a small network of policy entrepreneurs and education experts located at the interstices of a select range of international organisations, transnational education consultancy firms and global universities that include the World Bank Group (IBRD, IFC), the Asian Development Bank (ADB), the Centre for British Teachers (CfBT) and Harvard University in the US. Together they have been responsible for framing and promoting the idea of PPPs within the wider development domain. This network of education experts is behind the most well known publications, policy briefs and toolkits on PPPs, culminating in the widely disseminated WB report, *The role and impact of PPPs in education*, released in 2009 (see *Table 9.1* for a list of key influential publications and their authors). They also found their way into the World Bank Group's Education Strategy 2020 as a key development pillar for WB's education work over the next decade.

A central assumption made by this policy network is that '... education is a consumer good, and that the student is the principal consumer through parents' (WB, 2001, p 1). What follows from this assumption is that in order for parents (and students) to choose, the education sector needs to be organised so that it operates according to the logic of a free market. This includes information on the nature of the education offered by various providers including its quality; incentives that ensure the right kind of performance; regulatory guarantees to protect the interests of private investors and to ensure fair competition among providers; and an evaluation system that is able to feed back into the information system creating a virtuous circle.

Table 9.1: Core documents on public–private partnerships in education

Organisation	Authors Title Year
ADB and WB	Y. Wang (editor) *The new social policy* agenda in Asia, 2000
IFC	N. LaRocque, J. Tooley and M. Latham *Handbook on PPPs and education*, 2001
CfBT	M. Latham *Toolkit on PPPs and* education, 2008
CfBT	N. LaRocque *PPPs in basic education. An international review*, 2008
WB and IFC	J. Fielden and N. Larcoque *The evolving regulatory context for private educa*tion in emerging economies, 2008
IFC-Edinvest	M. Latham *Public–private partnerships in education*, 2009
WB	H. Patrinos, F. Barrera-Osorio and J. Guáqueta *The role and impact of PPPs in education*, 2009
WB	L. Lewis and H. Patrinos *Learning for all: Investing in people's knowledge and skills to promote development, World Bank Group Education Strategy 2020*, 2011
WB, CfBT (Centre for British Teachers)	L. Lewis and H. Patrinos *Impact evaluation of private sector participation in education*, 2012

Source: Adapted from Verger (2012)

These PPP policy entrepreneurs argue the public sector lacks the accurate incentives to operate services, and that public provision undermines competition and has a negative affect on the quality and the cost of education services (IFC, 2001). The role of the state in the governance of education is important, first, to ensure against the market failing, and second, to respond to concerns from critics about the inequities that have tended to arise when choice, markets, competition and standards policies are at work. In relation to market failure, the WB argues that the role of the state in PPPs is to provide oversight of the contract and to ensure the quality of the outcomes, that is:

> … government guides policy and provides financing while the private sector delivers education services to students. In particular, governments contract out private providers to supply a specified service of a defined quantity and quality at an agreed price for a specific period of time. These contracts contain rewards and sanctions in which the private sector shares the financial risk in the delivery of public services. (Patrinos et al, 2009, p 1)

Yet what is evident from the research literature (cf Ball, 2007, 2012) is that not only is it difficult for governments to properly write, and also oversee, contracts in the education sector because education itself is a complex service to provide, but that for-profit education firms have tended to hide behind claims of 'commercial sensitivity', in turn, making public scrutiny (and therefore open to being researched) more difficult.

In relation to issues of equity and opportunity, Scott (2013, p 6) argues that there has been a recent elision between the idea of choice and equity, and civil rights. In other words, PPP reformers have tended to appropriate the language of civil rights, yet distil the most individualistic aspects of civil rights aspirations while neglecting broader communitarian components. And it is around the individualising of education aspirations and the outcomes of decisions that we are able to see some of the negative outcomes in an equity sense of PPPs. Because education is a 'positional good', meaning, as Brighouse and Swift (2006, p 472) argue, a good whose value derives from their **scarcity**, then policies that intensify competition for desired places tend to increase tendencies to either rig the competition in such a way that it favours particular groups, or it encourages education providers to select those students (known as creaming) who will ensure the value associated with being a chosen provider. Leaving questions of equity and opportunity to the market has tended to exaggerate differences and outcomes for those groups unable to secure the outcomes they want, or who do not display the evident characteristics of those most likely to do well in school (such as the middle class).

How, then, have PPPs been promoted as desirable policy tool? Their legitimacy lies in their promise to resolve some of the intractable problems facing the development community. This includes *access* to quality education, a key part of the EFA and MDG agenda, and poverty reduction. Yet, as evidence shows, PPPs have often not favoured the very poor, and nor have they (in the case of the IFC) favoured low-income countries despite the fact that the IFC has argued that PPPs are pro-poor (Harma and Rose 2012; Mundy and Menashy, 2012).

The WB also seeks to legitimise its policy approach through 'evidence'. Yet it systematically overgeneralises from limited evidence, taking examples out of context, or smoothing out differences in research findings (see Robertson, 2012). For example, in the chapter, 'What do we know about public–private partnerships in education?', from the WB's report *The role and impact of public–private partnerships in education* (Patrinos et al, 2009), it notes a very mixed picture of evidence and that in many cases as it is not possible to overcome problems of student and school selection. Yet at the same time, it goes on to make strong claims about the efficiency and effectiveness of the private sector in education provision.

There is a great deal at stake for those who see the education sector as a new services sector, with major returns on investment, particularly when economies of scale and scope can be developed (see Ball, 2012). A specialist (increasingly corporate) industry has sprung up around PPPs, particularly in those developed economies that have taken the partnerships furtherest (for instance, Australia, the UK and US), and one that services the UN system (Bull, 2010; Greve, 2010). This industry, which is increasingly exporting its expertise globally, includes a rapidly growing number of private actors, from foundations, specialist PPP firms, global consultancy firms, banks, local consultants, think tanks, dedicated websites, rapid response teams and specialist law firms, increasingly acting as market-oriented sources of authority that '… establish rules, norms and institutions that guide the behaviours of the participants, and affect[s] the opportunities available to others' (Cutler et al, 1999, p 4). These dynamics also shine an important light on processes of globalisation, and on global policy making. Clearly alignments between global, national and local policies and practices around PPPs provide the means, motivations and mechanisms through which these policies are advanced globally. But we can also see that they are dependent on the activities and efforts of the policy entrepreneurs, whose framing, commissioning and selecting of evidence works to support their ongoing project. By also deepening and extending the activities of those with a growing private set of interest in the education sector, PPPs become embedded in policy lexicons and industry practices.

Conclusion

We conclude this chapter by revisiting the 'conceptual grammar' mentioned in the introduction. That pointed us towards a range of crucial differences associated with the globalisation of education policy by comparison with the 'traditional' means of approaching those issues. The most significant change brought about by globalisation is in the role of the national state in education policy making. While ostensibly little has changed over the last 50 years (we still have ministers of education, and frequent changes to national education policies), there have been major changes in both the state as an instrument of policy, and in the effective scales of both setting and framing educational goals. In terms of the first of these, the national state still provides the necessary political legitimacy that policies need to be effective – they cannot be seen to be wholly imposed from outside, in the interests of transnational agencies. This is most starkly evident in the case of PPPs, that make sure to involve the state in the funding of education, if not in its provision or regulation. Yet it is here too that we see the limits of the state's willingness, and capacity, to regulate private providers and their activities in the education sector, even when in receipt of public funds. The rise of private authority poses major questions around the idea of policy as both public and contested.

In terms of the second, the wider framing of national education policies, the broader political economic context within which they are set is now clearly global, driven by agencies and global firms, such as the WB, OECD, WTO and Pearson Education, all with an agenda that favours a limited view of learning, **global standards**, testing and ranking, competition and trade. Again, this is not achieved by 'force', but by such governance technologies as PISA, and the competitive comparison it generates. Beyond this, it is useful to ask where now do we find policy contestations, and between whom? While the protests around the WTO are notable for their success in stalling the global negotiations, the agenda has simply been run at a regional or bilateral level. It is interesting here to note that the apparent contests set up by PISA themselves accept, confirm and validate the basis of the contestations. It is also important to note that while we have emphasised the 'joint' elements of their activities, the international organisations, PPPs, and so on, themselves have different understandings of and goals for national education policies. Finally, we do find major ideational and empirical shifts in what is understood by 'education'. In the end, there have been major shifts in who is taught what, by whom, why and with what outcomes in schools and universities as a result of the globalisation of education policy.

Summary

- Globalisation has changed both the forms and objectives of education policy, and the conceptual means through which they have to be approached.
- Globalisation does not mean that national states no longer make education policy, but it does limit and shape their options.
- The main actors in these processes are major international organisations, such as the OECD and WB, whose main business is promoting the global economy.
- These organisations rarely influence national education policies directly, through prescription, but operate indirectly, by influencing their overall goals and governance.
- Education systems have become part of the global trading system.
- There is an overall trend in the direction of greater private sector involvement in education, as exemplified though the increasing influence of PPPs.
- The dual aims of education, promoting human rights and promoting economic growth, are increasingly heavily weighted in the direction of the latter.

Questions for discussion

- The international organisations that are most successful in promoting the globalisation of education policy do not have 'education' as their main business. What can be inferred from this about the nature and purpose of global education policy?

- What range of consequences of either (1) the introduction of global targets and benchmarks for education, (2) bringing education into the global trading system or (3) the emergence of PPPs are evident 'on the ground'? Can you point to local examples?
- What are the implications of constructing education as part of trade policy rather than as public services policy?

Further activities

- There is an enormous amount of information on PISA, EFA, MDGs and GATS available on the internet. It can be searched in any number of ways, by country, by date, by educational output, that enable you to give further substance to, or to challenge, what is written in this chapter.
- Compare the accounts of PPPs in education provided by the WB with those advanced by critics such as the Special Issue: 'Achieving Education for All through public–private partnerships?' of the journal *Development in Practice*, vol 20, no 4-5, 2010.

Further reading and resources

Robertson, S., Novelli, M., Dale, R., Tikly, L., Dachi, H. and Alphonce, N. (2007) *'Globalisation, education and development: Ideas, actors and dynamics', Researching the Issues*, vol 68, no 2.

Verger, A., Novelli, M. and Altinyelken, H.K. (eds) (2012) *Global education policy and international development: New agendas, issues and policies.* London: Continuum.

Dale, R. and Robertson, S.L. (eds) (2009) *Globalisation and Europeanisation in education*, Oxford: Symposium Books.

Lauder, H., Brown, P., Dillabough J.-A. and Halsey, A.H. (2006) *Education, globalization, and social change*, London: Routledge.

Olssen, M., Codd, J. and O'Neill, A.-M. (2004) *Education policy: Globalisation, citizenship, democracy*, London: Sage Publications.

Rivzi, F. and Lingard, B. (2010) *Globalizing education policy*, London: Routledge.

Simons, M., Olssen, M. and Peters, M.A. (eds) *Re-reading education policies: A handbook studying the policy agenda of the 21st century*, Rotterdam: Sense Publications.

YouTube resources: 'Debating privatisation in education' (www.youtube.com/watch?v=xRRA07v8hyg).

'Sponsored academies in the UK: A form of education public–private partnership' (www.youtube.com/watch?v=X8wNCMTisc0).

'Education in a globalised world (www.youtube.com/watch?v=ATWbef5ydml).

Notes
[1] See www.uis.unesco.org/Education/.../lmtf-rpt1-toward-univrsl-learning.pdf

References

Ball, S.J. (2007) *Education plc: Understanding private sector participation in public sector education*, New York: Routledge.

Ball, S.J. (2009) 'Privatising education, privatizing education policy, privatizing educational research: network governance and the "competition state"', *Journal of Education Policy*, vol 24, no 1, pp 83-99.

Ball, S.J. (2012) *Global education Inc*, London and New York: Routledge.

Barrera-Osorio, F., Guaqueta, J. and Patrinos, H. (2012) 'The role and impact of public–private partnerships in education', in S. Robertson, K. Mundy, A. Verger and F. Menashy (eds) *Public–private partnerships in education: New actors and modes of governance*, Cheltenham: Edward Elgar, pp 201-16.

Breakspear, S. (2012) *The policy impact of PISA: An exploration of the normative effects of international benchmarking in school system performance*, OECD Education Working Papers, No 71, Paris: OECD Publishing.

Brighouse, H. and Swift, A. (2006) 'Equality, priority and positional goods', *Ethics*, vol 116, pp 471-97.

Bull, B. (2010) 'Public–private partnerships: the United Nations experience', in G. Hodge, C. Greve and A. Boardman (eds) *International handbook on public–private partnerships*, Cheltenham: Edward Elgar, pp 479-95.

Bull, B. and McNeill, D. (2007) *Development issues in global governance, public–private partnerships and market multilateralism*, London and New York: Routledge.

Cammack, P. (2006) 'UN imperialism; unleashing entrepreneurship in the developing world', in C. Moors (ed) *The new imperialists: Ideologies of Empire*, London: Oneworld Publications, pp 179-92.

Carvalho, M. (2012) 'The fabrications and travels of a knowledge-policy instrument', *European Education Research Journal*, vol 11, no 2, pp 172-88.

Chabbott, C (1998) 'Constructing educational consensus: international development professionals and the World Conference on Education for All', *International Journal of Educational Development*, vol 18, no 3, pp 207-18.

Cutler, A.C., Hauflter, V. and Porter, T. (1999) *Private authority and international affairs*, New York: State University of New York Press.

Dunning, J. (2006) 'Towards a new paradigm of development: Implications for the determinants of international business', *Transnational Corporations*, vol 15,no 1, pp 173-227.

Greve, C. (2010) 'The global public–private partnership industry', in G. Hodge, C. Greve and A. Boardman (eds) *International handbook on public–private partnerships*, Cheltenham: Edward Elgar, pp 499-509.

Harma, J. and Rose, P. (2012) 'Is low-fee primary education affordable for the poor? Evidence from rural India', in S. Robertson, K. Mundy, A. Verger and F. Menashy (eds) *Public–private partnerships in education: New actors and modes of governance*, Cheltenham: Edward Elgar, pp 243-58.

Harvey, D. (2005) *A brief history of neoliberalism*, Oxford: Oxford University Press.

Hentschke, G., Lechuga, V. and Tierney, W. (eds) (2010) *For-profit colleges and universities*, Sterling, VA: Stylus.

Hodge, G., Greve, C. and Boardman, A. (2010) 'Introduction: the PPP phenomenon and its evaluation', in G. Hodge, C. Greve and A. Boardman (eds) *International handbook on public–private partnerships*, Cheltenham: Edward Elgar, pp 3-16.

Hood, C. (1991) 'A public management for all seasons?', *Public Administration*, vol 69, pp 3-19.

Hopmann, S. (2008) 'No child, no school, no state left behind: schooling in the age of accountability', *Journal of Curriculum Studies*, vol 40, no 4, pp 417-56.

IFC (International Finance Corporation) (2001) *Handbook on PPPs and education*, Washington, DC: IFC.

Jones, P. (1992) *World Bank financing of education*, London: Routledge.

Kelsey, J. (2008) *Serving whose interests? The political economy of Trade in Services Agreements*, London and New York: Routledge.

Kirkemann, P. and Appelquist, M.-L. (2008) *Evaluation study: Public–private partnership programme*, Nordic Consulting Company, Taastrup.

Klees, S.J. (2010) 'Aid, development, and education', *Current Issues in Comparative Education, vol 13, no 1, pp 7-27.*

Klees, S.J. (2012) 'UNESCO vs World Bank: The struggle over leadership in education', in L.C. Engel and D. Rutkowski (eds) *UNESCO without US funding? Implications for education*, Bloomington, IN: Worldwide Center for Evaluation and Education Policy, Indiana University (http://ceep.indiana.edu/projects/PDF/SP_UNESCO.pdf).

Leventhal, M. and Tang, I. (2013) *Mapping private equity firms in education* (http://equityforeducation.wordpress.com).

Lubienski, C. (2013) 'Privatising form or function? Equity, outcomes and influence', *Oxford Review of Education*, vol 39, no 4, pp 498-513.

McGrath, S. (2010) 'The role of education in development: an educationalist's response to some recent work in development economics', *Comparative Education*, vol 46, no 2, pp 237-53.

Martens, K. (2007) 'How to become an influential actor – the "comparative turn" in OECD education policy', in K. Martens, A. Rusconi and K. Leuze (eds) *New arenas of education governance – The impact of international organisations and markets on education policy making,* Houndmills: Palgrave Macmillan, pp 40-56.

Martens, K. and Niemann, D. (2010) *Governance by comparison – How ratings and rankings impact national policy-making in education,* TranState Working Papers No 139, Bremen: University of Bremen.

Meyer, H.-D. and Benavot, A. (eds) (2012) *PISA, power, and policy: the emergence of global educational governance,* Oxford: Symposium.

Mundy, K. (2002) 'Retrospect and Prospect: Education in a reforming World Bank', *International Journal of Educational Development,* vol 22, no 5, pp 483-508.

Mundy, K. (2007a) 'EFA and the new development compact', *International Review of Education,* vol 52, no 1, pp 23-48.

Mundy, K. (2007b) 'Contribution to moderated discussion', *Comparative Education Review,* vol 51, no 2, pp 237-8.

Mundy, K. and Menashy, F. (2012) 'The role of the International Finance Corporation in the promotion of public private partnerships for education development', in S. Robertson, K. Mundy, A. Verger and F. Menashy (eds) *Public–private partnerships in education: New actors and modes of governance,* Cheltenham: Edward Elgar, pp 81-103.

OECD (Organisation for Economic Co-operation and Development) (2006) *The Program for International Student Assessment* (www.oecd.org/pisa/pisaproducts/pisa2006/39725224.pdf).

Patrinos, H., Barrera-Osorio, F. and Guaqueta, J. (2009) *The role and impact of public–private partnerships in education,* Washington, DC: The World Bank.

Pigozzi, M.J. (2007) 'Moderated discussion', *Comparative Education Review,* vol 51, no 2, pp 240-2.

Reserve Bank of Australia (2008) 'Australia's exports of education services' (www.rba.gov.au/publications/bulletin/2008/jun/2.html).

Robertson, S. (2012) 'The strange non-death of neoliberal privatisation in the World Bank's education strategy 2020', in S. Klees, J. Samoff and N. Stromquist (eds) *The World Bank and education: Critiques and alternatives,* Rotterdam: Sense Publishers, pp 189-208.

Robertson, S. and Keeling, R. (2008) 'Stirring the Lions; strategy and tactics in global higher education', **Globalisation, Societies and Education**, vol 6, no 3, pp 221-40.

Robertson, S., Bonal, X. and Dale, R. (2002) 'GATS and the education service industry: the politics of scale and global reterritorialization', *Comparative Education Review,* vol 46, no 4, pp 472-96.

Rostow, W.W. (1960) *The stages of economic growth: A non-Communist manifesto,* Cambridge: Cambridge University Press.

Schultz, T.W. (1971) *Investment in human capital: The role of education and of research,* New York: Free Press.

Scott, J. (2013) 'A Rosa Parks moment? School choice and the marketization of civil rights', *Critical Studies in Education*, vol 54, no 1, pp 5-18.

Scott, J. and DiMartino, C. (2009) 'Public education under new management: a typology of educational privatization applied to New York City's restructuring', *Peabody Journal of Education*, vol 84, no 4, pp 432-52.

Steiner-Khamsi, G. (2004) *The global politics of educational borrowing and lending*, New York: Teachers College Press.

Tomasevski, K. (2005) 'Globalizing what? Education as a human right or as a traded service', *Indiana Journal of Global Legal Studies*, vol 12, no 1, pp 1-78.

Tooley, J. (2013) 'Challenging education injustice: "grassroots" privatisation in South Asia and sub-Saharan Africa', *Oxford Review of Education* (http://dx.doi.org/10.1080/03054985.2013.820466).

UNESCO (United Nations Educational, Scientific and Cultural Organisation) (2007) *General Conference, 34th; Medium-term strategy, 2008-2013*, Paris: UNESCO.

UNESCO (2012) *Education for all global nonitoring report youth and skills: Putting education to work*, Paris: UNESCO.

Verger, A. (2012) 'Framing and selling global education policy: The promotion of public–private partnerships for education in low-income contexts', *Journal of Education Policy*, vol 27, no 1, pp 109-30.

WB (The World Bank) (2001) *Handbook on public–private partnerships*, Washington, DC: WB.

Welch, A. (2002) 'Internationalizing Australian universities', *Comparative Education Review*, vol 46, no 4, pp 433-71.

Williamson, J. (1993) 'Democracy and the "Washington consensus"', *World Development*, vol 21, no 8, pp 1329-36.

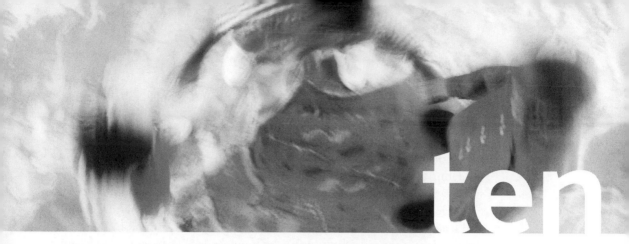

Global criminal justice

John Muncie

Overview

This chapter explores the nature and reach of 'global crime', international crime control and cross-jurisdiction cooperation, and the ways in which economic and political globalisation refracts through national systems. It shows that the global governance of crime and its control is multifaceted, involving many different actors, and is highly contested. Nation states continue to robustly protect their sovereignty. Tempering the emphasis on the globalisation of neoliberal penality evident in the criminological literature, ideas of penality based on social democratic notions of welfare and justice remain a significant feature of contemporary national criminal justice policy making.

Key concepts

Global crime; neoliberal penality; transnational justice; policy transfer; punitiveness; human rights; sovereign justice; social democratic penality; transnational policing

Introduction

Key arguments for a growing **transnational justice** are based primarily on developments in cross-border policing, **policy transfers**, the inauguration of the International Criminal Court (ICC) and international human rights conventions. Since the 1980s transnationalism is also assumed to have been cemented around a different and more punitive set of concerns, emanating from processes of US-inspired **neoliberal penality** and facilitated through international policy networks. However, the notion of 'global criminal justice' as a singular, completed and uncontested process is problematic. As in other areas of **global social policy**, global **governance** of crime and its control is multifaceted and highly contested, and involves diverse actors operating through spheres of national and cross-border governance. Nation states continue to robustly protect their own sovereignty, as expressed, for example, in various forms of neoliberal *and* social democratic penality and dialogues between them. Some key explanatory factors for continued differentiation appear to be correlations between levels of income inequality, welfare provision and rates of imprisonment.

This chapter argues for analysis which recognises (1) the uneven, multifaceted and heterogeneous nature of cross-border cooperation and rights compliance; (2) how the global, the international and the national are not mutually exclusive but continually interact to re-constitute, re-make and challenge each other; and (3) how the specificities of criminal justice are driven less by concerns for (global or local) crime control and more by idiosyncratic processes of political decision making.

Crime across borders

> [T]he more open our borders are, the more freely people can travel, the more freely money can move and information and technology can be transferred, the more vulnerable we are to people who would seek to undermine the very fabric of civilized life, whether through terrorism, ... weapons of mass destruction, organized crime, or drugs – and sometimes through all of the above. (President Bill Clinton, 29 April 1996, at www.fas.org/irp/offdocs/iccs/iccsviii.html)

Transnational illicit activity, say, in the form of smuggling, piracy, drug trades and slavery, is by no means new, and neither has it always been subject to criminal justice sanction. During the 1960s and 1970s the idea of transnational crime was indelibly attached to the US-led 'War on Drugs' inaugurated by President Nixon in 1971 and which in part led to the formation of the United Nations (UN) Convention Against Illicit Traffic in Narcotic Drugs and Psychotropic Substances in 1988. However, official accounts of contemporary '**global crime**' now place it firmly in the context of an assumed burgeoning of international networks of organised crime, which are far more extensive than previous or existing drug markets (Reichel, 2005). The UN Office on Drugs and Crime (UNODC, 1999) first brought sustained intergovernmental attention to the issue in its *Global report on crime and justice*. It identified transnational crime as 'a leading issue of the 1990s', involving not only the trafficking of drugs, but also of arms, children, women, immigrants, body organs, cultural artefacts, flora and fauna, nuclear materials and automobiles across national borders. In 2000 the UN Convention Against Transnational Organised Crime, together with protocols to prevent trafficking in people, the smuggling of **migrants** and illicit trafficking in firearms, established an apparent consensus that transnational crime was a paramount security issue, and encouraged states to create new domestic criminal offences (such as participation in an organised criminal group) and to adopt new frameworks for extradition, mutual legal assistance and law enforcement cooperation.

Nevertheless, 10 years later, the UNODC report on *The globalisation of crime* warned that:

> ... global governance has failed to keep pace with economic globalization. Therefore, as unprecedented openness in trade, finance, travel and communication has created economic growth and well-being, it has also given rise to massive opportunities for criminals to make their business prosper. Organized crime has diversified, gone global and reached macro-economic proportions: illicit goods are sourced from one continent, trafficked across another, and marketed in a third.... Crime is fuelling corruption, infiltrating business and politics, and hindering development. And it is undermining governance by empowering those who operate outside the law. (UNODC, 2010, p ii)

In the same report, Antonio Maria Costa, Executive Director of UNODC, identified the key concerns as:

* violent drug cartels, particularly in Central America, the Caribbean and West Africa;
* modern slavery (human trafficking), spreading in Eastern Europe as well as Southeast Asia and Latin America;
* cybercrime, threatening state infrastructure and state security;
* piracy and the holding of ships to ransom, particularly in East Africa;
* counterfeit goods undermining licit trade and endangering lives;
* money laundering corrupting the banking sector, worldwide.

A number of observations have been made about these developments:

* Traditional notions of the 'crime problem', which typically make up 'local' law and order agendas, such as burglary, theft, street violence and so on, are being tested and extended by crime that appears to originate from

overseas territories, particularly the trafficking of people and products around the world.

- The direction of trafficking is largely from the 'developing' world or states in transition to the 'developed' world. The world's biggest economies, the **G8** and the BRIC countries (Brazil, Russia, India and China), are also the biggest markets for 'global crime', which is overwhelmingly the product of market demand rather than the plotting of dedicated criminal groups (UNODC, 2010, p 18).

- Defining and locating 'global crime' is problematic because often there is no sharp separation of legitimate patterns of **migration**, internet usage and commodity exchange from criminal activities. There are significant grey areas populated by entrepreneurs who move from the licit to the illicit and back again as circumstances and opportunities dictate (UNODC, 2010, p 31).

- Such merging of the licit and illicit is not only economic but also political. Naim's (2011) report for the Global Commission on Drug Policies details the extent of involvement and complicity of some nation states and their leaders in various illegalities such as trade in illegal drugs, arms smuggling and human trafficking. He cites various government bodies, particularly in Russia, Africa, Eastern Europe and South America, as complicit in such trafficking. The collusion is such that he maintains that it is impossible to distinguish between the activities of some governments and that of organised criminal groups. The fundamental issue then becomes not one of, say, controlling markets for drugs, but of preventing 'criminals from taking over governments around the world'. In this analysis the 'real criminals' are not to be found among the impoverished and disadvantaged, but are members of political, military, business, cultural and media elites.

- The clear conclusion is that nation states' exposure to (and in some cases collusion with) organised crime has grown as economic **globalisation** has flourished. Castells (1998) warned that geopolitical change and economic shifts had facilitated the emergence of 'joined-up' globalised criminal networks and new forms of highly profitable crime. The global movement of capital and labour had created the very conditions in which cross-border criminality was made ever more possible, in turn heightening concern over the sanctity and vulnerability of the nation state.

- The perceived requirement for international cooperation and the harmonising of legal powers queries the independence of the nation state. Aas (2007, p 187) maintains that 'for a long time the power of criminalisation has been primarily vested in the nation state as a prerequisite of its sovereignty. Now however the power to put definitions of criminality on the agenda is moving to transnational and international actors.'

- The elevation of transnational crime as a key security issue worldwide has led to demands for significant international cooperation under the pretext that no one state could ever hope to deal with such problems on its own (Muncie, 2011). But the overall impression from the UN reports (introduced above) is that although governments may be responding to transnational criminal activities, they are doing too little too late (UNODC, 2010, p 18).

The sheer scale of the transformation of 'the social' implied by these readings of global crime, insecurity and crime control also calls into question criminology's traditional assumptions, rationales, ways of thinking and purpose. It has encouraged the discipline to look beyond its traditionally narrow nation-specific and legally defined contexts and concerns. While orthodox readings of (global) crime focus on the likes of drug and human trafficking and so on, another agenda is opening up about disorderly financial markets, poverty, environmental pollution, climate change and other realms of socially harmful behaviour that are potentially more serious and catastrophic than that which is strictly legally recognised either nationally or internationally as 'criminal' (Hillyard et al, 2004; Muncie et al, 2010).

The following sections discuss the different ways in which specific aspects of crime and crime control have become the subject/object of collective action by international, state and non-state organisations.

Transnational policing

The term '**transnational policing**' has been used to describe any form of policing that transcends national borders. This might involve cross-border police cooperation, 'knowledge work' and intelligence exchange between different nation states, including privatised (typically Western) police and security training for states in conflict or in transition (such as Iraq, Libya, Bahrain and Afghanistan). Although policing has transgressed national boundaries from time to time almost from its inception, particularly through the export of 'British policing' in the context of 19th-century imperialism and colonialism, it is generally agreed that transnational policing only became a regular and formalised development in the post-Cold War climate of the 1990s (Nadelmann, 1993; Sheptycki, 2000). Bowling (2009) has usefully delineated the increasing social–spatial spread of modern policing that now encompasses not only national (such as the Federal Bureau of Investigation, FBI) and sub-national levels (such as regional crime squads), but also forms of international and **multilateral** cooperation, such as:

- The International Criminal Police Organisation (commonly known as Interpol). Formed in the 1920s and now with a membership of 190 countries, its remit is to promote mutual assistance and information exchange between all police authorities while respecting and adhering to the limits of the laws existing in different countries.
- Europol was formed in 1994 with a brief to support member states of the European Union (EU) primarily in drug-related law enforcement, although it has since been extended to include the likes of illegal immigration, trafficking in stolen vehicles, money laundering and terrorism. Like Interpol, Europol officers have no powers of arrest. There is therefore no 'operational' international police officer. Their remit is devoted to collecting, analysing and disseminating intelligence among Europol signatories. It is left to national jurisdictions to act on whatever knowledge is gleaned about criminals and criminal activity. Unlike Interpol, Europol has legal recognition in European Law, and is politically accountable to the Justice and Home Affairs Council of the EU.
- In 1995, the Schengen Treaty formalised aspects of police information exchange across Europe in order to enable freedom of movement and the relaxing of border controls. The Schengen Information System allows police to access a shared database of wanted or undesirable people and stolen objects. It has been ratified by all EU member states except the UK and Ireland.
- The Amsterdam Treaty of 1999 advocated the establishment of an *area of freedom, security and justice* to ensure security, rights and free movement within the EU. As well as Europol it supports the work of Eurojust (for cooperation between prosecutors), Frontex (for cooperation between border control authorities) and the European Arrest Warrant (to facilitate extradition between EU countries). However, it also recognised the idea of *constructive abstention* whereby a member state could opt out of such security measures but without preventing other countries from going ahead.
- In 1997 UNODC was established to promote a coordinated, comprehensive international response to illicit trafficking in drugs, crime prevention and criminal justice, international terrorism and political corruption. These goals are largely pursued through training, research and guidance to governments to support and adopt relevant UN treaties and protocols.
- In order to tackle drug trafficking from Afghanistan, UNODC, together with Azerbaijan, Kazakhstan, Kyrgyzstan, Russia, Turkmenistan, Tajikistan and Uzbekistan, established the Central Asian Regional Information and Coordination Centre (CARICC) in 2006. Its aim is to facilitate information exchange and analysis, and to assist in the coordination of operational activities of the police, drug control agencies, customs, border guards and security services of the countries involved. A similar model

for the Gulf States – the Gulf Centre for Criminal Intelligence (GCCI) – for Bahrain, Kuwait, Oman, Qatar, Saudi Arabia and the United Arab Emirates – is being established in Doha, Qatar.

- The appointment of overseas police liaison officers (PLOs) who have a permanent presence in a foreign embassy or high commission is believed to have been notably expanded. Aydinli and Yon (2011) estimate that as of 2009 there were at least 54 countries deploying PLOs to 647 different sites. Their role is largely one of intelligence gathering and information management. For example, at that time the FBI has around 340 agents and support staff assigned to permanent overseas positions. The Australian Federal Police had 80 liaison officers in 27 countries, China had sent 38 PLOs to 23 countries, and the UK Serious Organised Crime Agency (SOCA) had 140 overseas PLOs in countries around the world. Other recent innovations include local police departments (such as the New York Police Department, NYPD, in New York) sending their own police officers to work in a variety of countries overseas specifically to develop counter-terrorist intelligence.

In the aftermath of the September 11, 2001 attacks in New York and Washington, police forces across the globe have developed new domestic and international counter-terrorism strategies, while international police agencies have likewise stepped up their efforts to combat terrorism. Because of the nature of the threat, many of these activities require greater international cooperation, and most significantly, it is argued, have enabled police organisations to act more *independently* of their national governments – and also of democratic control. The nature of transnational policing is also being further complicated by the role of private military companies (such as Blackwater in Iraq) in providing security for key economic facilities such as pipelines and power stations (McLaughlin, 2007).

For Loader (2002), these developments raise serious issues about police accountability and imbalances in law and order targets. Much of this activity involves networks of actors operating across national borders and lies outside of public, and in some cases political, view, and thereby outside of democratic control. The role of the CIA, for example, in a programme of extraordinary rendition and torture of terrorist suspects is perhaps the most extreme example of extra-legal activities practised by intelligence agencies seemingly operating beyond both international and national law (such practices are in clear violation of the European Convention on Human Rights and the UN Convention Against Torture). The concern is that fears about transnational crime are being deliberately fostered and exaggerated by private and public policing and surveillance agencies, either in the pursuit of profit or 'to colonize other domains of public policy and sideline/trump considerations of accountability and human rights' (Loader, 2002, p 293). Moreover the targets of transnational policing tend to be the 'usual suspects'. In particular, it is migrants, the disadvantaged and criminal syndicates (such as the Sicilian mafia) who are the usual object of its gaze rather than perpetrators of corporate financial and environmental crime (McLaughlin, 2007).

Transnational justice

The autonomy of nation states has also been queried by the growth of institutions of transnational justice, and in particular a proliferation of multilateral legal frameworks, conventions and treaties. The study of transnational justice was initially concerned with the meaning and application of international law to combat fascism and military conflict after the Second World War. The establishment of the UN and the UN Charter, which came into force in October 1945, set out basic principles of international relations based on peace, security, respect for human rights and cooperation between nations in addressing international problems. The Universal Declaration of Human Rights, adopted by the UN General Assembly in 1948, was the first statutory instrument of universal human rights.

The UN has since formulated many legally binding international human rights instruments. These treaties, and the principles and rights that they outline, have become legal obligations on those states choosing to be bound by them. Mechanisms have also been established to hold governments accountable in the event that they violate human rights. The six main human rights treaties are: the International Covenant on Civil and Political Rights; the International Covenant on Economic, Social and Cultural Rights; the Convention on the Rights of the Child; the Convention Against Torture and other Cruel, Inhuman or Degrading Treatment or Punishment; the International Convention on the Elimination of All Forms of Racial Discrimination; and the Convention on the Elimination of All Forms of Discrimination against Women. Every country in the world has ratified at least one of these, and many have ratified most of them (see www. unicef.org/crc/index_framework.html). Each has clear implications for the administration of criminal justice and crime control in the signatory states, by, for example, setting out minimum standards for the treatment and confinement of suspects and prisoners, the promotion of alternatives to imprisonment, the prohibition of torture and the abolition of capital punishment.

In 1945 the Nuremberg International Military Tribunal established new 'international offences' of crimes against peace, war crimes and crimes against humanity. In the early 1990s the mass murders witnessed in the former

Yugoslavia and in Rwanda led to the establishment of criminal tribunals to deal with these specific war crimes. In 2002 a permanent International Criminal Court (ICC) was legally established in The Hague, Netherlands. It issued its first arrest warrants in 2005. To date, all of the court's investigations have involved events in some African states, and none in the 'affluent West'. Its mandate is to prosecute *individuals* for genocide, crimes against humanity, war crimes and the crime of aggression (Pakes, 2004; Findlay, 2008; Drake et al, 2010). Its powers do not extend to the prosecution of governments or corporations. The investigation and prosecution of such crime is also supported by intergovernmental organisations such as Justice Rapid Response (JRR). First operationalised in 2009, this is a 'stand-by' body of criminal justice and human rights professionals who can be called on by nation states and international or regional organisations, and 'rapidly deployed' to investigate and analyse situations where international criminal law and human rights violations have been reported. A sub-section is trained to deal with sexual and gender-based violence in particular. To date, 69 states have participated in JRR activities and JRR has responded to 16 requests for 'expertise', including UN inquiries into war crimes and crimes against humanity, in Libya, Guinea, the Ivory Coast and Syria (see www. justicerapidresponse.org).

It is important to recognise, however, that states continue to have the primary duty to exercise their criminal jurisdiction over those responsible for international crimes. **State sovereignty** remains a determining international frame of reference. The ICC only acts as a last resort in cases in which national criminal law systems are unwilling or unable to carry out the investigation or prosecution. Moreover, the jurisdiction of the ICC is not recognised by numerous countries, including China, Israel and the US.

Supranational political structures, such as the EU or the UN, are, as we have seen, playing a significant role in 'shaping the environment within which policing and law enforcement takes place', while bodies such as the UNODC and the ICC are 'shaping ideas and practice in the delivery of criminal justice' (Bowling, 2009, p 152). However, the motives for such transnational activity are not always clear and not necessarily always inspired by crime control. Andreas and Nadelmann (2007, p 250) suggest that they may reflect more the ambition of powerful countries to export particular moral and ethical norms from one part of the world to another:

> Substantially driven by the interest and moralizing impulses of major Western powers, a loosely institutionalised and coordinated international crime control system based on the homogenization of criminal law norms and regularization of law enforcement relations is emerging and promises to be an

increasingly prominent dimension of global governance in the twenty first century.

Policy travel

The travel of criminal justice policy around the world has also been considered a crucial dimension and indicator of transnationalism. Indeed, some nation states appear increasingly seduced in looking worldwide in efforts to discover 'what works' in preventing crime and to reduce reoffending, readily believing that what might 'work' in other jurisdictions will inevitably 'work' back home. The development of trans-global communication networks has accelerated such processes of exchange (Baker and Roberts, 2005). In its most deterministic reading, the idea of cross-border policy transfer in the context of criminal justice implies the wholesale movement of various crime control strategies that have been developed in one jurisdiction and then imported and adopted by others. Of note has been a worldwide diffusion of the rhetoric, principles and practices of 'zero tolerance' (see below).

However, the possibility of a specific form of convergence around Anglo-American notions and practices of criminal justice tends to dominate the criminological literature on policy transfer (Jones and Newburn, 2007). In particular, Nadelmann (1993, pp 469-70) is convinced that the US has played the dominant role in a harmonisation of national criminal justice policy and practice:

> ... foreign governments have responded to US pressures, inducements and examples by enacting new criminal laws.. Foreign police have adopted US investigative techniques and foreign courts and legislatures have followed up with the requisite legal authorisations.... By and large the United States has provided the models and other governments have done the accommodating.

This vision appears particularly pertinent in accounting for major reforms in the UK since the mid-1990s. Zero tolerance policing, night curfews, electronic tagging, mandatory minimum sentences, drugs czars, the naming and shaming of young offenders, community courts, private prisons, Chicago-style policing based on neighbourhood focus groups, strict controls over parents, sex offender registration, elected police and crime commissioners and, for a short period in the 1990s, boot camps, have, in some form, either practically or symbolically, held a presence in parts of the UK, having all originated in the US.

A straightforward reading of such developments might be that it is only 'natural' for nation states to look worldwide in efforts to discover 'what works'. But it is also clear that particular lines and directions of transfer involve political choice and strategic decision making that are, moreover, not clearly informed by evidence as to what works. In the UK, for example, the incoming Labour government of 1997 shifted its ideological and policy attention away from Western Europe and towards the US. From this Garland (2001) is able to trace the emergence of a similar 'culture of control' in both countries. Wacquant (1999) notes how law and order talk directed at 'youth', 'problem neighbourhoods', 'incivilities' and 'urban violence' came to increasingly dominate the political and media landscape of the US in the 1990s. Neoconservative think tanks (such as the Manhattan Institute), foundations, policy entrepreneurs and commercial enterprises began to valorise the diminution of the social or the welfare state (in the name of neoliberal economic competitiveness) and the expansion of a penal or punitive state (in order to deal with the economically excluded) (Wacquant, 1999, pp 322, 333). This 'talk' eventually entered European public debate (through the conduit of the UK and through such think tanks as the Institute of Economic Affairs), and began to provide the framework for any broader political discussions of justice, safety, community, and so on.

Such argument suggests that there is some remarkable transnational criminal justice policy travel, but it is also clear that it occurs on several dimensions and proceeds in various directions (Jones and Newburn, 2007). The transfer of policy is not one-directional or one-dimensional. In a relativist version of the policy transfer thesis it is acknowledged that transfer will always be subject to 'local' conditions and is more likely to be 'translated' than adopted wholesale. Here the sensitising concepts are those of policy networks, 'flows' and divergence, rather than those of a hegemonic jurisdiction, 'transfers' and convergence.

The case of zero tolerance policing seems to substantiate such a view. Zero tolerance has attracted worldwide attention following its introduction in New York in the early 1990s. Valorised by New York's Mayor Rudi Giuliani and Police Commissioner Bill Bratton, it was widely claimed to have been the root cause of a significant reduction in New York City's crime rate. The idea of zero tolerance policing is based on a combination of assertive policing of minor offences (with the assumption that more serious crime will then be curtailed), and pressure on police districts to improve clear-up rates as measured by real-time statistical data afforded by new computer systems such as COMPSTAT. It was embraced not just by politicians keen to be associated with a quick and effective crime 'fix', but also by leading criminologists. New York attracted legions of overseas police visitors, particularly from Latin America and Europe, keen to learn how the 'New York miracle' could be emulated in their own countries. However, attempts at transfer have been far from successful. In the UK and the Netherlands, for example, initial enthusiasm was soon blunted by the realisation that such an aggressive policing style and management was counter and detrimental to existing policing strategies and cultures (Punch, 2007). Doubts were also made on its success given that crime rates in other US cities were also falling at the same time but without the introduction of zero tolerance policing. Such realisation led Jones and Newburn (2007) to conclude that the simple, deliberate transfer of complete policies, laws and practices from one jurisdiction to another is close to unachievable. The effects and outcomes vary greatly according to jurisdiction and also to the local circumstances in which they are applied. Differences in legislative frameworks and institutional architecture inhibit direct transplantation of policies, and deeply embedded differences of history, tradition and culture may prevent even partial replication.

Neoliberal penality

The concept of the 'neoliberal' has become a defining principle of much criminological study of globalisation and comparative criminal justice in the UK. In some contrast to the reactive and often descriptive accounts of purposeful transnational cooperation, neoliberal visions of a globalising world imply (particularly in their 'strong' version) that 'uncontrollable' economic forces have moved power and authority away from nation states and deposited it in the hands of 'external' multinational capital and finance. Shifts in political economy, particularly those associated with international trade and capital mobility, it is argued, have severely constrained the range of political strategies and policy options that individual states can pursue (Bauman, 1998; McGrew and Held, 2002; Beck, 2006). The need to attract international capital has compelled governments to adopt similar economic, social, welfare *and* criminal justice policies. This has generally involved a drawing back of commitments to social welfare. Unregulated free market economics have become established as sacrosanct 'natural order'. Neoliberalism, according to Wacquant (2009b, pp 306-7), is a 'transnational political project aiming to remake the nexus of market, state, and citizenship from above.' It is carried out by a 'new global ruling class in the making', spanning the heads and senior executives of transnational firms, high-ranking politicians and top officials of multinational organisations such as the **International Monetary Fund** (IMF) and The World Bank (WB).

For Castells (2008, p 82), the institutions of national governance are ill equipped to deal with such global developments. They are beset by crises of *efficiency* (major social problems such as global warming, financial collapse and terrorism are beyond nation state control), *legitimacy* (collapse in public faith in national politics), *identity* (state citizenship is subordinated to other community and religious affiliations) and *equity* (economic competition undermines redistributive welfarism and exacerbates inequalities within and between **populations**). Significantly the penal realm has expanded to monitor, control and punish increasing numbers in the population who have been rendered 'out of place' or 'undesirable'.

Wacquant (2008, 2009a) views increasing **punitiveness** not simply as a consequence, but as an integral part of the neoliberal state. His account of the 'punitive upsurge' notes six prominent features of the coming together of neoliberalism as a political project and the deployment of a proactive punitive penality. First, punitiveness is legitimated through a discourse of 'putting an end to leniency' by not only targeting crime, but also all manner of disorders and nuisances through a remit of zero tolerance. Second, there has been a proliferation of laws, surveillance strategies and technological quick-fixes – from watch groups and partnerships to satellite tracking – that have significantly extended the reach of control agencies. Third, the necessity of this 'punitive turn' is conveyed everywhere by an alarmist, catastrophist discourse on 'insecurity' and 'perpetual risk'. Fourth, declining working-class neighbourhoods have become perpetually stigmatised targets for intervention (particularly their minority ethnic, youth and immigrant populations). Fifth, any residual philosophy of 'rehabilitation' has been more or less supplanted by a managerialist approach centred on the cost-driven administration of carceral stocks and flows, paving the way for the privatisation of correctional services. And sixth, the implementation of these new punitive policies has invariably resulted in an extension of police powers, a hardening and speeding up of judicial procedures, and ultimately, an increase in the prison population (Wacquant, 2008, pp 10-11).

In this regard the epitome of contemporary neoliberal penality is widely assumed to be the US. Indeed, Wacquant has maintained that the US has been 'the theoretical and practical motor for the elaboration and *planetary* dissemination of a political project that aims to subordinate all human activities to the tutelage of the market' (2008, p 20; emphasis added). The US, however, also seems to epitomise the defence of nation state sovereignty, through its opposition to the authority of international courts and human rights conventions. The US refuses to recognise the legitimacy of the ICC. It is one of a diminishing number of countries that retains the death penalty, and remains the most incarcerating nation state in the world (see ***Table 10.1***). American punitiveness also appears the subject of an unprecedented political consensus where the once exceptional now appears commonplace (or at least US administrations rarely seem to regard their penality as 'abnormal'). However, as is now well established (at least in criminological academia), punitiveness and 'carceral hyperinflation' have little to do with any change in crime rates and rather more to do with highly politicised shifts in sentencing policy and practice, such as the introduction of mandatory sentencing, 'truth in sentencing' and 'three strikes and you're out' laws (Blumstein and Beck, 1999). Neoliberal penality has, far from weakening the state, involved a strengthening of the state (to enforce a social and moral order conducive to global capital accumulation; see Muncie, 2011).

Table 10.1: Comparing world prison populations (selected countries)

Country	Total 2011/12	Rate per 100,000 population	Increase/ decrease in rate since 1999
USA	2,266,832	730	+85
Russia	722,200	505	−180
South Africa	157,375	310	−10
New Zealand	8,433	190	+45
England and Wales	86,708	154	+29
Scotland	8,146	154	+34
Australia	29,106	129	+34
China	1,640,000	121	+6
Canada	39,099	117	+2
Italy	66,009	108	+23
France	67,373	102	+12
Netherlands	14,488	87	+2
Germany	67,671	83	−7
Norway	3,602	73	+18
Sweden	6,669	70	+10
Finland	3,189	59	+4
Japan	69,876	55	+15

Sources: International Centre for Prison Studies, 'World prison brief' (www.prisonstudies.org/info/worldbrief); Walmsley (1999)

Questions also remain of how far this vision and experience of neoliberal penality resonates beyond the rich industrialised Western countries of North America and Western Europe. Criminological research has, like many disciplines, remained blind to experiences outside the countries of the 'core'. Newburn (2010), for example, maintains that the parameters of neoliberal penality are highly differentiated and will always be shaped, translated and reworked through local cultures, histories and politics. There appears to be discrete and distinctive ways, for example, in which neoliberal modes of governance find expression in conservative and social democratic *rationalities* and in authoritarian, retributive, human rights, or restorative *technologies*. The neoliberal penality thesis then risks imposing a framework shaped by one part of the world onto others to which it does not readily apply, either partially or fully (Cheliotis and Xenakis, 2010; Lacey, 2012).

Social democratic penality

Wacquant (2009a, pp 172-3) acknowledges that while processes of diffusion and policy transfer are evident globally, 'neoliberalism is from its inception a multi-sited, polycentric, and geographically uneven formation.' In other words, there are sites of resistance where 'neoliberalism has been thwarted ... and the push towards penalization has been blunted or diverted.'

Cavadino and Dignan (2006) have attempted to shed some light on the prevalence of international divergence by relating criminal justice differentiation to *differing* political economies. They classified these as the 'neoliberal', (such as the US, South Africa, England and Wales), conservative corporatist (such as Germany, Italy, France and the Netherlands), social democratic corporatist (such as Sweden and Finland) and oriental corporatist (such as Japan). Such a typology (see ***Table 10.2***) clearly suggests that societies that may share a broadly similar social and economic organisation will 'also tend to resemble one another in terms of their penality' (Cavadino and Dignan, 2006, p 14). In short, those dependent on the 'free' market and a residualist welfare state will have extreme income differentials, a tendency

Table 10.2: Political economies and penal tendencies

Regime types			
Neoliberalism	Conservative corporatism	Social democratic corporatism	Oriental corporatism
Free market, minimalist or residual welfare state	Status-related, moderately generous welfare state	Universalistic, generous welfare state	Private sector-based welfare corporatism, bureaucratic, paternalistic
Individualised, atomised, limited social rights	Conditional and moderate social rights	Relatively unconditional and generous social rights	Quasi-feudal corporatism, strong sense of duty
Right-wing politics	Centrist	Left-wing	Centre-right
Law and order penal ideology	Rehabilitation	Rights-based	Apology-based restoration and rehabilitation
High imprisonment rate	Medium	Low	Low
Examples: US, England and Wales, Australia, New Zealand, South Africa	Germany, France, Italy, Netherlands	Sweden, Finland	Japan

Source: Adapted and abbreviated from Cavadino and Dignan (2006, p 15)

towards social exclusion, and consequently, high rates of imprisonment. Other advanced capitalist societies that have preserved a more generous welfare state will be more egalitarian and inclusionary, leading to relatively lower imprisonment rates.

O'Malley (2002) also considers that the anti-welfare neoliberalism of the US has little in common with other neoliberal countries such as Canada, New Zealand, Australia, and most of Western Europe, where welfare apparatus are substantially more intact, even if 'translated' into forms more compatible with market competitiveness. Critics of the 'inevitable' hegemony of US-inspired neoliberal punitiveness would, for example, point out countervailing 'restorative' tendencies at work in numerous criminal justice – particularly juvenile justice – systems across the world. In part this is expressed in various forms of family group conferencing in New Zealand and Australia, in healing circles in Canada and in Truth and Reconciliation community peace committees in South Africa. In 2002 the UN's Economic and Social Council urged all states to adopt the universal principles of restorative justice, including non-coercive offender and victim participation, confidentiality and procedural safeguards. There is also an increasingly important role being developed by the UN and the Council of Europe in harmonising policy in accord with the principles of human rights rather than populist punitiveness (Muncie, 2005). For example, the mandate of the Council of Europe's Directorate for Human Rights includes the prevention of torture and inhuman or degrading treatment or punishment; promotion of gender equality; safeguarding individuals against threats to their dignity and integrity; the protection of children's rights; bioethics; and the protection of freedom of expression and of information (see www.coe.int/t/dgi/mandat_en.asp). Economic neoliberalism, it seems, does not necessarily involve the simultaneous development of a proactive and repressive penal apparatus.

It is in these contexts that we must also acknowledge a persistent international social democratic penality, albeit contested and differentially expressed. In contrast to neoliberalism, this is based around the principle of universalism in welfare provision, rather than withdrawal or selective targeting, promotes rehabilitative and inclusionary interventions, rather than exclusionary and retributive punishment, prioritises the re-educative and reintegrative purposes of imprisonment and affords a centrality to the goals of social justice rather than criminal justice. With its roots in the late 19th century, social democratic forms of penality were, by 1970, the established policy framework for criminal justice in most Western nations (Garland, 2001). For some, they remain so.

The Scandinavian countries, for example, have long seemed to stand out as pinnacles of low incarceration and social democratic criminal justice.

Spending on social services, taxation, governmental legitimacy and trust are high, while imprisonment rates and income inequality are low. Criminal justice debates are less politicised than is common in other countries such as the US and the UK (Lappi-Seppälä and Tonry, 2011). The conditions of Scandinavian low imprisonment appear driven not simply by traditions of social democratic welfare state security, but by a reluctance to over-politicise and over-sensationalise issues of crime in political, media and public discourse. This has been made possible by the development of strong state bureaucracies with significant independence and protection from political and market interference.

Such diversity has also been explained with reference to income differentials and levels of social inequality. The more stratified a society, the more likely the resort to imprisonment. Wilkinson and Pickett (2007, 2009) suggest that more unequal societies are 'socially dysfunctional' in many different ways. It is striking that a group of more egalitarian countries (usually including Japan, Sweden and Norway) perform well on a variety of outcomes (including resort to imprisonment), while more unequal countries (including the US, Singapore and the UK) tend to have poorer outcomes (see *Figure 10.1*). Tonry concludes that: 'moderate penal policies and low imprisonment rates are associated with low levels of income inequality, high levels of trust and legitimacy, strong welfare states, professionalized as opposed to politicized criminal justice systems and consensual rather than conflictual political cultures' (Tonry, 2009, p 381).

Although there are clear dangers with rigidly accepting a neoliberal/social democracy dichotomy without acknowledging their coexistence and correspondence, some of the core principles of social democracy – not least a commitment to uphold universal human rights – clearly continue to inform some aspects of criminal justice policy and practice. For Brown (2013), it is such issues which might be more profitably scrutinised through a re-examination of their durability and persistence rather than assuming their inevitable decline or eclipse by the logics of neoliberalism. We should also remain mindful, however, that routes to social democratic welfarism do not always necessarily bring with them greater tolerance and leniency. Welfarism can also be a particularly insidious, penetrating and unaccountable form of social control (Cohen, 1985).

Conclusion

The landscape of criminal justice has become more complex and challenging through the identification of 'crime across borders' and the efforts of nation states to collaborate (largely to combat trafficking in all of its forms) and in the formation of new transnational agencies such as the UNODC (largely

Figure 10.1: The relationship between income inequality and prison rates

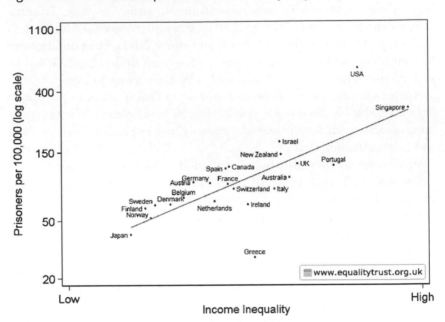

Source: www.equalitytrust.org.uk/why/evidence/imprisonment

to assist states in crime and terrorism prevention) and the ICC (largely to prosecute war crime and crimes against humanity). These intergovernmental initiatives promote new conventions, frameworks, guidelines and legislative actions, although the principal institutions of criminal justice remain grounded in nation states. In many respects it is clear that the specificities of criminal justice continue to operate within differing national frames of penality and in ways that are specific to local conditions and cultural contexts and reflective of the goals of particular policy makers and political agendas.

Not only is the impact and effect of intergovernmental crime control initiatives contingent on locality, neither are they uniform or consistent. Indeed, we may identify something of a 'clash of globalisations'. For example, neoliberal penality may speak of the import, largely US-inspired, of conceptions of the free market and community responsibilisation backed by an authoritarian state. On the other hand, social democratic penality, seemingly more favoured by the UN and EU, unveils a contrary vision of universal human rights delivered through more egalitarian societies and welfare systems (Muncie, 2005; Snacken, 2010). However, even in the latter, adherence to international directives is far from being fully realised. State ratification of human rights directives may for some simply operate as a means to signal membership of the 'international community' and without cost, given that there are few mechanisms to enforce compliance. For others the goal is to be accepted into world monetary systems or, in the case of 'peripheral' European countries, entry into the EU. According to Hathaway (2002), human rights stand out as an area of international law in which countries have little incentive to police non-compliance. Adoption of treaties by individual countries appears 'more likely to offset pressure for change in human rights practices than to augment it.' (Hathaway, 2002, p 2025). Human rights, it seems, can be compromised in the interests of 'national security', 'political stability' or 'financial prosperity' (Muncie, 2011).

The precise meaning of 'global criminal justice' then remains unclear. At one and the same time it conjures up *positive* images of enhanced law enforcement and an international commitment to take human rights seriously, or conversely *negative* images of events being out of national control and a perpetually disorderly world that requires ever more draconian forms of population and social control. A focus on the mechanisms and agencies of transnational crime control also risks losing sight of the continuing importance of the nation state and significant instances of 'de-globalisation', as some nation states militarise their borders, regulate and criminalise migration, retreat to the 'surety' of the familiar and resort to protectionist and parochial nationalism. It is also far from clear – despite claims for either US or UN hegemony – what justice on a world scale might actually mean, what standards it might adopt and through which agencies (or particular nation states) it might be put into operation.

Criminological study of 'global criminal justice' remains underdeveloped and has, notably, tended to proceed from, and been dominated by, Western analytical frames. For much that is claimed to be 'global', we might instead classify as Americanisation or Europeanisation. An inability to 'recognise' non-Western sites is pervasive (Muncie, 2011). The absence of any sustained analysis of the relevance of, or effects of, transnational criminal justice on the likes of China and India is notable, and given the likely future position of these countries on the world stage, a serious failing of anything that pertains to be a 'global criminology'. The desire to identify the parameters of a 'global criminal justice' might itself be rightly considered as peculiarly ethnocentric: an aspiration (or obsession) that still remains of most relevance only to the most powerful of Western (and Anglophone) nations.

Summary

• It is essential to distinguish between processes of transnationalisation and globalisation. While both are ill defined and often used interchangeably, globalisation suggests something of an emergent world order; transnationalism refers more obliquely to processes of international exchange and mutual cooperation. Neither should be read as necessarily implying homogeneity in criminal justice, either now or in the future.

- Criminal justice continues to be a powerful icon of sovereign statehood and remains a significant vestige of state power that may in other spheres of social and economic policy (for example, fiscal independence) be said to have been eroded (or indeed approaching imminent collapse). The state remains a key actor in resolving insecurities and uncertainties said to be brought about by (economic) globalisation. This is typically achieved by prioritising its role as provider of public safety in order to convince overseas corporations that any given country is a 'safe place' in which to do business.

- It is widely claimed that attempts to reassert sovereign autonomy, particularly since the 1980s and in deference to the neoliberal market economy, have been expressed in largely 'get tough' punitive terms. However, this thesis is expressed differently at different times and in different cultures and societies, and in some societies does not seem to apply at all.

- Global criminal justice, as a political practice, needs to be understood as a series of specific and contingent *relations*: its manifestation and effects are rarely uniform. It can take on various forms, both neoliberal and social democratic. It is also something 'on the move': an ongoing, uneven and negotiated *process* in a continual state of being realised and/or of being reversed, rather than one that is completed.

- Questions for future study in this area include: what are the different policy discourses and practices of crime control and criminal justice that are promulgated by transnational actors and circulated within spheres of cross-border governance? How do these influence the domestic politics of crime control and criminal justice policy making? And how would attention to the experiences of countries outside North America and Europe alter current understandings of the scope, experiences and significance of global criminal justice policy as a subject of study and research and as a political practice?

Questions for discussion

- Should crime and criminal justice be considered more 'globalised' now than previously? Why?
- Is the spread of neoliberal penality the *most* significant feature of globalised criminal justice?
- Can international human rights conventions create a global framework for criminal justice policy? What obstacles do you think might lie in its path?

Further reading and resources

David Nelken's (1997) article, 'The globalisation of crime and criminal justice' in *Current Legal Problems*, vol 50, pp 251-77, was among the first to explore this field. His edited volume, *Comparative criminal justice and globalisation* (2011), provides a detailed and critical expose of the myriad issues in comparing crime and criminal justice across different cultures in the context of globalisation.

Accessible introductions to this area can be found in the student-oriented texts *Globalisation and crime*, by Katja Franko Aas (2007, 2nd edition 2013) and *Criminal justice: Local and global* edited by Deb Drake, John Muncie and Louise Westmarland (2010).

United Nations' site for its human rights initiatives: www.un.org/en/rights

United Nations' site for improving recognition of children's rights in particular: www. unicef-irc.org

International Centre for Prison Studies, which provides the most comprehensive and up-to-date prison statistics from around the world: www.prisonstudies.org/info/ worldbrief

United Nations Office on Drugs and Crime (UNODC), based in Vienna: www.unodc.org

Amnesty (www.amnesty.org.uk) and Human Rights Watch (www.hrw.org) are two of the most influential non-governmental organisations concerned with protecting civil liberties and human rights worldwide.

References

Aas, K.F. (2007) *Globalisation and crime*, London: Sage Publications.

Andreas, P. and Nadelmann, E. (2007) *Policing the globe: Criminalization and crime control in international relations*, Oxford: Oxford University Press.

Aydinli, E. and Yon, H. (2011) 'Transgovernmentalism meets security: police liaison officers, terrorism and statist transnationalism', *Governance*, vol 24, no 1, pp 55-84.

Baker, E. and Roberts, J. (2005) 'Globalisation and the new punitiveness', in J. Pratt, D. Brown, M. Brown, S. Hallsworth and W. Morrison (eds) *The new punitiveness*, Cullompton: Willan, pp 121-38.

Bauman, Z. (1998) *Globalisation: The human consequences*, Cambridge: Polity.

Beck, U. (2006) *Power in the global age*, Cambridge: Polity.

Blumstein, A. and Beck, A.J. (1999) 'Population growth in US prisons, 1980-1996', in M. Tonry and J. Petersilia (eds) *Prisons: Crime and justice – A review of research*, vol 26, Chicago, IL: University of Chicago Press, pp 17-61.

Bowling, B. (2009) 'Transnational policing: the globalisation thesis, a typology and a research agenda', *Policing*, vol 3, no 2, pp 149-60.

Brown, D. (2013) 'Prison rates, social democracy, neoliberalism and justice reinvestment', in K. Carrington et al (eds) *Crime, justice and social democracy*, London: Palgrave Macmillan.

Castells, M. (1998) *End of millennium*, Oxford: Blackwell.

Castells, M. (2008) 'The new public sphere: the global civil society, communication networks and global governance', *The ANNALS of the American Academy of Political and Social Science*, vol 616, pp 78-93.

Cavadino, M. and Dignan, J. (2006) *Penal systems: A comparative approach*, London: Sage Publications.

Cheliotis, L. and Xenakis, S. (2010) 'What's neoliberalism got to do with it? Towards a political economy of punishment in Greece', *Criminology and criminal justice*, vol 10, no 4, pp 353-73.

Cohen, S. (1985) *Visions of social control*, London: Polity.

Drake, D., Muncie, J. and Westmarland, L. (eds) (2010) *Criminal justice: Local and global*, Cullompton: Willan.

Findlay, M. (2008) *Governing through globalised crime*, Cullompton: Willan.

Garland, D. (2001) *The culture of control*, Oxford: Oxford University Press.

Hathaway, O. (2002) 'Do human rights treaties make a difference?', *Yale Law Journal*, vol 111, pp 1935-2042.

Hillyard, P., Pantazis, C., Tombs. S. and Gordon, D. (2004) *Beyond criminology: Taking harm seriously*, London: Pluto.

Jones, T. and Newburn, T. (2007) *Policy transfer and criminal justice: Exploring US influence over British crime control policy*, Maidenhead: Open University Press.

Lacey, N. (2012) *Punishment, (neo)liberalism and social democracy*, Max Weber Lecture Series, Florence: European University Institute.

Lappi-Seppälä, T. and Tonry, M. (2011) 'Crime, criminal justice, and criminology in the Nordic countries', *Crime and Justice*, vol 40, no 1, Crime and Justice in Scandinavia, Chicago, IL: University of Chicago Press.

Loader, I. (2002) 'Policing, securitization and democratization in Europe', *Criminology and Criminal Justice*, vol 2, no 2, pp 125-53.

McGrew, A. and Held, D. (eds) (2002) *Governing global transformations*, Cambridge: Polity Press.

McLaughlin, E. (2007) *The new policing*, London: Sage Publications.

Muncie, J. (2005) 'The globalisation of crime control: the case of youth and juvenile justice', *Theoretical Criminology*, vol 9, no 1, pp 35-64.

Muncie, J. (2011) 'On globalisation and exceptionalism', in D. Nelken (ed) *Comparative criminal justice and globalization*, Farnham: Ashgate.

Muncie, J., Talbot, D. and Walters, R. (eds) (2010) *Crime: Local and global*, Cullompton, Willan.

Nadelmann, E. (1993) *Cops across borders: The internationalization of US criminal law enforcement*, University Park, PA, Penn State University Press.

Naim, M. (2011) *The drug trade: The politicisation of criminals and the criminalization of politicians*, Working Paper, Geneva: Global Commission on Drug Policies.

Nelken, D. (ed) (2011) *Comparative criminal justice and globalization*, Farnham: Ashgate.

Newburn, T. (2010) 'Diffusion, differentiation and resistance in comparative penality', *Criminology and Criminal Justice*, vol 10, no 4, pp 341-52.

O'Malley, P. (2002) 'Globalising risk? Distinguishing styles of "neo liberal" criminal justice in Australia and the USA', *Criminology and Criminal Justice*, vol 2, no 2, pp 205-22.

Pakes, F. (2003) *Comparative criminal justice*, Cullompton: Willan.

Punch, M. (2007) *Zero tolerance policing*, Bristol: Policy Press.

Reichel, P. (ed) (2005) *Handbook of transnational crime and justice*, Thousand Oaks, CA: Sage Publications.

Sheptycki, J. (ed) (2000) *Issues in transnational policing*, London: Routledge.

Snacken, S. (2010) 'Resisting punitiveness in Europe?', *Theoretical Criminology*, vol 14, no 3, pp 273-92.

Tonry, M. (2009) 'Explanations of American punishment policies', *Punishment and Society*, vol 11, no 3, pp 377-94.

UNODC (United Nations Office on Drugs and Crime) (1999) *Global report on crime and justice*, New York, Oxford University Press.

UNODC (2010) *The Globalisation of crime*, Vienna: UNODC.

Wacquant, L. (1999) 'How penal common sense comes to Europeans: notes on the transatlantic diffusion of the neo-liberal doxa', *European Societies*, vol 1, no 3, pp 319-52.

Wacquant, L. (2008) 'Ordering insecurity: Social polarisation and the punitive upsurge', *Radical Philosophy Review*, vol 11, no 1, pp 9-27.

Wacquant, L. (2009a) *Prisons of poverty*, Minneapolis, MN: University of Minnesota Press.

Wacquant, L. (2009b) *Punishing the poor: The neoliberal government of social insecurity*, Durham, NC: Duke University Press.

Walmsley, R. (1999) *World prison population list*, Research Findings no 88, London: Home Office.

Wilkinson, R.G. and Pickett, K.E. (2007) 'The problems of relative deprivation: why some societies do better than others', *Social Science & Medicine*, vol 65, no 9, pp 1965-78.

Wilkinson, R.G. and Pickett, K.E. (2009) *The spirit level*, London: Allen Lane.

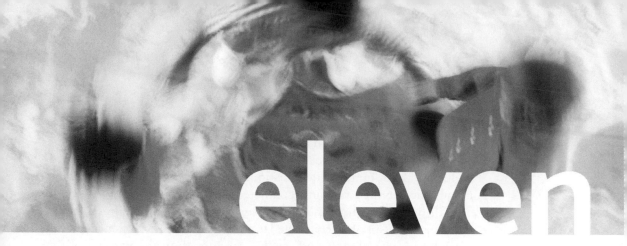

eleven

Global population policy

Anne Hendrixson, Nicholas Hildyard,
Larry Lohmann and Sarah Sexton

Overview

Population policy is one of the earliest examples of global social policy and draws on population theory dating back over 200 years. This chapter[1] outlines and explains the significance of this theory, showing how it has informed various policies and practices from the 19th century to the present day. It discusses 19th-century restrictions on welfare and famine relief; early 20th-century attempts in the US and Europe to restrict reproduction of the 'feeble-minded'; and later 20th-century attempts to limit the number of children to which poor, black or Third World women give birth. The chapter describes the rise in the 20th century of international organisations, both public and private, whose focus on overpopulation underpinned international development policies for several decades. In the 21st century, population theory continues to inform policies and debates on national security, environmental degradation and climate change, ageing and immigration, and in doing so it undermines the rights and interests of a wide variety of social groups.

Key concepts
Population control; Malthusian; neo-Malthusian; overpopulation; scarcity; eugenics; security

Introduction

Population, or **overpopulation**, has been held to be the ultimate cause of many current global social and environmental problems: deforestation, pollution, environmental degradation, poverty, hunger, climate change, urbanisation, crime, war and conflict, social instability, slow economic growth, insecurity, unemployment and **migration**. Tackling all these problems directly is often considered futile without external (often technical) measures to control, slow and stabilise the growth in the number of the world's people and their distribution across different geographical locations. Another view, however, holds that claims of overpopulation cover up more immediate causes of the problems – and invariably victimise and scapegoat already vulnerable groups in the process. Ever since English economist Thomas Malthus wrote his first *Essay on the principle of population* in 1798, his theory and arguments have been endlessly refuted by practical instances indicating that any problem attributed to human numbers can just as easily have a different explanation, or that the statistical correlation is ambiguous. Facts and figures have never had much effect on population debates or disagreements over policies. This is because, deep down, the disagreements are less about numbers than about ideology, values, power and economic interests, about rights, economic markets and welfare. They are political and cultural disagreements, not mathematical ones. Overpopulation arguments and the policies based on them tend to persist, not because of their intrinsic merit, but because of the ideological advantages they offer to powerful political and economic interests. In this sense, **population policy** could be considered as one that aims to minimise redistribution and restrict social rights.

This chapter looks at the reasons why the argument that there are 'too many' people in the world continues to manifest itself in a range of contexts. It first outlines the context in which Malthus was writing in the late 18th and early 19th centuries, and the uses to which his theory was put in the 19th century. Here we point to population policy as an 'early' example of **global social policy**, highlighting transnational ideational and policy transfers associated with the British Empire. The chapter then gives some examples from across the 20th century of how **eugenics** used population theory and influenced **global policy actors**. We show how the US deployed Malthusian arguments in the 1950s as a justification to contain communism in other countries and to pursue various development policies. We describe how **international organisations**, both public and private, have been instrumental in the transfer of overpopulation theory and in claiming the urgency of tackling **population growth** and **population decline**. The chapter concludes with a round-up of how population arguments are being deployed in the 21st century, particularly in global debates on security, conflict and climate change.

Origins of population control thinking

Underpinning many an overpopulation argument is the work of English economist Thomas Malthus, who is best remembered for the 'law of nature' he first set out in his 1798 *Essay on the principle of population* (**Box 11.1**). This was written against a background of major social and economic transformations in England, which led to an era of immense suffering. For example, large amounts of common pasture and forested land, over which an entire community had rights of use, were being fenced off for private use. The enclosure of common woodland alone amounted to shredding what was known throughout Europe as 'the poor's overcoat'. Denied access to common land on which their livelihoods depended, many of the 'dispossessed' were unable to find secure employment or alternative livelihoods, either in the countryside or in the towns, and so had to depend on poor relief from local parishes, the closest thing to social welfare at the time.

Box 11.1: Thomas Malthus's theory of population

Thomas Malthus's theory maintains that population increases will eventually lead to starvation. Malthus claimed that food production increases at an arithmetic rate (1, 2, 3, 4, 5 and so on), but the number of people doubles every 25 years because it grows at a geometric rate (1, 2, 4, 8, 16 and so on) – unless people delay and check their childbearing through later marriage and self-discipline. If they do not keep their numbers in check, warfare, epidemic disease and starvation will do so – and because Malthus believed that poorer people found self-restraint or self-discipline difficult, disease and starvation were not only inevitable but also 'natural': he originally presented his theory as a 'law of nature'. Malthus subsequently admitted that his mathematical and geometric series of increases in food and humans were not observable in any society, and that his famous 'power of numbers' was only an image, admissions that demographers have since confirmed.

A variety of explanations and proposals for action were advanced in response to this mass poverty, of which Malthus's *Essay* was one. Market forces and market reasoning, Malthus argued, bring discipline into the chaos that is nature. Without private property and with unchecked population growth, the world is catapulted headlong into **scarcity**. Scarcity did not result from periodic natural disasters: the *Essay* declared that it was a permanent feature of nature, always impinging disproportionately on the poor. By suggesting that the poor's fertility was the main source of their poverty – rather than the fencing off of common lands, chronic or periodic unemployment, or high food prices – Malthus's theory served the interests of property-owning classes. The solution to poverty, it was maintained, was a matter of individual responsibility: it had nothing to do with wider institutional structures and contexts. Social welfare, therefore, was little more than a subsidy for the fertility of the poor and brought about further misery. Malthus insisted that anything that humans might do to redress inequalities or to mitigate suffering would be counterproductive because it would only increase population and therefore place more pressure on productive resources. Private property, not the poor laws and not the commons, would provide the best possible deal for the poor, he maintained (Lohmann, 2003).

Within a generation, Malthus's population theory enabled English elites to argue that the underlying cause of distress among the poor was overpopulation. The Poor Law Amendment Act 1834 instituted a system of workhouses in which conditions were deliberately made as prison-like as possible so that people would choose to take the poorest-paid work rather than enter the workhouses. The Malthusian spectre of overpopulation was of central intellectual and political significance in shaping this law, which was, arguably, the first time a 'population policy' was introduced.

The global ramifications of this theory were almost immediately evident. A few years later, Malthusian thinking was exported to Ireland and India, two of Britain's overseas colonies, experiencing famines – with disastrous consequences (**Box 11.2**).

Box 11.2: Global policy transfer – the export of Malthusianism to British colonies

A decade after the Poor Law Amendment Act 1834, overpopulation was invoked by the British government as an explanation for famine and death, and as a rationale for policy (in)action, in Ireland. In 1845, a fungus ruined the potato harvest, the staple food crop that most peasants grew on the poor-quality land allotted them by landlords. Instead of attributing the resulting starvation to the peasants' lack of access to land or lack of access to food other than potatoes (during these famine years, Irish exports of wheat and cattle to England and its Caribbean plantations increased), the colonial British government, dominated by absentee landlords, maintained that too many peasants had caused the famine. Applying the tenets of Malthusianism, they argued that it was futile and counterproductive to intervene by allowing the peasants access to other food or land or by reducing their taxes so they could buy food; this would simply delay and exacerbate the impending crash when the number of people outstripped the amount of food available. As a result of the Great Famine, some one million people died while another million emigrated within five years (Ross, 2000, p 4).

Thirty years later, Malthusian principles were again invoked to legitimise British policies in India, turning a drought into a famine. From 1876 to 1879, India experienced a devastatingly destructive drought when the monsoon rains failed. Yet although crop failures and water shortages were the worst in centuries, there were grain surpluses that could have rescued drought victims. As in Ireland, however, much of India's surplus rice and wheat production had been exported to England. As in Ireland, those with the power to relieve famine convinced themselves that exertions against implacable natural laws, whether of market prices or population growth, were worse than no effort at all. 'The staggering death toll – 5.5 million to 12 million died in India despite modern railways and millions of tons of grain in commercial circulation – was the foreseeable and avoidable result of deliberate policy choices.... Malthusian explanations were not only wrong-headed at the time: they were also contributory causes of the deaths that occurred' (Davis, 2002, pp 3, 1).

Administrators in the Indian Civil Service after independence from Britain in 1947 often had quite consciously Malthusian attitudes that can be traced back to the 19th century. The 1943-44 Bengal famine, in which at least 1.5 million people died, not least because of British policies, contributed to India's 1951 decision to opt for a family planning programme, one of the first countries in the world to do so (Rao, 2004).

Malthusian transformation: eugenics

From Malthus's time onwards, the implied 'over' in population has invariably referred to poorer people, people from black and disadvantaged ethnic groups or people from the colonies or countries of the South – or a combination of all three. In practice, the 'too many' refers to the 'other', not to the speaker. It is not surprising, therefore, that **Malthusianism** found an intellectual ally in the late 19th century and early 20th century in eugenics. Building on Malthusian tropes about the poor, eugenics argued that poor's supposed moral deficiencies were innate (Ross, 2000, p 5).

In the US and UK, middle-class intellectuals and eugenic reformers proposed at first that birth control, including sterilisation, be used to prevent certain categories of the ill or disabled from polluting the 'national gene pool'. But it rapidly came to be viewed as a way of dealing with a broader spectrum of social ills. By the turn of the 20th century, control of the population of the 'feeble-minded' (a term first used in 1876 in the UK) was seen as a remedy for a wide variety of social problems, including prostitution, vagrancy and petty crime. Inspired by eugenic and Malthusian thinking, policy makers increasingly believed that science had demonstrated that poverty, too, was primarily the result of innate physical and moral debility.

Most eugenic-inspired policies focused on restricting births of certain groups. Although eugenicists recognised birth control as an important instrument of social policy, they were ambivalent about it because it was used primarily by the middle and upper classes whose fertility they did not want to limit. Stopping some people from reproducing altogether seemed more effective. By 1920, when much of the medical profession had absorbed eugenic and racialist ideas, 25 states in the US had enacted laws for the compulsory sterilisation of the criminally insane and other groups (Lifton, 1986, p 22). Drawing on British and US eugenic thinking, Germany introduced a sterilisation policy in 1933. This soon evolved into a programme of euthanasia of 'valueless life' and a pilot 'medical killing' scheme for the Holocaust, which transformed 'state remedies' for curbing fertility into systematic mass murder on an unprecedented scale (Ross, 1998, p 72).

Eugenic ideas went underground after the end of the Second World War following revelations about the Holocaust. Nonetheless, some countries and more than half of US states kept their sterilisation policies for decades, as late as the 1970s. Moreover, targeted sterilisation abuse continues today. In recent years, Roma women in the Czech Republic, Hungary and Slovakia have been targeted and sterilised without their consent, some during caesarean section operations. Many women living with HIV in parts of Africa and Latin America have been coerced into being sterilised on the grounds that otherwise any baby to which they might give birth will have HIV, even though mother-to-child transmission of HIV can now be effectively addressed with AIDS medications (OSI, 2011).

Just as sterilisation abuse continues, so too eugenic ideas are still common. In the 21st century, eugenic assumptions continue to circulate in debates about environmental degradation and immigration; biological determinism; rebiologising and geneticising 'race'; the use of reproductive technologies such as prenatal screening and prenatal genetic diagnosis; fears of future scarcities; national security; and ageing and population decline (Minns, 2006).

Population policies in the 20th century

Rise of population institutions

After the Second World War, the 'population issue' was raised by a variety of government, military and corporate interests, particularly in the US. In the ensuing decades, they disseminated the 'overpopulation' discourse across the countries of the Third World, particularly in Asia, directly and indirectly as they supported the development of key international organisations.

The principal vehicle for Malthusian fears became the threat of communism, and Malthusian and eugenic thinking quickly became enshrined in Cold War 'containment' policies from the late 1940s onwards. Population growth, rather than global social injustice or inequalities in resource distribution, was seen as the ultimate source of the conditions that attracted peasants to communism, particularly across Asia. **Population control** thus became part of national security planning, particularly in the US, then emerging as the dominant power in international politics. By the 1940s, US government bodies were recommending government financing of population research as part of security planning (Ross, 2000, p 9).

Population control was adopted as a major international development strategy in the 1950s. By the end of the 1960s, it had become pivotal to development strategies designed to address poverty, hunger and low wages. Since official international population assistance began in the mid-1960s, the US has been the acknowledged leader in the field. It has consistently been the largest donor (until recently), provided much of the intellectual leadership linking fertility reduction with economic development, and been the pillar of **multilateral** efforts through the United Nations (UN) system, The World Bank (WB) and organisations such as the International Planned Parenthood Federation (IPPF) (Connelly, 2008).

The WB, UN Population Fund, **World Health Organization** (WHO) and UN Children's Fund (UNICEF) entered the family planning area in the 1960s, when governments of many recipient countries became increasingly tolerant of efforts to create or strengthen international population assistance. In 1967, with financial support coming from the US, the UN established its Population Trust Fund, reorganised in 1969 as the UN Fund for Population Activities (UNFPA), commonly known as the UN Population Fund. By 1968, curbing population growth had become central to WB development policy, and has remained so ever since. The United States Agency for International Development (USAID) established an office of population in 1964 and began funding direct family planning activities in 1967. By 1971, USAID's annual allocation for population had risen to US$100 million, far more than was allocated for healthcare. Much of the population budget was channelled through the IPPF. Although international donors financed many family planning programmes, some Third World governments, particularly those in Asia, gradually began to provide an increasing proportion of the funding themselves. In many Latin American countries, however, both the church and state opposed modern contraceptives.

The 1974 World Population Conference was the first major forum on issues of population growth. Northern countries wanted to implement population control policies in the South; Southern countries shifted the debate to development issues, arguing that 'development is the best contraceptive'. By the 1984 International Conference on Population in Mexico City, however, there was more consensus among Southern countries, donors and non-governmental organisations (NGOs) about the need to limit population growth. Many Southern economies had deteriorated and their dependence on Western aid had increased. By 1991, 69 countries had officially endorsed comprehensive population policies (Nair et al, 2004).

Targeting women's fertility

For some 60 years, many countries implemented policies explicitly aimed at reducing their populations by reducing the number of children to whom women give birth, either directly by increasing the number of women using modern contraceptives or who are sterilised, or indirectly through women's education, employment and empowerment. While many countries simply provided contraception, others went further, introducing quantitative targets for the numbers of women to be sterilised or fitted with intra-uterine devices (IUDs). Some brought in financial incentives or disincentives for family planning providers and potential contraceptive users, while others employed outright coercion. The latter took various forms around the world, some of the more extreme measures resulting in: forced vasectomies in India in the 1970s (one of the few programmes focusing on men); a one-child policy in China introduced from the 1980s onwards that forced women to have late-term abortions; and implantation of women in Indonesia with five-year contraceptive doses in 'safaris' organised by the military forces.

Beyond violating women's **reproductive rights**, population control that targets women's fertility undermines health systems and entrenches gender biases. The focus on women's childbearing to the detriment of their underlying health can often cause more deaths than childbearing itself. A large proportion of maternal and infant deaths in India, for instance, are attributable to under-nutrition, anaemia and communicable diseases stemming from lack of food, poverty and social inequity. Diseases that are predominantly infectious cause some two thirds of women's deaths in India. Most women's deaths occur before they give birth, and nearly 30 per cent of women's deaths are of girls under the age of 15. Of women of reproductive age, nearly 30 per cent of deaths are caused by major infectious diseases, while about 12.5 per cent are due to childbirth and conditions associated with it. Indian public health activist and academic Mohan Rao argues that 'given the overall health situation among women, dominated by communicable diseases, anaemia and under-nutrition, to concentrate on reproductive health is to utterly miss the wood for the trees' (Rao, 2004, p 195).

Population policies seeking to enforce a one- or two-child norm have reinforced existing gender biases against women. China, for instance, introduced its one-child policy in 1979-80 in response to a 1972 report, *Limits to growth* (Meadows et al, 1972), which modelled the consequences of a growing world population on industrialisation, pollution, food production and resource depletion. The leaders of the People's Republic of China defined the country's population problem as too many people of too 'backward' a type. Struggles over the number of children soon became contests over the sex of those offspring; boys were the children who counted. Only a son could carry on the male-centred family line; sons would remain with their parents after marriage and look after them. From the early 1980s, peasant couples had reluctantly begun disposing of their daughters in an attempt to get a son. Although outright infanticide seems to have declined in the 1980s, infant abandonment persisted. The spread of ultrasound machines into every corner of rural China pushed the state gender norm back into the period before birth. Prenatal sex determination followed by sex-selective abortion became an attractive, high-tech alternative to disposing of already living infants.

Fierce resistance forced the authorities to revise the one-child policy in the late 1980s, allowing parents in the countryside with a daughter to have one more child even if it, too, was a girl. Today, the practice of prenatal sex selection followed by sex-selective abortion is the single greatest contributor to a growing dearth of girls in China. By the turn of the millennium, the abortion of female foetuses had become a thoroughly normalised practice in the villages, and the sex ratio at birth had soared to 120 boys per 100 girls – the highest in Asia and globally (the biologically normal ratio is 105-106 boys for every 100 girls) (Greenhalgh and Winckler, 2005).

'Feminist' population policy: reform or business as usual?

Many women's health groups supported contraception that contributed to human health, welfare and self-determination by enabling women and men to have greater influence over the timing and spacing of births, but opposed contraception that harmed women's health and welfare. In this respect, population policy has largely been a global social policy contested by national and transnational social movements rather than supported by them; it has been a top-down global policy that has often encountered bottom-up global resistance. In the early 1990s, however, some large 'multinational' women's health groups believed that cooperating with governments, international donor agencies or UNFPA might ensure better reproductive health and counter abuses in population policies. They targeted the UN's 1994 International Conference on Population and Development (ICPD), aiming to have women's **reproductive rights** and gender equity accepted as vital aspects of population policies.

UNIVERSITY OF WINCHESTER
LIBRARY

The ICPD, the largest and costliest of all the UN conferences on population, was marked by the unprecedented involvement of NGOs and women's organisations (Koivusalo and Ollila, 1997). Its Programme of Action, heralded as a paradigm shift in the discourse about population and development and endorsed by 179 countries, was intended to establish international and national population policy for the following two decades. The programme's main recommendation – that population programmes provide reproductive health services rather than just family planning – assumes that women's fertility will not drop until children survive beyond infancy and young childhood, until men also take responsibility for contraception, and until women have the right to control their fertility and enough political power to secure that right. It expressly rejected the use of incentives and targets in family planning services.

Despite shifts in language and focus – from population control to sexual and reproductive health – policies inspired by population thinking have not become a thing of the past. For instance, the Indian government has declared that it has abandoned the use of targets. But India's national population policy for the year 2000 aimed for 'replacement level fertility rates' by the year 2010 and a 'stable population' by 2045. Many states in India promote policies that include disincentives for having additional children, such as the two-child norm, and incentives for accepting sterilisation (see **Box 11.3**).

Box 11.3: The resurgence of coercive population control in India

Ten Indian states have policies aimed at deterring parents from having a third child. Third children in these states may be denied ration cards, education in government schools and access to welfare while their parents are excluded from government jobs and prohibited from sitting on *panchayats* (local governing bodies). Both Rajasthan and Maharashtra make 'adherence to a two-child norm' a condition of service for state government employees. The Andhra Pradesh policy links funding for construction of schools and other public works, as well as rural development schemes generally, to family planning. Allotment of surplus agricultural land, housing schemes and a variety of social programmes are also tied to acceptance of sterilisation. Women's groups stress that the two-child norm has increased the incidence of sex-selective abortions and female infanticide (Sama, 2005, p 15).

In 2006, the UK's Department for International Development (DFID) gave over £160 million to support India's Reproductive and Child Health Programme, which used the money to give incentives to clinics, doctors and NGO staff to carry out sterilisations. In the state of Bihar, after clinics had sterilised 30 women in any one day, they received a 500 rupee bonus (around £6) for every additional patient sterilised. The aid had been intended to support contraceptive dissemination, however, and has since been discontinued.

Population policies in the 21st century

Loss of political momentum and donor funding

Despite the momentum of the 1994 ICPD, increased funding for population programmes was not forthcoming. The ICPD's Programme of Action had estimated the annual costs of meeting basic family planning needs in developing countries and countries in transition (such as those of the former Soviet Union), but in 2009 the UNFPA revised the figures upwards. Whereas the Programme of Action had estimated these costs for the year 2010 at US$20 billion, the revisions more than tripled the amount to US$65 billion. But even as the estimated costs went up, funding for family planning decreased in the decade after the ICPD, as global funding went instead towards HIV/AIDS programmes.

With the demise of an overt population control agenda, political backing for population programmes waned, particularly given the AIDS epidemic. At the same time, in the US, religious fundamentalist interests opposed to abortion and women's reproductive rights became more dominant, and US government support for the ICPD lessened because of a lack of political support at home. Since the US is the largest donor country for family planning, the loss was significant.

In response, the UNFPA and other international organisations strived to keep family planning high on policy agendas with new rationales arguing the benefits of increased funding. Many of these use **neo-Malthusian** arguments to link population growth with poverty, such as the theory of 'demographic dividend' due to a 'bulge' of working-age adults. The WB, for example, maintains that:

> ... lower fertility and slower population growth, in combination with decreasing mortality ... increases the proportion of productive individuals relative to dependents. This change creates a "window of opportunity" conducive to economic growth. Countries that exploit this "demographic dividend" ... can experience economic growth and reduction in poverty. (WB, 2004, p 3)

A 2012 report from the UNFPA and the US-based Guttmacher Institute outlining the costs and benefits of contraceptive services argued for expanded contraceptive availability on the grounds that women's reproductive health could be improved with this fix. This report calculated the number of women in the global South who do not use modern contraception, a figure described as 'unmet need'. As such, it promoted quantitative targets for future contraceptive users (222 million women) and the number of unplanned pregnancies and births that could be averted (218 million pregnancies, 55 million births and 138 million abortions) (Singh and Darroch, 2012).

In sum, even if these days international organisations seldom market population policies in explicitly demographic terms, they have not necessarily dropped or modified their goals of reducing fertility. This is despite falling fertility rates among women around the world. Indeed, since the mid-1950s, in global terms, the 'average' number of children a woman will have has halved to around 2.5, and less than one fifth of the world's people live in countries where most women have four children.

Rebirth of family planning

In 2012 renewed efforts were made to rally international support for family planning. *The Lancet* published a special edition on the 'rebirth of family planning' in the run-up to a Family Planning Summit held in London in July. At the Summit, the UK government, the Bill & Melinda Gates Foundation (BMGF), UNFPA and other partners lobbied for 'universal coverage', aiming for an additional 120 million women in the world's poorest countries to be using contraceptives by 2020.

Women's health groups have criticised the London Family Planning Summit because of this contraceptive user target and because the main platform did not endorse safe and accessible abortion. Although Summit speakers openly disavowed population control and supported women's rights, as they have tended to do since the 1994 ICPD, women's groups have grave concerns about the implementation of the Summit strategy, given its emphasis on quantitative goals.

The primary focus of the Summit strategy, as with current international population policy more widely, was with the countries of sub-Saharan Africa with high fertility rates, even though these countries account for just 10 per cent of the world population. The emphasis on contraceptive delivery in population policies is undermining efforts to address AIDS in Africa, which is home to 64 per cent of all people in the world living with HIV. For example, from 2013 to 2016, the BMGF, the Program for Appropriate Technology in Health (a US non-profit organisation focusing on developing health technologies), UNFPA, DFID and USAID will partner with pharmaceutical company Pfizer to provide three million women in sub-Saharan Africa and South Asia with the injectable contraceptive Depo-Provera (PATH, 2012).

There is evidence, however, that Depo-Provera doubles the risk of a woman acquiring and transmitting HIV, while WHO has cautioned women who have received a Depo-Provera injection to also use condoms (WHO, 2012).

Forecasting a future of Malthusian scarcity

Since the 1950s, Malthusian fears had been expressed in terms of environmental catastrophe and mass starvation. Paul Ehrlich's 1968 book, *The population bomb*, for example, presented overpopulation as the greatest threat to global ecological survival (Ehrlich, 1968). Population alarmism is still common in environmental degradation and climate change narratives. One US political scientist warns that, 'Governing a parched and packed planet may prove to be the overarching political challenge of the twenty-first century' (Matthew, 2012, p 133).

In the past decade, these fears have justified more scientific and policy interest in promoting 'population stabilisation' (through control of women's fertility) so as to avert *future* climate change. Advocates have argued for increased access to contraceptives, particularly in the global South, as a way of reducing greenhouse gas emissions in a problematic calculus that equates more people with more emissions. This is despite the fact that per capita greenhouse gas emissions from richer countries are far higher than those from poorer ones, and that Northern countries, with only 20 per cent of the world's population, are responsible for 80 per cent of the historical carbon dioxide emissions that have accumulated in the atmosphere and that contribute to *current* climate change (The Corner House, 2009; Sasser, 2013). Indeed, the countries with the highest greenhouse gas emissions are those with slow or declining population growth, while the few countries in the world where women's fertility rates remain high have the lowest per capita carbon emissions. Aggregate per capita emissions figures, however, still tend to obscure *who* is producing greenhouse gases and *how*, by statistically levelling out emissions among everyone. One estimate is that the world's richest half billion people – some 7 per cent of the global population – are responsible for half the world's carbon dioxide emissions today, while conversely 50 per cent of the world's people, the poorest, are responsible for just 7 per cent of emissions.

The UNFPA argues that smaller family size in the global South will enable women to cope better with the challenges of climate change. Its 2009 *State of the world population* report claims, 'slower population growth in some countries has bought more time to prepare adaptation plans for the coming impacts of climate change' (UNFPA, 2009). Family planning and fertility reduction is stressed as a win for women and a win for the environment. A worsening climate situation, however, is driven by the continued extraction and burning of fossil fuels. Tackling human–caused climate change requires societies to turn away from their fossil fuel dependence. Yet fossil fuel burners raise the spectre of teeming Chinese, Indian and African citizens causing whole cities and countries to be submerged by flooding and rising sea levels because of their emissions, unless polluting companies are granted private property rights in the atmosphere through carbon trading and carbon offset schemes, many of which usurp land, water and air in the global South. These are the tools of the main official approach to the climate crisis, which aims to build a global carbon market worth trillions of dollars – and which gives incentives to polluting industries to delay structural change away from fossil fuels. Population numbers in fact offer little or no useful pointers toward policies that should be adopted to tackle climate change. Massive fossil fuel use in industrialised societies cannot be countered by handing out condoms and other contraceptives.

In addition to delaying structural changes in both the North and South away from the extraction and use of fossil fuels, overpopulation arguments serve to excuse the failure of carbon markets to tackle the problem, to justify increased and multiple interventions in the countries deemed to hold the surplus people, and to excuse those interventions when they cause further environmental degradation, migration or conflict.

The threat of future crises resulting from more people is also frequently raised in relation to food and water. A prediction of millions of yet unborn 'extra mouths to feed' (primarily dark-skinned ones) is used to justify genetically modified crops as a 'partial solution' to world hunger, just as Green Revolution agriculture was marketed in the 1960s and 1970s (see ***Box 11.4***).

Box 11.4: Green Revolution agriculture

'Overpopulation' was used to justify one of the most influential Western development and agricultural strategies of the post-war period, the 'Green Revolution'. Development planners maintained that the only solution to the Malthusian spectre of famine was enhancing output through technological means – irrigation, chemical fertilisers and pesticides, and high-yielding seeds. Peasant agriculture was subordinated to or replaced by a more commercial and capital-intensive mode of production geared towards agricultural exports. Western multinationals, such as fertiliser and chemical manufacturers, profited as suppliers of agricultural inputs.

Local food production in developing countries was reduced, and the US became the principal source of food grains for the Third World. In the end, the Green Revolution turned out to be less about producing more food and improving the food security for the needy than about securing the economic interests of Western multinationals. The Green Revolution denied the yield-raising potential of land redistribution and reoriented production to world markets rather than to local subsistence needs.

Despite the Green Revolution's failure to solve the problem of world hunger, the growing nutritional crisis in the Third World is still attributed to 'overpopulation' or 'environmental stress'. Leading agricultural research organisations claim that ultimately the only solution is the curbing of world population growth and an extension of the Green Revolution through genetically modified crops and privatised water supplies (Ross, 2000, pp 12-17).

Malthus justified the privatisation of communal land through predictions of population-induced scarcity. The privatisation of seeds, water and air is being promoted through a similar scarcity discourse. The belief that 'overpopulation' is a primary cause of resource scarcity is one of the most popular and pervasive. Yet differentiating between absolute scarcity – no food or water at all – and socially generated or manufactured scarcity – not enough food or water in some places for some people because others have the power to deny them access – is essential for any sensible discussion of the causes of food insecurity, lack of access to potable water and 'overpopulation'.

Population control as counter-insurgency

In the 21st century, connections continue to be made between population control and national security, but with varying targets. The concept of 'strategic demography' is increasingly used to frame national security threats in demographic terms. Claims are made that population pressures contribute to religious, ethnic and young men's violence, primarily in Africa and Middle Eastern regions, and that population pressures and climate change cause social unrest (Goldstone et al, 2012). Such population-based security arguments are used to justify military interventions, heightened national border enforcement, restricted migration, imprisonment and, in some cases, increased family planning.

Environmental and climate 'conflict'

After the end of the Cold War, national security analysts and scholars looking to identify new global threats increasingly identified population pressure on the environment as a cause of political instability. In the 1990s political scientist Thomas Homer-Dixon argued that scarcities of renewable resources such as cropland, fresh water and forests, induced in large part by population pressure, contribute to migration and violent intrastate conflict in many parts of the developing world. His ideas influenced US policy during the Clinton administration in the 1990s and persist today in ideas about population-driven 'climate conflict'.

In 2007, international organisations and the US military voiced their concerns about climate, looking at Africa as the primary hotspot and site for intervention and citing the civil war in Darfur as a cautionary study of future disaster, a conflict they attributed to population pressure coupled with (an assumed absolute) resource scarcity and climate change. A UN Environment programme (UNEP) report on the Sudan argued that overpopulation of both people and their livestock, compounded with water shortages due to climate change, drives conflict in the region. Left out of such narratives are issues such as the increased export of livestock to the Middle East after outsiders became more involved in the trade; the underuse of land and water in certain localities as well as its overuse (together with long-standing historic conflicts over land); imbalances of power between ethnic groups; and ethnicity itself becoming a contested resource. The growth of climate conflict discourse has dovetailed with the establishment of a US military command centre for Africa, AFRICOM, to protect US interests and to engage with the 'War on Terror' on the continent (Hartmann, 2010, p 236).

Ironically, ideas of environmental and climate conflict evade the fact that the US Pentagon is the single largest user of petroleum in the world, and that militaries around the world are primary agents of destruction. War invariably ravages natural landscapes and military toxins pollute land, air and water, often for many decades (Sanders, 2009).

'War on Terror'

Concerns about growing numbers of young people in the global South, and the decline of those in the North as people age, build on Malthusian fears of scarcity and have been dubbed the 'new population bomb':

> The world's expected population growth will increasingly be concentrated in today's poorest, youngest, and most heavily Muslim countries, which have a dangerous lack of quality education, capital, and employment opportunities; and, for the first time in history, most of the world's population will become urbanized, with the largest urban centers being in the world's poorest countries, where policing, sanitation, and health care are often scarce. Taken together, these trends are every bit as alarming as those noted by Erhlich. (Goldstone, 2010, p 31)

Several theories link youth with unrest in the global South. The 'youth bulge' theory defines the proportion of the world's people aged 24 and under, the majority of whom live in the South, as a 'political hazard' and a threat to social and economic stability and security. Developed in 1985 by geographer Gary Fuller at the US Central Intelligence Agency (CIA), the 'youth bulge' theory aimed to provide a tool to predict unrest and to uncover potential national security threats. It is now a mainstream concept, used by the WB, UNDP, UNFPA and USAID as a rationale for development programmes aimed at young people, including family planning services. In these programmes, the 'youth bulge' represents both promise and peril: using family planning to reduce fertility and increase their opportunities for education and employment, young people can become an economic bonus; without it, they are a dangerous element in an already chaotic mix (Hendrixson, 2012).

Similar arguments claim that sex-selection practices in Asian countries – aborting female foetuses or abandoning girl children – lead to 'surplus sons and missing daughters', resulting in male aggression because of a lack of sexual partners, employment and education. These claims skew policy and propagate images of dangerous men. In China, rural bachelors are treated as potential criminals and are marginalised socially and economically. In contrast, international organisations and the Chinese government have 'flooded into the field of girl care', calling for an end to gender biases, education for girls and the rescue of trafficked children (Greenhalgh, 2012).

The prison industrial complex as population control

The prison industrial complex also serves as system of population control, particularly in the US. The US prison population is the largest in the world with over 2.2 million people incarcerated in US prisons or jails, a 500 per cent increase since the 1970s. Sixty per cent of US prisoners are black or Latino. The US 'War on Drugs' has resulted in non-violent drug offenders comprising the bulk of those either in jail or on parole or probation. Prison population growth in the US can thus be linked not to serious crime rates – which have dropped since 1991 – but to economic stagnation, unemployment and the consequences of structural adjustment at home (see also **Chapter Ten** in this volume).

The 'War on Drugs', meanwhile, has not stopped drug use but has taken thousands of unemployed people off the streets, in a move that will legally deny them the opportunity to get jobs, housing and public assistance after their release. The disproportionate incarceration of black men – one in three black men can expect to go to prison if trends continue – has led to what civil rights lawyer Michelle Alexander calls 'a racial caste system', that is, a form of social control over black men (Alexander, 2011, p 2). For women, imprisonment can mean reproductive health abuses such as forced sterilisation and being made unable to care for their children, both of which occur in the state of California (Justice Now, 2012).

The US criminal justice system is also punishing undocumented **migrants** for entering the US and removing them from the country. Currently, more than half of all federal criminal prosecutions are brought for immigration-related crimes, including illegal entry and re-entry following a felony. Enforcement programmes seek to remove non-US citizens who are arrested for a criminal offence or commit one. Funding for such programmes leapt from US$23 million to US$690 million between 2004-11. According to the Migration Policy Institute, they 'have led to substantial increases in both the overall numbers of removals and in the proportion of removals of unauthorized immigrants with criminal convictions' (Meissner et al, 2013, p 7). Elsewhere many countries detain asylum seekers and migrants, particularly those from the global South. The UK immigration detention system is the largest in Europe, holding some 27,000 people in 2011.

Conclusion

This chapter has traced the entanglements of population theory and global policy formation over the past two centuries, showing that population policy is one of the earliest forms of global social policy. Here we see how one theory, developed in a particular historical period in a particular part of the world, was quickly adopted and transferred to a range of countries and contexts by state and non-state global policy actors.

From the theoretical work of Malthus in the 19th century to contemporary claims that overpopulation presents a fundamental threat to human security, population policy has mainly been directed at controlling women's fertility, especially that of women in 'developing' countries. While the policy applications of this theory and set of underlying assumptions and concerns may have changed, the thinking has remained constant. We have traced the changes in policy emphasis from population control in the 1950s to reproductive health in the 1990s, noting that over this time, US state and non-state transnational actors have remained prime movers behind the perpetuation of the overpopulation discourse and its influence on global policies. Indeed, despite persistent refutations of the theory and its assumptions, and various concerted social movement and NGO campaigns against it, neither population policies nor Malthusian thinking show signs of dying out: the targets of both policies and thinking continue to shift, reflecting changing demographic, economic and political realities, but also remain much the same. Throughout, the chapter has emphasised the ideological use of population theory, whether Malthusian, eugenic or

neo-Malthusian, to advance and legitimise various political and economic interests. In the words of Hartmann and Oliver (2007, p 4), this demonstrates:

> ... the need to remain vigilant about the construction, circulation and deployment of ideas about population. Ideas matter. They are not innocent or neutral. Ideas and theories about population have informed and shaped harmful policies and practices in the past as well as the present, and have the power to do so in the future.

Note

[1] The authors of this chapter are listed in alphabetical order. The work and thinking of several other scholar activists was indispensable to this collaborative research project, and thus to this chapter: Mohan Rao, Betsy Hartmann, Sumati Nair, Eric Ross and Mike Davis.

Summary

- Population policy is a long-standing concern of global social policy and an early example of how ideas and policies are transferred across national borders; it predates the emergence of international organisations in the 20th century.
- Global policy actors – international organisations, private institutions and global sources of finance such as Northern donor funds – constitute key channels through which population policy is promoted, even as it is enacted through recipient governments and NGOs.
- Population control policy has usually been directed at women's fertility and has involved the use of quantitative and qualitative targets, and voluntary and coercive techniques.
- Women's and public health movements have primarily opposed global population policies and practices, but in recent years some have attempted to use them to help achieve their own goals.
- The theory of overpopulation is currently finding new outlets, and is applied to issues of international security and conflict.
- Discourses on 'overpopulation' invariably obscure the real roots of poverty, inequality and environmental degradation, and overwhelm other explanations of poverty.

Questions for discussion

- What principal transnational policy actors are involved in the international spread of ideas about 'overpopulation'?
- How are ideas and theories about 'overpopulation' manifested in global policy responses?

- How do discourses on 'overpopulation' obscure the root causes of poverty, inequality and environmental degradation?

Further activities

Examine the debates around population from Cairo+20 (the ICPD 'Beyond 2014' conference), including perspectives from UNFPA and other UN agencies, governments and international women's health organisations. How does each sector understand population issues? How do their perspectives overlap and differ? What are the high-level UN recommendations for achieving sexual and reproductive health, and environmental sustainability?

Visit the Population Matters website (www.populationmatters.org/what-you-can-do/offset-carbon/), and critically examine their PopOffsets program. This claims that you can help curb population growth and offset your personal carbon footprint when you donate to their family planning program. What are the assumptions about population growth and the environment that undergird this claim? What sources of carbon emissions would you target to most effectively reduce emission rates?

Further reading and resources

Angus and Butler (2011) look at the social and economic causes of the environmental crisis, while exposing the shortcomings of population alarmism. Their book aims to spark debate among environmentalists to address the more direct causes of environmental destruction, poverty, food shortages and resource depletion.

Hartmann (1995) traces the history of population thinking and population control; describes the development, implementation and consequences of contraceptive technologies; and examines the political, economic and social contexts in which policies are deployed – and their impacts, especially on women in 'developing' countries.

Lugton, with McKinney, McKay Bryson, Pickbourn and Hartmann (2013), is a social justice curriculum on population, food, the environment and climate change. It contains background readings, up-to-date facts and figures, reasoned arguments, quotes, poems, cartoons and a comprehensive resource list.

Richey (2008) examines the interactions between global population discourse and local family planning practices across Africa (Tanzania in particular) against a backdrop of neoliberal models of development, and the dominant focus on HIV/AIDS.

Maternowska (2006) queries why so few poor people in Haiti attend health and family planning clinics run by foreign aid organisations despite wanting fewer children. It highlights the range of political dynamics that shape people's decisions about family planning, illustrating the complex interplay between global and local politics.

Krause (2005) traces fears about the potential societal consequences attributed to low birth rates, ageing and immigration to demographic reports that present their opinions about society, women and cultural identity as scientific truth.

Rao and Sexton (2010) present a collection of essays, each focusing on different parts of the globe, critically assessing the 1994 UN ICPD and population policies since then. The essays raise issues of politics, economics and ethics, all enmeshed with health and gender concerns.

Halfon (2006) explores how population policies during the 1990s gradually changed from focusing on 'population control' to advocating women's empowerment, and how an international consensus was built up around this transition.

Finally, Connelly (2008) presents a new global history on the global population control movement, highlighting how affluent countries, foundations and NGOs have supported it.

'Different Takes', a series of discussion papers, covers various aspects of population, social justice and global politics and policy and is available at the website of the Population and Development Program at Hampshire College, US (http://popdev. hampshire.edu).

The Corner House (UK) series on Overpopulation contains a range of papers arguing that the debate about 'overpopulation' is less about numbers of people than about rights (to land, water, food and livelihoods, for example), about markets, private property and inequality, and about relationships of power between different groups of people (www.thecornerhouse.org.uk/subject/overpopulation).

References

Alexander, M. (2010) *The new Jim Crow: Mass incarceration in the age of colorblindness*, New York: The New Press.

Angus, I. and Butler, S. (2011) *Too many people: Population, immigration, and the environmental crisis*, Chicago, IL: Haymarket Books.

Connelly, M. (2008) *Fatal misconception: The struggle to control world population*, Cambridge, MA: Harvard University Press.

Corner House, The (2009) *Climate change and 'overpopulation': Some reflections*, Sturminster Newton: The Corner House (www.thecornerhouse.org.uk).

Davis, M. (2002) 'The origins of the Third World: markets, states and climate', Corner House Briefing 27 (www.thecornerhouse.org.uk/pdf/briefing/27origins.pdf).

Ehrlich, P. (1968) *The population bomb*, New York: Ballantine Books.

Greenhalgh, S. (2012) 'Patriarchal demographics? China's sex ratio reconsidered', *Population and Development Review*, vol 38 (supplement), pp 130-49.

Greenhalgh, S. and Winckler, E.A. (2005) *Governing China's population: From Leninist to neoliberal biopolitics*, Stanford, CA: Stanford University Press.

Goldstone, J. (2010) 'The new population bomb', *Foreign Policy*, vol 89, no 1, pp 31-43.

Goldstone, J., Kauffman E. and Duffy Toft, M. (2012) *Political demography: How population changes are reshaping international security and national politics,* Boulder, CO: Paradigm Publishers.

Halfon, S. (2006) *The Cairo Consensus: Demographic surveys, women's empowerment and regime change*, Lanham, MD: Lexington Books.

Hartmann, B. (1995) *Reproductive rights and wrongs: The global politics of population control (2nd edn)*, Boston, MA: South End Press.

Hartmann, B. (2010) 'Rethinking climate refugees and climate conflict: Rhetoric, reality, and the politics of policy discourse', *Journal of International Development*, vol 22, pp 233-46.

Hendrixson, A. (2012) 'The "new population bomb" is a dud', *Different Takes*, no 75, Population and Development Program at Hampshire College (http://popdev. hampshire.edu/projects/dt/75).

Justice Now (2012) 'March 15 hearing on CDCR – Female offenders: Testimony submitted by Justice Now' (www.jnow.org/downloads/JusticeNow.3.15. BudgetTestimony.FemaleOff.pdf).

Koivusalo, M. and Ollila, E. (1997) *Making a healthy world. Agencies, actors and policies in international health*, London: Zed Books.

Krause, E.L. (2005) *A crisis of births: Population politics and family-making in Italy*, Belmont, CA: Wadsworth.

Lifton, R.J. (1986) *The Nazi doctors: Medical killing and the psychology of genocide*, London: Macmillan.

Lohmann, L. (2003) 'Re-imagining the population debate', Corner House Briefing 28 (www.thecornerhouse.org.uk/pdf/briefing/28reimagin.pdf).

Lugton, M. with McKinney, P., McKay Bryson, K., Pickbourn L. and Hartmann, B. (2013) *Population in perspective: A curriculum resource*, Amherst, MA: the Population and Development Program at Hampshire College (http://populationinperspective.org).

Malthus, T.R. (1993 [1798]) *Essay on the principle of population* (1st edn), Oxford: Oxford University Press.

Maternowska, M.C. (2006) *Reproducing inequities: Poverty and the politics of population in Haiti*, Piscataway, NJ: Rutgers University Press.

Matthew R. (2012) 'Demography, climate change and conflict', in J. Goldstone, E. Kauffman and M. Duffy Toft (eds) *Political demography: How population changes are reshaping international security and national politics,* Boulder, CO: Paradigm Publishers.

Meadows, D.H., Meadows, D.L., Randers, J. and Behrens, W.W. (1972) *Limits to growth,* New York: Basic Books.

Meissner, D, Kerwin, D.M., Chishti, M. and Bergeron, C. (2013) *Immigration enforcement in the United States: The rise of a formidable machinery,* Washington, DC: Migration Policy Institute.

Minns, R. (2006) 'Too many grannies? Private pensions, corporate welfare and growing insecurity', Corner House Briefing 35 (www.thecornerhouse.org.uk/pdf/briefing/35grannies.pdf).

Nair, S. and Kirbat, P. with Sexton, S. (2004) 'A decade after Cairo: women's health in a free market economy', Corner House Briefing 31 (www.thecornerhouse.org.uk/pdf/briefing/31cairo.pdf).

OSI (Open Society Foundations) (2011) *Against her will: Forced and coerced sterilization of women worldwide* (www.opensocietyfoundations.org/publications/against-her-will-forced-and-coerced-sterilization-women-worldwide).

PATH (Program for Appropriate Technology in Health) (2012) 'Innovative partnership to develop convenient contraceptives to up to three million women' (www.path.org/news/pr120711-depo-uniject.php).

Rao, M. (2004) *From population control to reproductive health: Malthusian arithmetic,* New Delhi: Sage Publications.

Rao, M. and Sexton, S. (eds) (2010) *Markets and Malthus: Population, gender, and health in neo-liberal times,* New Delhi: Sage Publications.

Richey, L. (2008) *Population politics and development: From the policies to the clinics,* New York: Palgrave Macmillan.

Ross, E. (1998) *The Malthus factor: Poverty, politics and population and capitalist development,* London and New York: Zed Books.

Ross, E. (2000) 'The Malthus factor: poverty, politics and population in capitalist development', Corner House Briefing 20 (www.thecornerhouse.org.uk/pdf/briefing/20malth.pdf).

Sanders, B. (2009) *The green zone: The environmental costs of militarism,* Oakland, CA: AK Press.

Sama: Resource Group for Women and Health (2005) *Beyond numbers: Implications of the two-child norm,* New Delhi: Sama: Resource Group for Women and Health.

Sasser, J. (2013) 'Empower women, save the planet? Science, strategy, and population-environment advocacy', Dissertation Abstracts International. B. The sciences and engineering [0419-4217] vol 74, iss: 2-B(E).

Singh, S. and Darroch, J.E. (2012) *Adding it up: Costs and benefits of contraceptive services – Estimates for 2012,* Guttmacher Institute and United National Population Fund (UNFPA) (www.guttmacher.org/pubs/AIU-2012-estimates.pdf).

UNFPA (United Nations Population Fund) (2009) *State of the world population: Facing a changing world: Women, population and climate,* New York: UNFPA.

WB (The World Bank) (2004) *A review of population, reproductive health and adolescent health and development in poverty reduction strategies,* Washington, DC: The Population and Reproductive Health Cluster, Health, Nutrition and Population Unit, The World Bank.

WHO (World Health Organization) (2012) 'Hormonal contraception and HIV: Technical statement', Geneva (http://whqlibdoc.who.int/hq/2012/WHO_RHR_12.08_eng.pdf).

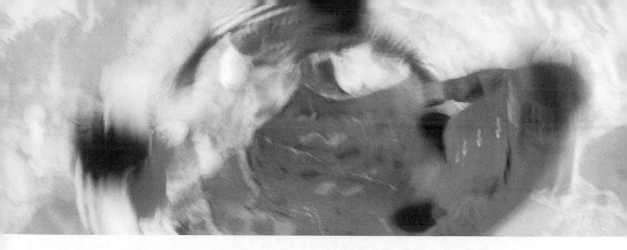

Glossary of terms

Anti-globalisation movement (also known as global social justice movement) Social movement that opposes neoliberal globalisation through summit protests and social fora.

Bilateralism Process of, or commitment to, forming an agreement between two states.

Bretton Woods The World Bank and International Monetary Fund are the key institutional bases of the Bretton Woods system, which was set up after the Second World War to stabilise the international economy.

Burden of disease The overall impact of diseases and injuries at the individual level or at the societal level. Also refers to the economic costs of diseases.

Business/corporate power The ability of business actors and organisations to influence others so that they act in ways they would not otherwise. Different kinds of powers are sometimes distinguished: **corporate agency power**, and **corporate structural power**.

Civil society (also known as civic society) Seen as a sphere separate from state and market comprising voluntary civic or social associations, groups or organisations that represent, defend or serve the interests of their members.

Civil society organisations include advocacy groups and networks, community groups, non-governmental organisations, registered charities, self-help groups and trade unions.

Comparative advantage A theory of international trade that states that countries will gain from trade if they transfer resources between industries to specialise in the sectors in which they are the most efficient. They need not hold an absolute advantage to gain from trade. Comparative advantage stipulates that countries should specialise in the products they are the best at producing.

Competitive advantage A theory that incorporates historical and cultural factors, including the structure of industry and the level of technological development, in explaining the internationally competitive position of industries in different countries.

Competitive comparison Comparison as a technology of global governance – not just to compare, but to contrast, and to rank, and thus provide a basis for international competition. It also extends to inter-institutional comparison – for example, schools, universities – and to interpersonal competition – rankings for jobs, desirable educational opportunities, etc.

Comprehensive healthcare An approach that emphasises full provision of personal health services on a universal basis, with a traditional emphasis on primary healthcare. Defined in the Alma Ata Declaration, it also provides the basis for Health for All policies.

Conceptual grammar All social scientific enquiry is necessarily based on some form(s) of conceptual grammar, such as what the object of study is, why and how it is important, and with what theoretical tools and understandings it is to be addressed. In social policy studies, a particular, nation-state based, conceptual grammar for the analysis of policy has become embedded in many analyses; it is taken for granted as a starting point, rather than being problematised. At its simplest, the conceptual grammar employed in this book problematises the nation state approach by asking where it came from, and how it has been altered and shaped by the entry of influential organisations at a supranational level

Conditionalities Attached to loans by multilateral economic institutions, which include requirements to open economic sectors to foreign investment, privatise state-owned enterprises and welfare services, and remove tariff barriers and food and fuel subsidies.

Contribution A payment made to a pension plan by a plan sponsor or a plan member.

Corporate agency power The capacity of a business actor to influence policy making in a given direction. Mechanisms of agency power include standing for election, membership of public decision-making bodies, use of the media and direct lobbying.

Corporate codes of conduct Policy statements that define ethical standards for corporate conduct. They are voluntary, have no legal standard and use a variety of monitoring and enforcement mechanisms.

Corporate social responsibility A range of business initiatives and policies that have the stated aims of contributing positively.

Corporate structural power The ability of firms to steer policy making towards their own ends through the simple pursuit of their own day-to-day economic interests. Power stems from the fact that decision makers depend on firms to continue to invest and make healthy profits.

Cosmopolitan approach/cosmopolitanism The idea that all human beings, regardless of nationality, belong to a single (moral, political or cultural) community.

Diaspora Dispersal of people throughout the world from their original location. Originally applied to Jewish people, it now refers to any national or ethnic group with members scattered around the world.

Displacement In the context of international trade, a process whereby imported goods substitute for those produced domestically, often leading to domestic unemployment. In the context of migration, displacement refers to people who are forcibly removed from their place of residence.

Double taxation The taxation of profits within a corporation's home country and another country where income is earned. Where agreements exist, profits may be declared and taxed within either country.

Epistemic communities Networks of actors that are significant in generating and transferring knowledge about policy between policy networks.

Eugenics The belief that the hereditary traits of a population can be 'improved' through various forms of intervention. It often refers to movements and social policies of the early 20th century that were concerned with perceived intelligence factors correlated with social class. Eugenic policies have been categorised as either positive or negative, with positive eugenics aimed at encouraging reproduction among those groups of people presumed to have desirable inheritable traits and negative eugenics trying to lower or stop altogether the fertility (by means of sterilisation, family planning or abortion) of those deemed to have undesirable inheritable or genetic traits. Most of these policies have been coercive to varying degrees.

Exchange rate system A system that determines the value of one currency when exchanged with another. In 'floating' systems, it is the market that determines the exchange rate, while in 'fixed' systems this is held constant over time.

Export-oriented policy Economic policy focused on producing goods for export.

Export processing zone Area of a country where labour standards, environmental rules or tax collections are reduced in order to attract the investment of transnational corporations. Products assembled in these zones are intended for export.

Financial Sector Adjustment Loan Loan provided under the Financial Sector Assessment Programme (FSAP), a joint International Monetary Fund–World Bank programme introduced in May 1999. It aims to increase the effectiveness of efforts to promote the soundness of financial systems in member countries.

Foreign direct investment Financial capital transfer from one country to another for investment in production of goods or services.

Free trade agreements Treaties between countries that commit each side to eliminating tariffs on each other's products and facilitating the exchange of goods and services.

Funded pensions Occupational or personal pensions that accumulate dedicated assets to cover liabilities.

G8/Group of 8 A forum for the governments of eight of the world's 11 largest national economies (Canada, France, Germany, Italy, Japan, Russia, the UK and the US). Representatives from these countries meet to discuss a range of policy concerns. 'G8' can refer to the member states in aggregate or to the annual summit meeting of the G8 heads of state

G20/Group of 20 A forum set up in 1999 to discuss issues of financial stability. It brings together industrial and emerging market countries from different regions of the world. Members of the G20 are the Finance Ministers and Central Bank governors of 19 countries: Argentina, Australia, Brazil, Canada, China, France, Germany, India, Indonesia, Italy, Japan, Mexico, Russia, Saudi Arabia, South Africa, South Korea, Turkey, the UK and the US. The European Union is also a member.

G77/Group of 77 Originally a group of 77 countries established in 1964 in the context of the first session of the United Nations on Trade and Development. It now comprises 132 developing country states. The group seeks to harmonise the positions of developing countries prior to and during negotiations.

GAVI A public–private partnership whose remit is to increase vaccination against preventable diseases in developing countries.

Global business Company or business organisation whose interests and operations extend beyond nation states and world regions to encompass the globe.

Global business interest association Associations that represent common interests of businesses worldwide, for example, the International Chamber of Commerce.

Global crime Criminal activity spreading across international borders in terms of its financing and/or organisation. Often used as a synonym for international organised crime, but in many usages global crime is specifically linked to globalisation. In particular, it draws analogies to how criminal organisations can prosper in global economies, and how their methods of activity and accumulation resemble those of transnational corporations.

Global division of labour Social arrangements whereby people around the world are grouped into particular types of jobs. The allocation of people to tasks can be based on ethnicity, caste, class, 'race', gender, historical or geographical circumstance, merit or talent.

Global philanthropy Financial or in-kind support by private donors to charitable causes provided by the public sector. Sometimes used by donors as a way to avoid tax because charitable giving attracts tax relief.

Global policy Policy formed by discussion between transnational actors.

Global policy actors Policy actors, such as non-governmental organisations, social movements, international governmental organisations, business organisations, governments and professional associations, that attempt to influence policy in multiple countries.

Global policy advocacy coalition Advocacy or campaigning coalition oriented around global policy reform. See also transnational advocacy coalition.

Global public goods Goods that serve the international public interest but that no one country or private actor left to itself might choose to provide – for example, the international regulation and notification of diseases. The consumption of global public goods is not exclusive to one state: it is available to many states.

Global public–private partnerships Global governance mechanisms that involve an agreement between an intergovernmental organisation (for example, a United Nations agency) and a private agency (for example, the Bill & Melinda Gates Foundation).

Global redistribution The process by which funds and resources flow across state borders. Normally this occurs from richer Northern states to poorer Southern ones, such as by the means of overseas development assistance. But it also occurs from poorer Southern states to richer Northern ones, as in (for example) the subsidies to Northern health systems provided by the migration of skilled health workers trained in Southern states.

Global regulation The process whereby international actors are required to confirm to global rules, procedures and standards. Commonly discussed in the context of the need for global regulation of business actors and practices in the interests of social protection and welfare.

Global social governance The complex process of global social policy formation and implementation involving the collaboration of a number of governmental, intergovernmental and global private actors.

Global social movement A social movement that is global in scale and scope. Examples include 'old' social movements – labour, peace – as well as 'new' social movements – the environment, women, human rights and development. The anti-globalisation movement is a prime example of a global social movement, as it unites various other global social movements.

Global social policy Examines how social policy issues are increasingly being perceived to be global in scope, cause and impact. The term encompasses the study of: how cross-border flows of people, goods, services, ideas and finance relate to social policy development; the emergence of transnational forms of collective action, including the development of multilateral and cross-border modes of governance and policy making; and how these modes shape the development and impacts of social policy around the world.

Global social rights Social entitlements, such as the right to social security, normally articulated within United Nations covenants. Such rights do not currently entail the right of redress to international courts if they are not met.

Global standards Minimum common standards that are agreed on by many countries, and/or promoted by international organisations.

Globalisation A term used to denote the economic, technological, cultural, social and political forces and processes said to have produced the characteristic conditions of contemporary life. Foremost among these characteristics is a dense network of interconnections and interdependencies that routinely transcend national borders. This interconnectedness is not only said to be more extensive in scope than in previous periods, but more intensive, and the speed at which such interactions are occurring is increasing.

Globalisation studies A multidisciplinary field of study and research focusing on understanding globalisation processes and impacts. Sometimes referred to as global studies by those who may accept the appropriateness of a global analytical framework but who do not accept the tenets of the globalisation thesis.

Governance Governance comprises the set of rules, norms, and practices that shape how government operates. Governance might be seen as the key mechanism through which international organisations influence national social policy.

Health status Level of health of an individual, group or population, measured according to morbidity, mortality or available health resources. More than the outcome of individual choice (such as lifestyle and diet), it is influenced by a range of social determinants of health, such as economic situation, nutritional status, education and quality of sanitation and housing.

Health system The functional expression of health policies. The formal structure that incorporates both health services and other measures whose primary purpose is to promote, restore or maintain health. It covers a defined population and is organised, financed and regulated by statute.

Healthcare reform A generic term for the reform of the organisation and/ or financing of healthcare services. However, a particular set of changes has dominated measures on healthcare reform, following broader new public management principles, separating purchasers and providers of services and utilising market mechanisms within healthcare services.

Human capital theory In education, the idea that 'the overall economic performance of the OECD countries is increasingly more directly based upon their knowledge stock and their learning capabilities' (Foray and Lundvall, 1996, p 21).

Individual pension fund A pension fund that comprises the assets of a single member and his/her beneficiaries, usually in the form of an individual account.

Influence mechanism The ways in which policy actors work to effect policy decisions. Examples of influence mechanisms include norms creation, persuasion and economic incentives.

Informal economy Economic activity that exists beyond formally regulated economic and legal institutions.

International governmental organisation See international organisation.

International Labour Organization Founded in 1919 and becoming the first **United Nations specialised agency** in 1946, it produces international labour standards in the form of Conventions and Recommendations, provides technical assistance and promotes the development of employers' and workers' organisations. It is governed by a tripartite structure in which workers, employers and governments cooperate as formally equal partners.

International migration Migration from one country to another. Also an academic approach to migration that downplays transnational aspects of migration. See also transnational migration.

International Monetary Fund A Bretton Wood institution, set up in 1944. The IMF works to foster global growth and economic stability. It provides policy advice and financing to members in economic difficulties and also works with developing nations to help them achieve macroeconomic stability and reduce poverty (www.imf.org).

International non-governmental organisation Part of the international voluntary sector, these are non-governmental organisations based mainly in Western countries. They operate in a variety of countries, sometimes in cooperation with local and national non-governmental organisations, often delivering government aid in emergency situations. Recent decades have seen the growth of 'super-INGOs' such as Oxfam and Save the Children, which dominate their areas of operation.

International organisation An organisation whose members include two or more states or the organ of such an international organisation.

Learning metrics The use of forms of measurement aimed at describing in quantitative terms learning, quality, productivity and efficiency in education.

Liberalisation The process of removing regulations and other restrictions on the operation of markets. Often used to refer to the removal of trade barriers.

Malthusianism A perspective drawing (selectively) on the 18th-century writings of English clergyman Thomas Malthus. It maintains that it is the number of people per se in any given area that causes food shortages, environmental degradation, water pollution, deforestation and so on. The obvious solution to such problems constructed this way is to reduce the numbers of these people (rather than also considering forces acting from outside the area, for instance).

Methodological nationalism A methodological approach to studying social phenomena that equates 'society' with nation states and focuses on social processes occurring within the confines of nation states. Pays little attention to the existence of transnational processes or the effects of these processes in shaping national social structures and impacts.

Methodological transnationalism A methodological approach to studying social phenomena that moves beyond national boundaries by emphasising transnational influences and links, together with the ways in which they play out in domestic and cross-border contexts.

Migrants People who move from one country to another or from one area of a country to another (as in rural to urban migration).

Migration Movement of people from one country to another or from one area of the country to another.

Millennium Development Goals Eight development targets agreed by the members of the United Nations in 2000 that aim to halve the numbers of people living in extreme forms of poverty by the year 2015.

Mixed reforms In a pensions and social security context, these partially replace the former social security-type system with individual accounts (see individual pension fund). Under mixed systems, popular in Central and Eastern Europe, participants contribute to both a scaled-down, pay-as-you-go pension system and to an individual account, and gain benefits from both systems over time.

Modernisation theory Modernisation theory emerged in the 1950s as an explanation of how the industrial societies of North America and Western Europe developed. The theory argues that societies develop in fairly predictable stages through which they become increasingly complex. Development depends primarily on the importation of technology as well as a number of other political and social changes believed to come about as a result. For example, modernisation involves increased levels of schooling and the development of mass media, both of which foster democratic political institutions. Transportation and communication become increasingly sophisticated and accessible, populations become more urban and mobile, and the extended family declines in importance as a result. Organisations become bureaucratic as the division of labour grows more complex and religion declines in public influence. Last, cash-driven markets take over as the primary mechanism through which goods and services are exchanged. Modernisation theory is controversial because it espouses a development path for poor countries based on the experience of countries that have industrialised. In the main, this calls for investment in manufacturing in urban areas so as to absorb 'surplus' rural labour. It has been argued that the wages earned by urban workers will be spent on consumption, thereby creating demand and more jobs. The benefits of growth would thus 'trickle down to the poor'.

Multilateral Between many states.

Multilateral agency/organisation An organisation that represents many countries (for example, International Labour Organisation). Some multilateral organisations are primarily oriented towards economic objectives and concerns and are often referred to as multilateral economic institutions (MEIs). Exemplars of MEIs are the International Monetary Fund and World Bank.

Multilateral system The classic definition comes from 1992: 'an institutional form which coordinates relations among three or more states on the basis of generalized principles of conduct' (Ruggie, 1992, p 571) but this does not include the idea that multilateral organisations often set out to address what were perceived as common problems that could best be addressed collaboratively. The distinction from globalisation is clear, in that globalisation cannot be reduced to the activities of particular groups of nations; globalisation assumes trans- or supranational, actions rather than international, as is assumed in multilateralism.

Multilateralism The process of, or commitment to, forming an agreement between many countries.

Multilevel governance The existence of levels of governance at world, world-regional, national and sub-national levels.

Multinational corporations See transnational corporations.

Neoliberal (noun) A person who believes in the untrammelled operation of the free market and a minimal role for the state in the economic and social spheres. Also used as an adjective – see, for example, neoliberal economic policy and neoliberal globalisation.

Neoliberal economic policy Economic policy resulting from neoliberalism, which favours the reduction of state involvement in economic and social regulation and supports the spread of free markets.

Neoliberal globalisation Prescription for, and description of, globalisation that emphasises the free movement of capital and a reduced role for states, including the privatisation of many state functions.

Neoliberalism A political philosophy of competitive individualism that calls for minimal state involvement in economic and social regulation. In practice, such involvement tends not to be minimal and is directed so that it benefits for-profit interests and the richer social groups. Associated with the emergence of the New Right (Reagan and Thatcher) in the 1980s and exemplified in the Washington Consensus. Sees economic liberalism as the most effective and efficient means of promoting economic development and obtaining political freedom.

Neo-Malthusianism A perspective similar to Malthusianism that advocates intervention by providing contraception and sterilisation, usually of women, to reduce human numbers by reducing the numbers of babies born.

New public management Denotes broadly the government policies, since the 1980s, that aimed to modernise and render more effective the public sector. The basic hypothesis holds that market-oriented management of the public sector will lead to greater cost-efficiency for governments, without having negative side-effects on other objectives and considerations. Ferlie et al (1996) describe 'New Public Management in Action' as involving the introduction into public services of the 'three Ms': Markets, managers and measurement (Wikipedia).

Non-state international actors Policy actors operating in the market, community or household spheres, acting across many countries. Examples of such actors include transnational corporations, international non-governmental organisations and households.

Notional defined contribution pension A pension system that continues pay-as-you-go financing but accounts for benefits via 'notional' individual accounts.

Outputs versus outcomes Outputs refer to the immediate product of a particular activity; outcomes refer to the consequences of that output. For example, students' individual test scores can be seen as outputs, but these do not determine what consequences (or outcomes) will follow from a particular level of output

Overpopulation Population often denotes, or is understood as, not simply 'the number of people' or even a natural force, but as 'too many people' – or rather, 'overpopulation'. This term implies that too many people live within any given area. Problems with this term are that the particular area is not usually defined, nor any quantity actually calculated as to how many people are considered 'over', nor which people are 'too many'. Calculations that do determine an 'optimum population' tend not to make explicit the assumptions underpinning the results. Questions asking 'too many for what?' or 'too many for whom?' are rarely posed.

Parallel reform In the pensions context, this refers to a reform that maintains public and private systems side by side and allows individuals a choice of system in which to participate, resulting in smaller private pension systems.

Pay-as-you-go pension system An occupational or **personal pension plan** that accumulates dedicated assets to cover the plan's liabilities.

Penality A reference not only to penal institutions but also to the broader political, cultural, economic, discursive and ideological conditions of their existence (the penal field).

Pension fund The pool of assets forming an independent legal entity that are bought with the contributions to a pension plan for the exclusive purpose of financing pension plan benefits. Plan/fund members have a legal or beneficial right or some other contractual claim against the assets of the pension fund. Pension funds take the form of either a special purpose entity with legal personality (such as a trust, foundation or corporate entity) or a legally separated fund without legal personality managed by a dedicated provider (such as a pension fund management company) or other financial institution on behalf of the plan/fund members.

Personal pension plan A pension plan that does not have to be linked to an employment relationship. Such plans are established and administered directly by a pension fund or a financial institution acting as pension provider without any intervention by an employer. Individuals independently purchase and select material aspects of the arrangements. Employers may nonetheless make contributions to personal pension plans. Some personal plans may have restricted membership.

Philanthrocapitalism Philosophy and practice of applying capitalist objectives, methods and criteria to philanthropic projects. Has been criticised for addressing the symptoms of poverty and need rather than the underlying causes, which many see as rooted in the capitalism.

Policy borrowing A conceptual framework that is similar to policy transfer. Work in this field has focused primarily on the movement of policy between the US and the UK.

Policy diffusion The process by which an innovation is communicated through certain channels, over time, among members of a social system.

It is a special type of communication in that the messages are concerned with new ideas.

Policy transfer Process in which policies/ideas in one setting (past or present) are used in the development of policies/ideas in another time or place.

Population Commonly understood as shorthand for 'the number of people' living within a specific bounded area, such as a city or country, or the world. The term 'population' became a statistical concept in 18th-century England and is now linked to many functions and factors that can supposedly be managed, such as population census, control, distribution, explosion, growth, planning, policy, pressure, survey and trend.

Population control Refers to programmes implemented by both public and private entities, state and non-state actors, that are explicitly designed to drive down the birth rates of certain groups of people, particularly in Asia and Africa, and, to a lesser extent, Latin America. Usually carried out through the aggressive promotion of sterilisation and/or long-acting contraceptives that women themselves cannot control (for instance, implants or injections rather than the Pill or condoms). Some population control programmes have called themselves family planning programmes, but population control is not the same as family planning. Family planning is a generic term encompassing many different types of birth control policies and programmes.

Population decline The rate at which the number of people in any given area is decreasing, although the term is also used to suggest a culture or people that is deteriorating in terms of its power or importance.

Population growth The rate at which the number of people in any given area is increasing is calculated by adding up the number of births and people who have moved to the area, subtracting the number of deaths and those who have left, and expressing the result as a percentage of the initial population level.

Population policy A policy (usually) pursued by government to influence the number of people within the territory it governs. It has commonly been understood as trying to influence (usually to reduce) the number of children to whom women give birth and raise, by means of contraception or sterilisation.

Post-Washington Consensus A political consensus emanating from the recognition of the failure of 'structural adjustment policies' (see also structural adjustment loan). Policies consist of social funds to 'highly indebted poor countries' and have, since the late 1990s, been extended to all countries eligible for concessional lending in the form of Poverty Reduction Strategy Papers.

Poverty Reduction Strategy Papers Documents prepared by governments in low-income countries through a participatory process involving domestic stakeholders and external development partners, including the International Monetary Fund and the World Bank. A PRSP describes the macroeconomic, structural and social policies and programmes that a country will pursue over several years to promote broad-based growth and reduce poverty, as well as external financing needs and the associated sources of financing.

Private pension plan A pension plan administered by an institution other than general government (see **public pension plan**). Private pension plans may be administered directly by a private sector employer acting as the plan sponsor, a private pension fund or a private sector provider. Private pension plans may complement or substitute for public pension plans. In some countries, these may include plans for public sector workers.

Protection (trade) The creation of barriers to trade in order to protect domestic industries from foreign competition.

Public pension plan A social security or similar statutory programme administered by the general government (that is, central, state and local governments, as well as other public sector bodies such as social security institutions). Public pension plans have been traditionally financed through the **pay-as-you-go pension system**, but some OECD countries have partial funding of public pension liabilities or have replaced these plans by **private pension plans**.

Punitiveness An extension of means of punishment that relies on an intolerance and a vindictive infliction of pain.

Race to the bottom The thesis that in response to a perceived threat to their industrial competitiveness, states are likely to engage in behaviour that results in the lowering of social, environmental and labour standards in order to attract new or retain existing investment.

Reproductive rights/reproductive justice Women's right to control their bodies in all matters of reproduction. This includes access to contraception, but also freedom from coercion. Women from the South and women of colour have expanded the concept further to embrace maternal health and mortality, childbearing and child-raising.

Scarcity Refers to insufficiency of resources, such as food, and is a key concept in Malthusianism. If attention is paid to what is actually happening in any locale, however, the causes of hunger are invariably shown to lie not in absolute scarcity – no food at all – but in socially generated scarcity – not enough food for some people in some places because other people have denied them access to food, land and water. This indicates that imbalances of power between groups of people in society generate 'scarcity' rather than 'population'. From this perspective, 'scarcity', as used in modern economics, is a means of legitimising existing inequitable social and political relationships, institutions and policies, and of blocking or diverting attention from other causes of poverty and hunger.

Selective healthcare The provision of targeted or selected services so as to provide the most effective means of improving the health of people in greatest need. It was originally considered an intermediary phase before primary healthcare for all could be made available.

Social determinants of health The health effects of the social conditions in which people live and work, in particular, the ways in which underlying social inequalities and poverty affect health status.

Social protection Aims to insure workers against the risks of unemployment or sickness through a system of welfare benefits, whatever the cause.

Sovereign justice Descriptively, state-based legislation and institutional arrangements regarding criminal justice matters. Normatively, arguments that states should have abilities and rights to pursue criminal justice matters.

State sovereignty A doctrine that dates back several hundred years and stipulates that states are the ultimate decision-making authority in their country. The governments of states define what is in the national interest and pursue this national interest in the international arena. Thus, most states are very hesitant to empower an international body to make decisions that bind the populations of their states. Since states often have different national interests, international agreements are often difficult.

Structural Adjustment Loan Part of the Structural Adjustment Programme, a World Bank instrument prevalent in the 1980s that focused on correcting major macroeconomic 'distortions' allegedly hindering development.

Substitutive reform In the pensions context, a reform that fully replaces social security-type systems with those based on individual, funded pension savings accounts.

Sustainable Development Goals Current term used to describe what is expected to replace the Millennium Development Goals after 2015.

Targeting/targeted provision Social programmes that concentrate resources on particular social groups of the population. Often, the poorest and most vulnerable populations are those that are the focus of targeted social programmes of provision, which is why targeting is commonly associated with residual forms of social provision.

Trade negotiations Negotiations between governments to agree trade rules and to reduce barriers to trade. Trade negotiations involve bargaining over the concessions to be made by each government.

Trade protectionism The practice or advocacy of trade protection. See protection (trade).

Transnational advocacy coalition or network A group of organisations structured on a transnational basis to campaign for policy changes or wider social reforms. See also global policy advocacy coalition.

Transnational corporations Private firms that produce or sell commodities and/or services in more than one country. The largest TNCs operate in global markets in hundreds of countries around the globe. They are also known as multinational corporations.

Transnational justice Transnational cooperation on matters of criminal justice, and engagement by international donors, campaign groups, criminal justice agencies, governments and international organisations on matters of criminal justice. Includes addressing legacies of historical abuses and arrangements for a broader global redistribution of rights and obligations.

Transnational knowledge networks A semi-coordinated alliance of scholars and professionals sharing a common understanding of an approach to a particular (policy) issue.

Transnational policing Engagement in policing reform by international donors, national governments, foreign police and law enforcement agencies in the domestic policing agencies and programmes of recipient countries. It includes peace keeping in post-conflict situations, reconstruction and capacity building as part of nation- or state-building exercises, and the provision of technical assistance in relation to certain aspects of law enforcement. In each instance, there is a cross-border provision of resources with a view to shaping the kind of policing provided in recipient nations (Goldsmith and Sheptycki, 2007).

Travelling and embedded policy A perspective developed from policy sociology stressing that policies that travel around the globe are contested and mediated in all countries before becoming embedded as policy settlements.

United Nations specialised agency An autonomous agency with special agreements with the UN. Several specialised agencies have normative and standard-setting functions with a truly global focus. Specialised agencies include the World Health Organization, International Labour Organization, Food and Agriculture Organisation and UN Educational, Scientific and Cultural Organisation.

Universal health care Refers to a system which provides health care and financial protection to all its citizens. It is organised around providing a specified package of benefits to all members of a society with the end goal of providing financial risk protection, improved access to health services, and improved health outcomes (WHO 2010).

Universal Health Coverage The goal of universal health coverage is to ensure that all people obtain the health services they need without suffering financial hardship when paying for them (www.who.int/features/qa/universal_health_coverage). Sometimes used interchangeably with **universal health care**.

Vertical In the health context, an approach, programme or measure that focuses on a particular disease or health issue. For example, malaria and HIV/AIDS have been dealt with through specific, stand-alone programmes. Vertical programmes often have their own funding, personnel and governance structures, separate from the main health system.

Washington Consensus A term used to denote a relatively specific set of economic policy prescriptions that constituted the 'standard' reform package promoted for crisis-wracked developing countries by Washington–DC-based institutions such as the International Monetary Fund, The World Bank and the US Treasury Department. The prescriptions encompassed policies to pursue macroeconomic stability (by controlling inflation and reducing fiscal deficits); getting countries to open their economies to the rest of the world (through trade and capital account liberalisation); and liberalising markets through privatisation and deregulation.

World Bank Institution comprising the International Bank for Reconstruction and Development and the International Development Association. It was set up in 1944 to assist with European reconstruction and promote economic development. This goal was made less necessary by the Marshall Plan. Its main goal later evolved to focus on the developing world. It provides loans for programmes and projects for which no private finance can be found.

World Health Organization Organisation established in 1948 as the specialised United Nations health agency whose objective is the highest possible level of health for all peoples. It is governed by its 192 member states through the World Health Assembly.

World Trade Organization Set up in 1995 to promote international trade, with executive and legal powers recognised in international law to enforce international trade and investment law and to adjudicate in international trade disputes.

References

Ferlie, E., Ashburner, L., Fitzgerald, L., and Pettigrew, A. (1996) *New Public Management in action*, Oxford: Oxford University Press.

Foray, D. and Lundvall, B.A. (1996) 'From the economics of knowledge to the learning economy' in D. Foray, and B.A. Lundvall, (eds) *Employment and growth in the knowledge-based economy*, Paris: OECD.

Goldsmith, A. and Sheptycki, J. (2007) *Crafting transnational policing*, Oxford: Hart.

Ruggie, J. (1992) 'Multilateralism; anatomy of an institution', *International Organization*, vol 46, no 3, pp 461-98.

World Health Organization (2010) *World health report: Health systems financing: the path to universal coverage*, Geneva: World Health Organization.

Index

Note: page numbers in *italic* type refer to figures; those in **bold** refer to tables.

UNIVERSITY OF WINCHESTER
LIBRARY